The Absent
SUPERPOWER

The Shale Revolution and a World Without America

Peter Zeihan

Peter Zeihan on Geopolitics
Austin, TX
www.zeihan.com

Book Design by Scott J. Doughty

Printed in the United States of America
First Edition: December 2016
ISBN: 978-0-9985052-0-6

10 9 8 7 6 5

To the team who makes not just this book, but everything that I do, possible.

Susan Copeland
Michael Nayebi-Oskoui
Melissa Taylor
Wayne Watters

You keep me wired.
You keep me on task.
You keep me honest.
You keep me grounded.
You keep me in the right state.

Some of these tasks are more difficult than others.

CONTENTS

INTRODUCTION

The Journey to The Absent Superpower

EVERYTHING IS CHAOS!

At least, that what it seems like every time you turn on your TV, radio, computer, or smart phone.

The European Union is falling apart, Syria is in meltdown, cybercrime is an hourly occurrence, the Chinese economy is gyrating wildly, Russia is on the march, the election of Donald Trump has Americans of all political stripes wondering what comes next, and the Kardashians get more press time than Congress. It's enough to give anyone a panic attack.

Well, not quite anyone. Unlike the average person, all this craziness puts me in my happy place. Where most see the world turning itself upside down and inside out, I see a long-overdue shift in the global order. New trends emerging. New possibilities unfolding. For me, change is good for business.

That's because my job is a bit…different than the standard. You see, I'm a geopolitical strategist. That's a fancy way of saying I help organizations understand what challenges and opportunities they will be grappling with across the world in the years to come. As such I'm sort of a professional apprentice, rarely a master of any particular craft but needing to be able to hold my own in conversations about manufacturing and transport and health care and finance and agriculture and metals and electricity and education and defense and such. Preferably without pissing off anyone whose living is based off of manufacturing or transport or health care or finance or agriculture or metals or electricity or education or defense.

In many ways those conversations make me who I am. From the Air Force to the Pickle Packers, every interaction gives me a good hard view of the world, yet each of these interactions originates from a radically different perspective. Combine all those angles and interactions and perspectives and the unique information that comes from them with my private intelligence experience, and I'm granted the privilege of seeing something approximating the full picture — how the world's myriad pieces interlock — and catch some telling future glimpses to boot. More than anything else, what I sell is context.

That picture and those glimpses and that context formed the bones of my first book, *The Accidental Superpower*, which was published in November 2014. In *Accidental* I made the case that the world we knew was at a moment of change: The Americans who had created, nurtured, enabled, maintained and protected the post-WWII global order were losing interest. As they stepped back the world we know was about to fall to pieces.

At any time in history such a shift would have had monumental consequences, but the American retrenchment is but one of three massive shifts in the global order. The second is the rapid greying of the entire global population. Fewer people of working age translates directly into anemic, decaying economies — enervating global trade just as the Americans stop guaranteeing it. Third and finally, the American shale revolution has changed the mechanics — if not yet the mood — of how the Americans interact with the energy sector. Surging petroleum output within the Lower48 is pushing North America toward outright oil independence; in the past decade the total continental shortfall has narrowed from roughly 10 million barrels of oil per day (mbpd) to about 2mbpd.

In the two years since *Accidental* published, I've had ample opportunity to re-examine every aspect of my work — some of my critics have been (over) eager to assist in such endeavors — and I fear that I may have been off the mark on a couple of points.

First, the American shale sector has matured far faster and more holistically than I could have ever expected.

Enough with the Abbrevs

I hate to do this to you, but there are going to be a whole bunch of numbers in this book, and the energy sector is second only to the military in generating acronyms. Here's your cheat sheet:

mbpd   =**m**illions of **b**arrels **p**er **d**ay

This is a straightforward measure of the volume of oil production and/or transport capacity and/or refining capacity and/or refining output. Because of the large scale (millions), you will see this acronym used most often in the context of large countries, and overall region and global product flows. This term mbpd is *not* industry standard — derivations of MMbd are more common — but in my work I've discovered that most folks don't internalize the internal nomenclature of others and a straight-up acronym is easier to wrap your head around. So mbpd it is.

kbpd   =thousands (**k**) of **b**arrels **p**er **d**ay

Exactly the same concept, but three orders of magnitude smaller. You'll see this used far more often in refining or when dealing with smaller countries.

natgas =**nat**ural **gas**

The two-word nature of natural gas often tends to sow a bit of confusion when the term is used in a lengthy sentence, so this is mostly for simplicity and clarity. That, and I got tired of typing out "natural gas" a bajillion times.

mboed =**m**illions of **b**arrels of **o**il **e**quivalent **p**er **d**ay

There are many different kinds of hydrocarbons, with oil and natural gas only being the most common. This term is used to merge everything into a single unit to ease comparisons among many different producers who have different production balances of the various "energy" products. It takes about 5,800 cubic feet of natural gas to make 1boed.

bcf/d   =**b**illions of **c**ubic **f**eet of natural gas **p**er **d**ay

The standard metric for communicating natgas production volumes and transport capacity.

Despite a price crash in oil markets, despite ongoing opposition to shale among a far from insignificant portion of the population, despite broad scale ignorance about what shale is and what shale is not, shale has already overhauled American energy.

In 2006 total American oil production had dropped to 8.3mbpd while demand was touching 20.7mbpd, forcing the United States to import 12.4mbpd, more than Japan and China and Germany combined. By 2016 U.S. oil output had breached 15mbpd. Factor in the Canadians and Mexicans, and total American imports of non-North American oil had plunged to about 2mbpd — and that in the teeth of an oil price war. And that's just oil specifically. Take a more comprehensive view and include everything from bunker fuel to propane, and the continent is less than 0.8mbpd from being a net energy *exporter*.

The end of American dependence upon extra-continental energy sources does more than sever the largest of the remaining ties that bind America's fate to the wider world, it sets into motion a veritable cavalcade of trends: the re-industrialization of the United States, the accelerated breakdown of the global order, and a series of wide-ranging military conflicts that will shape the next two decades.

This book's opening section contains the long and the short of this Shale New World, the greatest evolution of the American industrial space since at least 1970. For the financiers and accountants and policy wonks out there, this was written with your geeky brains specifically in mind.

Second, the isolationist trickle I detected in American politics has deepened and expanded into a raging river. Of the two dozen men and women who entered the 2016 presidential race, only *one* — Ohio Governor John Kasich — advocated for a continuation of America's role in maintaining the global security and trade order that the Americans installed and have maintained since 1945. The most anti-trade candidate on the right won his party's nomination, while the most anti-trade candidate on the left finished a close second in the Democratic primaries to the Clinton political machine. Last night (now President) Donald Trump and Hillary Clinton met in New York to debate economic policy. What struck me as self-gratifying and horrifying in equal measure was that their core disagreement on trade issues wasn't whether trade was good or bad for the United States, but how much to pare it back and which reasons for paring cut it the most with the electorate. (The pair of them obviously disagreed — colorfully, vehemently and often — on other issues.)

The world has had *seven* decades to become inured to a world in which the Americans do the heavy lifting to maintain a system that economically benefits all. The world has had *three* decades to become inured to a world in which the Americans do not expect anything of substance in return. As the Americans back away, very few players have any inkling of how to operate in a world where markets are not open, transport is not safe, and energy cannot be secured easily.

The stage is set for a global tailspin of epic proportions. Just as the global economy tips into deflation, just as global energy becomes dangerous, just as global demographics catastrophically reduce global consumption, just as the world really *needs* the Americans to be engaged, the United States will be…absent. We stand on the very edge of the Disorder.

The Disorder's defining characteristic is, well, its lack of order. Remove the comfortable, smothering American presence in the world and the rest of humanity has to look out for its own interests. As many of those interests clash, expect devolutions that are deeply-felt and disastrous in equal measure. Part II breaks down the breakdown. I'm equally proud and terrified to report that some of the darker shades in *Accidental* are happening sooner rather than later. For generals — armchair or otherwise — who prefer jumping directly into the fight, Part II is what you're after.

In the final section we will circle back at take a good hard look at the United States. Energy independent, economically robust, physically secure, and — above all — strategically unfettered, the United States will be taking a break from the world writ large for the most part.

Yet "for the most part" is a far cry from a full divorce from all things international. The Yanks will still find bits of the world worth their time, effort, money and ammunition. Section III explores the American Play: where the Americans will still be found, why they will be there, how they'll act, and what they'll be up to.

It may be small comfort, but the acceleration of the shale revolution as well as the American political shift towards populism has illuminated a great deal, sharpening my view of the future. The various glimpses that made up *Accidental* have somewhat merged, lingering to the point that they now constitute a bit of a road map.

That road map is the core of this book.

Peter Zeihan
September 27, 2016
Somewhere over Kentucky

PART I

Shale New World

CHAPTER 1

The First Shale Revolution

Let's begin with the basics: What exactly is petroleum?

Petroleum is a catch-all term for everything from crude oil to propane to natural gas (natgas). Petroleum is the fuel of modernity. It does more than keep the lights on and keep your car moving. Petroleum is an input in almost everything you have ever used or purchased. Without petroleum there is no Internet — and certainly no cell phones. No petroleum means no Christmas ornaments (and for many of us, Christmas trees themselves), no kids' toys, no clothes, no kitchen knives, no hunting rifles, no microwave dinners, no paper, no fire extinguishers, no bread bags, no perfume, no windows, no computers, no condoms, no chewing gum, no wall insulation, no paint, and so on.[1]

Without petroleum there would not be a meaningful agricultural industry — and in that I mean everything from the growing of crops to the harvesting of crops to the transport of foodstuffs from farm to table. Think organic food is petroleum-free? Think again — all going organic

---

1 For those of you who are super technically minded, yes, you *can* make many of these items using non-petroleum substitutes — but only at an exorbitant cost. One of the many contributions of petroleum to civilization is to provide many of the perks of being a 17th century monarch to the average person. Think we have an issue with income inequality? Imagine a world in which only the 1% can have 90% of the things you have within 10 steps of you right now.

does is partially remove petroleum from one sub-step of the planting-fertil-izing-harvesting-collecting-storing-transporting-packaging-distributing-re-tailing-pantrying process. Can you imagine electricity without petroleum? Keep in mind that in most places the time that you need electricity the most is in the winter and at night (i.e. when the sun isn't shining).[2]

Will we move beyond petroleum someday? Maybe. I sincerely hope so, but it will not be soon. For now, we are stuck with petroleum — so best to understand the future of petroleum.

That future is shale.

Shale Rocks

Shale is a type of rock formation that often — although certainly not al-ways — holds petroleum. Most of the world's petroleum is the long-dead remains of plankton and algae. Once these tiny critters die, they sink to the bottom of whatever body of water they swam in, settling in with the mud. Over the millennia, the microscopic bodies stack up and the lower layers of the sea- or lake-bottom muck turn to soft rock. Repeat the process ad nauseam and you end up with multiple stacked layers of sedimentary stone with untold trillions of itty-bitty corpses trapped within. All this organic material stuck in the new rock tends to congeal into a waxy substance called kerogen. Geologic pressure in some areas heats up the rock, and in some areas the balance of heat and pressure and rock type is perfect for cooking the kerogen into petroleum.

Depending upon the local geology, getting to this petroleum can be a bit of a nightmare.

In what the energy sector refers to as conventional petroleum reservoirs, the rock in which the plankton et al cook is somewhat porous. As the millennia stack up to form eras, the bits of petroleum migrate through the rock strata until they reach a formation through which they shall not pass. This rock caps the formation and is called, somewhat unimaginatively, a cap rock. Behind the cap rock, the oil concentrates and pressures rise. Drilling

---

2   Appendix I will cover the intersection of shale and green technologies.

through a cap rock releases that pressure, allowing the petroleum to gush out. That's called a ... gusher.

To tap conventional energy sources, a *lot* of things have to go perfectly. You have to have the right source rock to generate precursor materials, the right type of kerogen to generate petroleum, the right sort of middle rock layer that allows the petroleum to migrate into a pool, and a good cap rock to actually enable the petroleum to collect into a volume that is viable for drilling.

Shale doesn't need *any* of that. Of all the petroleum of which we are currently aware, only one-fifth has ever been able to use permeable rock or natural faults to migrate beyond where it formed, and less than half of that flows into those perfect packages that have hopes of being tapped. That leaves four-fifths (at least — some geologists believe the ratio is more than nine-tenths) of the petroleum trapped *within* the source rock, and most of those source rock are shales. What the shale industry is all about is developing technologies that make it possible to access the oil that isn't perfectly packaged.

Of course "possible" isn't the same thing as "easy."

Shale doesn't have big, easy-to-prick, high-pressurized pools of petroleum. Shale rock isn't porous. Any petroleum that forms within shale cannot migrate. It is stuck within the rock in tiny pockets that often are mere microns across. Drill through a shale layer and you will indeed release small bits of pressure and produce small amounts of petroleum, but only for a few days — and likely nowhere near that long.

No, the only way to get shale rock to give up appreciable amounts of petroleum is to turn conventional drilling techniques on their ear — literally. Instead of drilling vertically down *through* the formation, you must instead drill horizontally *along* the formation. Total reservoir contact between the wellshaft and the shale layer would be but a few dozen feet per well with vertical drilling, but by going horizontally you can now establish over two miles of contact.

Think of conventional drilling versus shale oil production a bit like drilling into ravioli versus lasagna. In conventional drilling, drillers just need to pierce the cap rock and they hit a big reservoir of oil (the ravioli filling). In shale, drillers have to drill between various layers of different geologies (the noodles in lasagna) in order to access a multitude of small bits of petroleum — a far cry from the fat pockets of oil contained within conventional oil fields.

You've now got a system that will produce petroleum for a few weeks. Still not stellar. The next trick is to coax the rock to give up more petroleum. Perhaps "coax'" isn't the right word. More like browbeat. Here's where hydraulics come into play. Using a mix of measures, operators punch some holes in the last few dozen feet of the well's lateral. Powerful pumps shove several million gallons of liquid spiked with sand into the well shaft all the way down to the toe of the lateral.[3] When the shaft is full, the pumps kick into overdrive and all that pressure pushes out through the pipe's holes into the rock.

The magic of the fracking process is hydraulics. Placed under pressure, gases compress. Liquids, however, *never* compress. With enough pump power, the rock itself will crack apart, spiderwebbing a fine mesh of cracks out from the well shaft and forcing the sand-laced water into the parts of the mesh that are closest to the pipe.[4] Operators then place a temporary plug at the beginning of the perforated section. They then repeat the process for the next few dozen feet of pipe, and so on until they reach the lateral's heel. The pumps are then turned off. Pressure within the well pushes the frack fluid back into the shaft and up the wellbore. But the sand is stuck in the cracks and so left behind, keeping those cracks wedged open.

Each of those sand-propped cracks now accesses a multitude of those tiny, isolated pockets of petroleum — and that now-untrapped petroleum can flow back to the horizontal shaft, laterally to the vertical shaft, and up and out into the field's surface gathering system.

That's the short version.

The *very* short version.

The truth is that there is a mammoth deal of variation within the world of shale.

3 Typical frack fluid is 90% water, 9.5% sand, and 0.5% other We'll talk about the "other" in Appendix II.

4 Typically, the sand can't make it past 50-100 feet from the shaft — these are really tiny cracks — with the water perhaps making it another 50 before hydrogen bonding prevents it from progressing further.

Every shale field is different. The Bakken in North Dakota is almost a pure oil play; the Haynesville in the Louisiana/Texas border region is almost entirely natgas; and the Marcellus of Pennsylvania is a mix of not just natgas, light oil and lease condensate, but also petroleum gases like propane and butane. The formations of West Texas' Permian and California's Monterrey are a jumbled mess of stacked and interpenetrating layers. The Woodford of Oklahoma is layered as well, but those layers are separated by slabs of semi-crystalline chert that scatters seismic waves and wears down drill bits. The Niobrara of Colorado is full of clay, while Michigan's Antrim is brittle. Some petroleum-bearing shale layers are within a mile of the surface, while others are more than three miles down. Much of the Utica isn't just under the Allegheny Plateau, it is under — several thousand feet under — another play, the Marcellus. Some like the Conasauga of Alabama and Tennessee are thick. Others like the next-door Neal are thin. Others, like the Chattanooga which stretches from Kentucky to New York, are

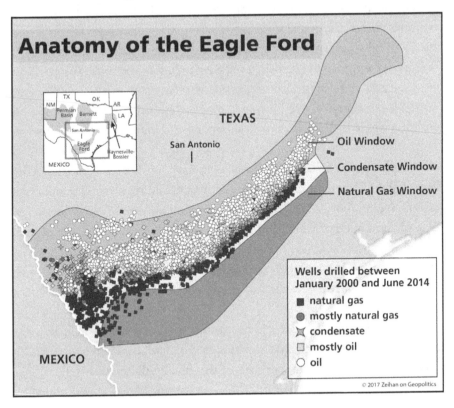

Anatomy of the Eagle Ford

TEXAS

San Antonio

Oil Window

Condensate Window

Natural Gas Window

MEXICO

Wells drilled between January 2000 and June 2014

■ natural gas
● mostly natural gas
✖ condensate
□ mostly oil
○ oil

© 2017 Zeihan on Geopolitics

both — ranging from under 80 feet thick to over 1,000. The Marcellus sprawls across over territory larger than the state of Oregon, while Oklahoma's SCOOP play is smaller than Connecticut.

And never forget that since shale is new, what we know keeps evolving. As recently as 2013 the U.S. Geological Survey thought the entire Permian Basin had only a few billion barrels of oil and natgas. Now they think its Wolfcamp sub-play alone has over 20 billion. Globally, *known* shale deposits are already more than the conventional deposits of Saudi Arabia and Russia combined.

Each field has its own characteristics and so requires not just a tweaking, but a re-imagination of the tools required to coax out the petroleum. More or less water, more or less sand, more or less pressure, different chemical mixes, different drill types, different outputs, different flow rates.

The differences hold true not simply among fields, but *within* them. The super-deep Utica mentioned above? Parts of it are nearly on the *surface*.

And there's the Eagle Ford of South Texas. Like all shale fields, not everything within the Eagle Ford is the same. There are three fairly distinct zones: an oil window in the north (where the temperatures that cooked the kerogen were somewhat cooler), a natgas window in the south (where those temperatures were higher), and a condensate window in the middle. And just to make things a wee bit more complicated, differences often abound within a single drilling pad; or even among the multiple stages of a single well.

A staple feature of the business is accepting that factors geologic, hydrological and technological (not to mention legal and regulatory) are not only ever-changing, but only rarely similar in even two places, much less across tens of thousands of wells that were drilled nationally in 2014. Anytime that anyone uses a data reference for well depth or production rates or frack systems and so on, assume a pipeload of caveats. Keeping on top of things from an analytical point of view is a bit like wrestling a stampede of balloon animals.

Luckily (for me) this book is not so much a book *about* shale as it is a book *inspired* by shale. I'll do my best to detail what's changing in the industry and why, and many portions of this book will certainly have a *Shale*

For Dummies[5] vibe. The real meat isn't how shale petroleum is produced, but how new production techniques are reshaping the energy politics and

---

5   ™

Know Your Energy

All petroleums are something called hydrocarbons — materials composed primarily of carbon and hydrogen atoms. The first step to understanding them is to realize that not all hydrocarbons are created equal.

First come the heaviest hydrocarbons, which we know colloquially as **crude oil**. The "oil" part is typically rather lengthy chains of those carbon and hydrogen atoms, while "crude" refers to associated components from carbon chains that have things other than purely hydrogen and carbon to a wide variety of contaminants ranging such as mercury and sulfur. The longer the hydrogen-carbon chains in the mix — not to mention the contaminant level — the thicker and gooier the oil. Most global crude oil streams are roughly the consistency of really oily peanut butter. Canadian tar sands are so low in quality that not only are they a solid at room temperature, they have to be heated to at least 300 degrees Fahrenheit to melt.

Particularly low-quality oil is typically **heavy** (indicating a high level of density and viscosity), **sour** (indicating a high proportion of sulfur) and jam-packed with a variety of impurities. Refining heavy crudes is very difficult; as a rule, only the most advanced industrial complexes in the world can even try. Since most of the "good" crude around the world — the stuff with a consistency of maple syrup — already has been used up, the average global crude stream has become heavier and sourer for decades, ergo the collective American decision in the 1980s to retool the local refining complex to process the thick, gooey stuff. America's most technically adept refinery complexes are located on the Gulf Coast of Texas and Louisiana. Most places that struggle with heavy/sour crude turn it into tar and asphalt, but American refineries are so high-end that they can actually turn even the heaviest crudes into gasoline.

Second, there are a sort of mid-level petrocarbons. Viscosity decreases to almost water-like levels of flow. Contaminants drop toward zero. Such **light** and **sweet** crude is liquid gold. Easy to pour, easy to process, and the best for making high-end distillates such as gasoline (which by itself accounts for 40%

of U.S. crude oil demand). Light/sweet used to be the global norm, but most of the good stuff has long since been tapped out. Or at least that was the case until the shale revolution.

It all has to do with the peculiar geologies of shale rock as opposed to the rock layers more common in conventional plays. In a typical petroleum formation, the petrocarbons can migrate through the rock. Though this allows them to concentrate and congregate in easy-to-tap pools, it also means they can pick up contaminants (like the aforementioned sulfur or mercury) on the way. But shale petroleum is trapped almost at the point it was born. Harvesting it in essence requires that you blast it out of its cradle.

Some of shale crude is so light and sweet it is actually in a slightly different, third category called **lease condensate**, a product so pure it has the consistency of nail polish remover and as such is child's play to refine. (I call it white chicken oil, because you can shake a white chicken over it and voila! Gasoline!) Add the light/sweet oils and condensates coming out of the U.S. shale patch together and the volumes are so high that the United States is now the world's largest producer of premium oils.

Fourth, often found co-mingled with crude are lighter hydrocarbons with much shorter carbon chains. Such substances are only liquid under high pressures. Names are familiar: propane, butane, pentane, and so on. Once separated from other hydrocarbons, these products are fairly easy to store and used in a variety of applications. Americans are most familiar with them for their use in cigarette lighters and backyard barbeques, but these **natural gas liquids (NGLs)** also are a leading ingredient in everything from anti-freeze to detergents to cosmetics to paint to packing foam to tires. As recently as 2007, the United States was the world's largest *importer* of nearly all of them. However, they are quite commonly found within shale formations. And so courtesy of the shale industry, as of 2015 the United States is instead the world's largest *exporter* of all of them.

Finally, the carbon chain shortens to one or two and you get methane and ethane, a.k.a. **natural gas (natgas)** or cow farts, which is a gaseous substance under all but the most extreme circumstances. Natural gas is the oddball in the chemistry world. On the plus side, it is the ultimate building block for almost any industrial process: paints, plastics and electricity production, to name three of the biggies. It is burned directly in many areas for residential heat. Some basic chemistry can turn it into an NGL should you have a propane shortage.

In a pinch — and if you have a lot of money — you can even turn it into more traditional oil-derived products like gasoline and jet fuel.

On the negative side, natural gas is a pain to corral because it is, well, a gas. As a liquid, oil is easy to move around. Truck, barge, rail car, bucket — you name it. But natgas is a gas and therefore requires absolutely dedicated, uninterrupted infrastructure. Natgas isn't just a primary product of the shale industry, it also is a *by*product of production from shale *oil* to the degree that the American market is glutted with it. We'll cover the reasons for and implications of that glut in Chapter 3.

Anatomy of Hydrocarbons

Common name Chemical formula	Boiling point (degrees Celcius)	Common uses	Chemical structure
Methane C_1H_4	-164	• Electricity generation • Residential heating • Chemical feedstock • Fuel additive	Carbon Hydrogen
Ethane C_2H_6	-89	• Ethylene production • Hydrogen production • Chemical feedstock • Pigments	
Propane C_3H_8	-42	• Off-grid residential and industrial heating, drying and power • Propellants • Adhesives	
Butane C_4H_{10}	-1	• Small-scale portable flame and heating fuels • Refrigerant • Solvents	
Octane C_8H_{16}	125	• Fuel additive • Paint additive • Solvents	
Hexadecane $C_{16}H_{34}$	287	• Fuel additive • Absorbents	

energy economy of the United States, and in turn the global system. We'll use the technical to inform the forecasts rather than the other way around. So considering this project's focus and in the interest of saving you, the reader, a lot of time and paper (and/or electrons) I'm still going to use words like "average" and "standard" and "typical" even though those terms are not completely correct. In the lexicon of this book, these figures represent my distillation of the collective best guess of the industry to date.

The Next Shale Revolution

One statement, however, needs no caveats. At the time of this writing, shale is hurting. In early 2016, oil prices bottomed out at about $30 a barrel, with the average price for the year well below $50. Considering that full-cycle breakeven costs were north of $90 just a few years previous, prognostications that the shale revolution had ended flowed fast and furious.[6] For someone like myself who has spent years researching, investigating and thinking about how shale will change the world, this proved a bit of a problem.

Luckily for the shale industry (and for me), news of its death has been somewhat exaggerated. During the past two years, the shale sector has evolved in dozens of ways, for the most part in a desperate effort to survive the current spate of low energy prices. The resulting changes have transformed the American shale patch from a critical piece of the American energy system to a globe-changing revolution. Understand those changes and you can understand just how transformative shale is about to become.

---

6 One of the endless challenges is defining what the word "cost" actually means. For the purpose of this book, unless I expressly state otherwise, I'm referring to "full-cycle breakeven cost." This is an aggregate of everything from prospecting and permitting on the front end, to drilling and gathering in the middle, to transport, royalties and taxes on the back end.

CHAPTER 2

The Second Shale Revolution

In June 2014, American shale faced a fundamental challenge that undermined every aspect of the process: oil prices crashed. From their annual peak of $114 a barrel they slid to $70 by the time of OPEC's summit Nov. 28. At that summit, many expected the Saudis to do what they had done for the past 15 years and lead up an effort to rein-in production and thus support prices.

Instead the opposite happened. The Saudi representative made it clear that unless other producers were willing to slash their own output, Saudi Arabia was fully prepared to fight a price war.

At first glance it was obvious that the Saudis would win, and win easily. Saudi Arabia and the other Arab states of the Persian Gulf boast the lowest production costs for crude oil in the world. The specific numbers are always hard to nail down since many countries treat the particulars of their energy industries as state secrets, but the broad consensus is that the Arab states of the Gulf probably have full-cycle costs of around $30 a barrel, with Saudi Arabia being roughly around $25. As of late 2014, the full-cycle break-even cost for the shale patch was probably around $75. Should the Saudis not merely cut production, but actually increase it, it would seem that the U.S.

shale industry would simply fall apart. That's certainly where the smart money lay.[1]

Throughout 2015 and up to the publishing of this book, doom for shale has been a common refrain — a conventional wisdom that goes hand in hand with failure for America's efforts at oil independence. Breathless stories about economic expansions in West Texas, Central Pennsylvania and Western North Dakota were replaced by apocalyptic teeth-gnashing of boom-towns turned bust. Even the Energy Information Administration (EIA) reluctantly climbed on board, predicting steady falls in U.S. output throughout 2015. Not one to let good conventional wisdom go to waste, media prognostications intensified.

There was just one problem: it didn't happen.

Throughout 2015, combined production of American oil and condensate didn't only remain stable, output ended the calendar year at a higher level — 12.7mbpd — than it had entered. Production didn't finally stagger until May 2016 — fully two *years* after the price crash started. At the time of this writing (in November 2016), U.S. petroleum output not only has yet to fall below the level at which the price drop began, it is within a few months of reaching record levels, despite ongoing low prices.

So what gives?

What nearly everyone missed is that something fundamental had changed.

The United States is experiencing nothing less than a Second Shale Revolution. This revolution will do more than "merely" reshape the American industrial base; it will reshape the global geopolitical environment, and it will continue to do so for at least the next three decades. What matters is that America's shale sector has *already* adapted to prices below $50.

Surviving the Plunge

The first thing to understand is that shale operators are hardly unaware or unimpacted by lower prices. After several years with their selling prices north of $90, shale firms became used to a lax environment. Production

---

1   We'll cover the full logic and details of the Saudi price war in Chapter 7.

was everywhere. Financing came easy. The biggest challenge most faced was locating all of the various inputs that make fracking possible: pipe, pumps, tanks, trucks, sand, cable, engineers, drivers, lodging, roads and so on. In nearly all cases, input inflation was far and away the biggest enemy. Yet with oil prices high, a mix of income and borrowing could manage that sort of problem.

Tank prices and everyone had to get a lot more efficient. This efficiency was gained in five ways:

1. *Contract creativity.* Enter the lawyers. Terms like "extenuating circum-stances," "force majeure," and "best effort" exist in most of the leases that enable the shale sector. There are myriad reasons payout of oil royalties can be circumscribed, delayed, or simply suspended. Many players touch each well, and many of them are paid directly from a well's income. Should one of these players face financial hardship, their liabilities — which include income payments to the lease/landholder — often can be put into jeopardy. This sort of financial … chicanery often hits the lease/landholder's income, but doesn't necessarily impact the operations of any of the firms that actually do the drilling or fracking. Most important, operator, supplier, leaseholder, and financier troubles — even bankrupt-cy — have zero impact on the production from wells that already have been drilled and fracked. Flows from shale wells do not require pumping. Once the well is set up, ongoing inputs are minimal — so in times of financial duress there's no reason to halt production.

2. *Crunching margins.* There are a large number of steps in the shale supply chain. Sand miners, railroads, foundries, specialty metals makers, ma-chine toolers, pipe layers, data crunchers, lease seekers, and manufactur-ers of trucks and pumps and tanks and on and on and on. Your average well involves inputs from more than 100 companies from start to finish. When prices slumped, every participant found ways to trim the fat. That meant work slowdowns, pruning inventory and ultimately reducing ser-vice fees. All of the padding that had been built into every aspect of the business to thicken bottom lines in a $100+ price environment was ruth-lessly shaved out. The four major American oilfield service companies — Halliburton, Schlumberger, Baker Hughes, and Weatherford — touch

nearly all wells drilled in the United States. Rather than hoard shale's income and risk a sector-wide collapse, the quartet found themselves cornered into issuing at least a one-fifth reduction in their overall fee structures. Firms across the entire industry found themselves similarly cornered into following suit. That factor alone triggered a technical recession in not just the energy sector, but the overall mining industry in the second half of 2015. But drilling only slowed — it did not stop. Margins shriveled, but output remained remarkably stable.

3. *Geographic consolidation.* All shale plays are not created equal, but with oil prices in the general vicinity of $100, many players could try many things in many places. Nearly all shale basins have multiple layers, or tiers, in their geologic structure — and each is its own play. Rather than a "mere" 30 or so shale fields in the United States, there are in reality about 100 discrete shale plays. With prices at $100 there were operators in *all* of them. Many were not profitable — even at $100 — but with easy financing everyone was trying out new techs and new approaches. Even if they couldn't break even, they could develop proprietary techs and techniques for sale elsewhere. When prices crunched, this fairly esoteric approach to profitability was forced to become demonstrably more practical. The more expensive shale projects simply closed down, and operators of all stripes relocated to the major plays that boasted the best infrastructure and lowest production costs: Bakken, Permian, Eagle Ford, Marcellus. All the tech explorers followed. For the first time in the shale industry's history, the trick wasn't to find your own patch of land and experiment with new things, but instead to take what you knew and merge it with other people working on the same project. Sometimes this was done willingly. Sometimes operators triggered something called "forced pooling," which forced their co-operators to either share their tech and commit to immediate drilling, or back out completely and hand over their portion of the well. Regardless of path, eight years of proprietary technological experimentation concentrated from 100 plays down to the Big4 and became near-communal property. Dozens of what were unheard of experimental technologies in June

2014 had become commonplace by June 2016, ruthlessly driving *output* rates higher even while they drove per-barrel production *costs* lower.

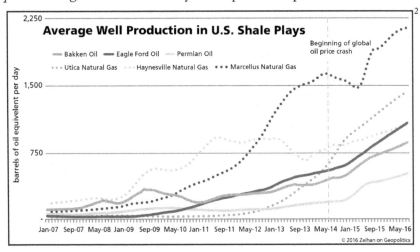

4. *Selective delays.* Some stages of shale production are more expensive than others. The fracking process typically consumes over half the cost, with drilling another quarter. Since shale wells push out their greatest flow rates in the first months of operation, the timing of when the well comes on-line is of critical importance. Why spend several million dollars to frack and complete a well with crude at $30 when you can drill now, but delay the fracking and completion for six months in the hope of making $50? Companies would figure out ways to lay claim to acreage, but then go slow in actually bringing the well on-line. As 2015 wound on, many producers took this a (huge) step further. It is rare to see a horizontal shaft with fewer than 20 stages — many push past 50 — and the current record is 124. All of these stages are fracked independently, so canny operators would only frack the first stage in order to fill the gathering pipeline network — and then defer on the rest of the frack until oil prices hit a number they considered more favorable. Drilling continued almost

2   Please note that this chart is the *average* hydrocarbon output for all wells in the relevant fields. It includes the 100,000 shale wells that were completed before all of these new techs became available in 2015, and the roughly 1,000,000 *non*-shale wells that were completed in the decades before the shale revolution. (The dotted lines are shale fields more known for their production of natgas than oil.)

unabated, but the *real* output was timed to take advantage of market moves. No firm data has ever existed for just how many wells are in this "fracklog," but the general industry guesstimate is that if they all were fracked to completion the United States would instantly add more than 500kbpd of oil production.

5. *Technological adaptation.* Though contractual manipulation, lower input costs, discounts from the service firms, and technique sharing probably reduced overall costs by as much as $30 a barrel, it was nowhere near enough. The nature of the business needed an overhaul. Saudi Arabia's price war inadvertently created a dream scenario for American innovation. What's happening now is a leaner, meaner, *greener* set of technologies that is allowing shale to tackle what detractors rightly see as its greatest Achilles' heel: high upfront production costs. Such tech advances comprise the bulk of shale's recent price advantage. We turn to them now.

Reduce, Reuse, Recycle

Each well requires millions of gallons of liquids to position frac sand and chemicals throughout the well formation. Since the United States is the third-most water-rich country in the world, this is not a particularly sensitive topic so long as operators don't do anything stupid — and that's largely because in the grand scheme of things, the shale sector actually isn't all that water intensive. In total, the shale industry uses less water than the United States' golf courses. But in arid regions water availability is simultaneously an environmental, economic, hydrological, and political issue. Triply so in dry locations where shale has emerged the dominant economic sector — and therefore the top water user. Put a shale industry in a region that was previously dependent on irrigated agriculture for its economic livelihood (such as western North Dakota) and you get two of the staunchest and testiest special interests alliances — energy producers and farmers — going head to head. In that sort of fight, environmentalists have a field day.

Yet simple economics are driving change across the industry. Water is an input, inputs cost money, and in a low-price oil environment money is in short supply. Even in water-rich Pennsylvania there isn't anyone in the shale industry who relishes the thought of using more water than is absolutely necessary. Somewhat ironically, it is decidedly non-environmentally conscious Texas that has been the leader in limiting water use. There are three main approaches.

First, anytime water can be **recycled**, it is. The initial step of the recycling journey is actually built into the frack process: At the completion of a frackjob, the water is pumped out of the well and back to the surface. This "flowback" water is not simply dumped — eight years of evolution in water management regulations have seen to that. Instead, it is treated, re-treated, and re-used whenever possible. And any water you can recycle is water you do not need to re-purchase.

As always, variation is the commonality. The rock strata in the Eagle Ford wells absorb so much liquid that flowback rates can be as low as 3 percent, so even recycling rates of 100 percent would not much budge overall water use. Marcellus rock is less thirsty, so the full recycling that is now standard there enables operators to reduce their surface water use by up to one-third. On the positive extreme, flowback rates in the Permian can be as high as 80 percent — quite the windfall considering how arid West Texas is typically.

Second, the water infrastructure of the shale site is changing. Previously, pre-treated water was trucked in, the chemical inputs were tweaked on site, and the frack fluid was then pumped into the well. When the water was removed it was poured into an on-site, plastic-lined liquids pit, where it remained until well operations were wrapped up. The pit would then be drained, remediated, and infilled.

Now the liquids pits themselves are going away.

As recycling has become more viable and more common, the liquids are in constant motion within the pumping infrastructure. Instead of a disposal or holding pit, the new norm is for the liquids to be held in giant tanks — with the water either linked via pipe to other wells within the same lease or the tanks themselves being trucked between leases. This sharply reduces the volume of liquid requiring remediation, simplifies the logistics of site set-up, operations and drilling, and allows water to be recycled across drilling pads rather than only among stages at the same pad. One system, one source of water, and that water is used again and again.

Third, the industry has learned that it doesn't actually prefer surface water, but instead *deep sub*surface water. I'm not referring here to water from the potable water table that many municipalities use to supply their local tap water needs, but instead deep, **brackish water** typically in excess of one-half mile down.

There are plenty of reasons to go after this alternative water source:

- It is mildly saline. Sodium chloride — plain old table salt — is the No. 1 additive in most frack fluids. Why add your own when you can source water that already has at least part of the necessary chemical mix baked in?

- Operators typically have to drill through the brackish water layer anyway as part of efforts to reach the shale formation they're after. They therefore know exactly the location of the water they need and can easily drill a second, shallower well to tap the saline water table with no guesswork.

- This subsurface water has no life in it. The utter absence of bacteria and algae makes it far better suited for fracking purposes than surface water, which must be filtered, treated, and purified before use.

- Since this brackish water is unfit for human consumption as well as useless for irrigation, there is little competition for it in most areas.

- The locals have noticed. Since late 2015, West Texas ranchers have started drilling for this brackish water and building the surface pipe infrastructure required to provide shale operators with steady supplies.[3]

Put together, these shifts theoretically could reduce overall per-barrel water use by as much as 80 percent. Considering that roughly three-quarters of the truck traffic at a fracking site is involved in moving water, even minor improvements on just this part of the shale supply chain have outsized impacts on reducing costs, limiting environmental impact, and reducing the noise and road traffic that so infuriates the neighbors.

---

3   For a fee, of course.

Combine, Consolidate and Extend

One drilling site, one well, one pipe. That has been the mantra of the energy sector since its earliest days in 1859 Pennsylvania. The segregation was a simple requirement: multiple vertical wells in close proximity would break through a caprock at similar locations and so tap the same reservoir with remarkable speed. Think of a malt being drained by two straws. At Spindletop, the first major oil development on the U.S. Gulf Coast, such overdrilling reduced the field's output — not the *well*, the *field* — by 80 percent in less than three years.

But in the world of shale we're not talking about traditional, conventional vertical wells. When a shale borehole reaches the petroleum-rich layer, it takes a sharp turn and then travels horizontally. And unlike a conventional reservoir that can be drained from multiple wells, shale petroleum cannot migrate from one part of the formation to another. It is trapped where it was formed. Frack cracks are no good if they are hundreds of feet long because the sand can't travel that far. That sand — by design — gets stuck no more than a few dozen feet from the well. A good frack is one that brutalizes the areas right around the wellbore but doesn't go beyond.

This geometry of petroleum geology has enabled operators to adjust how they operate at drilling sites, adding a second vertical well shaft to each pad spot with its companion horizontal turn down below. With such **pad drilling**, one well becomes two, two wells became three, and so on. At the time of this writing, most pads boast between four and six wells, but far from unheard of are pads with upward of 20.

Reduce the number of drilling sites by half — much less by a factor of 20 — and you reduce the cost of site set-up, tear-down and remediation by a similar proportion. **"Walking" rigs** were redesigned to relocate themselves from spot to spot on the pad without needing to be disassembled, reducing the lag between well drilling efforts from days to hours. Considering that crewed rigs cost $15,000 to $30,000 a day based on the market, this singular improvement probably shaved a few dollars off per-barrel production costs. **Simultaneous Operations** advances took things a step further. Now the fracking process can begin as soon as the first well on a pad is completed, instead of needing to wait for the entire pad to be drilled.

Meanwhile, drilling envelopes have expanded at just as impressive a pace as input needs have shrunk. In an "old"-style shale well at the dawn of the shale era in 2005, a single vertical shaft would lead to a single horizontal shaft of about 600 feet. Bit by bit, operators figured out how to extend horizontal shafts further. The current "norm" is getting longer by the week, with the 2016 average probably about 7,500 feet. The current record is 18,544.

Yet these **longer laterals** could be a mixed blessing. Combining surface infrastructure and increasing the lengths of a well's lateral components is great for simplifying logistics, increasing reservoir contact, achieving economies of scale and the like. But the longer a lateral gets, the greater variation of geology it encounters. A frack fluid and pressure profile that works beautifully at the well's toe may be idiotic at the well's heel.

But another technology under development holds the solution.

The Micro-Seismic Revolution

Even within the richest portions of a particular shale well — to say nothing of a particular shale basin — there are wildly variant levels of petroleum concentrations. The industry adage is the 20/80 rule: that 20 percent of frac stages produce 80 percent of the well's total petroleum output. The 20/80 rule's corollary is that over half of the frac stages actually produce no petroleum at all! Yet because operators don't know precisely where the petroleum is, all of those stages have to be fracked, wasting a great deal of water and manpower. One of the industry's Holy Grails has been to seek technologies that would enable drillers and frackers to focus their effort on the most productive geologies, and in particular let them know which portions of those geologies require which tools.

The solution is a new tool called seismic imaging, or more accurately, the solution is an improvement upon the seismic imaging that the energy industry has been using for a generation.

In traditional imaging, a burst of sound waves is directed down into the geologic formation. Initially this was done with controlled explosion, although more recently sonic emitters (think fancy stereo speakers) have come into fashion. The sound waves pass through different densities of rock at different speeds. Some will have their trajectories modified. Some will bounce back to the surface where sonic detectors (a.k.a. fancy microphones) will pick them up. Crunch that data through a computer and you usually get a grainy, two-dimensional view of portions of a formation. Such data enable petroleum engineers to guesstimate both where to position their drilling pads and where to send out their horizontal spurs. Before the advent of seismic tech, you were quite literally guessing where to drill and the vast, vast majority of efforts resulted in dry wells. Seismic drillers can (on a good day) identify a cross-section of a big bulb of juicy oil and know exactly where to send their steel straws.

Precision seismic technologies are far more important to the shale sector than the energy sector at large. Most shale layers are only a few dozen feet thick, and without seismic guidance it would be impossible to guess not simply where to drill, but where to turn the well shaft and start horizontal efforts. But seismic is *not* custom made for the shale industry. Nothing says that those sedimentary layers have to be perfectly horizontal. Uplifts and tectonic changes over the eons can tilt, warp, and fault them. It's less a stack of white printer paper with a few sheets of red cardboard within, and more a very badly made 11-layer cake that has fallen on the floor. Since seismic only gives you partial two-dimensional snapshots, all seismic does for the industry is grant a higher probability of drilling into a petroleum-rich zone. There is still a great deal of guesswork around how to direct horizontal efforts.

Since 2014 that has changed radically. Seismic tech has joined up with the information economy to overhaul how seismic works and redesign it with the shale sector's needs specifically in mind. With old-style seismic, a generated sound burst would reflect back a grainy slice of data for a single well. With new and improved **micro-seismic**, there is no sound burst. Sophisticated microphones listen to the micro-scale sounds made by the operators themselves during the drilling and fracking. This constant stream of data feeds into computers that sport processing power that didn't exist as recently as 2013, providing a wealth and depth of information that takes much of the guesswork out of petroleum production.

Drillers who use micro-seismic now know exactly where to place their pads for best results, exactly where and how sharply to turn horizontal, exactly what angles to drill and when to re-angle in the midst of a horizontal effort — at multiple times if it proves relevant. It's a bit like sending a drill into an arm-shaped formation, starting at the shoulder and going all the way to the end of the pinky — even if the elbow is bent and fingers curled. They also know enough about the micro-geology so that they can make some frack stages shorter or longer in order to maximize petroleum access and/or minimize input usage. And because the data are in real time, operators can adjust every part of their efforts — from the drilling to the frac mix — on the fly in order to achieve the best results on not just pad-by-pad and well-by-well but *stage-by-stage*.

Best of all, micro-seismic allows operators to ignore the half of the frac stages that don't actually hold petroleum. This last bit alone promises to halve the amount of frac pumps and frac liquids and frac sand required, while enabling operators to focus their efforts on the most productive stages of each individual well. Conversely, based on the availability of spare capacity in gathering infrastructure or overall oil/natgas price levels, an operator might not *want* to frack the most petroleum-dense stages right away, but instead simply mark down where the best stuff is and come back to it later.

It isn't all sunshine and unicorns for this new tech, however. Since micro-seismic is so new, there are only a few purveyors and most of them are not operators; micro-seismic is an add-on service. And it's not cheap. Micro-seismic requires the deployment of fiber-optic and geophone arrays, typically down a borehole — and that borehole cannot be used for drilling, fracking or production at the same time. This makes the tech far more attractive in areas where there are depleted wells that can be repurposed to seismic detection — such as the Permian — rather than virgin regions like much of the Marcellus.

Few doubt that micro-seismic is gaining acceptance, but the pace of those gains is hotly in question. It's really all about timing: Coughing up cash for a newish tech provided by a third party in an era of cost cutting is as problematic as it sounds. As of mid-2016 micro-seismic is used in somewhere between 1 percent of all U.S. shale wells (the number floated by firms that don't do it) and 8 percent (the number floated by firms that do).

Branching Out

Just as seismic techs are improving rapidly, so too are drilling techs — with the potential game changer something generally called **multilateral drilling**. The concept is that the operator drills the initial vertical well to the deepest layer of the formation in question, followed by a normal horizontal spur. But instead of recalling the drilling apparatus and drilling a new vertical well bore, the operator only retreats the drill back to the vertical shaft and then drills a second horizontal spur. And then a third. And then a fourth. And on and on. And when that entire horizontal layer is fully drilled, only then is the drill recalled up the well bore ... but not all the way. It is only pulled back up until it hits the next layer of undrilled shale where another horizontal spur is drilled. And another. And so on, until every horizontal shale layer all the way back up to the surface is fully exploited.

A multilateral-capable drill needn't ever reposition, and it need only drill a single vertical shaft for a wide area. Just one multilateral-capable drill can establish all the reservoir contact that an old-style drill could in less than half the time with half the pipe — and all from one pad.

Only when all of the multiple levels of multiple laterals are drilled do frack crews start work on the individual stages of each individual spur. All told, the 2004 norm was 600 feet of reservoir contact from a pad; as of mid-2016 a multilaterally drilled well can easily sport 6 *miles* of contact with upward of 30 miles being possible — all linked back to a single vertical well shaft.

There are no shale projects where multi-lateral systems do not vastly reduce per-barrel costs or vastly improve per-pad output, but the biggest boosts come from the most complex geologies. A quick comparison:

• The Bakken and Eagle Ford are famous for particularly petroleum-dense shale layers, but those layers are rarely stacked more than two high. This simplifies seismic work, but somewhat limits the wow factor for multi-lateral efforts. Operators can fan out spurs through their single- or dou-ble-layer of shales, getting the equivalent of four to ten times the activity that they could have normally gotten from a single shaft. Good. Great even. But not particularly mind-boggling.

- In comparison, some areas of the Permian have upward of *ten* petroleum-bearing layers. All those layers and faults and angles have limited seismic effectiveness until recently (thank you micro-seismic). A single vertical shaft could punch through *all* of them, and operators can put a multi-lateral spur system in at each layer. In such a multilateral well 40 spurs would be considered a below-average result. Unsurprisingly, it is the Permian that has not only seen the most intensive work of late, but even increased output in the teeth of the 2015-2016 price crash.

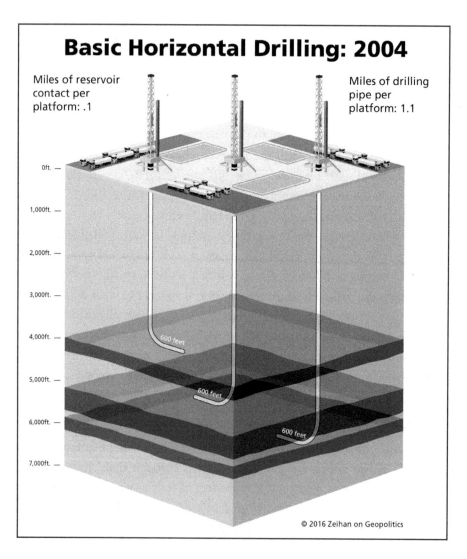

Basic Horizontal Drilling: 2004

Miles of reservoir contact per platform: .1

Miles of drilling pipe per platform: 1.1

0ft. —
1,000ft. —
2,000ft. —
3,000ft. —
4,000ft. —
5,000ft. —
6,000ft. —
7,000ft. —

600 feet

600 feet

600 feet

© 2016 Zeihan on Geopolitics

One of the big reasons the media is so obsessed with the shale-is-dead mantra is that the number of active rigs in operation has plummeted by more than 80 percent since November 2014. As the argument goes, fewer rigs illustrates an industry facing collapse.

Sorry, but no. Following the rig count is a bit like equating bicycles and automobiles.

Throughout the industry, the goal is greater efficiency. As shale technologies like multilateral drilling mature and evolve, more work is being done

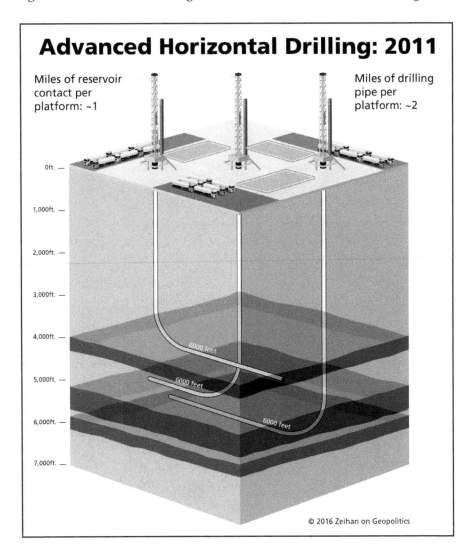

Advanced Horizontal Drilling: 2011

Miles of reservoir contact per platform: ~1

Miles of drilling pipe per platform: ~2

0ft. —
1,000ft. —
2,000ft. —
3,000ft. —
4,000ft. —
5,000ft. —
6,000ft. —
7,000ft. —

6000 feet
6000 feet
6000 feet

© 2016 Zeihan on Geopolitics

with fewer inputs per barrel of output and *rigs are an input*. Horizontal rigs that were the industry norm as recently as 2014 are losing viability because they are incapable of drilling multi-laterally. The media — and dare I say a certain geopolitical analyst — is only now scrambling to find new ways of gauging the new shale boom's activity.

This vastly improved production math also changes the way petroleum is collected and transported once it reaches the surface. When wells only produced a few score of barrels a day at initiation and there was only one well

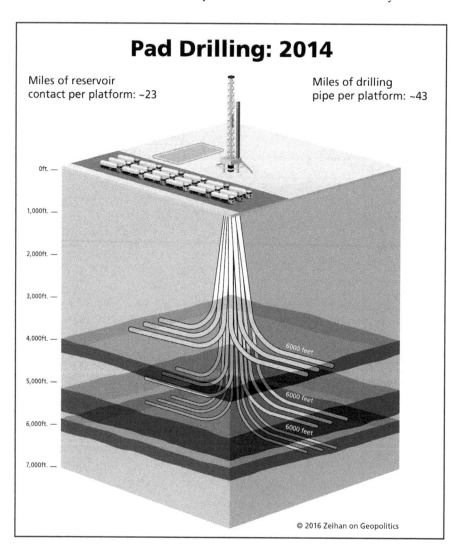

Pad Drilling: 2014

Miles of reservoir contact per platform: ~23

Miles of drilling pipe per platform: ~43

0ft.
1,000ft.
2,000ft.
3,000ft.
4,000ft.
5,000ft.
6,000ft.
7,000ft.

6000 feet
6000 feet
6000 feet

© 2016 Zeihan on Geopolitics

per pad, operating and collecting infrastructure was a crazy-quilt of back roads and small pipes that crisscrossed the landscape. Output per well has not only surged, there are now multiple wells on each pad. *Pad* output — as compared to *well* output — is already in the range of several thousands of barrels of oil equivalent per day (or more), all from a production footprint that requires less than one-tenth the area required a decade ago. More output from fewer production points requires far *larger* **trunk pipes** that are far *fewer* in number. The reduction in pipe footage, right-of-way requirements

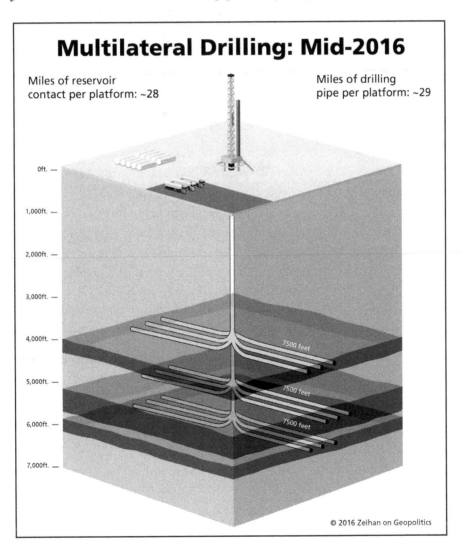

and installation equipment simplifies and cheapens the surface infrastructure process.

Are You Sufficiently Stimulated?

All of this is good — great even — but very little of it actually addresses
one of the ongoing challenges that shale presents: decline. Since the only
pressure within a shale well is that of those micro-pockets of petroleum
within the frack zone, once that pressure is depleted the wells rapidly wind
down. Wells give up 30 to 50 percent of their total 20-year output within
the first year. That number tends to tick up to 50 to 85 percent in year
two — from that point out, flows drop to a trickle. Drilling and fracking is
expensive, and for all the effort and expense to peter-out within three years
is somewhat … anticlimactic.

To date the best strategy to keep wells producing something closer to their
initial output for a longer period of time is to frack with more liquid, more
sand, and more pressure to crack up the rock more thoroughly so that more
petroleum bits are accessed right up front. Such **brute force fracks** free up
more petroleum bits that migrate toward the wellbore — a wellbore that
hasn't gotten any bigger — causing a bit of a traffic jam. The petroleum can
only exit so quickly, resulting in a flatter decline curve. This can be achieved
artificially as well by deliberately narrowing the well bore with something
called a **choke**, in essence a piece of constricting steel inserted into the well.

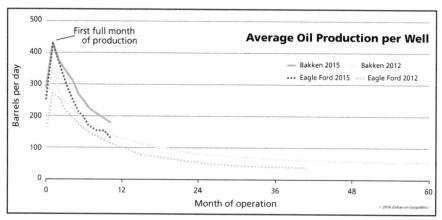

Such methods help operators get more reliable — and longer-term — output, but what truly is needed is the ability to reset a well back to its initial high specs in order to keep all of the attendant infrastructure operating at something closer to full capacity.

A newish stratagem is to go back to older well pads and add new wells to them. New efforts at old pads can apply advances in seismic and fracking and drilling to bring old pads well above old production levels — in essence turning an old single-well pad into a multi-well pad in which the new wellshaft is most certainly the bigger brother. Armed with micro-seismic, operators can even know where to drop in new shafts *between* existing vertical lines and horizontal spurs, with the new output being shunted into pre-existing collection networks. Such **infilling** can often bring a pad's output back up to prime levels without having to re-secure leases or pipe right-of-ways or build new roads.

Then there are ways of resuscitating the pre-existing well itself (rather than new drilling at an old pad).

Refracking is just what it sounds like. Operators return to an older well and recomplete the fracking process with today's technology. This does more than you might think. Big Data have really only been applied to well work since 2013, while micro-seismic is only began transitioning out of the fringe in early 2016. This means that in the initial shale boom of 2007-2011, not one well had meaningful during-production seismic work. This allows operators to revisit their entire well list and do the frack process all over again. For 25 to 75 percent of the cost of the initial work, stages are typically returned to their initial production levels.

As a rule, the biggest gains come from those wells that failed to impress the first time around, because this time around there are better data to guide the effort. It also is an opportunity to recomplete older wells with the best environmental practices of the current day rather than the free-for-all of the early boom years.

Then there is **waterflooding** ... which is also what it sounds like — operators force water down into a well shaft to flood out the oil. Waterflooding is a secondary stimulation that has been with the conventional energy industry for decades, heavily used in most on-land oil fields up to and including Saudi Arabia's superfield, Ghawar. In essence water is pumped down into the formation where it mingles slightly with remnant oil volumes. That oil-laced water is then pumped back up. The oil is skimmed off the top and the water makes a return trip in search of more petroleum.

The question for waterflooding is whether it is applicable to the geology of shale. Normally the water floods a conventional formation, scrounging for trace oil beneath the caprock. Shale has no such reservoir to access. But the tech has two huge advantages arguing for if not success, at least heavy experimentation. First, it has been the most common secondary stimulation method for decades, so there are plenty of engineers who can attempt to tweak waterflooding with shale in mind. Second, it's cheap. In theory, for as little as 2 to 5 percent of the original well cost, waterflooding can raise a well's output by 25 percent of its initial output.

Somewhat more esoteric systems also are in advanced experimentation.

Just as water can be injected to increase output at an older well, so too can carbon dioxide or methane. Both actually dissolve into crude and make it far less viscous, allowing the crude to flow more easily to the well bore. Such **gas injection** could source the carbon dioxide from cement and power plants or the methane from local natgas production, increasing petroleum output while vastly reducing local greenhouse gas emissions. The primary challenge is proximity. If your field isn't close to a population/industrial center, you might need a lengthy CO2 pipe just to get started, and depending on crude price points, the higher oil output might not be enough to justify the higher up-front infrastructure costs.

All of these additional stimulation efforts suggest a redesign of the entire well system with the intent of managing output not so much over the course of years, but decades. Such purposeful well-redesigns to include fairways for future indrilling, long-term seismic data monitoring and including infrastructure for enhanced recovery are all well and good and are likely to be a core tenant of the industry in just two or three years. All of that will certainly increase long-term output.

But for maximizing output from existing wells, the real breakthrough might be something much simpler.

Once a well is completed, the various stages are locked in place forever. That poses a problem for techs like refracking because the frac cracks from adjacent stages often cross paths, making it difficult to isolate — and thus concentrate — frac pressure in specific zones. A lack of such zonal isolation hugely limits what a refrack can achieve. Enter the **sliding sleeve**, a device that slides up and down the well bore as needed, allowing targeted, customized (re)fracking to happen at any point in the pipe. Even the stages themselves can be repartitioned as needed. The result — at least in theory — is a quantum leap in materials efficiency and the ability to simply open any sliding-sleeve to refrack at any time without needing to worry about well geometry or someone else's prior work or infrastructural debris. Sliding sleeve is certainly the newest — and least proven — of the techniques in play, but it too is already off the drawing board and in initial operation.

Shale's Next Stage

All of these changes are still rather young in terms of their dissemination throughout the shale patch. Sliding sleeve and micro-seismic, in particular, have a whiff of pixie dust about them.

The point isn't so much that this mix of techs will be *the* technologies that form the scaffolding of shale's new normal, but instead that these technologies are representative of dozens of similar technologies — all of which are being crafted and honed in fits and starts. All are creeping into operators' tool boxes, contributing to the formation of a new best practices suite that is far more price competitive than what exists today, much less two years ago. Best of all, most of these techs were already off the drawing board and in limited operation at the time the Saudis launched their price war, so the learning curve for their adoption is incredibly steep. No one has to invent the wheel.

In essence, an entire new subsector has been layered into the fracking industry that requires less work than the initial effort (surveying, leasing, permitting, drilling, road construction) that dominates the original well as well as less of the follow-up work (monitoring, collecting infrastructure). Yet it still produces as much — or more — of the initial well's output at a fairly marginal additional cost. With the technology that exists in mid-2016, each well now likely can be relied upon to at least *triple* its long-term output compared to 2014 norms for on average less than a 50-percent increase in

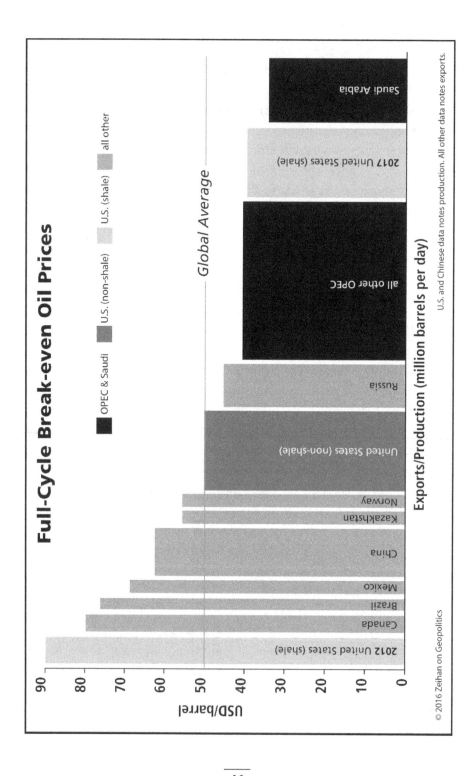

Full-Cycle Break-even Oil Prices

Legend: OPEC & Saudi | U.S. (non-shale) | U.S. (shale) | all other

Global Average

Exports/Production (million barrels per day)

USD/barrel

Saudi Arabia
2017 United States (shale)
all other OPEC
Russia
United States (non-shale)
Norway
Kazakhstan
China
Mexico
Brazil
Canada
2012 United States (shale)

90
80
70
60
50
40
30
20
10
0

U.S. and Chinese data notes production. All other data notes exports.

© 2016 Zeihan on Geopolitics

cost, with *less* surface infrastructure. Collectively these improvements will generate millions of additional barrels of crude daily over the next three decades, introducing the capacity to raise America's baseline output by half.[4]

All this tech means that the total input cost *per well* may be rising (sharply), but output is so much higher per well that the total production cost *per barrel* is plummeting.

In 2012, before any of these technologies had been operationalized, full-cycle costs were about $90 a barrel. In November 2014, when the Saudis launched their price war, the full-cycle break-even cost across the shale patch was probably about $75. Factoring in consolidation, the pursuit of efficiency and especially the development and application of new technologies, by August 2015 that figure had plunged to $50 in the Big4 fields. As operators started to redesign wells with the entire life cycle of production in mind (i.e. including plans for infilling and refracking), that per-barrel production cost for new wells dipped to vicinity of $40 at the time of this writing in November 2016, and that doesn't even include operators going back to exploit their fracklogs. Far from being some of the most expensive oil to produce in the world as it was in 2012, shale already is more cost-competitive than the global average. As these techs continue to mature and play off of one another, a price structure of around $25 sometime in 2019 seems within reach.

U.S. shale simply will not be swept away by a tsunami of Saudi oil. Instead U.S. shale is on the cusp of being cost-competitive *with* Saudi oil.

The Other Side of Shale

It isn't all good news. Every time an economic sector evolves, there are winners and losers. Shale is no exception. There are three general themes to keep in mind.

---

4   Oil production is ultimately price-dependent, so putting forward a firm output number on this is a sketchy exercise — particularly when dealing with technologies that are so young that their final cost envelope is not yet known. That said, back-of-envelope math suggests that these enhanced techniques could increase U.S. oil output by 6mbpd, more than enough to make the United States oil independent.

First, shale's drive for efficiency is a one-way process.

With the shale sector under price pressure, operators' goals are to get the most petroleum out of the ground for the lowest per-barrel cost. The industry is racking up success after success, producing more petroleum per foot of pipe, gallon of water, pound of sand, ounce of chemicals and man-hour worked. That's great if you are an operator, less so if you earn your living making pipe, supplying water, mining sand, fabricating chemicals, or in general working for said operator in some way.

Multilateral drilling isn't just reducing the need for pipe by half, it will reduce the need for welders by half. The shift from liquids ponds to water tanks not only has reduced the total volume of water by two-thirds, it will eliminate over half of the truck trips required to complete the well, taking a great many truck *driver* jobs along with it. Micro-seismic isn't just reducing the amount of fracking required by enabling operators to avoid fracking stages with no petroleum, but the reduction of sand inputs could well deliver an economic hit to western Wisconsin, where most of the industry's sand is sourced.

But all of this is happening without more than a marginal reduction in petroleum output. What's happened in 2015 and 2016 has not been so much a recession in the energy production sector, but a recession in the energy production *inputs* sector. As all of these technologies continue to evolve, the goal of ever-increasing efficiency will remain. This means that demand for all of those inputs is likely to never rebound to 2013 levels.

Second, much of the shale boom has been about building things that were not there before. This part of the boom is largely over — and not because of the price drop.

Think of where you live. Once someone (maybe you) made the decision to build, a flurry of activity follows. Lumberjacks got to work getting the trees, which generated business for lumber mills, which produced the planks for everything from the building frame to the particle board to the furniture. Quarries and stonecutters produced the rock façade and the inputs for the tile. Miners pulled limestone out of the ground, then transferred the rock to crushers who pulverized it to produce the base materials for cement. Miners of a different type went after bauxite and copper and iron ores that were sent to smelters who turned the rock into metals that were pulled into electrical wires or fashioned into brackets and nails and screws. Yet more miners produced high-quality sand that went off to be heated into sheets of glass. At every step of the process there was shipping: of timber and ores and metals and 2x4s and stone and siding and carpet and frames and so on. All these inputs and more converged upon a building site where they were poured, laid, hammered, glued, grouted, fixed, etc., to produce a structure. Every structure built touches more than 100 industries and thousands of people's economic well-being. For all those involved, the construction of your house or apartment building was a godsend. Your house made the economy — locally, regionally, nationally, even internationally — boom.

Then how long until you built your second house? *Did* you build a second one? The construction process typically only happens once. And unless you are part of the lucky group who owns multiple homes, even if you *did* build a second house, someone moved into your first house when you moved out and they didn't generate much of an economic bump at all. Sure you — or they — may have renovated or added on a room somewhere down the road, and that certainly stimulates economic activity — but nothing like the bonanza from the initial construction.

The same is true in any economic sector. You only build the basics once. Towns only need so many roads, sidewalks and power lines. Manufacturers only need so many fab facilities. This growth-from-investment pattern is a big reason Japan's economy did so well in the 1950s-1970s but hasn't grown at all since 1998. Similarly, that's part of why China grew so quickly from 1980-2015, but is in the midst of a jarring slowdown.[5] Similarly, the shale industry only needs so many roads and gathering pipelines, sand mines and chemical support. You only need to industrialize once.

In essence, some shale communities have taken a double hit. The various supporting infrastructure only needed to be built once — and that's done — while any new wells won't need nearly as many inputs. So any future expansions will seem downright languid compared to what's come previous. Towns in the vicinity of the more expensive shale plays — the ones that were largely abandoned in late-2014 — will see new booms when activity

---

5   And almost certainly headed for something far worse.

returns, but even collectively that is nothing compared to the 2007-2014 surge of construction at the Big4-producing zones.

Third, shale's ever decreasing break-even prices are driving many *conventional* energy producers out of business.

Nodding donkey in Montana

The *sale* price of shale natgas is roughly one-third the *production* cost of most conventional natgas plays in North America. Particularly hard hit are natgas producers in the Canadian province of Alberta. Albertan production sites are in excess of 1,500 miles from most of their core market in Ontario — a market less than 300 miles from the American Marcellus shale, a zone so prolific it is responsible for one-third of all U.S. natural gas production. Shale natgas also has devastated offshore natgas producers, most notably in the Gulf of Mexico, where costs are high, drilling times are long, and hurricanes can take production offline for months at a time. Shale faces none of these constraints, and so the Gulf natgas industry is for all intents and purposes dying on its feet with output down by half since just 2010.[6]

---

6   Which incidentally means that if shale ever actually runs out of natgas, the Gulf will still be there as a sort of energy piggy bank.

U.S. Hydrocarbon Production and Prices

Total Oil Production Moving Average   Natural Gas Production Moving Average   U.S. Natural Gas Price   U.S. Oil Price

Increased U.S. shale production

Thousand Barrels of Oil Equivalent Per Day

30,000
25,000
20,000
15,000
10,000
5,000
-

Dollars Per Barrel of Oil Equivalent

$160
$140
$120
$100
$80
$60
$40
$20
$-

Jan-1982
Oct-1982
Jul-1983
Apr-1984
Jan-1985
Oct-1985
Jul-1986
Apr-1987
Jan-1988
Oct-1988
Jul-1989
Apr-1990
Jan-1991
Oct-1991
Jul-1992
Apr-1993
Jan-1994
Oct-1994
Jul-1995
Apr-1996
Jan-1997
Oct-1997
Jul-1998
Apr-1999
Jan-2000
Oct-2000
Jul-2001
Apr-2002
Jan-2003
Oct-2003
Jul-2004
Apr-2005
Jan-2006
Oct-2006
Jul-2007
Apr-2008
Jan-2009
Oct-2009
Jul-2010
Apr-2011
Jan-2012
Oct-2012
Jul-2013
Apr-2014
Jan-2015
Oct-2015

Sources: World Bank and U.S. Energy Information Agency

The biggest losers are probably those nodding donkey (a.k.a. stripper) wells. It all has to do with the difference in old-style conventional oil production versus new-style shale.

The fracking process doesn't simply create pathways for oil and natgas to flow into the well bore, it releases tiny pockets of pressure throughout the frack zone. That pressure is what drives the petroleum output, and that process is not dependent upon any additional inputs.

That's not how a stripper well works. Stripper wells operate in fields that are well past their prime. All pre-existing pressure long since tapered off. Producing crude from these locations requires the *creation* of pressure. Nodding donkeys pump water up out of a largely-depleted oil formation, and that water drags a thin sheen of oil up with it. Since oil cannot dissolve in water — and since oil's density is less — the oil can be skimmed off the surface. Such oil production only generates tiny traces of crude — one barrel a day is the norm — and so it takes herds of donkeys to generate even modest volumes. All of this requires extensive infrastructure, constant pumping, and therefore constant electricity supplies.

Finding stripper wells is not hard to do. They exist in nearly any land-based oil-play that has been in operation for more than five decades, and are most commonly found in Texas, Oklahoma, Pennsylvania, and California (including on Wilshire Boulevard in Los Angeles). All told, U.S. stripper wells are responsible for roughly 1mbpd of oil output, but because of their high electric, water, and infrastructure needs, most have break-even costs in excess of $70 a barrel. Shale has found a way to live with lower prices, but nearly all of the iconic donkeys are operating at a loss.

There is one final loser of this increased efficiency: the shale operators themselves. In 2013, prices were high and the shale operators couldn't help but make money. In 2016, prices are low, consolidation is the watchword, and most operators are scraping by. In many ways today's shale patch is a victim of its own success. In driving up production, the industry has contributed to the price crash and so created the very environment that hobbles its businesses and forces an industry-wide consolidation. Every revolution has losers, and the shale revolution is no exception.

But the overall picture for the United States is stunning.

In the 10 years that shale has been commercially viable, U.S. production of oil and natgas has shot up from historical lows to historical highs. Moreover, the price structure of that production has fallen so low that shale is remaking the American industrial base. And for that, the real story isn't about oil, but natural gas.

CHAPTER 3

The Third Shale Revolution

Sometimes a picture is indeed worth a thousand words.

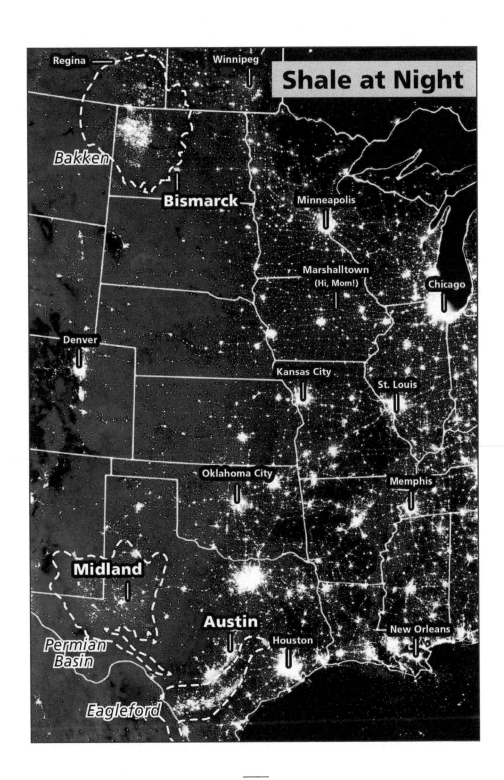

I call this the checkbook map, because every dot represents someone who has a checkbook and can pay an electric bill. There are three population centers to which I'd like to draw your attention. The northernmost arrow points to the hip town of Bismarck, North Dakota. The middle highlights the cultural mecca of Midland, Texas. The final arrow fingers the sleepy backwater of the Austin-San Antonio corridor, where I live.[1] People live here. They have checkbooks. There are lights. You can see the lights from orbit. Pretty straightforward.

Now look at some of the areas near these three cities — northwest of Bismarck, west of Midland, south of San Antonio. You'll notice fairly dense light patterns. These regions are some of the least densely populated places in the Lower48, yet they are lit up — in the case of western North Dakota and southern Texas, even brighter than many metropolitan regions.

Meet America's shale fields. The northernmost is the Bakken formation. In west Texas lies the Permian Basin. South of my Austin home is the Eagle Ford. The fields are lit up not because of they are packed with people who dutifully pay their utility bills, but because of flared natural gas (natgas).

It all comes down to transport. Oil is a liquid. It's fairly easy to move or store. You can put it into a rail car or tanker truck or bucket or simply leave it in an open vat. Just take the most basic of containment precautions and oil won't go anywhere. It is this simplicity of storage and transport — combined with the ubiquity of uses — that has made oil the backbone of the modern age. Unsurprisingly, oil is what the shale drillers are after.

Natural gas is different. It's, well, a gas. It disperses. The required volume of natgas at standard air pressure to achieve anything is massive. It'd take a container roughly the size of a walk-in closet to supply your oven for Thanksgiving dinner. The same volume of gasoline would allow you to drive from New York City to Los Angeles. And back.

Twenty times.[2]

---

1   Visit all you want, but don't move here.

2   My typical Thanksgiving extravaganzas tend to include both my posse and the in-laws, so the turkey has to be on the 20-pound side. Add in the spiral-sliced pineapple-maple ham, cornbread blue-cheese stuffing, wild mushroom stuffing, chipotle sweet potatoes, twice-baked ricotta potatoes, caramelized roasted root veggies, parmesan croissants, toasted cinnamon-agave pecans, bourbon-chocolate pecan pie, cranberry-eggnog cheesecake and

Mitigating natgas' volume constraint requires compressing it by a factor of 200 or more.[3] That requires specialized equipment, specialized transport systems and specialized storage vessels, making working with the stuff a general pain.

A successful natural gas industry, therefore, is based not on *storage* as oil is, but on *through*put: pre-existing points of pressurized supply shunting gas through pre-existing and matching pressurized transport networks to pre-existing and matching points of pressurized demand that can use the natgas at nearly the same speed that it arrives. If you lack such a complete and perfectly interconnected infrastructure, you lack a natural gas industry. The United States is the world's largest natgas producer, largest natgas consumer, and has the world's largest and most adaptable and interconnected natgas transport system — yet it cannot capture all of the natgas the shale fields are producing. In the Bakken, Permian, and Eagle Ford, the excess natural gas has to be burned off in such volumes that you can see the flares from space. At least 20 percent of the natgas used in the United States in 2015 was produced as a byproduct of liquids production, and that's likely a recent *low* considering that pipeline building is constantly playing catch-up with shale output.

Now We're Cooking With...

Think for a moment on the significance of that: natural gas, the most versatile industrial input in existence, the basic building block of modern society, in the United States is a *waste* product. As of New Year's 2016, natgas sold in the United States for barely more than $2 per 1,000 cubic feet, a fraction

....

a couple other things that vary from year to year and we're talking about using nearly 400 cubic feet of natural gas at standard temperature and pressure. One cubic foot can hold 7.5 gallons of liquid, so the fuel volume of that Thanksgiving natgas translates into 3,000 gallons of gasoline. The average American passenger automobile gets just shy of 37 miles to the gallon, so all that gasoline could move you 110,000 miles. The LA-NY trip is 2,770 miles one-way, making for 20 round trips between Long Beach and Manhattan.

3   For comparison your average party balloon is pressurized — at most — by a factor of three.

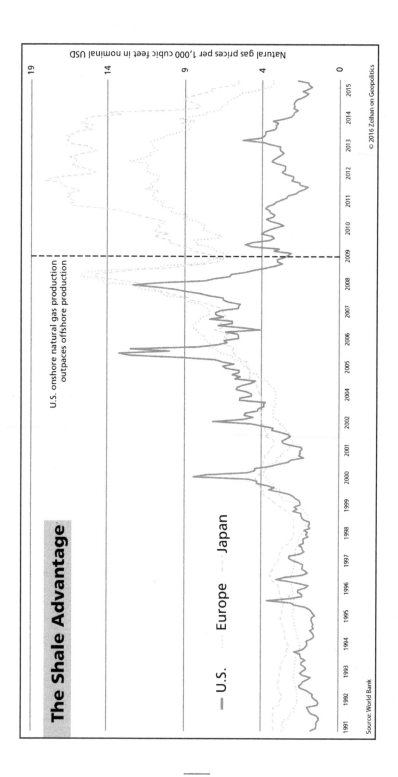

The Shale Advantage

Natural gas prices per 1,000 cubic feet in nominal USD

U.S. onshore natural gas production
outpaces offshore production

—— U.S.   ······ Europe   ---- Japan

Source: World Bank

© 2016 Zeihan on Geopolitics

the cost to other major economic players. The differential is in large part because so much of the natgas the shale industry produces is dumped into the transport infrastructure simply to get rid of it.

Though U.S. natgas prices are unlikely to remain in their current rock-bottom level over a decades-long timescale, the current pricing has legs.

The shale oil plays that tend to be the most productive have natgas comingled — "associated" in industry parlance — in with the oil. Since natgas is a gas, it exerts pressure that helps push oil from wherever it is held in the rock toward any sort of open space (for example, a well bore). So long as oil producers are trying to find efficiencies, they will tend to favor oil fields that have such associated natural gas. Even in areas like the Marcellus, which are known more for natgas than oil and so lack the halo effect of the main shale oil plays, operators heavily favor "wet" gas zones where the natgas is co-mingled with higher-selling price natural gas liquids (stuff like propane and butane). There is so much associated natgas in the Big4 shale plays that it's fairly reasonable the current price structure will endure for years to come.

For now this means that shale fields as varied as the Niobrara, Antrim, or Woodford can be held in reserve. Only when all of the associated shale natural gas is used up will producers then return en masse to sites with a reputation for having loads of low-cost "dry" gas, like the Fayetteville field of Arkansas or the Barnett field of Texas. And only when *that* is used up will secondary shale fields truly come into their own.[4] And only after *they* are tapped out will the conventional producing zones like the Gulf of Mexico once again have their day. Put all this together, and the United States is highly likely to have natural gas prices below $4 per 1,000 cubic feet for the next 30 years, assuming no new exploration at existing shale-producing zones, no new exploration in known shale zones that are not in production, no new technological advances, no application of recent technological advances to existing conventional natural gas fields, and no supplies from Canada, Mexico, the Gulf of Mexico or Alaska. More realistically, the

---

4   Again, keep in mind that there is no such thing as "typical." There are parts of the Utica and Barnett that are fairly "wet" even though those shales have an accurate reputation for being mostly "dry." Also, with technologies like those discussed in Chapter 2 continuing to evolve, what constitutes an economical field is most certainly a moving target.

United States is looking at 60 years (or more) of natural gas supplies that are eminently affordable.[5]

And natural gas prices will not be particularly volatile.

One of the massive challenges of the natgas industry has long been price swings. Everything that currently argues for natural gas prices being low — mostly the stickiness of transport infrastructure — also works in reverse. Should natural gas supplies prove insufficient, prices rise very quickly because there is no clean substitute. The only way to push prices down is not simply to expand exploration and production, but also to build new gathering and transport pipes to bring new sources of natural gas to end-users. With conventional fields, this explore-drill-produce cycle is a years-long process onshore, and takes at least a decade offshore. In contrast, a really complicated shale well takes about six weeks to complete. Should the production needle slide into the red, operators can mobilize within days and bring prices back down in a couple of months. Not to mention that the break-even prices for some of the larger and more natgas-intensive shale fields — primarily Marcellus, Fayetteville, and Barnett — already is well below $4, and in some sections of the Utica, it already is in the vicinity of *$1*.

Best of all, most shale fields — completely coincidentally — are adjacent to demand centers. The Barnett is *under* Dallas-Fort Worth. The Haynesville is just north of Houston. The Marcellus sprawls across the triangle of territory linking D.C., Chicago, and New York. The Niobrara is just outside of Denver. Conventional fields in North America aren't nearly as proximate. Albertan fields are at least several hundred miles from potential markets, and a cool 2,000 miles from the American refining hub around Houston. Fields in northern New Mexico require mountain drilling and lengthy trunk lines. Alaska's North Slope fields are literally on the wrong side of the continent. Shale's simplicity of transport logistics as compared

---

5   As to oil availability, the math is far simpler. Most shale oil firms indicate that their remaining reserves are in a bracket between 25 and 30 years. There's a reason for such a tight cluster. Should a company indicate that it has *more* than 30 years of reserves remaining, competitors believe the firm should increase its production rates. In essence when you claim more than 30 years, you identify yourself as a takeover target. So while the United States — officially — has "only" 30 years of shale oil supplies, that's only because of bookkeeping protocols. The number is certainly higher. Lord only knows how much higher.

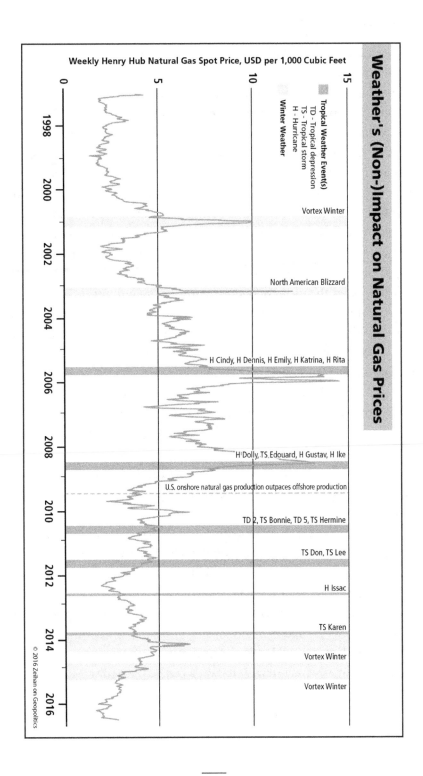

Weekly Henry Hub Natural Gas Spot Price, USD per 1,000 Cubic Feet

Tropical Weather Event(s)
TD - Tropical depression
TS - Tropical storm
H - Hurricane
Winter Weather

Weather's (Non-)Impact on Natural Gas Prices

Vortex Winter

North American Blizzard

H Cindy, H Dennis, H Emily, H Katrina, H Rita

H Dolly, TS Edouard, H Gustav, H Ike

U.S. onshore natural gas production outpaces offshore production

TD 2, TS Bonnie, TD 5, TS Hermine

TS Don, TS Lee

H Issac

TS Karen

Vortex Winter

Vortex Winter

© 2016 Zeihan on Geopolitics

to conventional plays adds up to faster reaction times at lower prices with less price volatility.

Consider the impact: In the time before shale, the second-largest nat-gas-producing province in the United States was the Gulf of Mexico off-shore.[6] On occasion, hurricanes would rip through the area, forcing the shutdown and evacuation of drilling and production platforms. This would do more than interrupt output for the few days that the hurricane was prox-imate; winds, waves, and subsea currents could wreck infrastructure both above and below the water. This necessitated not just lengthy and expensive repairs whose costs ultimately fed through to consumers, but actual short-ages that would spike prices for months. Americans could count themselves lucky if natural gas prices "only" doubled.

With shale in the mix, things have changed significantly.

First and most obvious, it is damnably hard to compete with free shale natgas. While shale natgas production has surged, total Gulf of Mexico output is down by more than half, demoting the Gulf to the country's sev-enth-largest natgas production zone.

Second, all shale production is *onshore* rather than *offshore*. Hurricanes haven't stopped occurring — Hurricane Issac in August 2012 and Tropical Storm Karen in October 2013 both roared through the middle of the Gulf's production zone — but Gulf output is far less important in both absolute and relative terms. Even large-scale Gulf disruptions barely make a ripple in national natgas markets because their impact on the shale industry is minimal.

Shale has provided so much insulation that even significant weath-er events that impact the entire country barely move the needle. During the winters of 2013-2014 and 2014-2015, frigid temperatures repeatedly gripped large portions of the country, stressing electricity and natural gas supplies — and so natgas prices rose. But there was only one price spike — in February 2014 — and it lasted a mere 11 *days*. Considering the onshore nature of product, the disassociated nature of shale production zones, and the sheer speed at which new shale wells can be brought on-line, the odds

---

6   This includes the federal offshore zone as well as the zones managed by Texas, Louisiana, and Alabama.

of serious disruptions — and more important, of sustained price rises — are very low indeed.

So natural gas is cheap, reliably cheap, and will be for decades to come. The only question is what to do with it?

The short answer is, well, a not so little bit of everything.

Economies of Shale

The electricity-generating sector has long been a major use of natural gas, accounting for roughly 30 percent of total American natgas demand at the onset of the shale era in 2007. Those in the industry of electricity generation aren't prone to making revolutionary shifts, and it is easy to identify with their skittishness. Power generators need long memories because electricity-generating plants' lifespans are measured in decades. Operators must game forward what natural gas (and coal, and uranium, and hydro, etc.) prices, supply reliability, and regulations will be not just for the next few years, but for the next generation.

The last major push into using natural gas to fuel electricity generation happened in the late 1990s. Prices then spiked in the early 2000s, rendering much of the investment uneconomic. It was a bit like buying a Hummer only to have gasoline prices triple on you. Utilities certainly noticed that natgas prices were crashing in the late 2000s, but no one was eager to take another jump into the natgas sandbox and risk repeating the pain of a decade earlier.

But electricity producers found it impossible to dismiss the non-event that was the February 2014 price spike, giving them confidence that the shale revolution had legs. In 2014, most electricity generators started committing to large-scale natgas usage and launching multi-year efforts to make natgas-burning power plants the core of their generation portfolios. The result has been one of the fastest buildouts of natgas usage in history, both for new generation and to displace existing generating assets that use fuels that are, well, not free.

This transition is still building momentum. Natural gas use for power generation increased more than 40 percent between 2007 and 2016, advancing it to the position of the single-largest source of electric power in the United States, with it now typically generating as much power as hydroelectric, solar, wind, and nuclear combined. The *increase* in natgas-fired power generation in the United States in the past five years is more than the *total* electricity usage of France, the world's seventh-largest electricity consumer. As soon as 2020, odds are that natgas will generate more electricity than *all* other forms of generation combined. And because cheap inputs mean cheap outputs, average American power prices have flatlined since the shale revolution began.

Cheaper electricity means pretty much cheaper everything. Just as natural gas is the primary industrial input, electricity is the primary input for everything in modern life.

In recent decades any number of power-intensive industries have relocated abroad to places where vast volumes of energy are produced locally and/or where electricity costs are heavily subsidized: refining to Venezuela, chemicals to Saudi Arabia, paperboard to Canada, rubber to Malaysia, plastics to China, aluminum smelting to Russia, methanol fabrication to Qatar. Courtesy of all the shale natgas, electricity costs are now low and stable in the United *without any subsidies*, and most of these industries are already moving back. Similarly, power-intensive industries that you cannot do without — things like food processing, water treatment, and water distribution — are discovering that the cost of one of their top inputs has, at worst, stalled.

Those savings will increase as infrastructure expands to capture more and more of the waste natgas. All told, American industry *already* has invested more than $400 billion in natural gas transport and usage infrastructure, all of which will be fully on-line by 2020. And making electricity is hardly the only thing you can do with natural gas.

Methane and ethane — the component molecules of natural gas — are the simplest, basest hydrocarbons in existence. By exposing them to different temperatures, chemicals, and catalysts you can create a bewildering array of daughter and granddaughter materials, which in turn form the basis of modern life. A (very) brief sampling of the typical chemicals (and products) that come from refining natgas and their associated liquids includes, but is far from limited to:

Petroleum Inputs into Common Goods

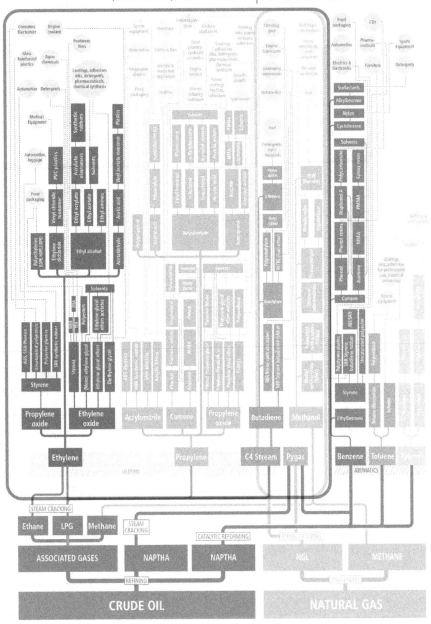

© 2019 Zeihan on Geopolitics

- Methanol: insulation, construction materials, dry cleaning chemicals, lighters, shavers, foam insulation, perfumes, pens, pencils

- Ethylene: fertilizers, films, plastic bags, milk jugs, cosmetics, anti-freeze, polyester clothing, synthetic lubricants, mouthwash, aspirin

- Polypropylene: safety glass, diapers, paint, solvents, carpet, rope/twine, tape, ceramics, paper, fiberglass, rubbing alcohol

- MTBE: fuel additives, industrial and medical solvents

- Butadiene: automotive components, diesel fuel, tires, hoses and belts, shoe soles, carpet backing, latex paints

- Isobutylene: chewing gum, lubricants, synthetic rubbers, caulking, glues

- Polyurethane: varnish, sports equipment, packing foam, artificial wood, shoe midsoles, solid plastics, coatings and varnish, planes, trains, automobiles

Because of the cheap/free inputs the shale revolution has made possible, the United States is massively expanding its natgas and natgas liquids refining operations. *All* of these chemical products are now cheaper in the United States than anywhere else in the world.[7]

And yet there is still loads more natgas to be used, which has allowed it to eat into the market share of other industrial processes. There are multiple fabrication routes to most modern chemical outputs — which route you pick is largely determined by the cost and availability of the inputs. For most of the petroleum age, it is oil that has proven the best input, largely because its status as a liquid makes it easier to produce, transport, store and manipulate. In oil-refining operations, a common early daughter product is something called naphtha, which can be in turn processed into nearly any chemical.

Methane and ethane *can* be used to make these same products, but because of constraints of infrastructure, storage, price and price reliability,

---

7 The one niggling exception is China, where subsidies and the phrase "world's largest" are as core to the national identity as beer and beavers are to Canada. Remove the subsidies, however, and these chemical products are considerably more expensive than not only U.S. chemicals, but also the global average.

Chill

Even with 10bcf/d ultimately going to Mexico and Canada, there is *still* more natgas! And so a number of firms have applied for the rights to export natgas from the U.S. Gulf Coast to global markets in a decidedly non-standard form.

Though more than 95 percent of the natgas used in human history has been transported by pipe, there is one other way to move it safely: freeze it first.

By running natgas through a giant refrigerator, it condenses into liquid form. This liquefied natural gas (LNG) then can be poured into specially-designed tankers and shipped across the ocean, opening new distribution horizons. Upon arrival at the purchasing port, the LNG is offloaded in liquid form into storage tanks, and when needed warmed back into its natural gaseous state and fed into pre-existing natgas pipelines.

LNG facilities face a series of hurdles:

- *Economic/financial.* Chilling a gas into a liquid in a specialized freezer before sending it across the ocean on a specialized boat to a specialized receiving terminal on the other side of the planet is as expensive as it sounds. For just 1bcf/d of LNG capacity, the freezing/shipping/regasification process costs about $8 billion in up-front capital costs, roughly $6 billion of which is just the freezing facility (for comparison, you could build 1bcf/d of natgas production *and* in-country transport infrastructure for about $2 billion). Even the supermajors often balk at such price tags, and only the largest of banks will consider financing.

- *Environmental/civic.* Liquefaction faculties are giant industrial facilities and cannot just be plopped down anywhere. In addition to requiring a ginormous volume of cheap natgas, they require solid electrical grid connections to power the freezers, nearly a square mile of land on a coast to house the facility and provide sufficient stand-off distance, deepwater access channels to support the tanker traffic, a state government that thinks LNG is a swimmingly good idea, and a local population that isn't prone to lying down in front of bulldozers. That largely limits LNG export points to the Texas and Louisiana coasts.

- *Precedent.* The one LNG exporting facility the United States has — Sabine Pass — only started operations in 2016. Simply put, the long-term economics of LNG export from the United States is unproven at present. Considering the scale of the bet participants must make, caution is understandable.

- *Time.* These behemoths don't go up quickly. The Sabine Pass export facility was originally an LNG *import* point and so began the export construction effort with the land, water access, storage tanks, pipe connections, and local political support already in hand — and it *still* took nearly a decade to bring online. Anyone who is considering building a brand-spanking-new *export* facility has to be utterly confident that U.S. natgas prices will be low for decades to come.

U.S. LNG will happen, and it will be big, but unlike the buildout of pipes to the neighbors or power plants or chemical facilities, it will take a lot more time. Don't expect U.S. LNG exports to reach Mexican or Canadian levels until at least 2025.

typically natgas is bypassed in favor of oil-derived naphtha. But not in the shale era. The magic number is about $4 per 1,000 cubic feet — at that point chemical and refining firms start to convert their naphtha cracking facilities to cracking natgas. And since shale has put natgas below that $4 ceiling almost without interruption since late 2011, natgas and its associated liquids are making inroads into the bulk of the American chemicals business, serving as a feedstock for the creation of everything from fire extinguishers to coolants to detergents to fertilizers to glass to luggage to tires to adhesives to textiles to furniture to paint to electronics.

And yet there's more. Any system that is physically linked to the United States has discovered that it has access to all this waste shale gas. Major pipeline expansions are underway to take Texas shale gas to Mexico to assist the Mexicans with a complete overhaul of their electricity systems. In 2006, U.S. natgas exports to Mexico were but 1bcf/d. At the time of this writing they have tripled, and new infrastructure coming on-line will enable them to triple again. By 2020 American shale gas imported into Mexico, nearly all of which will be used to generate electricity, will supply two-thirds of the country's total natgas demand. And since a lack of reliable, affordable

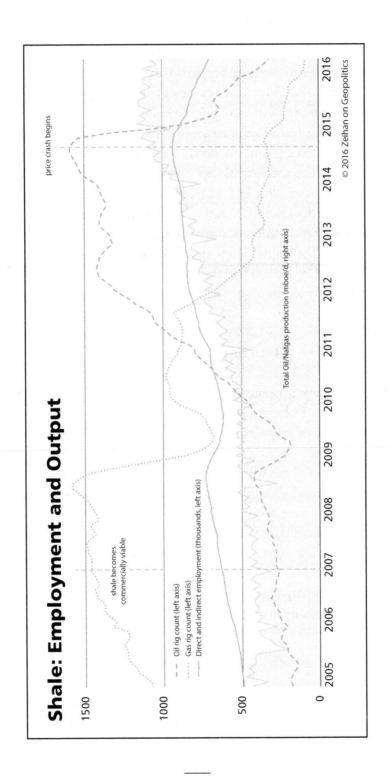

Shale: Employment and Output

1500

1000

500

0

2005   2006   2007   2008   2009   2010   2011   2012   2013   2014   2015   2016

price crash begins

shale becomes
commercially viable

- - - Oil rig count (left axis)
······ Gas rig count (left axis)
—— Direct and indirect employment (thousands, left axis)

Total Oil/Natgas production (mboe/d, right axis)

© 2016 Zeihan on Geopolitics

electricity long has been the greatest check on Mexican industrial development, expect shale to trigger a Mexican industrial boom.

Mexico isn't the only American neighbor taking advantage of the cheap natgas. Steadily expanding pipe connections between the American Northeast and the Canadian province of Ontario are funneling ever-increasing volumes of shale gas to the north. With the well-to-market distance from the Marcellus and Ontario only one-quarter that from Ontario's traditional Albertan supplier, U.S. shale gas has a total end-sale price that is often within reach of just the *transport* cost for Albertan gas. It should come as no surprise that the Albertans are finding themselves priced out of their "home" market. The United States already is eastern Canada's dominant natgas supplier, and by decade's end the volume of American supplies to eastern Canada are likely to match the volume of American supplies to Mexico.[8]

The Employment Pipeline

All aspects of shale generate more than "mere" economic activity, they generate jobs. A lot of jobs. An embarrassment of jobs.

The shale-is-dead conventional wisdom tells us that those jobs have come and gone, but the reality isn't a simple zero-sum game of "shale makes jobs" while "price drop destroys jobs." It's easiest to think about the sector's employment scenarios by breaking them down into five categories:

First, there are the core **production** jobs: the people employed directly by efforts to actually crack the shale open to get at the petroleum itself. Seismic experts, roughnecks, truck drivers, liquids specialists, layers of gathering pipe networks, and so on.

Second are the **input** jobs: the people who supply all the various ingredients to the shale industry from sand mines to steel foundries to drill bit manufacturers to water providers to road construction teams.

---

8   For (much) more on the intersection of energy politics and Mexican and Canadian affairs, as well as the future of Mexico and Canada, please see Chapters 12 and 13 of *The Accidental Superpower*.

Third is the **midstream**: this is the transport crew that takes the raw petroleum and ships it from the gathering networks to someone who can actually use it. Obviously long-haul pipeline firms — both builders and operators — fall into this category, but so too do the railroad and barge industries.

The U.S. Bureau of Labor Statistics estimates that pre-shale total employment in these **direct** job categories within the American energy complex numbered about 490,000. In September 2014 — two months before the Saudi price war — the sector clocked in at 934,000 positions, a 90-percent increase over the decade.

The above graphic illustrates the initial burst in production per rigs in 2005 at the beginning of the shale boom, and again in 2009 as production activities expanded throughout the Marcellus shale. Take a peek at 2015 — even as employment and rig counts dropped, each new rig, each new well, and each individual job became more productive. But in a low-price environment, "more productive" is synonymous with "we don't need as many workers." Multilateral drilling means fewer rig crews. In-ground water sourcing means fewer truck drivers.

Such job losses actually go beyond changes in price and technology to something wholly unrelated.

When a new drilling pad is established, a road is built to it and a gathering network is established. Every step of the process encourages employment. But regardless of whether the well is simple or multilateral, drilled once or 10 times, infilled, refracked, gas-injected, or otherwise bedazzled, there is never a *second* road or *second* gathering system. That initial build-out is never done again. A slowdown, even a retrenchment, in overall energy-related employment was due even before the 2014 price drop began. That this normal adjustment occurred at the same time as the price drop was just bad luck — and it makes the situation in the energy patch seem worse than it really is.

Simply put, many of these directly-generated positions fall as fast as they rise. Between 2007 and 2013, fully half of the new jobs created in the United States were shale production, input and midstream positions. Conversely, during the price drop of 2014-2015, fully half of the *lost* jobs in the United States fell into the same three categories.

But shale isn't done. It has (many) more jobs to create. It comes down to the final two employment categories:

Fourth are the **processing** jobs: the people who take the raw petroleum and turn it into something more usable. Refineries, electricity producers, chemical plants.

Fifth comes the **manufacturing** jobs: those who take advantage of the cheap and reliable inputs, transforming them to make everything from plastics to fertilizers to photo development to paint to pain killers to cosmetics to textiles to construction materials. Also included in this group are jobs that wouldn't have existed if not for the downward pressure that the shale industry has on electricity and raw chemical input costs.

The first three categories of job creation have fairly fast rollouts, and ebb and flow based on the pace of the industry; as a rule, the higher the energy price the faster these subsectors grow. In contrast, these final two categories — the **induced** jobs — take longer to get moving, largely because of infrastructure complexity: Drilling a shale well or laying a short pipe section can be done in weeks to months while building a new refinery or fab facility can take years. And since the end-users view energy as an *input* rather than as a source of income, lower energy prices are vastly preferred to high energy prices. What's bad for shale producers is oftentimes great for refiners and end-manufacturers.

Though induced jobs might not be characterized by the initial, dizzying surges in employment associated with direct activities in the shale patches, these job categories more than make up for it in terms of sheer size and durability. The U.S. Chamber of Commerce has far and away generated the most holistic estimate for total new employment as a consequence of shale. The Chamber estimates that the total of all new jobs across all categories — direct, indirect and induced — to already be 2.5 million as of 2015, with expected new additional jobs to total another 500,000 by 2020.[9]

It gets better.

---

9   In case you feel I'm being an industry cheerleader here, most energy industry associations put the number between 4 million and 6 million, while TIME has opined that 10 million is closer to the truth.

Roughly 70 percent of American economic activity comes from private consumption activity, and two of the six biggest expenses for American consumers are gasoline and electricity (mortgage/rent, taxes, health care, and food round out the top six). The shale revolution has saved the average family of four about $1,100 a year from cheaper gasoline and *another* $750 a year from cheaper electricity. For comparison, the W. Bush-era tax cuts — the largest in the post-WWII era — only saved them $315 annually. It is next to impossible to estimate the impact of all that savings on the job market, but somewhat easier to mentally process how much harder your life would be without that extra two-grand in your pocket.

Finally, the nature of forecasting actually argues for better outcomes than what I've just summed up. The problem with economic forecasts is that the forecaster has to pick a point at which he or she stops collecting data. In this case, the studies reviewed for this project were all published in 2015 and 2016, with the cut-off collection dates in mid-2014. In the middle of that year the best-guess break-even price for the American shale patch was about $75 a barrel, nearly double the actual break-even two years later. Which means 3 million fundamentally new jobs by 2020 isn't the average case.

It is the *low* case.

CHAPTER 4

Energy with an American Accent

The United States is unique, and that uniqueness has enabled it to dominate the world. Having the best parts of a continent overlaid with the world's best waterways make the United States rich. Having geographically coherent boundaries — those ocean moats are particularly nice — keeps America safe. Best of all, the most potent technologies of the modern age are best leveraged by the American geography.

Portugal and Spain developed deepwater navigation as a means of doing an end-run around European wars and Turkish middlemen in order to directly access Asia. In time the English — who, living on an island knew their way around a boat — proved they could use that technology better and constructed a global empire. But the United States essentially is a continent-sized island and can put far more capital and manpower and force behind any shipbuilding campaign than the British could ever muster.

Similarly, Imperial England launched the effort to shift from wind, water, and muscle for power to coal, oil, and steam — which in turn brought us everything from interchangeable parts to assembly lines. The transformation made it deeply powerful, but the technologies of industrialization found a better home in 19th century Germany, with its larger (and better educated) labor force and superior ability to marshal resources. That is, until industrialization immigrated to American shores, where it wallowed in the perfect mix of capital generation, skilled labor, cheap labor, and cheap transport.

Further, American markets were simultaneously large, growing, diversified, and — above all — *internal*, and therefore immune to the geopolitical competition that wracked Europe.

Advance to the topic at hand: There are a number of peculiar features of the American system that vastly empower a local shale industry and set the United States apart from the rest of the planet. Though some of these features could be duplicated, such duplication cannot be done quickly, easily, or cheaply. Even in places that might be able to foster a local shale boom, they will be merely temporary. Nowhere on earth will experience an American-style shale *revolution* in the next several decades.

Let's begin with the factors that are impossible to replicate and move into those that are easier.

Geology

All formations that hold petroleum are sedimentary, meaning that layer after layer of material — typically generated by runoff — stacks up, compresses, and solidifies into rock. But not all sedimentary rocks are created equal, and certainly not all sedimentary rocks contain petroleum. Petroleum-bearing sedimentary rock requires something more than mere runoff.

It requires organic material, and a lot of it at that. The ideal gestation lab is a huge area ringed with low-elevation lands of a sufficiently warm climate so that a vast area capable of supporting life can drain into a single massive delta system. It is within these deltas that thick layers of *organic-rich* sediment build.

In this, North America proved far luckier than the other continents.

During Jurassic times (roughly 195 million to 140 million years ago), North America was in the process of pulling away from Africa. Both continents drained much of their interiors to the same zone — a zone that currently includes what is now the Gulf of Mexico and portions of the Fayetteville, Haynesville, Eagle Ford, and Permian shale plays.

By the time of the early-Cretaceous (roughly 115 million years ago), North America and Africa had said their adieus, and a wide, shallow, north-facing bay opened between the Rockies and the Appalachians. The vast majority of the newly-emancipated North America drained into this new sedimentary basin that included everything from Canada's Horn River basin to the Albertan tar sands to the Bakken of North Dakota and the Niobrara of Colorado.

Tectonic shifting continually cracked the bay open until North America itself was split in two, with the gap between them called the Western Interior Seaway. Both subcontinents drained first into the seaway, adding layers of sediment that contributed to the many basins in the contemporary continent's interior: the Canadian Oil Sands as well as shale plays hard up against the Rockies such as the Mowry, Pierre, Niobrara, and the Bakken.

North America in the Early Cretaceous
c115 million years ago

Deep water
Shallow water
Dry land
Current Shale Plays

By the time of the Cretaceous-Tertiary extinction (65 million years ago, death of the dinosaurs), the subcontinents had reunited, with the connecting land bridge first forming in the north. For the next 5 million years, the remnants of the once-great seaway dropped the entirety of the continent's internal sediment in the former Seaway, atop what are now North America's most productive petroleum basins: the Bakken, Permian, and Eagle Ford.

Beyond formational geology, there is the far-from-minor issue that not all shales are created equal. Nearly without exception, North America's shales are all marine shales — meaning they developed in an oceanic environment, typically where river systems drained into an ocean. Many of the world's other shales are lacustrine, meaning that they formed in lakes. Technically,

North America in the Late Cretaceous
c85 million years ago

Current Shale Plays

there is no rule that lakebed shales have fewer petrocarbons than marine shales,[1] but the chemistry of the waters and rocks involved are substantially different. Lacustrine-sourced petroleum is trapped between or within waxy layers of clay. When you frack wax it doesn't crack, it just goos around a bit; any hydrocarbons within remain trapped. This doesn't mean countries with lacustrine formations will never be able to exploit their shales, but it certainly means they cannot do it with the technologies that exist today — those were designed for marine shales. The dawn of any "lacustrine revolutions" are at least 20 years away.

What is outstanding about the North American petroleum patch isn't so much that its geology boasts a near-perfect structure and geological age for generating marine-shale petroleum, but that it has sported *four*; in many cases, these different ages have deposited petroleum-bearing rocks atop one another. Not only can the same surface footprint service multiple plays (thank you pad drilling), new technologies like multilateral drilling can tap multiple plays *from the same borehole*. No amount of industrial effort could possibly duplicate such a fortuitous geology — either you've got it or you don't.

But that's only step 1.

Labor Pool

As of 2013 the 'typical' shale well produced less than 300 barrels per day over its 20-year productive life. Moreover, the tiny packets of petroleum trapped within the shale don't have much internal pressure. As soon as a well is brought on-line, the pressure rapidly drops off and the well's rate of output begins a steep decline. Though there are deep and ongoing technical improvements being made both to increase initial output levels and flatten out those decline curves, the fact remains that maintaining oil output from shale formations — to say nothing of increasing oil output on a nationwide

---

1   In fact, there's a body of evidence indicating that many lacustrine shales might actually hold a greater density of petroleum than your average marine shale.

scale — requires massive ongoing drilling efforts that in turn require hundreds of rig crews and tens of thousands of engineers.

This is harder to put together than it sounds. By the time an energy sector matures to the point that it is trying to crack apart rocks a mile underground, luck doesn't factor in all that often.

Though the sort of rote, book-learning that many countries excel at is important in the development of engineering skills, it is only the *beginning* of the shale skill set. Shale wells do not vary field-by-field or well-by-well, but stage-by-stage. Operating staff must function under wildly varying conditions in wildly varying geologies and geographies and make decisions on the fly without external supervision. Petroleum engineers who work the shale patch need (lots) of hands-on expertise in geology, fluid dynamics, metallurgy, and a host of other skills. The list of countries that teach such integrative, critical thinking en masse at all — much less that teach *engineers* how to think outside of the box — is very short.

None of this means that no one else can master the baseline techs. Horizontal drilling and hydraulic fracturing aren't new — both have existed for more than a century and been in semi-regular use since the 1980s — and while their combination represents a new way of doing things, the shale process *can* be learned and replicated.

But that would only get a country to the *first* wave of the shale revolution. By 2016 the American shale sector had largely moved past such "basic" skill requirements. All of the new techs like micro-seismic and multilateral drilling, all of the new pumps and drills and water management practices, require a much more advanced skill set than what happened in the American shale fields just five years ago.

It isn't so much that the United States has the best petroleum engineers in the world (although it does). It isn't so much that the United States has more petroleum engineers than the rest of the world combined (although it does). It's that anyone hoping to duplicate the end results of the American skilled labor market can do so only by building it from scratch. Shale's second revolution is only *now* being developed. No amount of study can help because there are no manuals to read just yet. You can only learn by *doing*, and you can only *do* within the confines of an already-active shale industry.

Private Ownership

Who benefits from shale?

I'm not talking here about the scads of firms involved, the scads of workers in various downstream industries or countries who can break away from problematic energy exporters, but instead what happens to the *money* at the time of production itself. Operators don't get all of the cash from what comes out of the ground. It gets spread around.

Or does it?

It sounds fairly basic, but most countries lack a basic concept of private ownership. In most places every parcel of real estate is the sole property of the government. Citizens (or corporations) may be able to take out century-long leases, but the land itself is wholly owned by the state. Even in those — mostly Western — countries where private ownership of land exists, not one actually allows for private interests to own the subsoil mineral rights. The landholder doesn't get a cent from petroleum production.

The reasons are twofold: in most places life is a struggle and the government must marshal all available resources to ensure the country's survival — one of those resources is land, and ownership of that land includes anything that is under it. Second, most foreign governments are built around supporting a single ethnicity or nationality, and the idea of allowing someone from a different background to own land is simply anathema. Changing attitudes on such issues is painfully difficult — in Mexico it only *started* to happen in 2015.

From an energy production point of view this actually is worse than it sounds. Because mineral rights are not a private prerogative you could find oil in your ancestral home and not gain a dollar from it. But because mineral rights are exclusively a *national* prerogative, your local government wouldn't gain any income either. It is purely up to the discretion (or lack thereof) of the national authorities whether your lands will come into production, and no one in the local area is guaranteed so much as a dime of income from royalties or taxes.

There is one exception. In just one spot on the planet can private interests (a.k.a. people like you) not only own land, but the mineral rights under the surface as well: the United States.

One of the primary reasons shale development has been able to proceed apace in the United States is that local governments get a double dose of income from the industry: first, directly in the form of local taxes, and second, indirectly in the form of taxation on income earned by local landowners who lease out their mineral rights. This income does more than mollify local governments and encourage landowners to participate; it also provides local governments with the funds they need to enable the shale industry to grow (such as road construction) as well as mitigate its impacts (such as regulation enforcement). Without private ownership and local taxation capability, locals receive all of shale's deleterious effects without reaping any of its benefits.

This local buy-in by landowners and governments also — massively — speeds a shale zone's development. Take a look at the difference between shale operations on private versus public land in the United States. In Texas, because the landowner and local governments actively advocate for shale developments, a drilling permit can be obtained within two days of application (that's two calendar days, not two business days — Texans drill on Thanksgiving and Christmas). On federal lands, because there is no landowner or local government pushing the process forward, the average timescale for application rulings in 2015 was 220 days (that's 220 business days, not 220 calendar days). Consequently, shale operations on public lands generate less than 1 percent of America's shale petroleum output.[2]

Capital

Shale ain't cheap.

Basic horizontal drilling rigs rent out at an excess of $100,000 per day once crew costs are figured in. Industrial power lines must connect to the

---

2   Fun update: The federal government is in the process of launching an on-line drilling application system, which it hopes will reduce the application time to ... wait for it ... a mere 115 days.

local grid … assuming the grid can handle the demand. If not, industrial generators need to be shipped in and hooked up. Trucks of all kinds — water, sand, and flatbed being the three biggest categories — must be procured and manned in the dozens. Thousands of people will need to be housed, oftentimes in areas that don't have thousands of extra apartments. Every hotel room will be bought up in bulk. Low-income housing will be emptied to make room. Man camps the size of medium-sized towns will be established by the same firms that build temporary military bases. Time with supercomputers and data analysts must be rented and mated with seismic crews. Acreage leases typically went for $5,000 to $15,000 per acre in the days of low-productivity wells, but in today's high-powered production, per-acre lease costs of more than $50,000 are far from alien. Workers need to be paid, taxes need to be paid, royalties need to be paid. All told, the average well in 2015 ran somewhere around $6 million to $7 million in the Big4 fields, and tens of thousands of wells are drilled a year.[3]

It's a ballet of not just physical logistics, but of financial logistics. While the ultimate responsibility rests with the operator, many pieces of the process are independent of the United States' 500-odd shale firms.[4] Sand miners, railway firms, server farms, and independent truck drivers all look after their own — and all need their own financial access. Worst of all, the low output per well means that most wells won't break even within the first six months with oil prices at $80 a barrel. At $40, payback can stretch out to two years.

---

3   Here's how average well costs have shifted of late according to my favorite branch of the U.S. government, the Department of Energy's Energy Information Agency:
Bakken: $7.1 million in 2014, $5.9 million in 2015.
Eagle Ford: $7.6 million in 2014, $6.5 million in 2015.
Marcellus: $6.6 million in 2014, $ 6.1 million in 2015.
Midland (Permian): $7.7 million in 2014, $7.2 million in 2015.
Delaware (Permian): $6.6 million in 2014, $5.2 million in 2015.
You can view the full report in all its gritty glory here:
https://www.eia.gov/analysis/studies/drilling/pdf/upstream.pdf

4   As with everything else, this figure is fairly squishy. Low energy prices have sparked off a consolidation wave, so while there are still technically hundreds of shale firms, the bulk of the work is completed by about 50 major players.

This, all of this, takes money. Lots of money. Or more to the point, it takes credit. Most countries simply lack the sort of financial depth required to even attempt a small shale industry. Of the maybe 60 countries that theoretically could attempt to finance a shale boom, all but a handful would see the cost of finance rise so precipitously that it would almost certainly cause a finance-induced recession in which the newcomer shale would also be a casualty.

The United States is not only in that handful of possibilities, it stands well away from the pack for many reasons:

- The United States is (by far) the world's largest financial power. Its stock market alone is worth in excess of $25 trillion, with another $8 trillion in the bond market and $9 trillion in bank loans.[5] It is (by far) the biggest financial power in human history, and its financial markets are, if anything, *too* good at coming up with new financial products to supply credit to new and rising economic sectors.[6] Exchange Traded Funds (ETFs) and direct stock emissions can bolster the bigger, publicly listed players. Companies often issue bonds direct to limit outside ownership (and thus prevent investors from taking too big a chunk of future profits). Bank loans — especially at the local level — can go to nearly any player in the system. And private equity firms always can swoop in and trade capital for a permanent slice of ownership. Deep-pocket options abound.

- Timing also is key. Shale really started taking off in 2007, the same year the United States fell into the Great Recession. In that year, the U.S. Federal Reserve was so concerned about financial meltdown that it started participating directly in the bond markets with something called quantitative easing (QE). In essence, the Fed printed currency and used that currency to purchase not just federal government bonds, but all kinds of publicly traded paper assets. The intent and result was to artificially generate demand for a wide variety of financial tools, so the extra cash would enable anyone with the stomach for borrowing to access credit at well-below normal rates. For economic sectors — like shale — that

---

5   All that is for 2015. Data courtesy of the Federal Reserve.

6   Subprime and its asset-backed securities being the most recent negative example.

were doing well *without* that extra money, it was the equivalent of putting rocket fuel in a minivan. Shale firms were able to tap the Fed flood directly in terms of the Fed buying their bonds, and indirectly because there was just as much private money lending to now a smaller number of lendees. And as the United States suffered through an 18-month recession, shale bonds — many of which issued dividends based on petroleum output — became attractive in their own right.

- The money flood isn't over just yet, it's just not coming from Washington. As the shale revolution started maturing in 2014, both China and Europe entered prolonged crisis — China because of the instability of its financial model and Europe because of the Greek crisis and the broader instability of the common currency. Both Chinese and European investors sent panicked torrents of capital abroad in search of safe haven, with the largest flows seeking American shelter. Some sought the rock-solid stability of U.S. government bonds. Others sought the hard assets only available in private real estate. Others wanted financial products backed by producing assets in a first-world country with strong contract and private ownership laws that also generated income streams — which lead them to pour over a half trillion dollars into the shale industry's own bonds between 2011 and 2014. As of late 2015, a host of other major players are in the midst of their own QE programs — most notably the eurozone, Japan, and China. These places have neither sufficiently profitable economic sectors that can absorb the liquidity directly nor financial industries that can process the liquidity into something their economies can easily use. A great deal of the cash is flowing to the United States, where the American financial community is packaging it for use by — you guessed it — the shale sector. America's ongoing energy expansion in general — and shale's ongoing expansion despite the 2014-2015 price crash in specific — are being partially funded by the rest of the world.

Infrastructure

Moving stuff around is hard. Really hard. But some stuff is easier to move than others. Solid objects can be moved individually or stacked, palletted, or containerized. This does far more than simply open up myriad options for moving them from points A to B, it also simplifies storage. You can hold nearly any sort of solid object in trucks, warehouses, barges, parking lots, train stations or whatnot for as long is practical.

Liquids are trickier. There's no putting liquids in a stack, but you *can* pour them into containers that could be stacked or moved about as if they were solids. It isn't as cheap or easy or simple, but it is possible. You also can move liquids via pipe, which is in essence a specialized container spliced into a dedicated transport system. Moving liquids by pipe is on average one-third the cost of moving liquids by rail and less than one-tenth that by truck.

Pipelines' primary limiters are pumps and elevation. As hard as it is to pump liquid up a hill, the crazy part comes when the liquid comes down the other side. Liquids have mass, mass builds momentum, and momentum tends to break things. Most pipes are in relatively flat areas as a result.

As different and more difficult as the logistics are between moving a solid and a liquid, they are far more complicated once you move a gas. Pressurizing gas into tanks is somewhat dangerous — certainly far more dangerous than stacking up solids or pouring liquids — and transporting pressurized tanks can get decidedly lively if there are any accidents.

Natural gas requires processing stations within the producing fields to separate the natgas from the oil. A separate gathering system is required to funnel gas produced to trunklines. For remote areas — such as the Bakken of North Dakota — this means building a ground-up transport network for natgas when one isn't even required for oil (the relative simplicity of moving liquids means that Bakken oil is often railed). A separate trunkline is required to move the collected natural gas across the country from the point of production to the point of consumption. Once the natural gas reaches its point of consumption, there must be a fully operational facility waiting to immediately use it.

Compared to the difficulty of training a deep and versatile workforce or having trillions of dollars lying around or the impossibility of developing a perfect geology, constructing a bunch of pipes and power plants is child's play.

Yet even in this "easy" prerequisite, the United States began with a massive lead. Before the shale revolution began, the United States was already the world's largest end-user of natural gas, with more than 300,000 miles of natural gas trunkline already installed. It already generated 20 percent of its electricity from natural gas and already boasted the world's largest petrochemical industry.

But even this proved insufficient to handle the influx. U.S. use of natgas for electricity has expanded by half. Dozens of new trunklines had to be built to link fields and cities. Nearly 1 million miles of new gathering pipe has been laid down, and now the United States has more than eight *thousand* natgas-burning power plants and chemical faculties — and yet natgas flaring still happens with sufficient commonality that astronauts on the International Space Station can see the shale fields.

Yes, all this can be built, and "all" it takes is time and money, but even this requirement — by far the easiest of the five — is a decades-long effort with a bill in the trillions.

In The Running, Falling Short

Add it all up and there are few places in the world that can attempt a shale sector, and even fewer that might be able to generate a boom of one-tenth the relative American outcome.

The North African states of **Algeria** and **Libya** have promising shale deposits, but the region faces a series of major obstacles to exploiting them. The local state energy firms — even Algeria's reasonably-competent Sonotrach — lack the funding required to construct, much less staff, a shale industry. Not only does the non-government workforce lack the skill sets to attempt shale independently of the government, the local educational system lacks the skills required to attempt to train up any relevant supplementary workers.

For its part, Libya is simply too unstable to support the sort of manpower-intensive, geographically-scattered operations that shale requires. And of course in the Sahara Desert the water required for fracking can be a bit

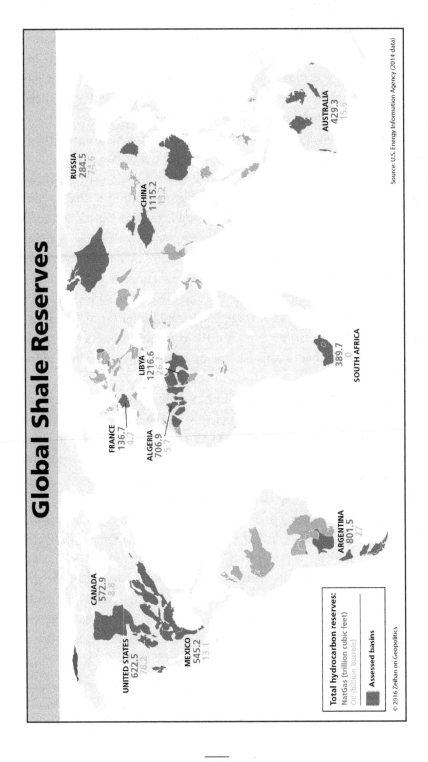

Global Shale Reserves

Total hydrocarbon reserves:
NatGas (trillion cubic feet)
Oil (billion barrels)

Assessed basins

© 2016 Zeihan on Geopolitics

Source: U.S. Energy Information Agency (2014 data)

UNITED STATES
622.5
78.2

CANADA
572.9
8.8

MEXICO
545.2
13.1

ARGENTINA
801.5
27

FRANCE
136.7
4.7

ALGERIA
706.9
5.7

LIBYA
1216.6
26.1

SOUTH AFRICA
389.7
0

RUSSIA
284.5
74.6

CHINA
1115.2
15.2

AUSTRALIA
429.3
15.6

hard to come by.[7] But even if a magic wand could solve all of those issues, why build up a shale sector when none of these restrictions apply to their pre-existing conventional energy plays? These countries will not join the world's shale club not so much because of reasons technical or financial, but because for them shale just isn't worth the effort.

The Bazhenov shale of **Russian Siberia** has a similar geology to the North American shale fairway, most notably the Bakken of North Dakota, and is probably the world's single most petroleum-rich shale play, holding — at least on paper — one-half as much petroleum as all U.S. shale plays combined. But the stuff is staying in the ground. Even if Russia had sufficient supplies of skilled labor (and Russia's state natgas monopoly is the poster child for corruption, inefficiency and groupthink), even if Russia was willing to pour in the money (and a Russia under sanctions is one that has to be choosy about what it splashes cash on), and even if Russia had full access to the best technology the U.S. shale patch could offer (and American sanctions against Russia expressly forbid their operation in Russia, much less their sale), the Bazhenov still has the problem that no one lives anywhere near it.

Shale exploitation requires a pad every mile or two with today's newest techs, or a pad every thousand feet or so with the tech of 2010. After that's done, a gathering network that links all the production sites must be cut through the terrain. That's easy in North Dakota, where the biggest obstacle is a wheat field.

No way anyone is doing that in the Bazhenov.

Russia's premier shale sprawls under northwestern Siberian permafrost, where the land is mushy during the brief Siberian summer and largely inaccessible even by helicopter during the long Siberian winter. Conventional permafrost plays can only see work done in the winter when the ground is frozen, and require the construction of 30-foot-tall berms for roads and pipes to run along — otherwise everything sinks into the summer swamp. It is one thing to build a large transport pipe through this area down the

7   There are extensive aquifers under the Sahara, so water might not be quite as rare as the stereotype of a few million square miles of desert might suggest, but that water is also needed to support these two countries' 47 million people.

spines of those berms — Russia can and does do this for its major conventional energy production sites — but it is quite another to run a mesh of thousands of connecting pipes through an area with no roads, no towns, and no solid ground. No matter the shape of Russia's economic or political future, shale will not feature.

China doesn't look all that hot either. Considering the country's on-paper shale natgas reserves (which at 1.1 quadrillion cubic feet are technically the world's largest), seemingly limitless supplies of labor, over-lubricated financial system, and penchant for stealing technology, it would seem that China would be primed for a shale revolution of a scale similar to the United States. Indeed, back in 2010 the Chinese government projected that by 2020 the country's shale gas industry would be producing somewhere in the vicinity of 10 bcf/d.[8] Yet in 2015 total Chinese shale natgas output was only 0.43 bcf/d and the 2020 estimate has since been (very quietly and unofficially) revised down by over two-thirds. The reason? Nearly all of China's shales are thin, dispersed, lacustrine, or some combination of the three and simply cannot be developed at present. The one promising petroleum-dense and geographically-concentrated marine shale China has lies in the Sichuan Basin, a region in the upper Yangtze region that is culturally distinct from the Chinese core territories around Beijing. Sichuan's shales are a stacked jumbled mess similar to America's Permian, and so might hold a motherload of energy supplies. However, in Beijing's lexicon, "culturally distinct" is a synonym for "potentially secessionist." Developing Sichuan to make the region functionally independent in energy markets is not high on the politburo's to-do-list.

The **Persian Gulf**, the world's premier oil production zone, undoubtedly has shales of dazzling quality. But, like North Africa, there is little reason to pour money into the unconventional industry when the conventional industry is cheaper, easier, and already developed. Note that I said the Persian Gulf "probably" has dazzling shales; no one really knows for sure because the locals have so much conventional petroleum they have no reason to prioritize shale exploration, much less development.

---

8   For comparison, in 2015 the U.S. shale gas industry was producing approximately 45 bcf/d.

The region also echoes two of Russia's complications: these shales are (probably) deep in the desert, and the shifting nature of the Arabian Desert's landscape would prove nearly as problematic for a gathering network as the Russian permafrost. And then there is simple climate: Regional desert temperatures regularly breach 120 degrees Fahrenheit. Unlike conventional construction efforts where working hours can be shifted into night, shale work requires a 24-hour-a-day effort to be cost-effective at anything other than sky-high prices.

The northern European states of **Denmark, the Netherlands, France,** and **Germany** all have promising deposits, advanced natural gas distribution infrastructure, lots of capital, and workforces brimming with technical skills. It would seem that if a region were to have a shale boom, Northern Europe would be an easy call. Yet such will not be the case, largely because the countries' shale deposits and population centers are simply too *well* co-located. In France's case, the sexiest shale field lies directly under Paris.[9] Add in the Continent's politically powerful Green movements and that no European state has a concept of mineral rights, and any shale developments will be sharply circumscribed.

That said, I do expect *some* movement in all four countries. All face rapidly declining domestic energy production, and in a world of circumscribed shipping and a more aggressive Russia, all four will have little choice than to explore what shale can do for them. Expect the fastest pick-up and the most output out of France. In addition to having the continent's best shales, French state(ish) energy firms Total and Gaz de France (the latter now part of GDF Suez) were by far the largest Continental energy firms to poke around in the world of shale.[10]

But don't expect booms, much less revolutions.

The best outcomes would be if shale somehow manages to compensate for the rapid declines across all Continental conventional energy production assets. Mainland Europe's production levels are already lower relative to needs than America's were in 2005, the rate of decline is steeper, the infrastructure

---

9   Can you imagine fracking at the Louvre?

10   Or at least they were until the French parliament essentially banned fracking technologies.

is less unified, and Europe's small-and-medium energy business list is a pale shadow compared to American norms. Even a stunningly successful shale boom would be the equivalent of running to stand still. Europe may see shale output, even significant shale output, but not nearly enough to change the economic or strategic posture of these states without a massive shift of circumstance.

Poland and **United Kingdom** look more promising, with both countries taking a fairly forward-looking view toward encouraging shale developments, but even here the outcome is not particularly robust. Poland's natural gas industry has been deliberately stunted; pre-shale, nearly all of Poland's natural gas imports came from the Poles' Russian nemesis, so Warsaw deliberately worked to keep natgas usage to a minimum. Even if Poland's shales were perfect — and like the United Kingdom's their shales are smaller and less petroleum-dense than America's — it would still take the better part of two decades to develop the infrastructure and end-use facilities required to metabolize whatever meaningful production the country might prove able to generate.

Finally comes the (very) short list of countries that can make a go of a shale industry. Their deposits may lack the scope of the American shale deposits, but they have the magic mix of factors — geology included — that will enable them to generate their own shale revolution. In no case will these "revolutions" be as huge as what's happening in the United States and in no case will their shale industries generate global impacts, but don't let that lead to underappreciation. The list is not a long one.

- Of the finalists **Argentina** absolutely looks the best. The shales are the most petroleum-dense, they are located among the country's pre-existing oil and natgas transport networks, domestic and international markets are already developed, local staff is fairly competent, and — somewhat shockingly considering the country's somewhat eccentric approach to regulation and private enterprise — the laws on the books provide regulatory clarity. The "only" problem is that Argentina is flat out broke. The exploitation of Argentine shales may require more American money — and all the things that go along with it — than the Argentines can stomach.

- The biggest challenge facing the energy sector of **Canada** is that it has traditionally seen the United States as not just its primary customer, but a customer who is willing to pay top dollar for access to reliable Albertan petroleum outputs. But now both global norms and U.S. energy's costs structures are lower than Alberta's. Since Canada's export infrastructure is hardwired into the United States, no matter what happens with global prices the Canadians are stuck earning domestic U.S. prices — prices that may well never again rise to a point that the tar sands are profitable. Alberta can and is moving into more cost-effective shale — and already some one-quarter of Albertan natgas production is sourced from shale formations — but Canadian success in shale almost by definition means the failure of Canada's conventional energy industry.

- The Burgos and Sabinas basins of **Mexico** are extensions of the American Eagle Ford shale, and as such have incredibly promising geologies. However, they lie in largely unpopulated, rugged, arid territories and Mexico certainly lacks the infrastructure, skill sets, and finances to push their rapid development. That said, as the Mexican energy sector liberalizes, not only will American money be crossing the border, but so too will be American drilling crews of all types. Mexican shale is part of Mexico's energy future, but it has a lot of catch up to do before it plays anything more than a supporting role.

- Shales in **Australia** are remote and therefore expensive, and Australia's labor force is small and therefore expensive. However, Chinese investment into the Australian energy patch has completely coincidentally run massive trunkpipes through Australia's newly discovered shale zones en route to Australia's previously discovered petroleum fields. As Australia's conventional energy industry enters natural decline, a new Australian shale energy sector can rise to fill the gap. But shale won't be needed Down Under within the next five years. And even when the time comes, Aussie shales have next to no oil in them. That's no problem for the country's prodigious LNG facilities, but is of little help to anyone who hopes that Australia can help increase global oil supplies.

Remaking the World

Geology is just one factor in determining the viability of success of shale — and to be fair, North America has some of the largest and most favorable shale reserves in the world. But only the United States has the magic blend of geology, legal and regulatory environment, available capital, and above all the experience and know-how to make shale work on a massive scale.

Will shale techs leak out from the United States to the wider world? Of course they will. But they will *not* generate echo revolutions anywhere. From a geopolitical standpoint, the shale revolution is a purely American development. Which means that the economic boom, reindustrialization, and energy independence it generates also will be purely American developments.

The question no longer is whether shale will be at the heart of American energy (it already is) but what the world will look like when the United States no longer is tied to global energy markets.

Answering that question requires taking a step back and not only evaluating the global system in its current form, but assessing *why* that system takes the shape that it does. Only then can we add shale to the mix and explore the new world that's just around the corner.

PART II

The Disorder

CHAPTER 5

The End of the (Old) World

The United States is the most powerful country in history and will remain so until long after your grandchildren are gone.

I do not make such a sweeping statement lightly. If you can understand *why* American power is so strong and durable — and wed that to an appreciation of the ins-and-outs of shale energy — you will possess the foundation of a deep, thorough understanding of how the world will (d)evolve in the years to come.

Let's start with the American geography.

The Geography of a Global Power

The middle of this map is why the United States is the global superpower, and will remain so long beyond the lives of your grandchildren. The Greater Midwest is the largest and most productive piece of arable land on the planet, out-producing the next two put together. But as important as that sounds (and is!) that's really the side show. The real deal is the Greater Mississippi River system that perfectly overlays the Midwest.

The first rule of geopolitics is that transport matters. Moving things by water is easy — so easy that today the cost of transporting goods by water is one-twelfth that of moving them by road. The Greater Mississippi system has more than 12,000 miles of interconnected waterways — more than the rest of the world put together. So long as this is true, the United States can move goods and grains and people about its system at a cost that seems laughably low compared to the internal transport costs of most countries.

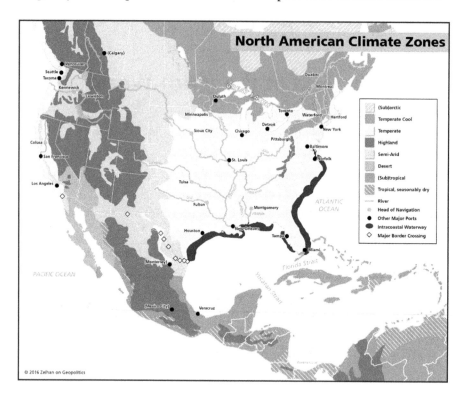

Low transport costs lower the cost of everything else. Save money on food and you have more to spend on educating your kids. Save money on building materials and you can afford that vacation. Reduce transport costs on water, and transport via other modes must be cheaper to compete. Those waterways also serve as distribution zones — particularly where two rivers meet, at the heads of navigation or where the rivers enter the ocean. Cities like Baltimore, Chicago, Kansas City, Minneapolis/St. Paul, Memphis, Mobile, New Orleans, New York, Philadelphia, Pittsburgh, Sacramento, San Francisco, St. Louis and so on, owe not just their existence but also much of their wealth to the cheapness of water transport.

All also are, to varying degrees, financial centers. All that cargo through-put requires back-end support in inventorying, repackaging, buying and selling, which in turn requires a 24-hour-a-day ability to process goods and money. As such, cities rooted in water transport almost without exception also have a strong local banking culture.

Since those banks were formed to service pre-existing economic needs rather than (geo)political ambitions, American banks also tend to be more measured in their borrowing and lending policies than banks created to serve the needs of the state, such as their peer institutions in Japan, China, Germany, or Greece. Put simply, American banks are independent institutions who see money as an economic good, while many of their foreign peers are little more than tools of state policy. That makes the foreign crowd far better at directing resources to achieve political goals such as maximum employment or infrastructure development or funding the government's deficit, but the American system is far better at achieving long-term economic stability — ergo it is the United States that holds the title of the world's financial superpower.

Of course waterways aren't responsible for moving all U.S. goods. In fact, the proportion of water-transported stuff in the United States has been dropping steadily for over a century.

The first limiter on American maritime transport is politics. In 1920 Congress passed the Jones Act, which barred any ship from plying the American waterways that was not American-built, American-owned, American-captained, and American-crewed. The idea was to keep America's maritime jobs with Americans and ensure the United States maintained a strong merchant marine, but like most protectionist measures, it had un-wanted side effects. The cost of water transport tripled, shipping shifted wholesale for rail and road (which were no longer so much more expensive than water transport), lower demand for vessels prompted America's ship-yards to fall into disrepair, and nearly a century later most Americans are not even aware that water played (and still plays) such a central role in their country's success. Washington and the state capitals also lost sight of this fact. America's maritime infrastructure has been creeping into decay for decades — the average age of the locks is more than 60 years, with many now well over a century old and in need of wholesale replacement.[1]

The second factor is far less onerous: the American economy has become far more advanced. As the American economy gradually evolved from a commodities-generating exporter at independence to a services-oriented importer in more recent years, the value of the products that Americans create has steadily risen. As the per-unit cost of American outputs has increased, transport as a percentage of the total cost of those outputs has steadily become less important. (Transport is a much higher percentage of the cost of a bushel of corn than it is for the cost of an iPhone.) It's also an issue of how do you transport services? You might ship lumber by water, but you wouldn't transport architectural designs. It's not that the United States is shipping less via the water (by value), just simply more via other modes. Most of what is still water-shipped these days includes bulk products like grains, petroleum, refined products, and construction materials like gravel, cement, and lumber.

As of 1993 the Americans only shipped about 11% of their cargo (as measured in ton-miles) by water, and with the subsequent shift of Midwestern agricultural exports from the Atlantic Basin (to which the Greater Mississippi flows) to the Pacific Basin (which can only be reached by road and rail), even that figure has since been cut in half.

But even with these changes and restrictions, the proportion of U.S. internal cargo moved by water is still above well above global norms. Only trade entrepots like the Netherlands — the Dutch live around the mouths of the Rhine, Europe's primary export artery — or developed archipelagic states like Japan regularly use water more. And so long as the river network remains navigable, it places a cap on the cost of non-water transport throughout the American system.

Physical security comes just as easily to the United States as wealth. In the north, forests and lakes separate the United States from Canada, a country with too little good land to be a meaningful security threat without massive

---

1 The total bill for a complete one-time replacement of all locks and dams on all navigable U.S. waterways is probably about $225 billion. For comparison, the United States spends about $450 billion a decade maintaining its interstate road network.

outside sponsorship. Canada has not had such sponsorship since the British Empire started loosening ties in the aftermath of the War of 1812 in favor of a more productive relationship with the United States. In the south, deserts and mountains block Mexico. The Mexican state has never invaded the United States[2] while the Americans have flat-out occupied Mexico City. Twice.[3]

To the east and west, moats of quite literally oceanic size prevent European and Asian powers from typically doing more than contemplating attack. Only one power has ever attempted an invasion of the United States — the British Empire in the War of 1812 — and it failed. On the flip side, all successful extra-hemispheric peer invasions were American shows.

The American system, with the Greater Midwest and Mississippi network at its core, is not only the richest piece of territory in the world, it also is the single-most secure.

Americans. Cannot. Mess. This. Up.

They've tried.

And now that you've got the quick-and-dirty of why the United States is the world's premier power, let's take a look at what they've done with it.

Trade and the World We Know

In what the Americans think of as ancient history, the world was imperial. The French Navy protected French trade between the French colonies and the French mainland. The English Navy did the same, as did the Japanese Navy, and so on. It was a sequestered imperial system. You didn't trade with your neighbors if you could help it because you never knew when some idiot on a different continent whose language sounds to you like an injured animal would throw a war. Even if you were not the target, you could lose access to whatever product, shipping route, or end market that you believed was so important. The only solution was to keep everything in-house, and if

---

2   For all you Texas history purists, Pancho Villa most definitely does *not* count.

3   Once in a war, once to secure overdue debt payments.

you needed something that wasn't in-house, you went out and confiscated it. Colonized it. Militarized it. And you folded it into your proprietary system.

The result were empires. These empires competed. Over resources. Over trade routes. Over end markets. Those competitions naturally (d)evolved into wars. Those wars culminated into the Second World War of 1939-1945, which brought the entire imperial system crashing down.

As the war was drawing to a close, the Americans looked around at the carnage and devastation and had three thoughts.

First, the United States was emerging from the war largely unscathed, and not simply because they were not drawn in until December 1941. The combination of the Midwest, the Greater Mississippi system, and the mineral-rich Appalachians and Rockies meant the Americans had nearly everything they needed at home. They didn't *need* an empire because they already had a *continent*. And it didn't hurt that there was no fighting whatsoever on the American mainland. America sent bombs. Its core territories didn't receive any.

Second, as the only man left standing, the United States had the opportunity to reboot the world. And so the Americans brought their allies together at a ski resort in Bretton Woods, New Hampshire, and imposed a fundamentally new global economic system.

The new American-birthed system was free trade. The U.S. Navy — the only appreciable navy to survive the war — would patrol the seas for everyone and protect all merchant commerce. Anyone who partnered with the Americans could sell any good to anyone else in the network. Additionally, the U.S. market was opened to everyone who was willing to play by America's rules. At war's end, the U.S. economy was one-third of the global total — and its consumer market was bigger than everyone else's put together because it was the only one that hadn't been carpet-bombed or strip-mined. It was quite the sweetener.

The third thought was that all this came with a singular catch: you had to let the Americans run your security policies. The core goal of American strategic thinking was that this military alliance would rule the new era — which quickly evolved into the policy of Soviet containment. For the next half-century, American foreign and strategic policy fixated on building, maintaining and expanding this global system of free trade as a means of waging the Cold War. The principle was a simple one: no matter how powerful the United States was, the Soviet Union had more men and more tanks closer to America's European allies — most of which had seen their countries razed during the Second World War. A head-on fight with the Soviet Union simply could not be won, and so the Americans needed to build an alliance that would both pay for itself *and* limit the direct exposure of American forces to Soviet forces. And the best way to build an alliance to serve as the front line was to flat out bribe one into existence.

The gambit worked — beautifully. NATO may have been a military alliance, but it was the economic aspects of Bretton Woods that made it stick. Soon after the war, the dual American poles of economic and military alliance were extended to the defeated Axis powers, the countries that would in time become known as the Asian tigers, and the bulk of the developing world up to and including Communist China.

The American-dominated free trade system ushered in the greatest era of peace and prosperity in human history. Global GDP expanded by a factor of ten. The global population tripled. The massive, civilization-threatening wars of the past, (whether they be Franco-German, Russian-Turkish, Japanese-Chinese or imperial predation) all simply stopped, held in abeyance by the smothering security and wealth of the American network. The Soviet Union never had a chance.

And then suddenly, it was gone. In 1989 the Berlin Wall fell, and the Central European states escaped the Soviet bloc. Less than three years later the Soviet Union itself shattered. The Bretton Woods system had achieved its goal, and it was time to revamp American strategic policy. Then-President George Bush Sr. put together a task force that included names such as Colin Powell, Brent Scowcroft, James Baker, and Dick Cheney to figure out what was next.

The American people were so impressed that they booted the senior Bush out of office. The next three presidents — Bill Clinton, George W. Bush, and Barack Obama — were all domestic presidents uninterested in foreign policy unless the world rudely intruded upon their plans. None of them expressed an interest in replacing the Cold War strategic doctrine with anything new. Free trade was maintained as a hallmark of American policy, albeit now without the attached security prerogatives. There was no Bretton

Woods II. The world became accustomed to the Americans maintaining the global system for their benefit, but not to the Americans demanding anything in return.

The result was "the end of history." The various European countries quasi-merged into the European Union, achieving an echo of the economies of scale that the Americans had started with a century previous and using it to export higher volumes. The Chinese liberalization doubled down, with "communist" being removed from everything save the letterhead; in time China overtook the United States as the largest manufacturing power. Large swathes of the developed world accessed foreign capital to fuel their development and foreign markets to sell their exports; Brazil began providing stiff competition to U.S. farmers. All this activity generated so much economic growth that the producers of industrial commodities made a killing, encouraging many to challenge traditional power structures. Venezuela agitated against the American-led order while Russia under Vladimir Putin amply demonstrated that throwing your weight around on the international stage is far from a purely American prerogative.

The growth was real. The stability was real. The evolutions were real. But one thing was *not* real.

The foundation.

You must remember five things:

1. *The success of America's challengers is dependent upon the Bretton Woods system.* What is China without the ability to import raw materials and energy, and export its products to global markets? What is Brazil without international financing and the ability to safely access the global ocean? What are Venezuela or Russia without global energy markets? All this and more is dependent upon the United States keeping global maritime transport cheap and safe. A change of mind in America means the end of these countries' ability to be challengers in the first place.

2. *The Americans did not create Bretton Woods to become rich.* The Americans already *were* rich, and had been the world's richest country since the completion of Reconstruction in the 1870s. In the decades since, the United States' economy never really internationalized: As a percentage of GDP, the United States is the most self-sufficient economy in the

world. As of 2015, only 8.25% of GDP came from merchandise exports, and over one-third of that is bound up in America's NAFTA partners. And that's with old data. With the massive re-shoring and industrial manufacturing boom currently underway, many of the remaining aspects of Americans' foreign "dependence" are being gutted without mercy or preamble.

3. *The Americans created Bretton Woods as a bribe.* Since Bretton Woods was about swapping economic access for security control, the United States could not have used it to force-feed its products to its allies — instead it had to allow its allies to access U.S. markets unilaterally. The United States *had* to be a net importer. It *had* to run a trade deficit. To do otherwise would have eliminated the incentive for countries as wildly divergent as Korea and China and Sweden and Germany and Argentina and Morocco to participate in the first place. For the Americans, free trade wasn't about economics at all, it was a *security* gambit that was designed to solidify an alliance in order to fight a war. But that war ended three decades ago. America's security *needs* have evolved, and soon so will its security *policies* — and that spells the end of globalized trade.

4. *The United States dominates the oceans regardless of what the global power structure looks like.* One American aircraft carrier battle group sports more projection-capable firepower than the combined navies of the rest of the world. As of 2016, the United States maintains *ten of them.* The Americans' decision to put this force differential at the service of the global commons is what makes free trade work. When the United States does finally adjust its strategic policies and no longer makes global transport safety its top concern, it still will hold the capacity to intervene anywhere on the planet at a moment's notice. It will become a country with global reach without global interests. For the 4 billion people whose economic and physical security are utterly dependent upon global trade, this is perhaps the worst possible outcome.

5. *Americans are panic-prone.* Every country has a series of early experiences that shape the national mindset. For the Americans it was century-long pioneer era: for the cost of a used car in today's dollars, Americans could

Conestoga the family out to the Midwest, break ground, and within six months be exporting grain for hard currency. It was the greatest cultural and economic expansion in human history, and it taught Americans that things will get better every single year. Of course that's not actually true. And so when the world reaches out and touches Americans on terms more familiar to the rest of the world, Americans have no frame of reference. They can't process. They lose their minds. The result is an overreaction, as Americans fear that the end is nigh, and in a panic they reinvent themselves in an attempt to forestall disaster. The aluminum grapefruit of Sputnik generated hysteria, which in turn triggered the greatest industrial and educational overhaul in American history. The Vietnam war funk led to the creation of precision-guided bombs and satellite communications. The 1980s recessions forced corporate redesigns that generated the capital to enable the Internet revolution. At the time of this writing, Americans haven't been scared since the September 11 attacks (which induced them to place the sharp end of American power on either side of every trade and energy artery on the planet). They are due.

Everything about the global system — the system that allows Germany and Korea to be major exporters, that keeps British and Japanese from being imperial, that makes Singapore and the Netherlands major global hubs, that enables China and Saudi Arabia to exist as unified states — is maintained by a power that designed that system to fight a war that ended a generation ago. And should the Americans lose interest for whatever reason, it will all come tumbling down and the Americans might not even notice.

The world we know is one bad American hair day from collapse. Order is giving way to Disorder.

And that's the good news.

There's an unrelated crisis lurking just around the corner that has nothing to do with maritime transport or global navies or American mood swings.

Demography and a World in Flux

We all know that teenagers behave differently than grandparents, but have you ever thought of the implications of that on the wider world? Start by splitting the economically interesting parts of any population into three primary chunks.

First, you've got your young workers, roughly aged 20 to 45. For this group it's all about spending: houses, college, kids, cars, pot. (Not necessarily in that order). All these first-time spending sprees are what fuels a modern economy. But all this spending simply can't happen in a vacuum. Young workers are by definition early in their careers, so their wallets are smaller than their bills. The result? Borrowing: mortgages, college loans, car loans, and so on. It's a high-growth demographic, yes, but also high-debt.

Second are the "mature" workers, roughly aged 40 to 65. This group's debt-fueled spending years are behind them. On the spending side it is because the kids are leaving home, the house is being paid down, and the house itself is likely slated for downsizing. On the income side it's that their paychecks are at the highest they ever will be. Put it together and mature workers are as capital-rich as young workers are debt-wracked.

As such, mature workers' money is typically slated for one of two destinations: their retirement savings and the tax man's bucket. But look at it however you like, this group is where the world's dynamic capital comes from — "dynamic" in that its owners are willing to take risks to help it grow. Mature workers will invest in things like Kickstarter and second homes and petpsychotherapy.com. Sounds a bit pithy, I know, but the willingness to take risks with your money is what makes things like capitalism and California *work*.

Third there are retirees. This group has little appetite for risk. As a cohort they've pulled out of stocks and bonds and foreign holdings and redirected their savings into cash and T-bills because they can't stand the volatility. If they hold stocks at all they are in decidedly unsexy firms like Wal-Mart or AT&T. While they are still net creditors to the system, their income has all but stopped (as opposed to mature workers who are socking away as much of their paychecks as they can stomach). And as retirees age not only do their savings dwindle — reducing what little positive impact they have on things like stock and government debt markets — they also increasingly draw from the system in the form of pensions and healthcare.

(Technically there's a fourth group — kids — but they really don't factor economically in the modern age. They used to serve as free labor on farms, but once most populations relocated into urban environments children essentially transformed into luxury goods. Think of them as more expensive Shih Tzus.)

In a normal system there are more mature workers than retirees, and more young workers than mature workers. Stack them all up by age group with the youth at the bottom and the elderly and the top and you get a pyramid. In such a system there are more consumers (young workers) than investment generators (mature workers) than resource absorbers (retirees). There is a medium-sized, capital-rich generation (mature workers) that is generating the financial capacity that enables the young workers to borrow and consume, and the retirees to live in retirement. There typically isn't enough to go around, so money is tight. Governments face limits. Loans require credit checks and collateral and business plans.

That's *not* what the United States is like right now.

I'm sure you've heard of the Baby Boomers. They comprise the largest population cohort the Americans have ever generated as a proportion of their population: 75 million. There are so many of them that they have contorted the American system all their lives. When they entered the workforce they absorbed all the available jobs, and many had to take jobs that were below their skill sets. That flooding of the labor market depressed wages for two decades and forced many households to obtain two incomes — depressing wages even more — in order to get by.

By 2000, the vast majority of the Boomers were in the "mature worker" phase of their lives. This is most certainly a mixed bag for the United States. Firmly in the plus column is that the large generation is saving massive volumes in preparation for their retirement.[4] The result has been a wealth of investment capital surging through American financial markets, keeping

---

4   They are not saving nearly enough, of course, but I'll leave that well-worn topic for others.

borrowing costs low whether that borrowing is for a new car for your spouse, a new phone for your child, a new road through your state, a new aircraft carrier for the Navy, or a new universal health care policy for the president. Borrowing hasn't been this cheap since 1950.

But just as too many workers depress wages, too much capital depresses rates of return. Lower returns have nudged the Boomers to make investment decisions that were riskier than they should have been. In the financial industry this is the classic "seeking yield" problem. Boomer investors deliberately chose riskier investments in the hope of getting better returns. As more money poured into riskier sectors, businesses and geographies, yields only went down more. The Boomer cohort is so big that the United States cannot metabolize all their capital, and so Boomer money splurted out beyond the country's borders, going global. Rwandan municipal bonds and Kazakh energy investments became all the rage. Consequently, growth rates in the developing world have been at record highs for much of the 2000-2015 period.

This isn't healthy, and it certainly isn't sustainable. Bubbles emerged almost everywhere because of the Boomers' investment choices, and in time those bubbles have burst. You can lay most of the financial bubbles (and busts) of the past two decades at the Boomers' feet — everything from dot-com to Enron to subprime to Brazil, Russia, India, and China — all were only possible because the Boomers were ignoring risk in the quest for that extra 1% of yield.

There's more to the story than investment, however. High incomes plus high investment means high *tax* receipts. During the same period, government coffers swelled right alongside the still-gently-aging Boomers. The presidencies of George W. Bush and Barack Obama presided over the Boomers' primary taxpaying years. But rather than use that extra tax income to fill up America's three retirement-related programs — Social Security, Medicare, and Medicaid — and prepare for the day that the Boomers' aging wasn't nearly so gentle, the two presidents did the opposite. During their terms Washington indulged in spending binges, running up the national debt from $6 trillion to just shy of $20 trillion.

As of 2016, the oldest boomers have been in retirement for a decade. The heyday of runaway government income is over, and the heyday of runaway government spending on retirement and healthcare spending is about to begin. The impact will not be limited to America. As the Boomers' savings shifts into retirement mode, all that capital they have deployed to all those investment products – whether they be in Silicon Valley or Detroit or Bolivia or Turkey or India – will be recalled, and the growth that it has fueled will collapse.

The next generation to consider are the Boomers' kids: Generation Y, a.k.a. Echo Boomers or the Millennials. They face precisely the same problems that their parents do; there are too damn many of them — certainly more than there are available jobs — and so they face precisely the same pressures their parents did back in the 1960s and 1970s. Luckily for the Millennials, they have a couple of advantages that their parents lacked:

- They are by far the best-educated generation that the United States has ever assembled. As the American economy evolves into a dynamic, service-oriented system, as careers give way to jobs, jobs give way to part-time work, and as part-time work gives way to hobbies that happen to generate income, the Yers are actually fairly well-prepared socially, politically, and psychologically for the new era.

- Second, one-third of GenY still lives at home — which saves them more than a bit of scratch. Of those who have moved out, nearly half of *them* were only able to do so because the Bank of Mom&Dad is helping pay the bills. Such deep and broad financial support for the Millennials means that the United States is in the midst of the greatest generational wealth transfer in American history without anyone actually dying yet.

Which all sucks for the last major generation, GenX, by birth rate and numbers the smallest generation as a percentage of the population in modern U.S. history. The Xers face a series of catastrophes:

- First, their incomes are lower than they "should" be. GenX started entering the workforce in the late 1980s only to discover the Boomers had already taken all available employment opportunities. GenX became the eternal intern generation, and has been fighting to recover from their late start ever since.

- Second, as GenX ages into the mature-worker role, they are expected to pay for the entirety of pension and healthcare costs for 75 million retiring Boomers. They also will be expected to make up — via higher taxes to fund government services — for all of the money the Boomers transferred (and are continuing to transfer) to their children. Balancing the budget will require the biggest and most sustained tax increases — or most egregious debt build-ups — in American history outside of wartime.

- Third, GenY is as large as GenX is small. There simply won't be enough GenX investment capital — especially once you consider how big a chunk of GenX's income will be required to pay the enlarged tax bill — to fully fund the private sector. The result will be sharply higher borrowing costs for everyone.

- Fourth, there never will be any meaningful changes to Medicare, Medicaid, or Social Security. The GenX cohort is roughly one-fifth smaller than the Boomers — considering that GenX is younger, they should

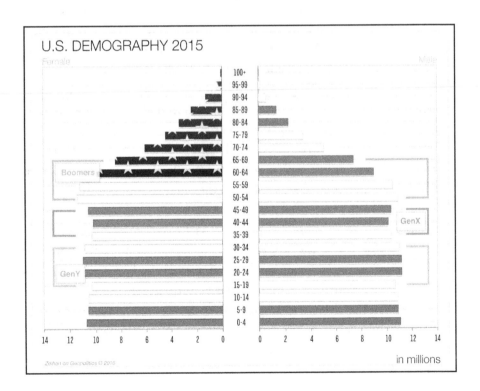

U.S. DEMOGRAPHY 2015

in millions

be one-quarter *bigger* — an imbalance so extreme that GenX will not outnumber the Boomers until most of the Xers are in their *sixties*. GenX will never be able to vote away the benefits the Boomers have voted for themselves. Nor can GenX count upon GenY as an ally in rationalizing the federal budget, for if meaningful reform were to happen, the cuts in government outlays would be so extreme that the Boomers would have to move in with their kids. From GenY's perspective, the child-parent living experience is an inviolably one-way process.

But as much as I dog on GenY, thank God they are there — for three reasons. First, GenY are currently in the "young worker" phase of their lives and are consuming like mad. Their raising of kids and building of homes and buying of cars and carpet and chairs to put into those homes are why the U.S. economy has been growing at such a steady clip since the end of the Great Recession in 2009. All that beard butter and all those bedazzled flip-flops add up. Without their hordes, the U.S. economy would be flat. At best.

Second, in 15 years when Xers start becoming the new retiree class — one far smaller than the Boomers — and GenY matures[5] into the new tax-*paying* class, we will again have a large generation paying the bills. So, yes, budgets are tight in the United States and will remain tight for another decade and a half, but then the United States transitions into a more normal system; one in which the shrinking Boomer bills and deficits will become more manageable with every passing year.

Third, as omnipresent as those narcissistic, neurotic Millennials might seem to be in the United States, they are actually all alone in the universe. The huge Boomer cohort — as well as the smaller Xer cohort — is not unique. Nearly every advanced economy in the world has a similar top-heavy population structure among people aged 35 to 70. But *only the American Boomers had kids.* There are no German Ys or Canadian Ys or Korean Ys or Thai Ys or Italian Ys or Japanese Ys. Even among the "younger" countries like Poland and Romania and China, it's as if there were a line drawn between 1980 and 1985 — 5 to 15 years after the line was drawn in the core developed countries — when everyone simply stopped repopulating. The

---

5   And I use that word in its loosest possible definition.

result is not just a baby bust, but accelerating population falls unparalleled in speed and depth by any peacetime event in human history with the singular exception of the Black Plague. Barring a breakthrough in medical technology that enables people in their 50s to have children — and a breakthrough in social dynamics that makes them *want* to en masse — the relative *scope* of the coming depopulation could well prove even bigger.

To which the Americans of GenY are nearly the sole exception among the rich countries. And one of only a handful of exceptions among the world writ large. As of 2016, the average American is already younger than the average citizen of every first-world country in the world except Australia, New Zealand, Ireland, Cyprus, and Iceland.[6] By 2019, the average American will be younger than the average Chinese. By 2040 younger than the average Brazilian, with the average Mexican well on course to age past the Americans just past the mid-century mark.

The impact upon the global system is already mammoth. The Japanese economic breakdown of 1990 wasn't demographic in origin, but Japan has since aged past the point that it will again be a consumption-led economy. Ever. Taiwan and Korea may seem more dynamic — and they are — but the pair's success is only because of their access to the wonders of the Bretton Woods system; they can export the veritable pride's share of their economic output. Demographically, the pair are two of the four major countries aging most quickly into mass retirement. (Canada rounds out the top four.)

Europe's financial crisis came from a mix of financial, geopolitical, cultural, and demographic factors, but with every passing year demography is a bigger component behind the Europeans' inability to put the crisis behind them. As soon as 2022, Germany, Belgium, Greece, Austria, and Italy will not be past just the point of not just demographic recovery — they and more have already crossed that threshold — but financial and economic recovery as well. By 2030 they will be joined by Bulgaria, Croatia, the Czech Republic, Estonia, Finland, Latvia, Lithuania, Luxembourg, Hungary, Malta, Poland, Portugal, Romania, Slovakia, Slovenia, and Spain.

---

6   Whose combined populations are less than one-tenth that of the United States.

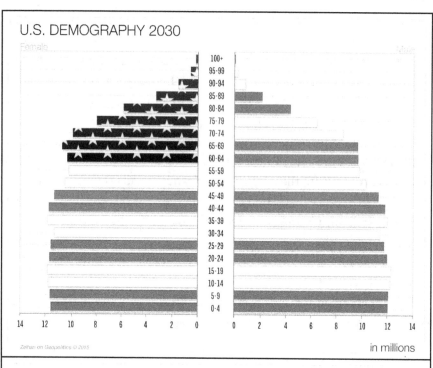

U.S. DEMOGRAPHY 2030

Female   Male

100+, 95-99, 90-94, 85-89, 80-84, 75-79, 70-74, 65-69, 60-64, 55-59, 50-54, 45-49, 40-44, 35-39, 30-34, 25-29, 20-24, 15-19, 10-14, 5-9, 0-4

14   12   10   8   6   4   2   0   0   2   4   6   8   10   12   14

Zeihan on Geopolitics © 2015

in millions

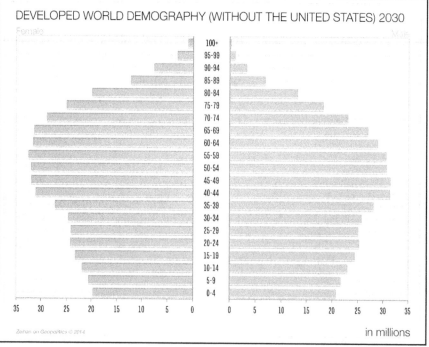

DEVELOPED WORLD DEMOGRAPHY (WITHOUT THE UNITED STATES) 2030

Female   Male

100+, 95-99, 90-94, 85-89, 80-84, 75-79, 70-74, 65-69, 60-64, 55-59, 50-54, 45-49, 40-44, 35-39, 30-34, 25-29, 20-24, 15-19, 10-14, 5-9, 0-4

35   30   25   20   15   10   5   0   0   5   10   15   20   25   30   35

Zeihan on Geopolitics © 2014

in millions

And finally there is China. The adoption of the one-child policy has not only gutted the next generation of Chinese workers (and consumers[7]), it has merged with Chinese culture and the Chinese development strategy in a most damning way. Chinese industrialists discovered quite some time ago that they faced labor shortages. Indeed, the cost of Chinese labor has increased by a factor of ten since 2000; Chinese labor is now twice the cost *and* less skilled than Mexican labor. Those industrialists went inland, away from the expensive coastal cities, to find new workers. But they only brought back the women.

The reason is simple. You can cram young women into dorms like ants. Doing so with young men generates crime and security concerns. Chinese men and women of child-bearing age are not simply separated by socio-economic status, they are separated by physical province. China may still be younger than Europe, but its demography is already past recovery and its rate of aging — fourth-fastest of the world's significant countries — will place it among the European rarified age brackets within two decades.

7   And taxpayers.

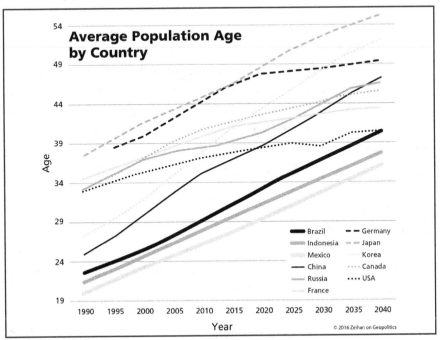

The transformation of the American system is a consequence of primarily domestic changes, rendering it largely immune to international developments. These changes will ultimately untether the United States from the global system. Yet the changes *beyond* the United States are largely caused by shifts in the *American* system, making international stability hostage to a country that no longer sees a link between its own economic and security well-being and that of the rest of the world.

Bereft of local consumption, bereft of local financial strength, the only option for these and so many other of the world's nations is exports … just as the United States is losing interest in the global trade system writ large. Order is giving way to Disorder.

Making matters (much) worse, the world's dependence upon merchandise exports to maintain economic well-being, social-stability, pension plans, and national coherence is only one side of the coin. The coin's other side brings us back to the energy question.

The Strategy of Energy

At issue is the fact that there is more to global trade than selling the *out*puts of the manufacturing process. There are also *in*puts, the most important and strategic of which is crude oil. But Bretton Woods did more than open markets and let countries export their way to wealth via safe sea lanes. An equally huge part of making Bretton Woods work is enabling all of its constituent participants to have access to ample supplies of energy on a sufficiently-reliable schedule so that they can keep the trains running, the lights on, their factories cranking, their cars driving, and in general their economies humming away.

The amount of oil required is legion. The EU countries suck down a combined 12mbpd, with *11*mbpd of that being imports. The heavily industrialized Northeast Asian quartet — China, Japan, Korea, and Taiwan — require nearly 19mbpd, with a whopping 75% of that sourced from outside of the region, mostly from the Persian Gulf.

It didn't start this way. In 1950, total global oil production was only 11mbpd, of which *half* was produced *in the United States*. Most international maritime oil shipments, therefore, were from the United States to the Western European allies. As the years ticked by, however, three developments transformed the politics of oil supply from a logistical regional issue into a massive global one.

First, Europe ran out of oil. Initially European oil supply was an issue of local distribution, but don't confuse "local" with "simple." That distribution issue was one of the key geo-economic factors guiding military strategy during World War II. The Nazis needed to capture Romania and Baku (in then-Soviet Azerbaijan) in order to secure larger and more reliable oil supplies. Allied strikes against Nazi-occupied Romania and the failure of the Nazi advance at Stalingrad (just shy of the oil fields of Azerbaijan) are leading factors as to why the Nazi war effort so catastrophically failed in late 1944 and 1945 — the Germans found it nearly impossible to keep their forces fueled.

Post-war, Western Europe lost access to both Romanian and Azerbaijani oil, yet they could still supply themselves via their own imperial supply networks. But one of the (from the Western Europeans' points of view) less desired details of Bretton Woods is that no one was supposed to have an empire any longer. There was a lot of nodding and smiling as the Europeans assumed that the Americans didn't actually mean *them*. That would be silly.

For a few years the new free trade and the old imperial systems lived somewhat uncomfortably alongside each other, but a hard break came quickly. In

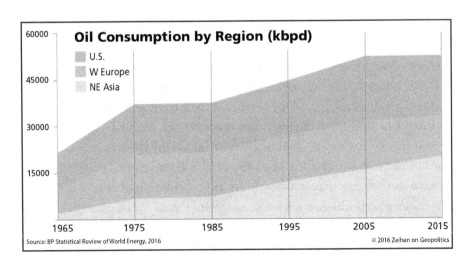

Oil Consumption by Region (kbpd)

Source: BP Statistical Review of World Energy, 2016   © 2016 Zeihan on Geopolitics

the 1956 Suez crisis the United States formally — and *very* publicly — refused to provide military assistance to the joint British-French-Israeli effort to capture the Suez Canal from a newly independent Egyptian government. Further, the Americans formally — and *very* publicly — threatened to enact financial, economic and even military sanctions against London and Paris if they continued with their Suez efforts.

The result was a fast-paced shattering of the entire European colonial network. The Europeans, by American design, became almost completely dependent upon the Americans for the security of their ongoing oil imports. And those imports were skyrocketing independently of the shift in sourcing paradigms. By the time of the Suez crisis, Europe's post-WWII export-led economic boom was already flying high. With rising economic activity and affluence came more energy-eating industry and a newly car-mobile citizenry. Within Europe, local demand rose even as domestic supplies petered out. Abroad the Americans systematically broke apart the Europeans' imperial oil supply chains, making their allies wholly dependent upon the American Navy to keep their systems running.

Second, the Americans expanded Bretton Woods to an ever-widening list of countries in every part of the world: the defeated Axis, Scandinavia, Latin America, Southeast Asia, and more. American foreign policy fixated upon expanding the alliance network wherever and wherever it could, for every country that was in the American camp denied the Soviets a toehold. Within a generation America's containment policy was a global phenomenon.

For the vast majority of the alliance's new members, their membership in the global trade regime was their first taste of industrialization — their only previous "participation" in the global economy had been under European colonial rule, a system fixated on extracting resources and wealth from them rather than developing modern systems in their territories. Now these newly independent states were laying down roads (which enabled a car-and-truck driven economic model[8]), building industrial bases (which required electricity and petroleum inputs), and establishing modern military forces (which needed jet fuel, gasoline and diesel). An entirely new set of economies joined America's global alliance network, an entirely new set of countries joined

---

8   Heh. Car-and-truck driven. See what I did there?

Major Oil Importers

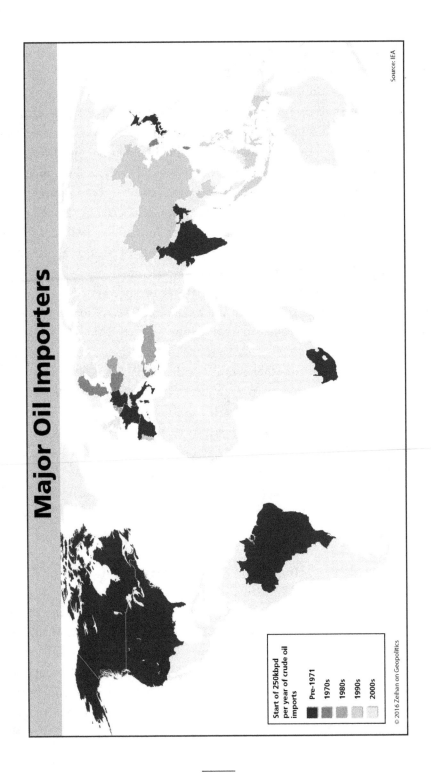

Start of 250kbpd
per year of crude oil
imports

- Pre-1971
- 1970s
- 1980s
- 1990s
- 2000s

Source: IEA

the global trade system, and an entirely new list of energy importers added their demand to global energy markets.

Third, most of the easy oil everywhere in the world got used up. And some of it wasn't all that easy to acquire. Rising demand pressured all of the world's pre-WWII supply centers: the Dutch East Indies (now a newly independent Indonesia), British Malaysia (as of 1973 known simply as Malaysia), Pennsylvania, and Texas. There just wasn't enough in these few supply centers to make up the difference. Exploration into new zones brought new supplies on-line, but only for a decade or four: China's Daqing maxed out at 1.1mbpd in 1997, the Alaskan North Slope at 2.0mbpd in 1988, the North Sea peaked at 6.4mbpd in 2000, and the U.S. Gulf of Mexico hit 1.8mbpd in 2009 and has been falling ever since.

The only "reliable" producers of global significance ended up being in Russian Siberia, where the climate and topography was so hostile that local populations would never outstrip local supplies; and the Middle East, where the petroleum reservoirs were so large, shallow, and easy to develop that they could produce for another century or three.

With every passing decade, the number of oil importers rose, the volume of oil required rose, and the more the globe became dependent upon a small number of sources. Just between 1980 and 2007, global oil demand increased 40%, from 61.4mbpd to 87.1mbpd, while the proportion of what was *imported* increased from one-half to two-thirds. Without the Americans keeping supply sources — and in particular Persian Gulf supplies — forced open, nothing about the modern era could have happened.

2007: The World at the Dawn of Shale

Scope aside, it isn't like the Americans themselves didn't see the benefit to themselves — and not simply because of the rubric of the Cold War and the necessity of the alliance system. The United States itself is one of the countries that saw its economy grow and its domestic oil production decline. Though American oil fields played a critical role in fueling the WWII Allied war effort, by 1973 the United States became a net importer of crude and by 2008 it was forced to ship in 15mbpd, triple that of the second-largest oil importing country and amounting to an oil import bill of 2.8% of GDP — over $400 billion in that year.

The Americans had little choice but to establish and maintain tight links with Algeria and Saudi Arabia, despite human rights records which best can be characterized as boisterously atrocious. The Americans found themselves assisting Angola in producing crude even as the United States agitated against the Angolan government in the 1975-2002 civil war. The Americans' generation-long face-off against the Iranians in the aftermath of the 1979 Iranian revolution forced them to keep an aircraft carrier battle group in the Persian Gulf to keep that region's various players from each others' — or from the oil flows' — throats. Simply put, it didn't matter what the Americans thought of these places or their politics. The Americans' energy dependency meant they simply had no room to maneuver. Dependency forced engagement.

They were hardly alone.

At the dawn of the shale era, the global energy picture consisted of more than just the large importing region of the United States. There also were the countries of the European Union and the Northeast Asian states of Japan, China, Korea and Taiwan. Bretton Woods allies all. Collectively these regions *imported* approximately 31mbpd of crude oil and refined products. That's double the American total — fully half of all globally traded energy.

For the Americans and the Europeans, the energy map was ridiculously complex. Each imported large volumes of crude from a dozen different sources, with additional supplies coming in from twice that many more. Canada was America's top supplier, while the Americans tapped Mexican, Saudi, and Venezuelan supplies in roughly equal quantity, but also sourced very high-quality crude oils — ideal for refining gasoline — from Algeria and Nigeria. Other significant suppliers included Angola, Iraq, Russia, Kuwait, and Libya. The Europeans relied upon Russia as their single-largest source overall, but where you lived on the continent — and the particulars of your colonial legacy — heavily colored your import patterns. North African crude flowed to Italy. West African crude to France. Norwegian crude supplied the United Kingdom. High-quality Azerbaijani crude was sought out by less-advanced refiners. Iranian crude — partially discounted because of sanctions — held market share in places like Greece, Italy, and Spain.

The commonality within and across the United States and European Union was that there was no commonality. Dozens of crude streams supplied scores of refineries. Hundreds of contracts a day made for a bewildering mix of blends and delivery schedules, particularly for major regional refining hubs like Italy, the Netherlands, New Jersey, and Texas.

The energy supermajors — America's ExxonMobil, Chevron and ConocoPhillips, and Europe's BP, Royal Dutch/Shell, ENI and Total — thrived in this world. All produce crude from hundreds of sites in dozens of countries. All manage oil flows of a bewildering array of qualities and quantities. The internal logistics required to keep track of such internal diversity perfectly meshed with the external diversity that were the global energy supply chains of 2007. Such vertically-integrated, horizontally-diversified firms could not simply earn profit supplying the dozens of local American and European markets, but they could play the numbers and shuffle their supplies around within and among those markets to earn the top dollar. An Italian refinery was short of medium/sour crude from Angola? Ship them some Kazakh crude that was originally bound for Spain. A New Jersey refinery is undergoing maintenance and cannot take delivery of a tanker of Algerian light? Redirect that cargo to a subsidiary refinery in northern France. A hurricane hits the Gulf of Mexico, taking a few Texas refineries offline, and driving gasoline prices up in the American interior? Increase refining runs in Germany and ship refined product across the Atlantic to take advantage of the regional price spike.

And if there were any unloved cargos of anything — light/sweet, heavy/sour, gasoline, jet fuel or anything else — the supermajors could always ship them to Northeast Asia. A quirk of petroleum geology and geography left the entire arc of maritime Asia from Pakistan to Japan, and in particular Northeast Asia, with very little in the way of petroleum deposits. China alone has large-scale reserves, but the country's rapid economic growth transformed it from an oil exporter to importer as long ago as 1993, while petroleum output in Japan, Korea, and Taiwan has never covered more than a tiny percentage (typically less than 1%) of their energy needs. That just leaves Southeast Asia, and of those countries only Malaysia and Brunei remained as net exporters in 2007.[9] And most of the major Asian importers found themselves heavily dependent upon not just crude from outside the region, but from the maelstrom of issues that is the Persian Gulf.

The opportunity for profit gouging proved — consistently — phenomenal. Unlike the corporate structures of oil firms in the United States, where multiple interests regularly compete for attention, a fully state-owned national oil company dominates every one of the Persian Gulf states. These companies majority-own every aspect of the exploration/production/transport/loading/refining supply chain, so the sole purpose is to maximize income for the government.[10] It was child's play for the Emiratis, Iranians, Kuwaitis, Omanis, Qataris, and especially the Saudis to exercise oligopolistic pricing. Based on the supply patterns of the day, the Asians — and especially the Northeast Asians — were forced to pay 3%-10% a barrel more for their imported crude than other importers simply because they had no other options. This Asian Premium regularly transferred some $50 million a day from Northeast Asia to the Persian Gulf above and beyond what one would normally expect the crude to cost. The Persian Gulf states slathered themselves in such financial gravy, applying the income to whatever task on which they set their minds. The Saudis purchased social unification with bottomless subsidies. The Persians funded their spy and militant networks in places as far afield as Afghanistan, Iraq, Lebanon, the Palestinian Territories, and Yemen. The Emiratis built their own, less classy, version of Las Vegas — calling it Dubai. The Kuwaitis saved for a rainy day.

The Asian Premium benefited more than the Persian Gulf states, however. It also encouraged anyone who could rustle up spare cargos to sail them to Northeast Asia and levy similar surcharges. Because of the premium, the Northeast Asians couldn't afford to be overly picky. They would take almost any cargo that was on offer, even if their refineries couldn't process it. The Northeast Asians would maintain extra storage capacity at their refineries so they could blend multiple crude streams on-site, primarily to thin out

---

9   With combined exports under 0.4mbpd.

10   Technically, the Iraqi oil sector isn't state-owned since the Americans wrote private enterprise into the Iraqi constitution. Functionally, however, the Oil Ministry out of Baghdad controls all aspects of the country's southern energy industry while the Kurdish authorities in northern Iraq control everything within their zones of control.

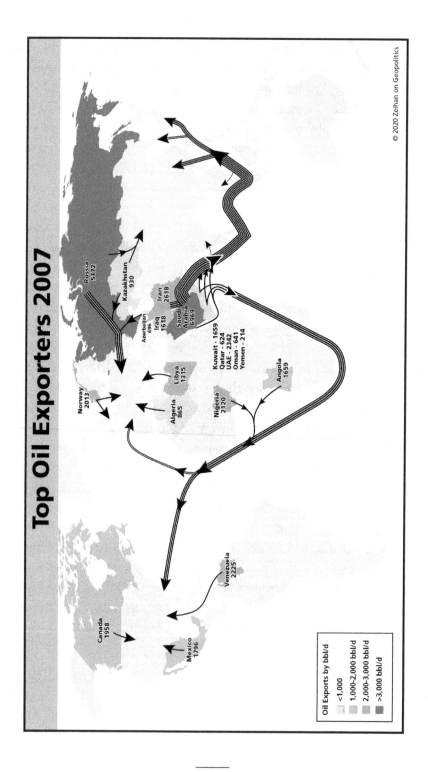

Top Oil Exporters 2007

Russia 5172
Kazakhstan 930
Azerbaijan 696
Iraq 1618
Iran 2618
Saudi Arabia 6969
Kuwait - 1659
Qatar - 624
UAE - 2342
Oman - 641
Yemen - 214
Angola 1659
Norway 2013
Libya 1315
Algeria 865
Nigeria 2120
Canada 1958
Mexico 1796
Venezuela 2225

Oil Exports by bbl/d
<1,000
1,000–2,000 bbl/d
2,000–3,000 bbl/d
>3,000 bbl/d

© 2020 Zeihan on Geopolitics

particularly heavy or sour crudes into something that their refineries could stomach. Alaska's medium crudes were a regular visitor. Russia shelled out tens of billions on a pipeline corridor through virgin Siberian territory to Vladivostok in the Russian Far East so it could tap the Premium. Chinese firms signed questionable deals with Latin American states to bring expensive-to-produce crude streams on-line. Angola, fresh from its genocidal civil war, found Asian buyers willing to pay almost any price for anything it could ship.

2015: Shale and a World in Flux

Oh, how times change. Four unrelated factors have reshaped the face of American energy since 2007, and from that, global energy.

First, SUV-obsessed, midnight-oil-burning Americans are using less energy, and in particular less crude oil.

When you believe that oil prices will be higher for longer you start changing your consumption patterns and investing in things that will reduce your footprint. I'm not talking habits here like carpooling, but hard and fast changes that remain with you for years: things like buying energy-efficient appliances or switching your car out for a hybrid.

And it isn't just your personal actions. Manufacturers discover that their customers want products that use less energy, and so tweak their own processes to cater to the shifting demand. Take your pick — pretty much any of the standard fare in your average house uses but a fraction of the electricity that was required a decade or two ago. Since the 1990s television power demand is down by 35% despite massive increases in quality and size. Dishwashers use 40% less electricity, air conditioners 50% less, refrigerators 60%.

Casa Zeihan has experienced all these evolutions and more in the past few years. My Prius will burn 100 fewer barrels of crude over its lifespan than the average car on the road. My solar panels generate about 60% of the electricity that I typically use and will pay for themselves in just seven years. The new windows and siding reduced the electricity required to heat and cool the house by nearly 40%.

Literally thousands of products that we use every day have been tweaked with energy conservation in mind. Government policy plays a role here — things like nudging up the minimum gasoline mileage requirement obviously has an impact that is global in scope — but for the most part it is the average consumer's natural responses to high prices that makes all the difference in the world.

The best part is that when energy prices fall back, the result is *not* an immediate surge in demand. Sell your energy-efficient car, and it is still part of the vehicle fleet. Sell your solar-enpaneled house, and it is still part of the housing stock. And many of the older, more energy-intensive products just are not around any longer. (I'm certainly not trading in my new energy-efficient flat screen for an old-style energy-hogging tube.) Neither are many manufacturers going to go back to the older energy-intensive methods of production or energy-gobbling product lines. All those high-efficiency dryers and hybrid cars aren't the highwater mark of energy savings, they are the new baseline.

The technical term is **demand destruction**, and the shifts in energy consumption patterns that it generates are permanent. The price point at which people in the developed world start being energy conscious to the point that it impacts their spending patterns is about $80 a barrel. The average price

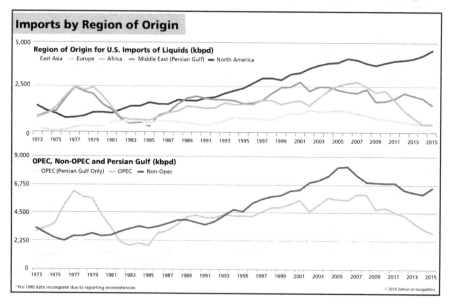

Imports by Region of Origin

Region of Origin for U.S. Imports of Liquids (kbpd)
East Asia — Europe — Africa — Middle East (Persian Gulf) — North America

OPEC, Non-OPEC and Persian Gulf (kbpd)
OPEC (Persian Gulf Only) — OPEC — Non-Opec

*Pre-1990 data incomplete due to reporting inconsistencies

© 2016 Zeihan on Geopolitics

of oil was above that level for 10 of the 11 years from 2004-2014. Simply from the purchase and implementation of the gadgets and cars and home improvements and updated industrial processes the United States has already installed and paid for, American primary energy demand will stay essentially flat for a couple more *decades*.

The second major shift limiting American energy exposure is a powerful **demographic** component. Think on the patterns in your life and those of the people around you. Once you take that first big job, your life starts getting bigger. Your roommate arrangements go away and you get your own place. A bicycle becomes a car. A significant other becomes a spouse and you need a bigger place and probably a bigger car. Pretty soon someone gets a bump and you need to move again so the baby will have a room. That bigger place requires a longer commute. One kid mysteriously becomes 2.3. Your life enters a phase that can best be described as hectic: piano lessons, soccer practice, PTA meetings. Shuttling the rugrats about becomes a new part-time job. And all the time in your work schedule hasn't let up. Buy this. Drive there. By the time you are 35 everything is go go go!

Now fast-forward a bit, to about age 55. Things are calming down. Work is still work, but the kids are moving out and (finally!) starting to take care of themselves. That big house doesn't seem so necessary. Rooms are closed off. Maybe you downsize. The minivan goes away, replaced by a toy car. Your transport schedule — blissfully — becomes less operatic.

Fast-forward again to age 75. You're fully retired. No more commute to work. You're a grandparent, so aside from popping in to a few extra-curricular events you don't need to worry about baseball or the mall or those god-awful 6:30 a.m. college prep classes. In fact, because of that silly fender bender you're not driving much at all because your damn kids keep hiding your damn keys.

Oil demand peaks at about 35, and then it steadily declines with age. In 2007 the oldest of the American Baby Boomers retired. In 2021, half of the American Boomer cohort will have followed their leader, and by 2030 the Boomers will be gone from the American workforce. For demographic reasons alone, American energy demand should slide for at least another 15 years.

Banning the Ban

In October 1973 a wide array of Arab oil exporters announced an embargo on all oil sales to the United States in protest of American military assistance to Israel. By March 1974 global oil prices had quadrupled and Americans had their first taste of energy rationing outside of wartime. As part of an array of mitigating polices, the United States banned the export of crude oil. The fear created by the Arab embargo and the fear manifested in the U.S. oil export prohibition have been the guiding lights of global energy ever since.

Or at least, they were until shale came along. In December 2015, in the ultimate expression of confidence that the Americans are no longer concerned about energy security, the American export ban was lifted,

For producers struggling with low oil prices, the end of the export ban was a godsend. Instead of all shale output being bottled up in the U.S. interior, at least some could make it out to international markets. By late-2016 the United States was exporting a few hundred thousand barrels daily of high quality light/sweet shale crude. The spread between U.S. oil prices and global energy prices narrowed somewhat. Considering that every $1 rise in crude's selling price adds some $5 million to the operators' collective daily bottom line, this is no small issue.

The end of the export ban has also been a boon for the American consumer. Pre-shale the conventional wisdom was that all the world's high-quality conventional crude was gone. For decades the global crude stream was becoming sourer and heavier. Rather than be hostage to the producers of high-quality oil (most of which were the instigators of the 1973 Arab embargo) U.S. energy firms invested some $1 trillion into overhauling the country's refining industry so it could handle the thickest, dirtiest crude the world could produce.

Shale crude didn't just overturn the conventional wisdom, it overturned the economics of American refining. While the refiners certainly enjoyed the financial impact of the shale crude glut, they didn't particularly enjoy how their facilities were faring. The new shale crude streams were simply too high-quality to be run in refineries designed to process sludge. By re-enabling crude exports, the glut of high-quality shale crude was lessened, improving the economics of importing heavy/sour, U.S. refineries' preferred diet. So even as U.S. *crude* prices rose a bit because of the export ban's end, U.S. *gasoline* prices have actually fallen a touch.

Don't get too used to the change. In 2016 there is an oil price war in full swing, one consequence of which is that global spare oil production capacity is at record lows. Should there be any disruption to output or transport of crude anywhere in the world, no one will be able to make up the shortfall. Oil prices will skyrocket, which will prompt the U.S. Congress to reinstate the export ban. To do otherwise would expose U.S. voters to energy prices both high and erratic. Considering the populist nature of U.S. politics of late, that's a non-starter.

The third major factor behind the transformation of the American energy picture is much more prosaic. The Americans have found themselves being supplied by a new player, their northern neighbor. Starting in the 1960s, the Canadians of **Alberta** started experimenting with producing a type of oil called heavy bitumen, more commonly known as oil sands. Unlike more traditional crudes, bitumen isn't a liquid at room temperature, and the oil sands' production zones in Central Alberta tend to be more than a bit colder than 70 degrees.

As such production typically follows one of two methods. In the first the bitumen is strip-mined, relocated by trucks roughly the shape and size of Connecticut, dumped into massive industrial upgraders that melt the oil out of the sand so that the oil can be transported by more traditional means. In the second process, some sort of energetic stimulation — whether steam-injection or a funky form of electrification — is pushed into the deposit, heating and loosening the bitumen so it can be extracted somewhat like more normal oil.

With American energy demand a very clear "known," the Albertans invested billions into supplying their southern neighbors. Canadian crude exports to the United States were but 400,000 in the late 1970s, but by 2015 they'd reached 3.8mbpd, making it the largest state-to-state oil relationship in the world.

And, of course, the final change in the American energy picture is **shale**. Shale oil and condensate output in the United States increased in excess of 500kbpd per year for a *decade*, taking gross output from 6.8mbpd in 2006 to 13mbpd in 2015. Taken together with declines in demand during the same period, total U.S. oil/condensate imports declined from 10mbpd to a mere

Top Oil Exporters 2015

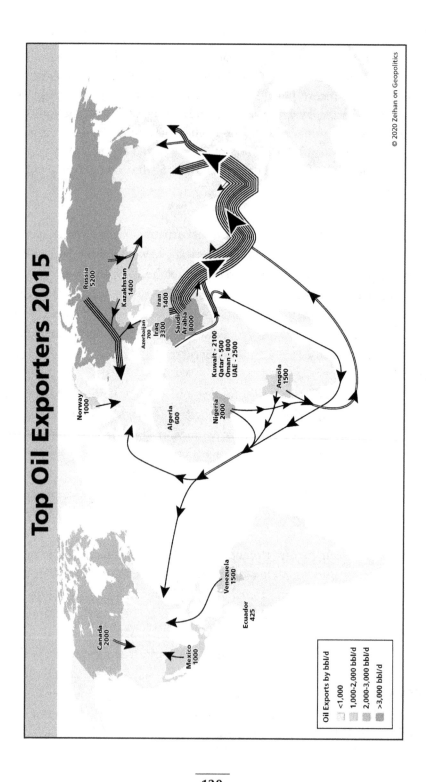

Russia 5200
Kazakhstan 1400
Iran 1400
Azerbaijan 700
Iraq 3300
Saudi Arabia 8000
Kuwait - 2100
Qatar - 500
Oman - 800
UAE - 2500
Norway 1000
Algeria 600
Nigeria 2000
Angola 1500
Venezuela 1500
Ecuador 425
Canada 2000
Mexico 1000

Oil Exports by bbl/d
<1,000
1,000-2,000 bbl/d
2,000-3,000 bbl/d
>3,000 bbl/d

© 2020 Zeihan on Geopolitics

5.4mbpd. Factor in the Albertans' displacement of more traditional crude sources, and the overall North American energy import tally was just over 2mbpd by the end of 2014, an amount less than China or Japan or Germany or Korea. Had Saudi Arabia not launched its price war in November 2014, U.S. shale output was on track to bring North America to outright oil independence somewhere around New Year's Day of 2017.

Would-be suppliers were not treated equally. The United States continued to use whatever Mexican crude was available, while Canadian crude imports hit fresh records every year. The Saudis, hyper-cognizant that their physical and economic security was directly related to how useful the Americans found them, continually pre-positioned crude supplies in the Gulf of Mexico both to supply refineries they owned there and to ensure Saudi crude would be immediately available should any American ever want it.

Beyond that short list, all suppliers suffered. Ironically, it had been the previous winners who fell the furthest; producers of highly-sought light and sweet crudes were shocked to find the Americans drowning in shale crude, which was even lighter and sweeter. In particular, places like Algeria, Equatorial Guinea, and Nigeria saw their shipments to the United States nearly fall to zero.[11]

And there's no small impact elsewhere in the world.

Across the Atlantic, the European financial crisis proved to be less a one-time thing and more the new normal. It wasn't until 2015, a full decade into the crisis, that overall debt levels peaked and the overall economy finally recovered to pre-recession levels. But it is already too late: Belgium, Germany, Greece, Italy, and others are all rapidly aging toward mass retirement. Overall, consumer and energy demand both aren't simply stagnant, but instead falling steadily.

With the North American and European energy markets no longer accepting massive volumes — indeed, with combined deliveries to those mar-

---

11   Calendar year 2015 witnessed a hiccup in this trend. The price crash discouraged no-holds-barred shale output, somewhat alleviating the North American light/sweet oil glut. This has encouraged American refiners to again purchase cargos of high-quality foreign crude, particularly from Algeria and Nigeria. U.S. refineries, however, continue to retool to run shale crude, so even in the unlikely circumstance that prices never rise, this import fallback is only a temporary blip.

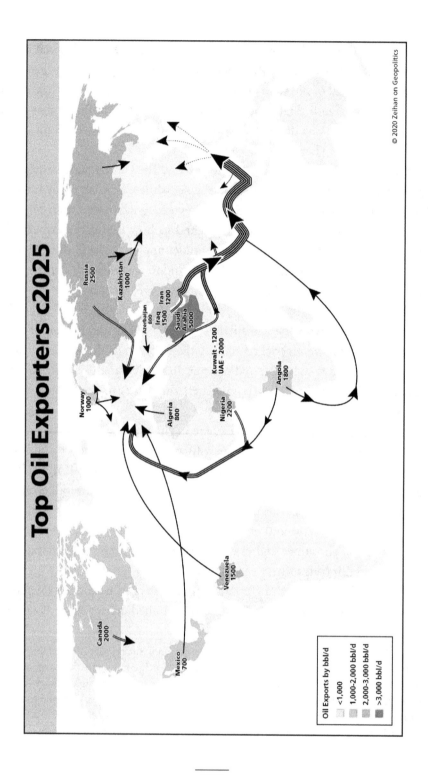

Top Oil Exporters c2025

Oil Exports by bbl/d
- <1,000
- 1,000-2,000 bbl/d
- 2,000-3,000 bbl/d
- >3,000 bbl/d

Canada 2000

Mexico 700

Venezuela 1500

Norway 1000

Russia 2500

Kazakhstan 1000

Azerbaijan 800

Iraq 1500

Iran 1200

Saudi Arabia 5000

Kuwait - 1200

UAE - 2000

Algeria 800

Nigeria 2200

Angola 1800

© 2020 Zeihan on Geopolitics

kets a full 9mbpd down in just eight years — the world's various energy producers needed to find new markets to sell their products.

Which left the big importers as the familiar names of Northeast Asia.

But this wasn't 2007 any longer. In 2007, the Northeast Asians were bottom feeders, accepting whatever supplies they were lucky enough to be offered. By 2015, they were the *only* dynamic energy markets left in the world. All players are now attempting to reach Northeast Asia not because they can make more money there, but because it is the only place that can even pretend to take large deliveries. The premium had not only shrunk to less than $1.50 per barrel, but from time to time crude sales to Asia even sold at a *discount*.

The Wars of the Disorder

Here's the crux of the matter:

The American disengagement is already deeply underway. As of 2016 the number of Americans in uniform serving abroad is at lows not seen since 1941. The U.S. economy is the least connected through trade to the rest of the world of *any* of the world's significant countries. As of 2016 the United States is the only advanced economy, and one of only a small handful of economies of any type, that is generating meaningful economic growth — and unique in the world in that nearly all of that growth is based off of activity within its own borders. And if that weren't enough on its own, a populist, isolationist, anti-trade bent has insinuated itself into American politics on both the Left and Right. The 2016 American presidential race was fought between a man who wanted to forcibly renegotiate every trade deal and alliance in place and a woman opposed to every free-trade deal completed in the past quarter-century — including those she personally negotiated.[12]

---

12   If it makes you feel any better, it isn't just the United States that is dipping into nativism. Japan is amending its constitution to make it easier to bomb people. China is crowning a new Mao. Britain voted itself out of the European Union. The Turkish president's leadership makes Donald Trump seem shy by comparison, Poland's government exudes the worst characteristics of Pope Innocent III and Kanye.

Directly or indirectly, today's world is American-managed and American-protected. Most countries are dependent upon the system that the Americans created and now maintain, and so lack the capacity to impose a replacement system for themselves. Remove that management and protection, and most countries lose vast swathes of their economic and security wherewithal.

For energy exporters it means getting their product to market no longer is a sure thing. For energy importers it means perhaps having to fight for access and cargos. Many will have little choice but to take their economic and security prerogatives into their own hands. That's a very sanitized way of saying that for many, war will be the only path forward. Disruption will be the new normal.

All that remains to fully cleave energy markets apart is a sharp supply disruption somewhere — anywhere — outside of North America. When that happens, North American prices will certainly bounce around, but shale output will come on-line quickly. Once technical oil independence is achieved, prices will have a functional ceiling of about $70 a barrel, a price point at which every U.S. shale play is profitable.

The wider world will be a different story. Every interruption and shot fired and tanker captured will result in prices both sky-high and erratic. Each disruption will not only enhance the absolute advantages that shale has already brought to the U.S. economy, but will layer in a relative advantage in supply security and price levels and stability versus the rest of the world. A functional floor on global oil prices of $150 is probably a good starting point, although that may prove to be too low.

There are three leading conflicts that will trigger just such a divide.

The first of these shifts is a new Russian-European war. The conflict is rooted in Russian insecurity and is not only inevitable, it already has begun. Shy of an American combat deployment that is as massive as it is unlikely, the Red Army will push across the near-entirety of its western frontier, forcing the Europeans to take up arms. This Twilight War is nearly upon us. We will explore both its origins and its outcomes — regional and global — in Chapter 6.

Chapter 7 will delineate the second major conflict with global consequences: a brewing war between Saudi Arabia and Iran, with the Saudis already the clear aggressors. The United States has long smothered the mutual animosity felt by these two Persian Gulf countries in the name of global stability. As American forces — both land and maritime — evacuate the region, what is in essence already a back-alley knife fight will spiral out of control into a general regional war.

Neither of these conflicts will occur in a vacuum. Disrupt that much energy export capacity and there simply will not be enough left to supply hungry importers the world over. The result will be a catastrophic realignment of national and corporate power as countries and companies adjust to and/or attempt to pre-empt the global convulsions. Chapter 8 lays out the third of the three great regional conflicts: the Tanker War that will consume East Asia.

CHAPTER 6

The Twilight War

In college I had the occasion of entertaining a Russian exchange student named Ivan. Once over vodka we were playing "what-if," debating how the world might have turned out differently if this or that detail had been altered. What if Kennedy hadn't been assassinated? What if Hitler had died before taking over Germany? What if the Soviets had won the Cold War?

On the last one, Ivan insisted that no changing of the details could have led to a different outcome. It may have been the alcohol, but I just couldn't wrap my head around why he was so convinced of the inevitability of the Soviet fall. Like most Americans I wasn't really sure why the Americans had walked away from the Cold War without so much as the memory of a limp while Russia was a dismembered mess. Even today Americans flinch more visibly when they think of Vietnam than they do when they think of Russia, a country that still possesses the nuclear wherewithal to end American existence.

So Ivan — still remarkably cogent a half-bottle of Novosibirsk Special Blend in — laid it out for me: you cannot swim across the Atlantic, so the United States would always be safe and not have to pay much for that safety. But anyone can walk across Poland, so the Soviets always had to be on alert — and being on alert is expensive.

For the sake of my liver, my interactions with my Russian associate pe-tered out shortly thereafter.[1] But Ivan's crisply logicked — if slurrily-deliv-ered — argument has stuck with me ever since.

The Russian Geography: A Lesson in Pain

Russia's geography, in a word, sucks.

Russian lands are barely temperate, with all but one Russian city lying at a higher latitude than Minneapolis.[2] Moscow itself gets under 20 hours of sunlight for the entire *month* of December. Russia only has one commer-cially navigable river, the Volga, which is frozen one-third of the year and empties to the landlocked Caspian Sea rather than the ocean. Short growing seasons make full tables something the Russians will never take for granted, while lack of easy movement condemns the country to being capital poor.

But the real difference is the shape of the land itself. Russian lands are wide open. Roughly 80 percent of the Russian population lives in European Russia, a region some 1,500 miles north-to-south but at most points only 1,000 miles east to west that is the flattest on earth.

On the western edge, the Russian plains merge almost seamlessly with the plains of Estonia, Latvia, Belarus, and especially Ukraine. There are no mountains or hills or even rivers separating them from each other. The southern border is even more open. Russia shares a 4,200-mile border with Kazakhstan, most of which is bereft of features more vertical than a Kansas interstate on-ramp.

In the southwest there is a "real" border in the Greater Caucasus chain — a mountain range that paved roads breach in but four places, only two of which remain open year-round. But most of the people in the northern slopes of the Greater Caucasus are not actually Russians. Instead the re-gional populations are a Halloween candy grab bag — complete with hid-den razor blades — of conquered peoples ranging from the Kabards to the

---

1   Ivan's drinking was a clear and present danger to my work ethic, so I started hanging out with a French student.

2   The singular exception is Makhachkala, the capital of the dangerously untidy province of Dagestan.

Ingush to the Circassians to the Chechens to the Dagestanis.[3] Only one sizable Russian-populated metro center — Rostov-on-Don — sits within 350 miles of the border.

What barriers Russia does have are in the wrong places: the forests and swamps and mountains of the Arctic and Siberia aren't between the Russians and rivals, but between the Russians and even crappier land. When the Russians look out across their world they don't see lands brimming with potential or ocean moats granting stand-off distance or impregnable deserts and mountains guarding flanks, but instead a relatively thin slice of civilized lands surrounded by patches of chaos with richer, hostile lands beyond.

Russian security only comes from conquering everyone nearby in order to establish buffers around the Russian core. If you can Russify these conquered peoples so that they identify with Moscow's goals (and fears), excellent! But this is not required. Or expected. The intent is not for them to be productive, but to instead transform these conquered peoples into a different sort of barrier — a sort of strategic road bump between more distant foes and the greater Moscow region. Since few people tell their children nursery rhymes about the joys of serving as other people's cannon fodder, the Russians often have to find ways to motivate their conquered populations — or more to the point, to intimidate their subjects into accepting the role the Russians demand of them. The Russians do this with a deep, intrusive, and cruel intelligence service. Under Lenin it was the Cheka, under Stalin the NVBD, and Brezhnev the KGB, after the Cold War the FSB, and now it's the FSB backed up with the social-monitoring techniques Edward Snowden brought with him from the American NSA. It's not a kind system, but history has not been kind to Russia.

Russia's territory is nearly the size of South America. Russia's borders stretch for more than 12,000 miles. Yet Russia's population is less than half that of the United States. The huge swathe of lightly populated lands means that Russia can never afford the dense infrastructure footprints so common in the Western world. This dictates the sort of military Russia must field: The lack of infrastructure prevents Russia from maintaining a small, technically advanced, highly mobile force that could be quickly redeployed to

---

3   Who are themselves more an amalgamation of peoples that just happen to live in the same area (and loathe one another) rather than a typical ethnic group.

where it is most needed. Instead Russia must maintain massive, ponderous forces hard on its borders.

Both of these strategies — the intensive intel operations and the static military stationing — are incredibly manpower-intensive. It's a task that requires — at a minimum — a million-man-strong intel system and another 4 million for the army. As of 2016 Russia sports roughly 770,000 active-duty troops. Its 2 million reservists could fill the gaps in an emergency, but a standing force they are not. To a degree, good tech penetration to sniff out dissidents and some snazzy propaganda to win over the masses can somewhat mitigate the intel cost, but in a land of poor infrastructure and endless flatlands, there is no substitute for a gigantic army.

It's about to get a lot worse. The Russian birth rate plummeted around the end of the Cold War. The health system has collapsed. Heroin addiction runs rampant. Russia suffers the world's worst infection rates of drug-resistant tuberculosis, and near-the-worst for HIV.[4] All this would be bad enough by itself, but the Russian system crashed in 1989 — children born in that year turned 18 in 2007. By 2022 everyone in the Russian military will have been born during the disease-ridden and drug-addled baby bust. The result? An army that is likely no more than half its 2010 size in functional terms, and considerably less than that in terms of operational capability.

Russia has already entered Twilight: There are barely enough men under arms and cloaks to maintain and defend Russia as it is. Cut those numbers by half, and the end of Russia itself is nigh.

The Soviet Solution

Geography — and recent history — offers a way forward. Though Russia's current borders are not defendable, as recently as a generation ago Russia's borders were fairly strong. Or more to the point, the Soviet Empire's borders were solid.

---

4   Technically, the Russians are "only" in the bottom fifth, but since the Kremlin's method of dealing with the epidemic was to stop testing, I think it is safe to say that the situation is much worse than the "data" suggests.

The Soviet Union anchored itself beyond contemporary Russia in a series of robust geographic barriers. In the northwest, Soviet territory went right up to the Baltic Sea. In the west, Soviet forces reached through Poland and into East Germany, the narrowest point of the North European Plain. In the southwest, the Soviets absorbed the Carpathians and the Danube valley, gaining the Balkan Mountains as their southern border land and pushing right up against the Austrian Alps. In the Caucasus the line wasn't the ridge of the Greater Caucasus — that became an internal border — but instead the ridge of the Lesser Caucasus further south. In the southeast, Soviet power stretched over 2,000 miles across the Central Asian steppes before anchoring in the Karakum Desert and the Tien Shen Mountains. It was the most secure the Russians had ever been. Of the Soviet Union's 12,000 miles of border, the only truly vulnerable bit was a few hundred miles where the two Germanies met, which is why Germany in general and Berlin in specific was such a hot point all throughout the Cold War.

It all fell apart in 1991. In the west, Russian power retreated from the Baltic Sea, the German frontier, the Alps, the Danube valley, and even the Carpathians. A generation on, most of the successor states are vehemently anti-Russian, and nearly all are in the same military alliance with the Russians' Cold War rival, the United States, and World War rival, Germany. In the south, the Russians lost the Caucasus and Central Asia in their entirety. Of the nineteen non-Russian countries that emerged from the Soviet wreckage, only two — Armenia and Belarus — would welcome the return of Russian power.

Even the shape of the new border structure played against the Russians. Despite a massive reduction in land area from the old Soviet system to the new Russian state, the new Russia actually has borders a bit *longer*. With more to defend, less cannon fodder, shorter distances from the frontier to Moscow, and a rapidly declining population, the strategic calculus has degraded from merely dangerous to apocalyptic.

What Is To Be Done?

There are a few theoretical approaches.

The first is to figure out how to achieve more with less. In other countries facing steep demographic decline, the goal is to vastly ramp up productivity in order to earn more income via exports. Unfortunately, this option isn't available. Russia's industrial sector is a mix of low value-added raw materials largely produced in remote Arctic and/or Siberian regions; value-added manufacturing accounts for but one-eighth of the Russian economy and one-sixth of Russian exports. Simply building the additional infrastructure required to shift onto a higher-value footing would require hundreds of billions of dollars of investment in infrastructure, industrial plant and education, millions of young people and decades of time that Russia simply doesn't have.

The second is to encourage inward migration to address the demographic imbalance. The challenge is that there just are not enough Russians living outside of the country to attract. Using 2016 Russian government data — constantly reimagined to provide the most flattering view possible — the baby bust is so deep that the average Russian is already 40 years old and will hit 46 within two decades. Simply holding the country's average age steady will require the import of 2 million 25-year-olds every year. At such a pace Russia would exhaust the entirety of the world's Russian diaspora in less than a decade.

A quick glance at Russian data suggests that Moscow is attempting to substitute with non-Russians — Russia sports the third-largest migrant population in the world. Most foreigners working and living in Russia are citizens of the Central Asian states that were formerly part of the Soviet Union. As a rule, they are part of the Russian-language legacy of the Soviet period and so can work in Russia without too much cultural friction.

But this flow is neither sustainable nor permanent. The Central Asian states don't just face demographic crunches threatening their raw numbers, but economic dislocation (and even collapse) has gutted their educational system. The quality of workforce that these states can provide Russia has steadily eroded since 1992. Add in that the Russian language isn't being maintained in any of the five states and that most of these migrants are Muslim, and the degree of populist/nationalist backlash within Russia has steadily risen. As such this migrant population is truly *migrant* — it comes and goes with the season and so its presence does little to address Russia's underlying problem.

And of course Russia faces a pair of other social complications. Between the demographic implosion and sense of besiegement, the Kremlin is attempting to close ranks. Non-Russians are being made to feel decidedly unwelcome. And when half of your national security strategy is based upon the conquering, monitoring, and impressment of your neighbors, *attracting* skilled immigrants isn't exactly part of your cultural milieu.

The final option — and the one the Russian leadership has settled on — is to find a way to change Russia's political geography sufficiently so that a smaller army will suffice. In short, the Kremlin wants to alter Russia's borders so they are easier to defend. Unfortunately for the Russians (and their neighbors), there is no internal fastness to which they can *retreat*. The more securable borders that Russia desires can only be achieved by *expanding*.

The Russians need to forward-position their military in five zones: the Baltic Coast, the Polish Gap, the Bessarabian Gap, and the western and eastern reaches of the Caucasus Mountains. Because the Russians would then be anchored in a series of geographic barriers, the portions of the frontier that actually require large-scale defenses would shrink from some 3,000 miles to under 600 — something the Russians can achieve with a military substantially smaller than it is today.

If Russia is to survive its demographic Twilight, it must do nothing less than absorb in whole or in part some 11 countries — Estonia, Latvia, Lithuania, Poland, Romania, Belarus, Moldova, Ukraine, Georgia, Azerbaijan, and Armenia. This Twilight War will be a desperate, sprawling military conflict that will define European/Russian borderland for decades.

Stage 1: Wreck Ukraine and Divide the Europeans

The first shots of the Twilight War have already been fired.

In February 2014 the Russians launched a multi-vectored invasion of the country of Ukraine. Beginning the day after the last athletes left the Sochi Olympic site, a mix of amphibious assaults and paratroopers ejected Ukrainian forces from the Crimean Peninsula within a matter of days.

Within two months, Russian paramilitary forces with at least some support from regular ground units ripped most of the Ukrainian provinces of Luhansk and Donbass away from Kiev.

While the Russians formally — and proudly — claim credit for the Crimean campaign, and have already formally incorporated it into Russia proper, they are far less direct in their Donbass/Luhansk assertions. The official Russian position is that what is going on in eastern Ukraine is an uprising against the Ukrainian authorities in Kiev. That while some Russian troops have resigned their commissions and as volunteers crossed the border without permission or coordination, Moscow itself is doing nothing in Ukraine proper. Considering the number of Russian troops that have been captured with equipment and written orders, considering the ongoing transfer of Russian military vehicles and materiel, and considering the heavy degree of military and intelligence communication across the international border, such claims are of course not even believed within the Russian information ministry.

But there is a method to the madness. After all, this is only the first stage of the war. The Russians see a veritable flock of birds they plan to kill with their Ukrainian stone. They break out into three general categories.

First, the Russians wanted the Crimea back — badly.

The Crimean port of Sevastopol is/was home to Russia's Black Sea Fleet. Russia had been leasing the port from Ukraine since the Soviet breakup; now the Russians directly hold it. It is more than "merely" a big-ass naval base. Tactically, think of the Crimea not so much as a piece of land, but as forward-positioned unsinkable aircraft carrier. As such Soviet/Russian investment in Crimea's naval infrastructure is, in a word, immense. Any naval or air assets stationed there are capable of threatening the entirety of Ukraine's sea-borne connections to the wider world. Since Ukraine's largest exports are metals and agricultural outputs like steel and wheat — commodities typically shipped via water — Russia now has a knife to the throat of the entire Ukrainian economy.

But the most important reason for snagging the Crimea is even more broadly strategic. Historically, when Turkey has invaded Russian territory, it has done so via the Crimea. The Russians are well aware that any naval force that dominates the peninsula also dominates the northern half of the

Black Sea and can use it as a forward base for the invasion of Ukraine and Russia proper. As such Russian forces have been stationed there ever since its capture by Catherine the Great in the late 18th century. From Moscow's point of view, only a quirk of internal Soviet politicking shifted the Crimea to Ukraine in the first place. For the Kremlin, bringing the peninsula back under direct control didn't just make heaps of tactical, economic, historical, and nationalistic sense, it allowed the Russian state to re-secure the first of those many geographic gaps through which invaders flow.

Second, Moscow wants to eliminate the Ukrainian military as a consideration before the "real" fighting begins.

All of the constituent components of the Soviet Union had a tough time in the 1990s, but many managed to turn themselves around. The Baltic Trio of Estonia, Latvia, and Lithuania reformed and ultimately joined the European Union. Azerbaijan, Kazakhstan, and Russia made oodles of cash during a period of high energy prices from 2000 to 2008. Ukraine faced no such turnaround. Old infrastructure, a collapsed educational and health care network, depressed regional demand for its main exports, and a deeply entrenched system of corruption all combined to steadily erode post-Soviet Ukraine's already dim prospects.

Through it all Ukraine's military wasn't so much cut to the bone as it was abandoned. The country had a fair amount of forces on paper, but troops weren't paid and there was no money for exercises. It isn't that new equipment was never purchased (although it wasn't) as much as the equipment that existed wasn't maintained. In terms of operational capacity and deployability, the Ukrainian military ceased functioning around 2005.

With the invasions of Crimea, Luhansk, and Donbass, the Ukrainians weren't just faced with an unwinnable war against a vastly superior force — they were faced with a trap they could not avoid:

- Most of Ukraine's remaining units of reasonable competence were ethnic *Russians* with tighter links to Moscow than to Kiev. When Ukraine mobilized to resist the Russian assault, many of Ukraine's best troops defected — taking with them not just much-needed equipment, but Ukraine's order and plan of battle.

- Ukrainian loyalists mostly hail from the western half of the country, while the country's eastern half is largely populated with either ethnic Russians or Russofied Ukrainians — many of whom were rooting for Moscow, if not actively colluding. The 500-mile journey from Kiev to Luhansk is a long one for Ukraine's poorly-equipped, poorly-trained, poorly-supplied troops. What loyal, competent forces remained in the Ukrainian military quickly identified themselves (they were the ones who fought effectively and didn't cut and run). Considering the general hostility of the surrounding population to those few good remaining troops, Russian (para) military forces found it a simple matter to isolate and chop them up.

- As the Russians were fighting an unofficial war, Moscow felt it would be a little too obvious if Russian air power came to play. This encouraged the Ukrainians to deploy their entire remaining air force to the east to help repel the Russian assaults. Once fully committed, the Russians moved several anti-aircraft batteries over the border and shot down the entirety of what was left of effective Ukrainian air assets.

As of late 2015 the goal of gutting the Ukrainian military had already been met. While the conflict seems quiet from the other side of the world, with "only" about a hundred soldiers dying a month, this is the maximum tempo of operations the Ukrainian military can sustain. For all practical purposes, the road to Kiev is open. When the time comes for the Russians to make their big push for the entire country of Ukraine, the Russians will be able to (easily) make good on Putin's promise that Russian tanks could be in Kiev in a month. Only then can Moscow get to the more serious business of the war that will need to be fought even further to the west.

Third, the Russians want to hand the Europeans not just a fait accompli, but to establish in European minds that it simply isn't realistic to resist Russia. There are a lot of angles to the Russian effort.

A big part of the Russian approach is all about baby steps.

Using irregular forces and formally denying that any regular Russian forces are present in Luhansk/Donbass provides European leaders who don't want to get in a war with a (remarkably flimsy) bit of political cover. By moving into eastern Ukraine a bit at time, Russia makes more stalwart Europeans question whether getting into a major war 1,000 miles from the

EU border for this or that tiny town is really worth the cost. And most of all, by going after a non-NATO state, the Russians know the Americans are certain to *not* get involved as a belligerent actor. Yet NATO members like Poland who (rightly) fear that they might be next, are left begging the Americans for support the Americans have no intention of providing. All around the Western alliance the result is doubt, confusion, and discord.

The best example of just how well this overall strategy is working — and just how loathe the Europeans are to confront Moscow — occurred in July 2014, when a Russian-operated missile system in Donbas shot down a Malaysian Airlines jetliner carrying 298 people, two-thirds of whom were Dutch citizens. The Netherlands is perhaps the most reliably pro-American country in mainland Europe, enjoys some 1,200 miles of buffer between its lands and the Russian frontier, and has minimal economic or energy dependence upon the Russian system. And yet even here, within days all

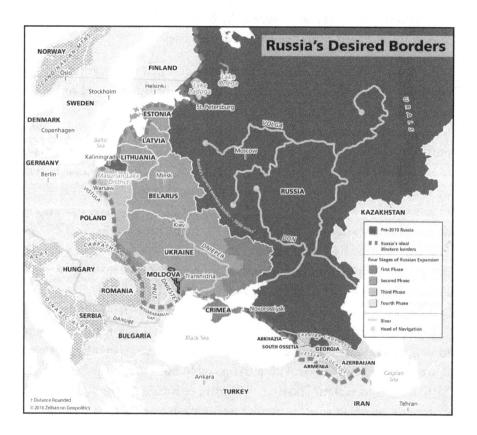

the Dutch government and press could manage was some indignant resignation. Between national bickering and the unsettling feeling that they lack leverage, all that the Europeans have managed to erect versus Russia are a few sanctions that have minimal impact on Russia's financial situation and a negligible impact on the war effort.

The Russian military position has only strengthened in the time since, and in June 2016 Moscow received a windfall. In a referendum the majority of British voters opted to remove the United Kingdom from the European Union. The United Kingdom has long served as the strongest connective tissue not just between NATO and the European Union, but also between the United States and Europe. London has also been the loudest voice arguing that the eastern edge of Western civilization in general, and the EU and NATO in specific, should continually be pushed further east. By removing themselves from the EU, the Brits have all but guaranteed that Western support for all things Ukraine will take a back seat to simple internal Western civilizational damage control. The Kremlin couldn't have asked for a better outcome.

Stage 2: The Scandinavians

While much has been made over the decades about European and NATO unity, the firmest relationships on the Continent are not France and Germany or the United States and the United Kingdom, but instead the Scandinavian family. Norway, Denmark, Finland, and Sweden have not only all been part of the same empire in ages past, but have dovetailed their economic, energy, foreign, and military policies without prodding from either the EU or the Atlantic alliance. Their militaries often co-train; their diplomats share embassies; they vouch for each other in organizations in which they are not all members.[5] All four are advanced technological democracies boasting extreme levels of social equality, and powerful senses of national and regional cohesion and identity.

---

5   Norway is not in the European Union, while Sweden and Finland are not in NATO.

There are many, many things that this cluster of countries agree on, but as regards this discussion there are three that truly stand out.

First, *all* are fixated on Russia as a military threat to the near-exclusion of everything else. Major European powers such as France, Germany, and the United Kingdom have a range of interests in a range of theaters, and so it is odd for them to focus fully on a single concern. In contrast, any Russian effort to push into the Northern European Plain or the Baltic Sea region requires Russia to neutralize Scandinavia; Finland, Sweden, Denmark, and Norway control the maritime approaches to the Plain's eastern half as well as the flows from the Baltic to the wider ocean. As such the defense sectors of the Scandinavian states are expressly geared toward countering Russian power. Norway and Denmark do this hand-in-glove with NATO, Sweden chooses an independent military strategy, while Finland's entire defense industry is geared toward inflicting as much pain upon Russian forces as is humanly possible to deter invasion.

Second, all consider the Baltic Trio of Estonia, Latvia, and Lithuania as long-lost relatives who are finally being returned to the Scandinavian fold. Russian success in its border expansion efforts by default would mean the elimination of the Trio as independent states. From the point of view of Oslo, Copenhagen, Stockholm, and Helsinki that will not be allowed to stand. The fact that the mere existence of the Baltic Trio as independent states on the east shore of the Baltic Sea hobbles Russian power doesn't hurt either.

Third, they will need help. All four of the Scandinavians punch well above their weight militarily, but Russia — sporting over five times their combined population — is simply beyond their ability to contain. Luckily, they are not the only states that will feel threatened, and not the only states that will act to counter Russian power.

The Scandinavian Quartet will be joined first and foremost by the United Kingdom. In part this is because the risk is fairly low. The United Kingdom is both not on Russia's target list, and it has a number of major countries between it and the Russians. In anything shy of a nuclear exchange, the Russians just cannot hurt the Brits all that much.

But mostly it is about grand strategy. As a maritime power, the one thing that can threaten the United Kingdom is a land power that faces so few land-based rivals that it can dedicate energy to floating a navy. Were Russia successful in reconsolidating its western borderlands, it would enjoy sufficient resource savings and strategic freedom to potentially become a naval power. Every time that has happened in Russian history, London has found itself in a broad struggle with Russian interests. Best to nip that potential threat in the bud by preventing the consolidation in the first place.

U.K. assistance is precisely what the Scandinavian Quartet needs. London commands sufficient naval power to utterly wipe Russian power from the northern seas and make civilian shipping to or from Russia's Arctic Ocean coast impossible. It has amphibious troops to help the Scandinavians reinforce the Balts (or raid the coasts of Russian-occupied Baltic states), and aircraft that can provide overflight and deep strike for all Baltic Sea operations. On the diplomatic front, London also could serve as a critical channel for unofficial American assistance to the anti-Russian coalition.

The Baltic Front will take four forms.

Sea. Collectively, the four Scandinavian states boast impressive economies and militaries that are more than a match for everything the Russians have on the Baltic Sea. The Baltic is nearly enclosed and ringed by countries hostile to Russian interests. In wartime any Russian forces on the sea would in essence be battling in a bottle. As such the Soviets gave their Baltic Sea Fleet lowest priority in terms of manpower, ships, and faculties — the Northern, Pacific and Black Sea fleet were more strategically viable — and in the post-Cold War world the Russians haven't changed that prioritization. In contrast, the vast majority of the Scandinavian navies *only* ply the Baltic while the remainder is in the adjacent North Sea. With such concentration mismatches, Russian military activity on and under the sea itself would likely be eradicated in a matter of days, if not hours.

And that is before the Brits are taken into consideration. While the Scandinavians dispatch Russia's Baltic Fleet, the British Navy will sink the entirety of the one Russian naval force that might have been able to sail to the Baltic warzone: the Northern Fleet, based near Murmansk. With all Russian naval assets in Northern Europe dedicated to reef-forming, the coalition will be able to launch maritime landings at the times and places of their choosing. This will enable the coalition to wreck Russian infrastructure, tying up Russian forces while limiting their own exposure.

Russia's second city of St. Petersburg will fall under full naval embargo. That's worse for the Russians than it sounds. The St. Petersburg area is both Russia's single-largest product import point as well as the largest of its three major oil export zones. In the war's opening days Russia will face large, irrecoverable hits to its income as well as consumer goods and food shortages.

Land. Ukraine is for all intents and purposes a broken state incapable of mounting a full-scale defense. The only meaningful barrier is the Dnieper River, which roughly bisects the country. Russian paratrooper capabilities should be able to conquer the Dnieper crossings in short order, enabling the Russians to conquer the country in its entirety in a matter of weeks.

In the same push that the Russians secure the bulk of Ukraine, regular Russian forces will also take command of Belarus — another post-Soviet state that utterly lacks the ability to defend itself. Unlike Ukrainians, however, Belarusians don't simply view the Russian government positively, they suffer a deep culture cringe and are highly likely to welcome the Russians in with open arms.

Beyond Belarus, Russia will have few difficulties conquering the Baltic Trio in short order. While all have oversized militaries, they are only oversized by their own tiny standards: the Trio have a combined population of just 6.2 million, lengthy borders with Russia and Russian-dominated Belarus, and lack a land border with any of their Scandinavian guardians to facilitate ground support. Add in large Russian minorities who cannot be relied upon to resist the Russian invasion, and the complete capitulation of Estonia and Latvia would likely happen within a few days, and no more than three weeks for Lithuania.

Russian tanks may be able to (literally) roll over any regular Baltic opposition, but that hardly means the Trio's formal subjugation is the end of the story. Sweden quite literally invented amphibious warfare during the Viking age, and the successors of that legacy include Denmark and Norway as well. All three states' defense staffs have been crawling all over the Baltics since 1992, establishing relationships and learning the geography. Modern anti-tank missiles can be smuggled by the score, and are almost as point-and-shoot as your phone camera. Introduce Scandinavian and British weapons, trainers and intelligence to Baltic freedom fighters, and Russian forces will find themselves under harassment as constant as it is lethal.

And do not forget Finland. In the 1939-1940 Winter War, Finland often inflicted 40-to-1 casualties upon the Red Army at a time when Finland was a recently-incorporated state, no one was coming to Finland's aid, the Soviet Union had no other fronts, and the Soviet Union was fully consolidated under Stalin himself. Give Finland strategic partners, a far stronger sense of purpose, deep national unity, and a foe not nearly as powerful as Stalinist Russia, and you get a painfully effective combatant. Finland and Russia both are about to rediscover history. What one of them feels will *not* be nostalgia.

Energy. A central pillar of Russian power for the past several decades has been Russia's massive natural gas and oil export network. During the late Cold War years the Russians regularly sought to build massive export trunklines to European countries — most notably Germany — in order to build economic links that could be twisted to political use. In the post-Cold War era, Russia *began* with such pipes and dependencies in place in nearly all of the former Soviet satellites and constituent Soviet states: most notably East Germany, Poland, Hungary, the Czech Republic, Slovakia, Romania, Bulgaria, Estonia, Latvia, Lithuania, Belarus, Moldova, Ukraine, Armenia, and Georgia. Between 1992 and 2015, many of these pipe links were expanded, and Moscow demonstrated a deep and abiding glee at translating those dependencies into political and strategic advantage. If Russia established a natgas or oil monopoly in a location, that country would suddenly find itself paying premiums. If a country using Russian supplies enacted a policy that Moscow disliked, the supply infrastructure would spontaneously require "maintenance" that could last years.

But the Russians realize they cannot cow the Scandinavians with the energy weapon. Sweden imports some Russian oil that could easily be sourced elsewhere. While Finland is somewhat dependent upon Russian natural gas, it has both mothballed and under-construction nuclear power generation that could quickly close the gap (and Finnish paranoia about all things Russian has induced it to maintain three months of backup supply for just this sort of emergency). Denmark is not only broadly self-sufficient, but serves as the region's trans-shipment hub and so can greatly ease any required energy-flow reshuffling. All use some Russian coal, but all could easily expand sea-borne imports from other sources. Best of all, Norway is part of the quartet. As one of the world's largest energy exporters, Norway could — easily — displace every molecule of Russian petrocarbons that the Scandinavian quartet could possibly need, and still have plenty of extra supply to firm up the United Kingdom's participation in the coalition.

So somewhat surprisingly, at this point the impacts upon global energy would probably be somewhat limited. Sure, the Scandinavian blockade will cease all activity from Russia's Baltic Pipeline System — that's 1.5mbpd of oil flows that simply cannot reach markets without the Scandinavians firing a shot, and a like amount of refined product that at a minimum would need to be railed or trucked to ports on other seas. But since the Norwegians can fill the local gap, the shortages would be felt by countries that the Norwegians would have otherwise supplied. In essence, Norwegian oil that used to go to Germany, Poland, France, Belgium, and the Netherlands — potentially 750kbpd worth — would be redirected to Norway's belligerent allies to compensate for the 250kbpd of oil and other energy inputs that the Scandinavians used to get from Russia. By spreading the pain, the overall impact will be somewhat mitigated. Global oil prices will certainly hike up by $40 per barrel or so, but that is far from a global catastrophe. For *that* the war has to get worse.

Air. The Russians will win handily the land war but become bogged down in a pacification campaign. The Russians will lose their local naval forces and become the target of incessant amphibious raids. The Russians will watch helpless as their single-largest energy outflow point — and thus single-largest income inflow point — is taken offline. But in the air the Russians could well prove dominating, and it all has to do with the Russian geography — and how the Russians see the Americans.

The United States is a long way from its rivals, and so its military is designed to operate from well beyond arm's length. This is triply true for the U.S. airpower: American jets have to fly thousands of miles to reach their targets. With smaller numbers, those jets have to have excellent survivability, excellent stealth or both. They also need extreme hitting power to justify such a long trip in the first place. Consequently, American military jets are the toughest, strongest, fastest in the world, able to operate without supporting ground or naval forces. But there aren't nearly as many of them as you might think, largely because of the extreme financial and technical expense of developing, building, and maintaining such advanced pieces of machinery.

Russia, as a land power, follows the opposite strategy. Unlike the Americans, who operate from well over the horizon, Russia occupies large pieces of flat land; airfields are very common throughout the regions the Russians care about. In an offensive war Russian jets operate hand-in-glove with its land forces, while in a defensive war Russia's foes come to Russia. In either case Russian jets just don't need to worry about range — or even survivability. So Russian jets are cheap. Nearly disposable. And there are a *lot* of them.

Russia's air force has declined precipitously in the years since the Soviet fall, but that air force was designed to counter the full force of an American-led NATO. It might fail — horribly — at that task today, but that is not the task of the moment. The coalition facing Russia may all have air forces qualitatively superior to their Russian equivalents — in particular the Swedes who design their own and the Brits who field carrier-based aircraft[6] — but even in their diminished state the Russians can still swamp their foes with hordes of cheap, capable fighters. Russia will enjoy air superiority over both its own territory and the territory it conquers. It also will be able to engage in air reconnaissance in force over the Arctic Ocean and Baltic Sea to hunt for enemy naval assets.

Worst of all, spamming the sky with aircraft is only half the Russian's air strategy. Moscow is painfully aware of how far behind the United States its aircraft are. To compensate Russia has developed what is quite possibly the world's most advanced integrated anti-aircraft missile systems, with the S-400 being the most impressive. Even if the Scandinavians and Brits can eat away at Russia's aircraft, pilot, and air crew numbers to the point that flying into the teeth of the Russian swarm becomes something more like batting away stray mosquitos, those missile batteries will still make for deadly Baltic skies. Scandinavian/British air power can and will be able to punch holes in Russian coverage — typically to coincide with their amphibious efforts — but those holes won't remain open for long, and each one will come at a stiff price.

There is nothing clean about this conflict. Russia will dominate the air, while the coalition dominates the sea, and both will struggle over the land.

---

6   The Brits have two supercarriers under development that are scheduled to become fully operational in 2017 and 2020.

But neither can deliver a knockout blow. The result will be a nasty, highly mobile little war in which both sides can consistently strike the other where it hurts the most.

Stage 3: The Central Axis

The leading reason the Russians will target the Baltic Trio first is because it is easier, not because it is the sum total of the territories that the Russians feel they must secure. To the Russians the most important zone of expansion is the North European Plain itself — a wide highway of flat lands from Bordeaux to Belarus and beyond. As one moves west from Moscow the plain radically funnels down, from more than 2,000 miles in the Russian heartland to about 250 miles in eastern Poland, a spot where the plain is constricted by the Carpathian Mountains to the south and Poland's Masurian Lake District in the north. The Kremlin believes that if this funnel can be plugged, then defending Russia's core territories would only require a very limited amount of static forces. The ideal anchor would be along the line of the Vistula River, which roughly bisects Poland in general and the Polish capital of Warsaw in specific.

Unlike the war between the Scandinavian alliance and Russia, which would be a dynamic dance of air, sea, and amphibious power, the war in Poland would be a furious, bloody melee. The Polish Land Forces may be larger than that of any three other "new" European states combined, but they simply lack the numbers and technology required to do more than slow the Russians down. There's a resignation to this fact in the design of the Polish Air Force: rather than focusing on the sort of close air support that might help the Polish Land Forces' survivability, it is instead heavy on long-range bombers. The idea is that Polish territory is so flat and open and the Russians so much more powerful that the tide of the ground war cannot be won with just Polish forces. So better to strike deep — make the Russians feel pain in Moscow! It's a strategy that is half-deterrent, half-spite. Any version of Polish-Russian war is one in which the Poles are limited to engaging in such acts of glorious futility to dissuade invasion, followed by gritty guerrilla tactics against a country and people for whom the Poles hold nothing but contempt.

But the Poles will not be alone.

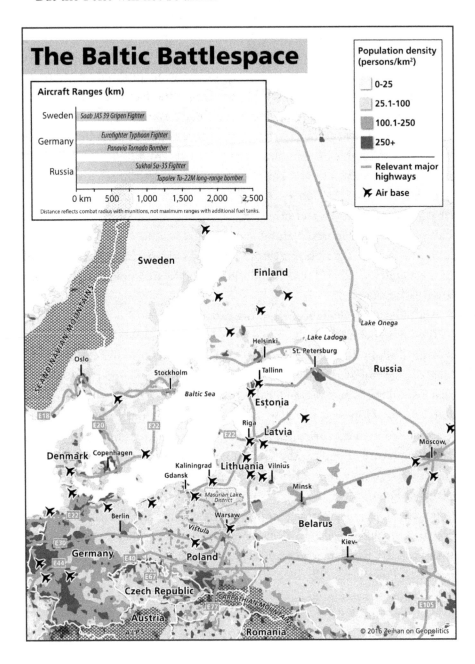

First, the Scandinavian Alliance will massively share weapons, technology, and intelligence with the Poles, along with the odd amphibious raid to target exposed Russian forces. Anything that expands the arc of coastal territory that the Russians must defend plays well to the extremely mobile forces the Alliance wields.

Second, the Germans will have no choice but to enter the war. If all else were equal, the Germans would (desperately) want to avoid belligerence. Leaving aside the horrors of World War II and the fact that the Germans are culturally gun-shy about facing down the Russians after a generation of post-Cold War peace, the Germans fully realize they are broadly incapable of keeping the lights on without souring imports from multiple players.

German oil and oil product imports — which account for 2.1mbpd out of a total demand of 2.3mbpd — come from all points of the compass. Eastern (that is to say, Russian and other former Soviet) supplies account for fully half of those oil imports. Natural gas exposure isn't nearly as onerous, as it accounts for less than one-sixth of Germany's electricity generation. Still, of the country's 7.2bcf/d of demand, fully 6.1bcf/d are imports and 4.4bcf/d are Russian-sourced.

Alas, German reluctance will prove moot.

The Germans might be a couple steps past nervous when Russian tanks roll into Tallinn, Riga, and Vilnius — and doubly so once the Scandinavians start dogfighting with the Russians within sight of the German coast — but that just isn't sufficient reason for the Germans to start beating Volkswagens into swords. However, put Russian forces in the country most critical to German-led manufacturing supply chains, only 350 miles from Berlin itself, and the picture changes. The Germans will have no choice but to rouse themselves, reforge their army, and once again battle the Russians on the plains of Poland.

For the Poles, Germany's entrance in the war is a Dr. Jekyll / Mr. Hyde scenario. In their heads, all Poles know full well that they cannot possibly turn back the Russian advance without massive German help. Yet in their hearts all Poles loathe the idea of German boots on Polish soil as much as the idea of Russian boots. Historically, whenever Germany or Russia has helped "liberate" Poland, the "liberators" have tended to wear out their welcome in fairly short order.

As soon as the Russians cross into Polish territory, all infrastructure that supplies Europe with energy via Poland will cease functioning either because the Russians shut it down, the Poles destroy it, or both. The Yamal-Europe and Nordstream natural gas lines and the Druzhba North oil line would cease operations, shorting Europe of an additional 8.5bcf/d of natural gas and 1.5mbpd of oil.[7]

Yet even with all that shortage, the Norwegians will — again — be able to come to the rescue. Even after supplying the Scandinavian Quartet and the British, they will still have 750kbpd of surplus that could be redirected. Using that to wipe out most of the 1mbpd the Germans import from the former Soviet space would — by far — be the best use of those supplies.

There are still a few things to which the Germans would need to see. Germany is a major manufacturing power, manufacturing requires electricity and 12% of the German electricity system runs on Russian natural gas. Luckily, the Germans have an ace up their sleeves: nuclear power. In the aftermath of the 2011 Fukushima nuclear disaster in Japan, the German government began shutting down its entire nuclear power sector — a sector that provided Germany with just under a quarter of all of its electricity needs. Add in problems with the Russians and the situation seems disastrous. Right?

Wrong. While the orders have been given and the *mothballing* is underway, as of October 2016 only one of Germany's nuclear power facilities has begun the actual *dismantling* process. Manufacturing and logistical complications will certainly crop up as regards the refueling and reconnection process, but Germany is the world's premier manufacturing and logistical power — it even has the capacity to enrich its own uranium, typically the trickiest step in the nuclear power supply chain.

The only piece of the puzzle for which there is no easy solution are oil supplies into eastern Germany and Poland (like Germany, Poland uses relatively

---

7   I say "upward of" since this is the total capacity of the various Russian oil and natgas pipelines into Poland and Germany. Russia has considerable spare capacity in its export network, and it shifts routes and usage rates based on everything from pricing to politics. As a rule the pipes in question are only used at about half capacity, but with the Scandinavian theater already hot by this point, the Russians would undoubtedly need a much higher rate of utilization.

little natural gas and has sufficient coal-burning capacity that a natural gas shortage is not a major inconvenience). This area is completely dependent upon Russian oil supplies and broadly lacks the port facilities required to bring in alternate supplies by water (one of East Germany's major refineries is owned by Russian state oil firm Rosneft, so you can imagine the sort of iron-grip the Russians hold on crude supplies). The only option would be to instead become dependent upon refined products from points further west. That is no small concern — especially in wartime — but needing to secure substitute sourcing of "just" 250kbpd of crude and 125kbpd of products like gasoline, diesel, and jet fuel to replace the products you'd normally refine from FSU crude is a far cry from Moscow being able to dictate German strategic policy per Moscow's original plan.

Poland, unfortunately, could well be left to twist in the wind. The country needs just over a half million barrels of crude daily to maintain operations, and it is hard to see anyone putting such valuable supplies so close to Russian lines to help out a regional player who has no chance of maintaining its independence without extensive outside support of every kind imaginable.

Globally, ignoring the spreading conflict has become all but impossible. Between the redirections and Russian cutoffs, at least 3.1mbpd of crude, 1.5mbpd of refined product, and 7bcf/d of natgas is no longer available for global consumption. Fuel switching within the belligerents — from natgas to either nuclear or coal — can cover half of the natgas shortage. However, that still leaves the largest energy disruptions since World War II to be dealt with, resulting in an energy supply kickline:

- Norway can fuel its allied belligerents, but only if it stops selling oil and natgas to its pre-existing clients in northwestern Europe, primarily the Netherlands, Belgium, and France.

- The Netherlands, Belgium, and France can cover their unexpected shortages by gobbling up all available LNG and oil supplies out of North and West Africa — places where European proximity, colonial legacy, and a whiff of war pricing will encourage everyone to prioritize European shipments.[8]

---

8   More on this in Chapters 8-10.

- The countries that used to absorb African energy exports — primarily in Northeast Asia — will have to eat the entirety of the *European* shortages, and in doing so become that much more dependent upon Persian Gulf suppliers.

At this point the Russians have ample reasons to expect victory. The Scandinavian Alliance may be capable and motivated, but they lack the bulk to roll-back Russian land forces in any sustained way. The opposing forces may be qualitatively superior in every way that matters, but the Russians have overwhelming numbers and a willingness to suffer casualties that the Scandinavians and Brits simply cannot match.

If they can get the politics right, Germany and Poland — with a combined population of 120 million to Russia's 140 millionish[9] — *do* have the numbers to force back Russian forces, but their militaries are not starting from a point where they are prepared for this sort of fight. Poland's military isn't expeditionary and will be struggling simply to maintain coherence in the face of the Russian onslaught. Aside from some lakes and forests in Poland's northeast, the country's eastern half and border region boasts excellent tank-driving and infantry-marching terrain. Just as problematic, a quarter-century of German demilitarization cannot be unwound in a day. At the time of this writing in 2016, the German army only has 63,000 men under regular arms — not all that many more than Poland, a country with half the population and less than one-sixth the economic heft. Rearming will take the Germans — bare minimum — a year, and only then can the long, brutal slug match to push the Russians out of Poland and the Baltics begin. That time lag buys the Russian military a great deal of flexibility in dealing with Sweden and its allies, and plenty of time to destroy the infrastructure across the Vistula and so retard any German-led counterattacks.

But the Russians are still not done.

Stage 4: The Southern Tier

In military terms, securing Russia's southeastern flank is actually the simplest:

- In the Caucasus region, Georgia is a military pigmy that Russia last defeated in 2008 — during the Olympics no less — in a mere five days.

- Azerbaijan has a powerful military on paper, but it has been continually shown as unable to defeat the far smaller and lesser-armed Armenia. Against the far larger and more heavily-armed Russians, it stands no chance whatsoever.

---

9 "ish" because whenever the Kremlin needs a propaganda victory, the State Statistics Committee tends to find a couple million extra Russians. Officially, the Russian Federation has 146 million people in 2016.

- Armenia already is home to a major Russian military detachment, and would enthusiastically cooperate with the Russians in subduing its neighbors, most notably Azerbaijan.

- Moldova is even less militarily functional than Georgia, and it is unclear if the country could even mount *political* opposition to a Russian invasion. Of the country's 3.5 million inhabitants, nearly half regularly vote for pro-Russian parties — and that doesn't count the sliver-shaped statelet of Transnistria, which has existed in a Russian-sponsored (and Russian-garrisoned) legal limbo since a civil war in 1993.

- That just leaves Romania. After Poland, Romania is undoubtedly the most capable state that Russia will target, but the Russians have significant advantages even here. Russia doesn't need to conquer all of Romanian territory; it just needs to snag the extreme northeastern sliver from the Carpathians down to the Danube delta. Though for Romania this is hardly insignificant, the Russian grab doesn't threaten the Romanian core territories along the Danube itself — and the omnipresence of the Carpathians and Danubian tributaries mean the areas in question have

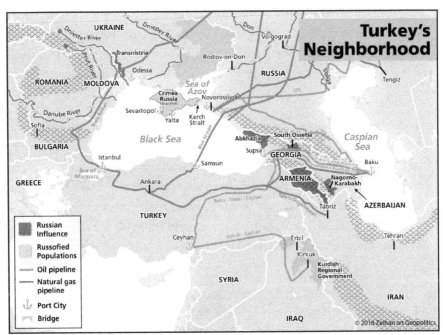

firmer infrastructure connections to Ukraine and Moldova than they do to the Romanian core (which is the whole point of why the Russians want these lands in the first place).

No, the challenge with these southern acquisitions is not so much conquering the targets, but instead making sure that no one is willing and able to fight the Russians on their behalf.

The country that keeps Russian strategic planners up at night is Turkey:

- Turkey's naval forces may seem paltry by the standards of Japan or the United Kingdom, but unlike the Russian fleets, they can all easily concentrate in the Black Sea at will. Combined with air power, the Turks could actually remove Russian naval forces from the Black Sea more easily than the Scandinavian Alliance could from the Baltic.

- As Russian forces occupying Ukraine would face more resistance than Russian forces occupying the Baltics — it's just an issue of numbers: 35 million ethnic Ukrainians versus less than 5 million ethnic Estonians, Latvians and Lithuanians — Turkey could translate its naval dominance into regular amphibious raids on the entire Ukrainian coast. The choicest target would be the Crimean Peninsula. Not only does the Tatar minority there view the Turks as ethnic kin, but the Russians lack a bridge to the Crimean Peninsula.[10] The Turks could likely capture the entire Peninsula fairly easily, and barring that continually bleed the Russian garrisons there.

- Turkey enjoys professional, if somewhat cool, relations with Bulgaria and Romania, and would have few problems negotiating and implementing military basing agreements that would force the Russians to keep more troops in northeastern Romania than they would like. The Turks might even be willing to provide air cover for Romanian attempts to retake their territory, since such an effort would greatly limit what Russians troops Turkish forces would face elsewhere.

---

10   A monster of a bridge to cross the 10-mile-wide Kirch Strait *is* under construction — the Russians estimate it will be operational by 2019 — but the Turks would only need to put one hole in it to eliminate the bridge from consideration.

- Turkey could also be counted upon to surge ground forces into Georgia and Azerbaijan. Total Russian forces south of the Caucasus number in the vicinity of 10,000 — and there is nothing in the area that Russia couldn't conquer with twice that number. Yet that's a laughable number of strategically isolated troops in the face of Turkey's *five-hundred-thousand man ground force*, which doesn't even count the country's 380,000 reservists. Especially when a handful of Turkish air strikes could sever the only two functioning rail lines that can ship troops and materiel from Russia into the Caucasus region.

The Swedes and the Scandinavians Moscow feels it can handle. Add in the Germans, and the Russians get twitchily introspective, but their determination holds. The real problem comes on the southern tier: the Russians feel that combating the Swedes *and* the Germans *and* the Turks simultaneously is simply beyond them. And they are right. Moscow *must* keep Turkey out of the Twilight War if Russia is to prevail. And for that, Russia must keep the Turks' attention firmly elsewhere.

The Syrian Distraction

Syria's geography is a topographic grab bag: scathing deserts, forested mountains, abbreviated coasts, and a steppic zone with surprisingly reliable rainfall. While making any generalities about a region so diverse is problematic, the short version is that the ruling Assad family's power base is among the various minorities that live on the coast and in the mountains. The primary opposition to the government is in the steppic zone, which constitutes the country's populated agricultural heartland, while the militant/terror group known as the Islamic State (IS or ISIS or ISIL based on who makes your acronyms) rules the desert.

Beginning in 2011 the Assad government and its primary opposition had fought over the strip of cities and arable land between the coastal mountains and the desert. In late 2013 both sides found it nearly impossible to dislodge the other. The rebels commanded the ancient cities of Homs, Hama, and Aleppo, while the government remained entrenched in the mountains and

Damascus. Fighting remained heavy, but strategically as of 2014 the war had become locked into stalemate. Additionally, since both the government and the rebels could rely upon relatively stable supplies of food and water and weapons from various quarters, neither side had too tough a time resisting IS attacks. IS doesn't have much in the way of heavy weapons like tanks and artillery, and while waves of pick-up trucks are magic in highly mobile desert warfare, the only thing impressive about a pick-up truck attack on a reinforced position is how short the battle is. IS' ideology, ability to recruit psychopaths, and brutality may be terrifying, but that does not translate into a functional military force capable of ousting battle-hardened, well-supplied forces from entrenched, urban positions.

And IS was weakening. Its version of puritanical Islam is not exactly the most economically sophisticated creed to ever attempt to rule the region. After a few months of selling women into slavery and executing non-believers en masse, the basic building blocks of civilization — most notably food production and the logistics of food distribution — tend to break down. IS desert fiefdom is flat out incapable of feeding the people who live under IS' control, and it is only with rampant smuggling that it is able to continue operations.

In this Moscow sensed an opportunity, and so in August of 2015 the Russians deployed about 1,000 servicemen to Syria. According to the Kremlin, the deployment was about battling international terrorism. According to Western and Arab governments and media, the deployment was half to bolster the failing Assad government (a longtime Soviet/Russian ally), and half to inject Russian interests into the Middle East in general.

The reality was somewhat more complicated. And sinister. For the first nine months of Russian involvement, Russian forces barely took notice of IS forces, instead concentrating their airstrike campaign on the coalition of rebel groups facing off against the Assad government in the Syrian heartland. While the Syrian government was certainly able to take advantage of some of these strikes, the real goal was to transform the static conflict into a war of movement. And in a war of movement, IS could play. As a result of the airstrike campaign, IS was able to advance from the desert along several vectors into the Syrian heartland, threaten both the government and the rebels directly, and expand the reach of its particular version of economic and cultural management.

The result, as the Russians intended, was the generation of a wave of refugees.

There was really only one way they could run. Israel doesn't take Syrian refugees. Jordan is blocking more from entering, and flirting with widescale ejections of those already there. Tiny Lebanon is full. Iraq — on the other side of the desert and IS-held territory — has a civil war of its own. That just leaves Turkey. As Russian calculations go, the Turks have three unpalatable choices:

1. Invade Syria outright to impose a security reality that would keep the Syrian population in place. This would keep the Turkish military preoccupied with issues to the south of Turkey, granting Russia a free hand in the Caucasus, Ukraine, and the Balkans.

2. Absorb the Syrian refuges. Such a task would engage all of the Turkish government's political bandwidth, granting Russia a free hand in the Caucasus, Ukraine, and the Balkans.

3. Pass the refugees on to Europe. This would wreck Turkey's relationship with Europe, making any coordination between the Turks and Europeans on, well anything, nearly impossible, and granting Russia a free hand in the Caucasus, Ukraine, and the Balkans.

As 2015 folded into 2016, it became clear that the Turks had opted for a mix of options 1 and 3. By late 2016 the Turks have deployed roughly 700 troops into Syria in order to shape the battlespace more to their liking. Talks between the Turks and Europeans on Turkey's European accession, expansion of visa-rights to Turks, the Syrian civil war, and even Russia's actions in Ukraine are for all intents and purposes suspended. All it cost the Russians was the deployment of a small batch of military personnel and some surplus ordinance.

Best/worst of all, the Russians can do it again. There are another 12 million Syrians living in now-fluid combat zone.

Should Russia's Syria ploy fail and Turkey turn its guns north, Moscow has a failsafe. In 2015, Turkey imported all of its natgas needs, some 4.2bcf/d.

Of these imports, 58% came from Russia with another 12% from Azerbaijan through zones the Russians will control early in the war. The remainder is a mix of piped gas from Iran — 18% of the total — into Turkey's far east, with the final 10% imported as LNG into its far west.

Fuel and import source switching will not work nearly as well for Turkey as it will for Northern Europe; Turkey lacks much in the way of energy storage, most notably for natural gas. Seasonal blackouts already are quite common even without import disruptions. Turkey also lacks backup electrical generation capacity, so switching fuels as needed isn't even an option. The bulk of Turkey — especially eastern Turkey — would face rolling blackouts for the conflict's duration.

And yet the impact *upon* Turkey is nothing compared to the impact *beyond* Turkey.

It's all about oil.

Four oil pipelines — Baku-Tbilisi-Supsa, Baku-Novorossiysk, Baku-Tbilisi-Ceyhan, and the Caspian Pipeline Consortium — ship nearly 3mbpd of Kazakh, Russian, and Azerbaijani crude to and through lands and seas under complete Turkish control. On Day One of Turkish involvement in the war, *all* of it would stop. Ironically the singular country that would not suffer would be Turkey. While Turkey imports nearly all of the crude it uses, at about 800kbpd the Turks could easily cover their needs with supplies from Iraqi Kurdistan. The problem is for the many countries further downstream that don't have such simple supply solutions.

For the first time in the petroleum era, there will be a war in which the combatants actually have the energy they need with the near entirety of the burden being borne by countries further abroad from the fighting. With Russian energy unable to access the Baltic, Black, or Mediterranean Seas, and with the Europeans willing and able to substitute Norwegian and African energy for Russian energy, the rest of the world will need to eat the loss of roughly 6.7mbpd of oil and 16.3bcf/d of natural gas. The near entirety of the energy shortage will be borne by the East Asian countries and India.

Betting on Twilight

This is admittedly a long shot for the Russians. Conquering — and *holding* — all or part of 11 countries, five of which are part of a nuclear-armed, American-backed security alliance, isn't exactly unambitious. Additionally, success would involve the forcible incorporation of some 70 million non-Russians, almost all of which would resent their new circumstances. But three thoughts come to mind.

First, there is no government on earth that has more experience in managing restive minorities than Russia. Since the earliest days of Muscovy, the Russians have known that the only way for them to achieve some semblance of security is to conquer their neighbors and their neighbors beyond, turn their lands into strategic buffers, and their people into cannon fodder. As such, Russia has always maintained the world's most intrusive intelligence network to keep these conquered populations pacified. It might sound labor-intensive — and it is — but it requires a lot fewer resources and personnel than defending a few thousand miles of indefensible border. And most important, courtesy of liberal bouts of privation and even more liberal doses of propaganda, the Russian population buys into the strategy.

Second, Russia has a lot more money than you think. Many believe that Russia cannot afford a war. It's a reasonable conclusion: a war would cost Russia some $350 million dollars per *day* in lost energy export revenue.[11] However, in 2016 Russia still had some $450 billion in currency reserves and various rainy day funds — enough to replace that lost energy income for four *years*. And even *that* figure assumes that the Russians haven't hidden anything away and they never liquidate any of their non-cash holdings such as their diamond, platinum, or gold stockpiles. Even more notable is that Russia has changed the laws governing its pension system so that the retirement age is now *after* the average male age of mortality. An additional

---

11   Assuming that crude is priced at $50 per barrel of oil and natgas at $10 per thousand cubic feet, the breakdown would be $250 million from oil sales and $100 million from natural gas sales. This data also includes exports that are dependent upon Turkish demand and Turkish export routes, as well as everything that sails out via or flows by pipe under the Baltic Sea.

legislative tweak has allowed — indeed, encouraged — government-managed pension funds to invest in Russian national government debt. If Russia turns away from this conflict, it won't be because of money.

Finally, Russia faces a hard deadline. Russia's demographic decline is so advanced that Russia as a state will likely break down within 20 years, and that assumes no fall in its macroeconomic position and no foreign intervention within Russia proper — neither of which are solid bets. The year 2020 is the year in which everyone under the age of 30 — those of an age that can reliably fill out the military's ranks — will have been born after the baby bust. The bottom line is that the Kremlin doesn't feel that it has a choice but to move, and to move before its demographic collapse robs it of the chance to even try.

The American Play in the Twilight War

The American instinct will certainly be to oppose the Russians. The Soviet Union has been the only entity to fundamentally threaten the American mainland since the American Civil War, so fear of Moscow will always lurk in a special, dark place in the American subconscious. But it takes more than mere antipathy to get someone to commit armored divisions. The Americans will not feature as belligerents in this war for a mix of reasons:

In part it is because post-Bretton Woods the Americans don't know what they want their relationship with the world to be, and it will take them at least a decade to figure it out. In part it is because Americans see few compelling reasons to become involved in a land war across a 2,000-mile front with a nuclear-armed power that feels it has nothing to lose. In part it is because the Europeans have shown few indications of weaning themselves off of Russian energy imports even as the Russians undermine the Continent's long-term physical and economic security — even in the countries that are in the Russians' cross-hairs. In part it is because the Russian government isn't stupid. It realizes that if it moves piecemeal, European resistance will not gel until it is too late. And if the Europeans are not sticking up — and together — for their own defense, it is hard for the Americans to feel motivated to do so for them. By all meaningful measurements, the NATO alliance *already* is no more.

This does not mean the Americans will be completely hands off in this or any other part of the Disorder, and there are any number of ways that the Americans can assist the various forces resisting the Russians.

- The United States will be happy to sell weapons and other materiel to pretty much anyone who is participating in the war against Russia. Many of the anti-Russian belligerents are/were NATO members and so have gobs of experience using American-made equipment. Of the handful of belligerents not in NATO, Sweden and Finland are/were part of several NATO programs, including some designed to maximize equipment interoperability. The particularly sexy weapons systems that would have the best splash:rock ratio would be the (in)famous Stingers to kick the teeth out of Russian aircraft and Javelins to kick the teeth out of Russian armor. Both are small, lightweight, lethal and about as easy to operate as a Nintendo controller.[12]

- The United States maintains the world's most advanced satellite and signals intelligence system, and one of only four countries that the U.S. shares that intelligence with — the United Kingdom — will be in the war. That will assist with everything from amphibious raid planning to deep-penetration missions to anti-aircraft system targeting to spawning resistance movements throughout the Russian sphere of influence (U.S. intel agencies are likely to play a more direct, if quiet, role on that last).

- For those on the wrong side of the line dividing West from East — most notably Ukraine and Georgia — the 1980s Afghan conflict offers some interesting parallels. During the Soviet occupation of Afghanistan, American intelligence agencies bought *Soviet* weapons systems from various players around the world and arranged for them to be delivered into the hands of anti-Soviet fighters. Toss in a few portable anti-aircraft devices and the result was a steady attrition of assets the Soviets couldn't afford to lose. Play that same strategy in 2010s and 2020s Eastern Europe,

---

12   That's more the old-style Super Mario controller rather than the newfangled Halo controller.

and Russia would face critical challenges in the most sensitive portion of its logistics: moving materiel and airpower from Russia proper to its western front.

- And judging from America's past, just because it doesn't become formally involved in a war doesn't stop American military personnel from volunteering to help out like-minded forces.

The largest role for the United States, however, will center on the energy question. In 2015 the United States was the world's second-largest exporter of refined oil products, and refineries across the country are undergoing ongoing expansions to take fuller advantage of the shale revolution. Should Washington and/or Houston feel so motivated, the American refining complex can *already* supply *all* of the gasoline, diesel, jet fuel, and the like to keep the tanks rolling, the jets flying and the lights on in Sweden, Poland, Germany, *and* Turkey.

Aftermath: Europe and Russia

There are too many moving parts to put any firm stakes in the ground as to the specifics of how such a wide-ranging conflict will progress, much less the texture of the European, Turkish, and Russian regions at war's end. The Germans might see the writing on the wall and start rearming early and thus speed Russia's defeat. Or they may wait too long and have to fight a long, painful war without meaningful Polish assistance. Turkey might sense what is coming down the pipe after Latvia falls and forward-deploy troops into Azerbaijan, wrecking much of Russia's southern strategy. Or it might feel compelled to surge forces into Syria and Iraq, leaving the Caucasus and Romania twisting in the wind. Poland might find a way to sneak a nuke into the party and throw everyone's plans into disarray.

The details will matter to a great many people for a great many reasons. But I find it more relevant — and certainly more depressing — to keep my eye on the bigger picture.

The fact is, with the obvious exceptions of the territories over which the Russians are struggling, it doesn't overly matter who wins or loses the Twilight War.

Win or lose, Sweden will no longer be a neutral country, but instead the centerweight of a new economic and military alliance that de facto rules Northern Europe. Win or lose, Germany will have re-emerged as a "normal" country — and one that once again has an army worthy of the name. Win or lose, the United Kingdom will have demonstrated that it simultaneously stands outside of Europe by preference, yet can intervene within Europe when its strategic needs dictate. Win or lose, Turkey is still the only Muslim country with a modern industrialized economy, the only European country with a strong demography, and the only country in either Europe or the Middle East that has everything that it needs within a few dozen miles of its borders. And whoever wins or loses, France will have had the duration of the conflict to reshape Western Europe and Africa into whatever shape it wants.[13]

What is particularly shocking is that triumphant or defeated, the war doesn't even matter for Russia when viewed from the (very) long term at (a lot of) distance.

The primary reason for the Twilight War is Russia's demographic collapse. It is the Russian *ethnicity* that is dying out, and that ethnicity is taking the Russian *state* with it. But that does *not* mean all citizens of *Russia* are ethnically *Russian*. Non-Russian minorities within the Russian Federation — most noticeably Turkic groups such as the Tatars, Chechens, and Bashkirs — have hearty demographics and their numbers are expanding rapidly. They are the future of the territory the world currently calls Russia.

A Russia defeated in a broad-based war would shatter quickly — certainly in less than a decade. The subsequent scattering of successor principalities would all have borders as indefensible as that of an amalgamated Russia, triggering decades if not generations of skirmishes, blood feuds and shifting, slippery, multi-sided wars. Such conflicts wouldn't "merely" be over who would get to wear Moscow's crown, but whoever won would then face the same damning geographic challenges that forced the Russian Empire, the

---

13   Stay tuned for *The Intentional Superpower: The Rise, Fall and Return of France.*

Soviet Union, and the Russian Federation on their centuries-long expansionist quest for physical security. The cycle will begin again with a new ethnicity in charge.

Yet if Russia *wins* the Twilight War, the Russian ethnicity will still be dying out. A Russian win takes us to the same end result: a Russia broken, just from within instead of from without — and with a few decades' delay.

Beyond Russia, beyond Europe, the rest of the world also faces precisely the same end result: energy shortages. Regardless of outcome, the Russian-European borderlands will be devastated, with the former Soviet energy transport infrastructure among the victims. It took the Soviet Union and its successor states the better part of a half century of peace along with hundreds of billions of dollars of domestic and foreign investment to construct that network. It would take — bare minimum — a couple of decades to bring that network back to specs.

Why so long? If for whatever reason Russian oil output cannot make it out of the pipeline system, production sites have to be shut down — just as they would have to be anywhere else. However, unlike output in Texas or Brazil or Libya, Russian oil is mostly produced in the Siberian permafrost. When permafrost production is shut-in, the wells freeze solid. Bringing that production back on-line requires re-drilling the well, a process that requires nearly as much effort in labor and money as the initial build-out. It takes as much time too: Permafrost can only be drilled when it is frozen solid, so for half of every year no work is even possible.[14]

Whoever wins, whoever loses, the world is just going to have to get by without most of the oil that this region has traditionally supplied for a good long time.

And for the world of oil, Siberia, the Twilight War and the Russian doom are just the beginning.

---

14   Incidentally, this is a leading reason why Russia has never once cooperated with OPEC in reining-in oil production. (On occasion Russia promises to reduce production, but it has never actually happened.) For OPEC, reducing and expanding output isn't much more complicated that remembering which direction to spin a few wheels. In Russia, recovering shut-in output requires years.

CHAPTER 7

The (Next) Gulf War

The Middle East has been a core region of global concern for the better part of recorded history. Civilization first took root in the soggy riverbanks of Mesopotamia. Humanity's first empires rose and fell in its lands, and their successors often found themselves returning, whether due to proximity, the need for foodstuffs, or control over trading routes. Three of the world's great religions formed here. Since time immemorial, there's been something to do in the Middle East.

The Bretton Woods era is no exception. The primary reason for involvement in recent decades can be summed up in one word: oil. Sure, there are other reasons too. General strategic competition certainly played a role. The Western world backed Israel against its Arab neighbors. The Cold War witnessed ongoing competition for regional loyalties, with the Americans buddying up with Morocco, Algeria, and Saudi Arabia; the British creating and befriending the Gulf Arab states; the French supporting Lebanon; and the Soviets influencing Libya, Syria and Iraq. Meanwhile, Egypt, Jordan, and Iran shifted their affiliations around a bit. But the primary reason was always oil, and the primary region has always been the Persian Gulf.

The Persian Gulf region wasn't just another cog in the clockwork of America's alliance strategy, it was *the* central piece that enabled the rest of it to work. The Americans used global trade to buy themselves a global alliance, global trade requires oil, the Persian Gulf has oil in spades, and so the

Americans had no choice but to be involved. At first the Americans just kept the oil flowing for their Bretton Woods allies, but in 1973 the Americans became net importers themselves, giving them a much more visceral reason to be obsessed with all things Middle Eastern.

2015 Average Daily Production and Exports (kbpd) of oil exporters

		Production	Exports			Production	Exports
Americas	Canada	4385	3283	Eurasia	Azerbaijan	841	742
	Mexico	2588	1248		Kazakhstan	1669	1398
	Colombia	1008	677		Norway	1948	1235
	Ecuador	543	418		Russia	10980	7867
	Venezuela	2626	1480		Turkmenistan	261	118
	Total:	11150	7106		Total:	15698	11360
Africa	Algeria	1586	803	Persian Gulf	Iran	3920	1359
	Angola	1826	1676		Iraq	4031	3005
	Congo-B	277	263		Kuwait	3096	2582
	Equ Guinea	289	285		Oman	952	732
	Gabon	233	215		Qatar**	1898	1574
	Libya*	432	207		Saudi Arabia	12014	7392
	Nigeria	2352	2225		UAE	3902	3001
	Total:	6995	5674		Total:	29813	19645
Asia	Brunei	127	120				
	Total:	127	120				

*Production/exports disrupted due to local conflict
**Significant volumes of NGLs and condensates among crude production Sources: 2016 BP Statistical Review of World Energy, Joint Organisations Data Initiative (JODI)

Standard American operating procedure was to spare no expense in entertaining regional diplomats and to sell regional allies weapons systems reserved for America's closest allies. Washington's backing proved central to bolstering the Shah's Iran against the Soviets. After the Shah's fall in 1979, American support proved equally critical to the Arab states of the Persian Gulf standing up to Islamic Iran. Massive outlays of American power were on occasion deployed in order to preserve or alter the regional balances of power in order to maintain energy flows. U.S. Naval forces kept the 1980-1988 Iran-Iraq war from spilling onto the waters of the Gulf. The U.S. Army ejected Iraqi forces from Kuwait in 1991. The full might of American power destroyed Iraq in the 2003 invasion.

But perhaps the best measure of commitment are the deployment patterns of the supercarriers, the backbone of American power projection. American global strategy could not risk the local powers engaging in a conflict in which oil flows and oil assets might be inadvertently damaged, much less directly targeted. And so the Americans have kept a permanent naval presence in the Persian Gulf since 1971 to quash — or at least sequester — local competition, to ensure the oil would continue flowing no matter what. Recent decades have seen permanent basing of a supercarrier group, and at times a second carrier would even stop by at particularly sensitive moments.

How times have changed.

As far as the Americans are concerned, most of its alliance network has outlived its usefulness, the Middle East's oil isn't needed, and the trade powered by oil was never directly used by the Americans in the first place. Every link in the logic chain that has kept American power tethered to the Persian Gulf has broken at more or less the same time. Even the managed withdrawal of American troops is well advanced.

Since 2007 the total number of American military personnel in the region across the belt of countries from Morocco to Afghanistan has shrunk from a high of over 250,000 to under 15,000. Contrary to popular belief, the withdrawal isn't an issue of an ideological split in American political thought. Yes, the majority of the withdrawals from Iraq and Afghanistan may have happened under Barack Obama, but the withdrawal started under and followed the withdrawal plans of Obama's predecessor, George W. Bush. As 2016 draws to a close, the majority of remaining U.S. forces in the region at U.S. Central Command's (CENTCOM) forward headquarters in Qatar. CENTCOM's established its Qatari facility to oversee operations in Iraq and Afghanistan. Now that American efforts in those two locales are largely closed down, CENTCOM is highly likely to return its regional operations command to American territory in the not-too-distant future. As to the all-important supercarriers, in calendar year 2015 the platforms were in the Persian Gulf for less than five months. This isn't the new normal. This is merely the transition to the new normal. The transition to the Disorder.

There still may be many reasons for many powers to have interests in the region, but since none of those powers is the global superpower, the strategic stasis that the region has existed in for the past 40 years is breaking like river ice in spring. The region will be left to sort out its own local geopolitics. And those geopolitics are, in a word, nasty.

Meet the Neighbors

Relationships throughout the Greater Middle East and Islamic world — from Morocco to Israel to the Philippines — are in the process of being reset, and there are literally dozens of stories to be told. For this chapter, however, we will focus in on the Persian Gulf specifically; it isn't simply most critical to global energy supplies, it also is most dynamic in terms of its local geopolitics.

The Gulf is home to seven countries that collectively produced 30mbpd in 2015, a touch over 30 percent of the global total. Our focus will be on the two major powers: Saudi Arabia and Iran. The governments of these territories have been strategic rivals for the better part of the past 1,500 years. Today they are in total, hostile opposition to each other on nearly every matter of principle or practicality imaginable, and the American withdrawal heralds the bloodiest competition between the two in at least the past two centuries.

Religion. Citizens of Iran predominantly practice Shia Islam, while the Saudis follow a militant, puritanical strain of Sunni Islam. Clerical interpretation on both sides labels the other as heretical. Saudi Arabia holds Holy Cities of Mecca and Medina, locales sacred to all Muslims regardless of denomination. Riyadh has on several occasions denied Iranians access. Globally the Sunni outnumber the Shia 6:1, which encourages major Sunni powers (like Saudi Arabia) to claim to speak for Islam as a whole; but within the Persian Gulf the Shia outnumber the Sunnis, which encourages Iran to claim to run the region.

Government. Saudi Arabia is a dictatorial monarchy ruled with an iron fist by the House of Saud, a dynasty that in part draws its legitimacy from its self-described role as the leaders of Sunni Islam. Iran is a semi-democratic theocracy with political authority rooted in the thousands-strong religious leadership of Shia Islam. In both cases, religious rulership and political rulership is fused; religious edicts often carry the full weight of the state behind them. Both take a brutally hard line toward political dissent, particularly toward religious practice that doesn't match state sanction. Primary means of enforcement include the use of autonomous religious police, public executions and large, internal intelligence services expressly designed to maintain civil control.

Ethnicity. Saudi Arabia sees itself as the natural rallying point for Arabs everywhere. Its biggest competitor for that role is Egypt, the most populous Arab state and the Middle East's longest-lived Arab culture. Egypt's attempts to export its secular, military-backed Arab nationalist state model throughout the Middle East region earned it the enmity of any governments that were not secular, military-backed and nationalist — which includes Saudi Arabia. Egypt's peace with Israel in the 1978 Camp David Accords sealed Egypt's fate as persona non grata at Arab gatherings. That fall, coupled with Saudi Arabia's staggering oil wealth, launched Riyadh's rise to prominence as the premier Arab power.

For its part, Iran is a Persian power swimming in a sea of Arabs. Persian identification is less strict than Arab (ethnic) or Saudi (family) identification — after generations of living in Persian lands many groups start to consider themselves Iranian while still retaining distinct non-Persian cultural markers. But the key word there is "generations." Even after millennia of such grinding assimilation, non-Persians still account for half of contemporary Iran's population.

Economics. Iran's population mostly lives up on the Iranian plateau and nestled against the country's many mountains, where the elevation is sufficiently high to wring out a bit of rain to support agriculture. That base has enabled Iran to develop a differentiated workforce and a fairly broad industrial base — by far the most varied and sophisticated in the Middle East (with the sole exception of Turkey). In contrast, Saudi Arabia sits atop a pillar of sand mortared with oil. Total manufacturing (not including oil-intensive operations like refining and chemicals) is only $30 billion. The Saudis import nearly everything, including nearly the near-entirety of their labor force (skilled or otherwise) and in excess of 80% of their foodstuffs.[1]

Saudi Arabia is the world's largest oil exporter, and has often used that position to regulate global oil prices per its domestic and foreign policy

---

1   A percentage that is increasing as the Saudis belatedly give up growing crops in the desert. At one point the Saudis' cost simply for wheat irrigation was running around $10 a bushel (traditionally, wheat sells in the $5-$10 a bushel range on the global market).

needs. For most of the past generation, Iran has been the world's third-largest exporter of crude oil and natural gas liquids, and often finds itself collateral damage when Saudi Arabia manipulates energy markets. On the flip side, Iran almost never cooperates with OPEC when the decision is made to limit output, choosing to cheat on its quota to maximize income and make Saudi Arabia eat the difference.[2]

Making matters worse, the shale revolution has largely excised North America from global energy markets. The Saudis and Iranians are now exporting the same commodity along the same routes to the same customers. The two are fiercely competing for those customers' orders, using everything from pre-positioned storage to unheard of discounts to undercut the other.

Culture. The Iranians are the heirs to Persia, an entity that stretches back to the very dawn of human civilization. In nearly every historical period when Persia has been ascendant, it has conquered the bulk of its wider region, which of course includes most of what is contemporary Saudi Arabia. With their rich cultural history, the Iranians consider themselves not only the natural leaders of the region, but also the peak of the human experience.

In contrast, the Saudis are a Bedouin family that just happened to cut a deal with the British at the right time and have yet to celebrate their centenary celebration. Yet they command the world's largest oil industry, wield power that is global in scope, and are the custodians of the Holy Cities.

The cultural arrogance on both sides, especially when considering the other, is staggering. The Saudis think of the Iranians as barbarians fit for little save death, while the Iranians consider the Saudis to be hillbillies with better teeth.

Persian Dreams and Peculiar Schemes

And if all that were not enough, developments in more recent times have set the two countries firmly against each other.

---

2   To be fair, Iran is hardly alone in cheating. Only the Kuwaitis and the Emiratis tend to follow the Saudis' lead. But as OPEC's second-biggest producer, the Iranians certainly cheat more than all other members in terms of volume.

During the early Cold War years, the Americans forced the reluctant Saudis and more reluctant Iranians to be on the same side. The Americans could not suffer regional infighting since such infighting would endanger global energy flows and the entirety of America's strategic policy. Luckily, everyone in the Persian Gulf faced the same existential threat: the Soviet goal of breaking the Americans meant breaking the American alliance structure meant breaking the Persian Gulf. The Saudis and Iranians didn't like being allied, but there wasn't much choice.

But in 1979 a revolution overthrew the Iranian Shah, transforming Iran into an Islamic republic. This not only ended the Iranian-American alliance, but transformed Iran into a country allergically hostile to U.S. interests. Consider the shift: Iran is a major oil exporter with a long coastline that parallels the world's densest energy production zone, Iran is pathological hostility to Saudi Arabia, Iran commands the Strait of Hormuz (through which nearly half of all maritime oil exports flow). With the Iranian flip, the entire American alliance structure faced pressure. It is no wonder that Iran remains a burr in the mind of Americans four decades later: Iran is the only country aside from the Soviet Union that has ever constituted an existential threat to American-maintained global order.

Of course the global superpower was more than capable of pushing back. Iran's ample overseas assets were frozen. On occasion the American navy would shell Iranian offshore oil assets. Sanctions forced the Iranians to sell their crude to a smaller pool of buyers, and thus at a discount. One particularly nasty American (and Saudi) counter was to quietly urge Saddam Hussein's Iraq to invade Iran, triggering an eight-year war with 1 million Iranian casualties.

After the Cold War ended, the Persian Gulf was the one aspect of America's trade-powered strategic policy that still made complete sense. The Soviets, now Russians, might have stopped threatening the global order, but *Iran* still could. After Iraq's 1990 invasion of Kuwait, Iraq was elevated to co-equal status as a threat to the global order. With the American overthrow of Saddam Hussein in 2003, Washington assumed direct responsibility for maintaining the safety of regional energy flows.

From the Saudi point of view the situation wasn't exactly ideal, but it was workable. With the Americans in Iraq, there was absolutely no way that Iran would even contemplate invading Iraq, which meant that there was no way Saudi Arabia itself could be threatened.

But then everything changed. In the last months of the George W. Bush administration, a wholesale American withdrawal from Iraq began, a strategic position which would have been impossible without America's rising disenchantment with maintaining the global order. Barack Obama was elected on the platform of accelerating that withdrawal. Then the shale revolution made disentanglement from both the Persian Gulf and the wider world economically and strategically possible — even wise. The Obama administration prioritized a nuclear deal with Iran, which would enable to the United States to quite simply wash their hands of the region in its entirety. One of the prices of that divorce was the ending of financial sanctions and the unfreezing of Iranian assets that had been sequestered since the 1980s. Instead of the Americans maintaining regional security, or a Saudi-led coalition being able to weaken and overwhelm a contained Iran, the American withdrawal was managed in such a way as to restore the pre-Bretton Woods balance of power with the Persians and Arabs glaring at each other across the Gulf.[3]

The Saudis fought the American disengagement every step of the way, and when Tehran and Washington began implementing the nuclear deal in early 2016 the Saudis threw a public snit, publicly leaking that should the United States proceed, they would divest their entire holdings of U.S. government debt. The response out of Washington was a disinterested shrug colored with a liberal tinge of good-riddance-to-bad-rubbish.[4] Congress magnified the insult in September 2016 by overriding a presidential veto to enable American citizens to sue foreign governments for their alleged role in terror attacks, a law specifically intended for use against Saudi Arabia.

The Saudis are passionately aware of just how close to full divorce the Americans now are, and (rightly) see the American disentanglement as an unmitigated disaster.

---

3   Whether this re-establishment of the balance of power was done intentionally is of course the subject of piping hot debate.

4   Total Saudi holdings of U.S. T-bills in March 2016 were $117 billion. On an average day some $500 billion in U.S. debt is traded, so the markets shrugged off the threat nearly as much as the U.S. government.

In modern times, the only local player with the potential to hold the Iranians back is Iraq. But while Iraq may still exist, it does so barely. Right from the beginning of the American occupation in 2003, Iranian influence surged into the country and quickly garnered commanding influence in much of the country and its institutions. Two-thirds of the Iraqi population is Shia, the same religious denomination as the bulk of Iran, greatly easing Iranian efforts. Iraq's third-largest city — the southern regional capital of Basra — is both solidly Shia and solidly pro-Iranian. During the 2000s the Iranians developed deep links to all aspects of Iraqi governance, up to and including the army, the intelligence services and the prime minister's office itself. Pro-Iranian militia not only operate with impunity throughout Iraq's Shia regions, regular Iranian forces are often embedded with the militia *within* Iraqi borders.

Iran is far and away the superior regional power. In Iran's nearly 40 years of strategic competition with the United States it established underdog positions in a dozen different countries. With the Americans vacating, each of those positions is making a bid for local dominance, and even the Iraqi firebreak may well have turned into a springboard for Iranian influence.

Riyadh looks at the broader region with rising horror.

Riyadh fears that every setback the Iranians have suffered since 1979 is about to be overcome by reintegration with the global system. And then — flush with cash that allows mass re-armament and bolstered by a diverse economy, the likes of which the Saudis cannot even dream about — Saudi Arabia will be forced to watch as every geopolitical tool that Iran has developed becomes stronger until House of Saud itself is threatened.

A change of strategy was required. The Saudi response strategy is twofold.

Step One: The Sword

First, the Saudis have spawned and reinforced a plethora of resistance movements, using their well-honed policy of exporting Islamist militants.

The House of Saud has its roots in the deep desert. Before the 20th century they were the nomads of Arabia, raiding the various oasis towns and on occasion even the more civilized Hijaz region — that's the western fringe of contemporary Saudi Arabia that gets a bit of rainfall and is home to Mecca and Medina. Desert life is hard, and maintaining a social structure in the desert is harder still. One of the many ways in which the Saud clan coped was the adoption of an ultra-strict version of Islam, which glorified combat and tightly regulated personal freedoms. Locals call it Salafist Islam while many outsiders know it as Wahhabism, referring to the movement's founder, one Sheikh Ibn Abdul Wahhab.

During World War I the Saudis were exactly what the Brits needed: a local group skilled at hit-and-run desert warfare who could be bribed to attack the Ottoman Turks. A British-Saudi alliance formed, and when the war ended the Saudis had enough organization, weaponry, and British backing to make a bid for security control of the area. An alliance of convenience with the descendants of Wahhab brought the major power brokers under one tent.[5] The state of Saudi Arabia was born.

Less than a decade later oil was discovered, and the new Saudi Arabia followed a development process fairly recognizable by other newly independent states. The freshly minted leaders engaged in an infrastructure spending boom — nearly bankrupting the state — in an effort to modernize the kingdom that was mostly without non-oil resources. The nomadic Saudis quickly settled down into a very urban, very comfortable lifestyle. The oil-based economy may have generated a lot of income, but it didn't generate a lot of jobs for people whose primary skills sets were raiding on horseback and beheading. As this is well before the arrival of Atari, PlayStation, or the Internet, options for filling free time were somewhat more basic. The population boomed.[6]

Certain discrepancies arose. If your culture is based on jihad and raiding but now you all live in apartments, what do you do with your unemployed youth who have been taught all their lives that violence in general and military action in specific is a good thing? Early efforts to expand Saudi territory quickly came up against the British military or British proxies,

---

5   Literally.

6   Fun fact: In contemporary times, Saudi Arabia has adapted to this somewhat by becoming among of the most pervasive global users of platforms such as SnapChat and Instagram. Such tools serve as the country's Tinder and Grinder. If you don't know what those are, ask your (college-aged or older) kids. Maybe have a stiff drink first though.

quashing most thoughts of conventional territorial expansion. That boxed up the energetically violent youth at home, causing no end of civil control issues.

The more vicious tribes were brought into the national guard or military. Those with a penchant for religion manned the religious police. The less violent bloated up the bureaucracy, while oil money was used to subsidize everything to keep the population pacified. And should anyone step out of line, Saudi jails were designed to hold a *lot* of people.[7]

In time, Saudi Arabia struck upon a new population-management system: exports. Riyadh started sending abroad youth with a particularly strong taste for violence to fight for the greater glory of the House of Sa-, er, Saudi Ara-, um, Islam. So long as the young men were beheading people and blowing things up elsewhere, they weren't causing problems back home.

Riyadh discovered that this "export" could be a powerful tool, and the Saudis started being more tactical in where the fighters were sent, choosing to direct the flows toward ideological, religious, and strategic foes. The most (in)famous cases were the Saudi sponsoring of the Afghan Mujahedeen against the Soviet Union, and later the Chechens against the Russians. What started as an effort to maintain internal stability emerged as a central tenant of Saudi strategic policy.

This is only a problem for the Saudis if these groups select targets that are at odds with Saudi goals. If a Chechen splinter group targets Russian forces in Dagestan (as they did in 1999), no biggie. But when al Qaeda operatives hijacked civilian airliners and flew them into buildings in New York City and Washington, the full power and rage of the Saudis' security guarantor nearly descended upon Riyadh. Even worse, in the post-9/11 environment, American diplomatic and intelligence efforts to destroy al Qaeda forced the Saudis to suspend their militant-export strategy for a decade. With Saudi militants stuck at home, the Saudis found themselves with a horrible civil safety issue. The six-figure-salaried Western expats responsible for keeping Saudi oil flowing were literally being shot in their homes. It took a brief civil war in 2003-2004 to mop-up the mess.

---

7   The Saudis were hardly alone in facing this challenge. Violent non-state actors in the Middle East have a long and colorful history in a region that has always had poorly-defined borders and weak states.

Step Two: The Checkbook

Second, the Saudis have money. A *lot* of money. And they aren't shy about spending it.

Various Saudi government accounts easily have in excess of $2 trillion, and that's not counting the personal stashes of the House of Saud itself, which are probably even larger.[8] Once the Saudis were faced with the threat of Iraq becoming a fully owned-and-operated Iranian satellite they wrote an encyclopedia of how-to books on checkbook diplomacy. Reaching out diplomatically — often via their militant links — the Saudis ingratiated themselves with every Sunni faction they could find, quite literally paying them to rise up and strike against the now Shia-dominated Baghdad.

Yet as a trailblazer in checkbook diplomacy, the Saudis fully understand that there are two sides to any financial struggle. The first is to splash money out to cause problems for and combat the influence of Iran in as many places as possible. With Saudi pockets so deep, the Iranians are constantly putting out fires, having to re-commit allies and proxies to Iranian goals, fighting groups that used to be neutral versus Tehran or even finding themselves battling groups that didn't exist a few days previous.

The second side of financial conflict is to hit Iran's own income at the source, which brings us to the Saudi price war. The Saudis have absolutely no love for the American shale industry, and should Riyadh's price war succeed in reducing American energy output, the Saudis would pop a veritable fleet of champagne bottles. But shale is *not* the primary target of the Saudi price war.

The real target is much closer to home.

Just as the Saudis gain the bulk of their income from oil sales, so too do the Iranians. The Saudis' 7.5mbpd of oil exports means that with crude at $40 per barrel their annual oil income is about $110 billion. That generates

---

8   And that doesn't count the $2 trillion wealth fund that the Saudis have indicated they intend to form with their partial privatization of state oil monopoly Saudi Aramco. To give you an idea of scale, that's more than the combined market value of the world's four largest companies by market capitalization: Apple, Alphabet/Google, Microsoft, and Amazon. com. The Saudis have loads of problems. Money isn't one of them.

so little (from the Saudi point of view) that the country must run an annual budget deficit of in the vicinity of 15 to 20 percent of GDP, or more than $100 billion.

It sounds horribly extreme. It is. But considering all of the various funds that the Saudis have socked away for rainy days, they can survive this sort of upside-down financing for almost three *decades* — and that assumes no austerity, no creative financing, no repatriation of the royal family's foreign holdings, no borrowing from extra-Saudi sources, no liquidation of any rogue prince's assets, and no borrowing against their future oil exports. This last point is particularly critical since it is how the Saudis pushed through the 1998 oil price collapse when oil was less than $20 per barrel for nearly three years. Riyadh since has repaid all of that debt, and as of the end of 2015, total foreign liabilities were but 1.6% of GDP. Put simply, from a financial standpoint the Saudis can keep this up as long as they need to.[9]

Iran's financial buffer is far less robust — or transparent. As a country that has operated beyond the rules and structures of the international financial system since the Ayatollah's rise, and doubly so since the onset of financial sanctions in 2013, Iran probably has a fair amount of cash stashed beyond the prying eyes of book authors. Yet among accounts being unfrozen by the go-slow normalization of Iranian-American relations, oil held in storage and a few other line items, as of late 2016 the Iranians probably have little more than $50 billion in total — half of the assets that were unfrozen by

---

9   A secondary target of the Saudi price war is Russia. Whether it is selling anti-aircraft tech to Iran, backing militant groups in Lebanon, or selling tanks to Syria or Iraq, the Russians/Soviets often use their strategic influence to stir up trouble for the Americans in the Middle East as a means of distracting the Americans from the Russian/Soviet periphery. The Saudis view such interference with silent rage and so have returned the favor whenever possible. Economic methods include oil price wars like the one that started in 2014 as well as the Reagan-supported price war of the mid-1980s. More violent methods included backing the mujahedeen during the 1980s Afghan war or the rebels in the 1990s Chechen Wars. In the current round, the Saudis have offered targeted price discounts to Chinese, Swedish, and Polish refineries that normally use only Russian crude grades to rob the Russians of both income and market share. One thing is for sure — so long as Russia continues to stick its chocolate into the Saudis' peanut butter, such tit-for-tat actions will remain hardwired into Mideast — and Russian — geopolitics.

the end of the sanctions regime have already been used to pay down short-term debt.

By any measure — relative to their economic size — savings are miniscule compared to Saudi Arabia, and their burn rate will chew through them in short order. Tehran already is scrambling to find the funds to maintain its internal subsidy regimes, which total at least $65 billion annually (so probably in the vicinity of 15% of GDP). And that's just the at-home costs. The region's hot wars — more on that in a minute — don't come cheap. Iran's sprawling network of proxies probably has an annual price tag of another $20 billion, and that doesn't even begin to include more conventional costs such as weapons transfers.[10]

The Saudi price war has hit the Iranians where it hurts. American and European sanctions reduced Iran's oil exports by half as measured by *volume*. Couple that reduction with the oil price drop, and several estimates suggest Iran's oil *income* plunged something like 80 percent between 2010 and 2015. The gap between Saudi and Iranian finances — already hilariously wide — widens yet more in a time of protracted low oil prices. In a dollar-to-dollar fight — hell, in a 10 dollar-to-dollar fight — the Iranians will lose every single time.

And so contemporary Saudi Arabia's strategy is pretty simple: export militants and use checkbook diplomacy to target Iranian proxies and allies everywhere, and try to wreck everything that the Iranians touch. It has both weaknesses and strengths.

The primary weakness is that while this strategy gives the Saudis *influence* over a wide spread of territory and a wide variety of groups, it grants them *control* over nothing. Worse yet, put a bunch of well-armed and well-funded sociopaths (who were selected because of their propensity for violence) into a target-rich environment, and sometimes they start selecting their own objectives. Over time such groups can, and do, break away. The two

---

10   These stats are sourced from a mix of places such as the IMF, World Bank, State Department, and other organizations that tend to be in the know. They are extremely squishy, heavy on the guesswork and most definitely not GAAP-compatible.

most famous groups to evolve beyond Saudi influence are al Qaeda and the Islamic State (IS).[11]

The strategy's primary strength is that the margin of error is exceedingly wide. So wide in fact that in contested areas, failure so catastrophic that it destroys the industrial, electrical, agricultural, and infrastructure pillars of society — threatening the very integrity of civilization — actually is considered a win. Saudi Arabia has the benefit of sizable desert buffers north of all of its population centers. The lands on the other side of those deserts can burn to the ground for all the Saudis care, because if they are reduced to ash, then the Iranians cannot benefit from them — or use those lands as launching pads against Saudi Arabia itself.

The Field of Combat

Pair off Saudi money-and-militant strategy against the decades-old Iranian geopolitical expansion and you get a *seven*-front cold war that in many places is already raging quite hot.

Syria. For decades, rulership of Syria has been held by the Assads, a clan of Alawites — a strain of Islam that many Muslims, especially Sunnis, consider heretical. In Iran this distaste was personal: Ayatollah Khomeini refused to allow Syrian President Havaz Assad to even visit Tehran because Khomeini considered Assad *kafir* (non-Muslim). But that didn't stop Khomeini from making the geopolitical choice of supporting Syria against the broad array of Sunni powers throughout the region. Tehran was rewarded when Syria became the first — and only — Arab power to support Iran against Iraq in the 1980-1988 war.

Since the Syrian civil war erupted in 2011, the Iranians have supplied the Assad regime with everything from food to weapons to intelligence to trainers to soldiers. Support has been so significant that several Iranian *generals* have been killed on Syrian battlefields. In recent years the Saudis

---

11   It isn't as if the Saudis are fully alone in this. Though Saudi Arabia may provide the most money, recruits, weapons, and strategic guidance, Kuwait actually is the processing hub for most of the cash destined for both al Qaeda and IS, and citizens of the United Arab Emirates probably contribute the most cash in per capita terms.

have matched the Iranians step for step, backing opposition forces of all stripes. The Iranians may have the advantage of backing the strongest single conventional force in the war — the Syrian government itself — but the Saudis have a distinct advantage in that they don't overly care what Syria looks like when the war finally ends.

So far the war has claimed more than 400,000 lives and resulted in more than 5 million external refugees. Considering the war damage to the country's infrastructure, the ever-shifting lines of control, the mass killings, prolonged sieges, and the fact that IS controls the bulk of the country's oil fields, meaningful oil exports from Syria have long-since stopped.[12] The most likely end-result is state collapse, with a few groups — like the Alawites — ruling tattered rump states in a sea of anarchy. Such an outcome would reduce Iran's pull by at least two-thirds, and push the sharp end of Iranian power in Syria as far from Saudi Arabia as is physically possible. It also will probably mean the death of at least another million people from war — and many times that from system breakdown.

Iraq: Never forget that the most feared faction in the Syrian civil war — IS — actually began in and commands far more (and far more useful) territory and populations in Iraq. IS' precursor was none other than an affiliate of al Qaeda, bolstered by a few disenfranchised Sunni factions such as the Baathists, Saddam's cadre of former rulers. Both the original and its offshoot were only made possible with heavy infusions of money and fighters from Saudi Arabia, even if both ultimately broke ranks and went their own way. During the Iraqi civil war that began during the American occupation, the Islamic State in Iraq — as the group was known 2006-2013 — transformed from being an irritant to U.S. forces to being the center point for Sunni opposition to the Shia-dominated government in Baghdad. American-brokered efforts failed to bring the Sunnis into the government on a sustained basis, and the result was the group's transformation into the IS we know today.

---

12   IS captured many of Syria's oil fields early in the war and was selling the crude on the black market to raise funds. However, once the U.S. State Department brought in a few economists, efforts were made to target IS' petroleum supply chains. This has greatly reduced the flow, starving IS of both funds and fuel.

As the months ticked by IS-controlled territory expanded like a stain, at times including major population centers including Mosul, Ramadi, and Fallujah.[13] The result, in practice, is a civil war every bit as wide-ranging and brutal as Syria's. Various Saudi interests — although not formally the government in Riyadh — retain links to various IS factions and continue to help them against their common foes in Damascus, Baghdad, and Tehran.

An independent IS isn't perceived in Riyadh as being all that problematic. As a radical militant group, IS has committed itself to the eradication of any who do not espouse its somewhat wackadoo version of Sunni Islam. While that undoubtedly includes some 99 percent of the human population, the strict Salafist strain of Islam the Saudis follow is fairly similar to IS' own religious ideology, putting the House of Saud at the bottom of IS' to-massacre list. One step above the Saudis are Sunni Muslims in general. In contrast, *Shia* Muslims — especially *Persian* Shia Muslims — are enemy No. 1, ranked well above Europeans, who are themselves ranked well above Americans. For the most part IS' top target sets are the very groups the Saudis would love to see taken down a few pegs, most notably the Iran-friendly Shia government of Iraq and the Iran-sponsored Alawite government of Syria.

The goal posts for measuring Saudi success in Iraq are very far apart. On one extreme is a semi-functional IS government that is able to hold power throughout the bulk of Sunni Iraq and constitute a direct check on both Iran's efforts to influence Baghdad, as well as Baghdad's ability to govern the whole of Iraq. This was more or less the state of affairs between March 2015 and March 2016. Out-of-the-park success would actually see IS conquer Baghdad itself.

On the other extreme is the Islamic State as a wide-ranging terror organization that holds little territory but has the ability to strike throughout not just Iraq's Sunni belt but deep into Baghdad on a regular basis. This was more or less the state of affairs between 2005 and 2007, when the Americans found themselves playing whack-a-mole with IS' predecessor during the first phase of Iraq's civil war.

---

13   IS was ejected from Fallujah and Ramadi in mid-2016, and at the time of this writing the Iraqi government is in the midst of a protracted campaign to liberate Mosul.

Both are bloody, but far more important (for the Saudis), both are effective. An Iraq that is tearing itself apart is not one that can be used as a springboard for Iranian ambitions.

Lebanon: The Syrian civil war has merged not only with the conflict in Iraq, but also with Lebanon. Stretching back to the very beginning of the ayatollahs' reign, Tehran has poured vast volumes of funding and staff into the Lebanese Shia militia known as Hezbollah. Since Hezbollah's founding in 1985, it has steadily expanded in numbers and military power until becoming the premier political-military force in the country, commanding such strength that it even stood up — successfully — to the Israeli military in a brief war in 2006.

Compared to such power, Saudi Arabia's levers in Lebanon are scattered and weak. Checkbook diplomacy only works so well when there isn't a clear Sunni majority; Lebanon is a fractious multi-ethnic polity where the Shia and Sunni communities are tied at about 27% of the population each. Checkbook diplomacy also cannot insulate their beneficiaries from explosives. In 2005 Hezbollah killed the Saudis' point man — Lebanese Prime Minister Rafic Hariri — with a one-*ton* car bomb that left a crater some 40 feet across and 10 feet deep.

But as with many things, the Syrian civil war has changed the calculus. Hezbollah was originally envisioned by Tehran as a means of facilitating Syrian control of Lebanon — "Iranian-owned, Syrian-operated" being the joke in the diplomatic lexicon — and to harass Israel. With the Syrian government besieged on all sides in the civil war, Iran was forced to fully commit Hezbollah to the Syrian fight instead. Hezbollah's forces are now fully consumed within the Syrian civil war, vastly reducing their bandwidth for dominating the Lebanese military and political space. This provides the Saudis with a wealth of opportunities to penetrate.

Palestinian Territories: The Saudis and Iranians are also picking sides in the Palestinian movement. As with everything in Levantine politics, drawing clear lines is at best a confusing endeavor, but here's the simplified version: The Saudis back the Fatah faction that rules the West Bank; Fatah is broadly willing to come to a diplomatic agreement with the Israelis over the future of the Palestinian territories. For their part, the Iranians gravitate toward Hamas — a faction far more willing to take up arms — which rules the Gaza Strip, in essence an open-air refugee camp that survives on goods smuggled through tunnels from Egypt.

Since the start of the Saudi effort to root out Iranian influence throughout the broader region, this balance of power has shifted. Now an odd-fellows partnership of Cairo, Jerusalem, and Riyadh has formed to keep Hamas and Tehran apart. Everyone gets something: Cairo limits smuggling (and IS penetration) in the Sinai, Jerusalem limits rocket shipments into Gaza, and Riyadh gets to excise yet another Iranian foothold. In the Palestinian sphere that just leaves Iran with links to the smaller, less-capable, and more-radical Palestinian Islamic Jihad.

Bahrain: A less dramatic contest has unfolded directly between the two rising regional superpowers in Bahrain. The only state of the Persian Gulf with no meaningful volumes of oil, Bahrain was long on lockdown because it was the base of the U.S. Fifth Fleet. But with American commitments to the Middle East steadily shrinking, Bahrain has slid back into play. The Iranians took advantage of the fact that the Bahraini are 70 percent Shia and were able to sponsor a popular uprising during the general chaos of the Arab Spring. Saudi Arabia quickly used the local geography to its advantage. Bahrain is not only far closer to the Saudi shore than the Iranian shore, but since 1986 there has also been a causeway connecting Bahrain to the Saudi mainland. That causeway does more than allow Saudis to go on truly epic benders — Saudi Arabia is often referred to as the world's driest country, and Bahrain the world's largest bar — it also enables the Saudis to deploy troops to de facto occupy Bahrain and crush the Iranian-inspired uprising. Toying with Bahrain is a cheap and easy way for the Iranians to keep 1,000 or so Saudi troops out-of-country.

Yemen: On the far opposite side of the loud conflicts in Lebanon, Syria and Iraq, a war has erupted in a place that makes Lebanon look like a suburban book club. From time to time powers local and foreign have attempted to unite the country currently known as Yemen into a more cartographically pleasing form, but after a few years the place reliably degenerates into a morass of brutal tribal infighting. The Saudis treat Yemen as a backward client state, typically sponsoring efforts at unification so Yemen's particular brand of chaos stays on its side of the border. Of late, the Iranians have gone on the offensive, sponsoring groups — most notably the Houthis — that the

Saudis have shut out of the halls of power, ripping to shreds a decade of Saudi efforts and triggering a full civil war.

Normally at this point the Saudis would have broken out their checkbook and hired an army just as they have paid American, Iraqi, and Egyptian forces in years past. But this time the Americans are uninterested, and the Iraqis and Egyptians unable. The Saudis have had no choice but to send in their *own* forces, and their forces are *not* trained for, well, combat. The result has been a Saudi-led anti-Iranian coalition in Yemen that includes military assets from Bahrain, Egypt, Jordan, Kuwait, Morocco, Qatar, Senegal, Sudan, and the United Arab Emirates.[14]

Saudi pacification of the Houthis — the Yemeni faction that absorbs most of the Saudi effort's time and ammunition — is far from inevitable, and certainly is not imminent. But while the Saudis may not be able to *win* this war, there is no way they can *lose* it. Yemen is on the far side of Saudi Arabia from Iran, so Iran simply cannot be a major factor in the war unless the Americans allow the Iranians to ship weapons in by water. The Americans may have no intention of getting involved in the ground aspects of a civil war in what is at best a failed state, but they are still sufficiently involved in the region to assist with a low-risk naval blockade. The result is a three-way war between a very well-funded and well-equipped — if somewhat militarily sophomoric — Saudi Arabia and their Gulfie allies, the battle-hardened Iranian-supported but ill-equipped Houthis, and the local branch of al Qaeda whom the Saudis are largely ignoring because the affiliate is more interested in fighting the Houthis than the Saudi coalition.

Pakistan: Even in Pakistan the two sides are starting to face off. As a perennially poor, energy-importing country that faces a chronic military standoff with the vastly-superior India, Pakistan has long been an eager target of Saudi Arabia's checkbook diplomacy. As such, the two enjoy relations so cordial that Pakistanis make up the largest single category of foreign workers in most portions of the Saudi system, up to and including the oil industry and the pilot teams of the Saudi air force.

Of greatest concern to Iran is the potential nuclear balance. Much has been made of Iran's nuclear program, but the reality of Iran's "interest" in

---

14 ... and Blackwater.

going nuclear is not what most believe. Iran is far and away the superior *conventional* military in the Persian Gulf region, and in a fair fight could easily defeat Iraq, Saudi Arabia, and all of the Gulf States combined. It doesn't need a nuke to be the dominant power in the region. If anything, the process of testing a nuke would invite an Israeli pre-emptive strike, making the entire effort counterproductive. As such Iran is fully willing to trade its nuclear program for entente with the United States, because if the Americans and Iranians agree to live and let live — and the Americans leave the region — then the tide of history (and economics and politics and demographics) favors Iran. (This is *not* to say that Iran wouldn't find a nuclear weapon a useful thing, just that a functional nuclear arsenal isn't nearly as useful to Iran as a Middle East without the United States.)

Which brings us back to the Saudi-Pakistani alliance. Pakistan, *already has* nuclear weapons. The Iranian nightmare isn't so much a war with

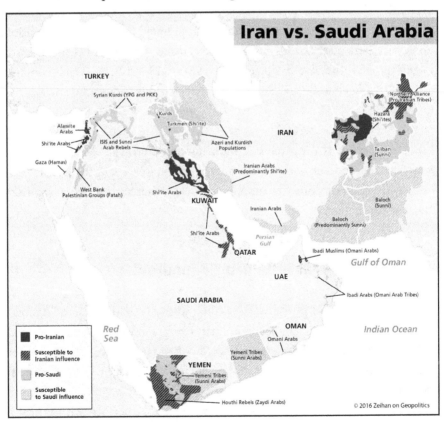

Iran vs. Saudi Arabia

© 2016 Zeihan on Geopolitics

Pakistan that goes nuclear, but that the Pakistani-Saudi alliance is so firm and the Saudi bank accounts so deep that Saudi Arabia could simply *buy* a nuke or five from the Pakistanis in order to fend off Iran. To counter that potentially crippling alliance, Iran is subtly extending its influence across the Pakistani border to court the Balochi minority — a group that has long been (violently) opposed to Islamabad. It's a double-edged sword. There are Balochis in Iran as well and the Saudis, on behalf of their Pakistani allies, are already returning the favor.

Oman: And there may be an eighth front soon. Omani Sultan Qaboos bin Said Al Said is one of the most talented leaders in the world, and certainly the Middle East's premier statesman. He deposed his father in 1970, then took a nearly Yemenesque mess of communists, militants, tribal groups, Islamists, monarchists, and generally disagreeable folks of all stripes and forged them into a modern, peaceable state. Keeping his country an oasis of stability, however, requires Said's near-constant attention. At the time of this writing, he is 75 and has no publicly designated heir. Per local tradition, upon his death the various factions have three days to select a successor. When they fail they are to open an envelope Said left behind that contains the name of his chosen successor, whom the various groups are encouraged to follow.

This is not a good secession plan.

A far more likely outcome is a multi-faction civil war. As Iran shares a long maritime border with Oman and Saudi Arabia a lengthy land border, both will be able to provide support to this or that faction with impunity. The war could get very ugly, very quickly.

The Iranian Conundrum

While Iran's regional position is splashier and louder than Saudi Arabia's, Iran is both strategically and economically overextended while Saudi Arabia enjoys strategic insulation, a fatter checkbook, a bigger income stream, and little concern about the amount of damage inflicted on any of the countries caught in the crossfire. And so the House of Saud is engaged in a full-court press to bleed and to crush Iran *now*, before the American withdrawal is completed, before the end of the sanctions can grant Iran fatter income streams, *while* the Syrian government and its sponsors in Tehran are still demonized in global public opinion. In the Saudi mind Iran is currently as weak as it will ever be, and so the Saudis are going for the throat.

While the Iranians cannot miss the massive uptick in Saudi aggression or the general Saudi goal, the Iranians have not quite yet registered just how much economic — and even military — trends favor the Saudis. There is a powerful belief in Tehran that as soon as they bury the hatchet with the Americans, foreign investment will flood back into the Iranian oil patch and their financial position will radically improve.

This is a massive miscalculation. Iran's investment environment is, in a word, hostile. Current regulations put all of the risk on foreign investors, yet offer no upside should oil prices be strong. American/European sanctions implemented in 2011-2012 were less the primary cause of killing foreign interest in Iranian oil and more the final straw. Tehran *did* announce in 2014 its intent of overhauling its contracting system in order attract foreign investment, but timelines keep being extended. At the time of this writing they are now over a year overdue, and there seems little hope that the first real draft will be available before mid-2017. Even if everything goes swimmingly, between deferred maintenance, degraded systems, and reservoir damage, Iran likely needs $200 billion in new investment to make even modest long-term improvements in output.

In fact, it is likely already too late. By mid-2017 U.S. shale's full-cycle break-even prices will likely be *equivalent* to that of Iran's conventional crude. Few firms are likely to risk an investment into a persnickety political environment and an uncertain legal environment where war risks are high. It would be easier to get iron-clad legal guarantees in Oklahoma where the biggest security risk is a beer shortage in a man camp.

Iran's default setting is to double down on insurgent tactics. However, barring a civil breakdown in Saudi Arabia's oil-producing region, this does nothing to alleviate the price war and certainly does not attract the direly needed investment into the Iranian oil complex. Meanwhile, Iran's expensive, painstakingly crafted regional presence is being rolled up bit by bit.

Iran's core problem is that its playbook is out of date. Iran's strategy since the rise of the ayatollahs in 1979 has been disruptive — sponsor or foster insurgent groups among the region's various minorities who can tear down the American-maintained regional order. But the game has changed, and the new game is one that Iran cannot win.

The Americans no longer care about the regional order, leaving the Saudis as the major combatant. But the Saudis don't care about regional stability either (outside of the rich bits of the Arabian Peninsula). Riyadh is solely concerned about eradicating Iranian power, and they themselves are using an insurgent strategy to do it.

It is now a numbers game. Iran's proxies are all *minorities* in a sea of Sunni Arabs, while the Saudis are backing the *majority* Sunni Arabs *and the Saudis don't care if the whole thing burns down.* There is no way Iran can win in a contest of dollars or bodies. With anti-system insurgents battling anti-system insurgents, there isn't going to be a lot of the regional order left. And as that order burns, it will take all of Iran's influence with it.

If Iran is going to be more than a poor, isolated kingdom high in its Zagros Mountains fastness, a change of strategy is required.

At some point it will dawn on the Iranians that the Saudis have truly turned the long-term strategic picture against them, and that the only possible way they can resist is to go to war.

Iran boasts a million-man army, an air force substantially larger than Saudi Arabia's and a willingness to tolerate hardships the Saudis don't even like to read about. On paper it appears that Iran should smoke Saudi Arabia easily in a fair fight. But a fair fight it will not be. The war the Iranians have prepared for will bear little resemblance to the war they will be forced to wage. The result does more than inject a great deal of uncertainty into the conflict, but also promises to make the impact on global oil far more horrific than it would otherwise be.

Stage One: Closing the Gulf

The war will commence with Iran implementing the strategy it has long prepared for: shutting down the Strait of Hormuz.

Iran has a phalanx of varied missile systems that could reach any point within the strait itself, with many of them capable of reaching the Saudi shoreline even across the wider points of the Persian Gulf. What Iran lacks, however, is the ability to deliver ordinance *accurately*. Iran has missiles, but they are ballistic and dumb, not cruise and smart. A missile barrage is loud and splashy, but is unlikely that the Iranians could hit any moving targets — even ones as large and slow as oil tankers. And Saudi (and Kuwaiti and Emirati) missile defense will most certainly have a chance to blunt any barrages.

Iran boasts more than 300 air superiority multi-role and ground attack planes flown by a cadre of experienced pilots, but the numbers are not the true story. Iran's air force is a franken-fleet of jets from Russia, the United States, China, and France — the bulk of which were acquired in the 1970s. Iran is the only current operator of the F-14 (a somewhat squirrelly piece of machinery that was never easy to maintain in the first place) and so spare parts haven't even existed for the things in years. Many of the other planes in its hangars (such as the Su-24 or MiG-29) are only operated by countries that haven't *ever* added new jets to their order of battle (like post-Soviet Kazakhstan and Ukraine).

Saudi Arabia, in contrast, has "only" about 225 available aircraft on hand, but its F-15s and Eurofighter Typhoons are among the most advanced aircraft operating outside of Russia and the First World. Neighboring UAE's F-16s and Mirage 2000s are similarly snappy, and Emirati pilots are some of the best outside of NATO.

Iran can threaten and scare, but its air and missile capabilities are insufficient to shut down maritime activity on the Gulf for long. Particularly when one considers that most Kuwaiti, Saudi, Qatari, and Emirati tanker traffic will hug the Saudi side of the Gulf until the last possible mile to limit exposure to Iranian weapons systems — and Kuwaiti, Saudi, Qatari, and Emirati air force assets can provide at least limited cover the entire way.

The Iranians, however, have more than one card to play.

An aggressive mine-deployment program would come next (or more likely, at the same time). Iran commands a veritable swarm of small vessels that could deploy hundreds — maybe even thousands — of mines into traffic lanes to deny ships the ability to safely enter, exit, or otherwise move about within, the Gulf. However, the chances of a single mine actually sinking something as large as a VLCC — your average supertanker has a bigger volume than the Chrysler Building — are slim. Iran's best chance will be to concentrate its mining efforts on the Strait itself, where ships will be further from Kuwaiti, Saudi, Qatari, and Emirati air support, where they will be forced to sail very close to Iranian shores, where they will be forced into a funnel by the Strait itself, and where they will be most vulnerable to the greatest concentration of Iranian naval and air power.[15] At Hormuz, Iranian speedboats based at and near Bandar Abbas could easily harass tanker vessels, and perhaps even capture a few.

While loud and 'splody, Iran's Hormuz strategy is actually diplomatic, not military: Threaten Gulf shipping to trigger a global energy panic that sends oil prices sky-high. Countries the world over will then pressure the United States to sue for peace. At that point Iran will press for a diplomatic reimagining of regional security and political structures.

But the Iranians are in for an ice-cold shock. The Americans are out of the global stability business, and will not feel much motivation to speak with the Iranians about a revised regional order that they find utterly disinteresting. The diplomatic play will fail on day one.

And if that were not enough, the Saudis too are working from a different playbook. Rather than attempt to mitigate Iran's efforts to close the Strait, Saudi Arabia will instead carry out almost identical strategy — using its own missile systems, its own naval assets, and its qualitatively superior air force to take shots at tankers steaming to and from Iran's oil-loading facilities. Iran will discover, much to its confusion, that the Saudis are *helping* Iran close the Strait.

What Tehran does not yet understand is that with the departure of the Americans, Iran is now *more* dependent upon keeping Persian Gulf oil flowing than Saudi Arabia. And as much as the Iranians have been aggravated by all things American for over a generation, Iran now needs the Americans between them and the Saudis more than the other way around.

It is all about the peculiar geography of the region's energy infrastructure.

---

15 Since Iraq is a sort-of Iranian satellite it is unlikely that Iran would target Iraqi oil assets intentionally. But on the seas mistakes happen all the time, so Iraqi tankers would be unlikely to escape damage altogether.

Iran's primary export point is Kharg Island, a location that presents the Iranians with three critical problems. First, Kharg is deep in the Persian Gulf, almost all the way to Iraq. Any ship that disembarks from Kharg must evade Saudi efforts for roughly 500 miles before it is clear of Hormuz. Second, there isn't a bridge connecting Kharg to the mainland, so any repair equipment or workers — not to mention emergency crews and *their* equipment — would need to be ferried in rather than simply drive to the site. A solid sortie from a Saudi pilot (or 30 — this being *the* high-profile economic target) could blow up a storage tank or pumping station and take Kharg completely out of the equation for weeks. Third, more than 90 percent of Iran's oil exports flow from this singular point. Significant damage to Kharg is the end of Iran's foreign earnings.

Saudi Arabia faces no such constraint. While its largest oil-loading facility — Ras Tanura — is actually bigger than Kharg, it is far from the

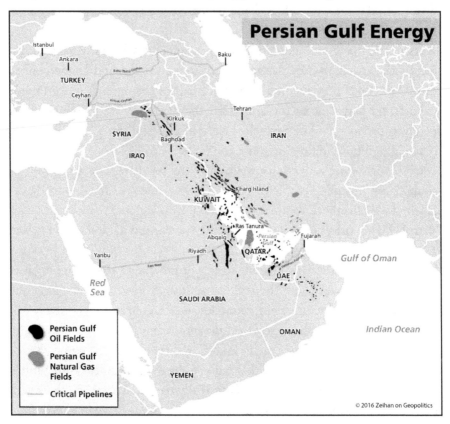

Saudis' only loading facility. Most important, Saudi Arabia has the ability to trans-ship 5mbpd of crude across the Arabian Peninsula via its East-West line to its Red Sea loading terminals. That takes roughly two-thirds of Saudi Arabia's oil exports and puts them beyond the reach of Iran's interdiction capacity. And Saudi Arabia isn't alone. The United Arab Emirates has a pipe that similarly can move 1.6mbpd — two-thirds of UAE export volumes — direct to the Arabian Gulf, bypassing Hormuz.

This is (very) small comfort to the Arab states of the Persian Gulf who don't have bypass pipes. Kuwait and Qatar are, in a word, screwed. All of their petroleum production facilities, storage facilities, refineries and export facilities — not to mention their combined 2.3mbpd of oil and 1.0mbpd of refined product exports — are closer to Iranian missile launchers than any locations in Saudi Arabia. And considering Kuwait City's and Abu Dhabi's general anti-Iranian position when it comes to all things American, Iraqi, Saudi, or oil, they are likely to find themselves under considerable target by Iran's interdiction efforts.

Assuming the Saudi and Emirati bypass pipelines are fully utilized; the Saudis target Kharg directly; and the disjointed Saudi and Iranian efforts to seal the Gulf prevent the shipment of half of the region's remaining oil exports, on Day One of the Gulf War the disruption to global energy is nearly as bad as it will be from the height of the Twilight War: 6.2mbpd of crude, 2.0mbpd of refined product and 5.5bcf/d of LNG.

Even with these reductions, financially the result will be a net *gain* for some. Fully 7.5mbpd of Saudi and Emirati crude will be able to bypass Hormuz — and those volumes will be sold into a global market with such sharply higher prices that Saudi and Emirati income will be sharply *up*. War, apparently, is good for business.

For the others, the only possible means of protecting their shipping is to secure outside naval help. The strategy is straightforward: reflagging and convoying. Navally competent countries would dispatch warships to the region, which would then escort oil tankers flying their flags. Any belligerent who targets such reflagged tankers or their escorts would be picking a military fight with a country that has the capacity — at least in a limited way — to retaliate. The Kuwaitis successfully recruited the U.S. Navy with this strategy during the Iran-Iraq war.

There will be a lengthy list of countries outside the Persian Gulf that are as desperate to get Kuwaiti and Qatari oil and LNG as the Kuwaitis and Qataris are to ship it. Unfortunately for Kuwait and Qatar, desperation does not equal capability to do something about it. One of the (many) side effects of living in an American-dominated world since World War II ended is that most countries balked at the cost of floating capable long-range navies. Why protect your shipping when the Americans will do it for you for free?

Those who choose to float a navy capable of independent, long-range operations makes for a short list. In order of capacity they are the United States, Japan, the United Kingdom, France, China, Russia, Australia, Korea, and Taiwan. That's *all* of them, and not all of them could (or would) play in the Middle East. The British, French, and Russians have all the petroleum they need closer to home, with the British and Russian navies likely already in play in the Twilight War and so unable to mount a Persian Gulf expedition. Australia is far more likely to tap Southeast Asian or South American supplies rather than run the Persian Gulf gauntlet without the political cover of its traditional allies.

Japan, China, Korea, and Taiwan are the only players with both the need and military capacity to intervene. Everyone in the Gulf — including the Saudis and the Iranians — are likely to bid for reflags and convoys, as much to deny escorts to the other side as to secure their own shipping. Regardless of who pairs up with whom, within several days of the war's outbreak, the world will enter a chronic oil shortage and what extra-regional players there are will have chosen sides. This East Asian involvement in the Persian Gulf is only one piece of what will be a wide-ranging struggle to secure energy supplies. We will examine this Tanker War in-depth in Chapter 8.

Phase 2: Rebellion

This portion of the war is somewhat less about guns and bombs, and more about knives and cloaks.

Though Iran might get some lucky shots off at Saudi Arabia's Persian Gulf coastal facilities, the simple fact is that anything less than a score of lucky shots will do little to inhibit Saudi Arabia's income, much less its war-fighting capacity. And so, the Iranians will very quickly move into the war's gritty second phase: sponsoring rebellion.

Iran's army is an expression of its geography. The mountains of Persia have given rise to not just the Persians who constitute 50 percent of the population, but a dozen other major ethnicities as well. As such the Persians always have been concerned about the threat of civil unrest. A few angry Kurds or Manzandarani or Turkmen can quickly escalate into a Kurdish or Manzandarani or Turkmeni rebellion. The solution is for Iran to maintain a large standing army that never leaves home. Its primary purpose is to prevent those few angry Kurds or Manzandarani or Turkmen from living long enough to spark an uprising. The last time Iran's army experienced a moment of weakness was in the aftermath of the Shah's fall, which quickly devolved into free-for-all civil war, which sufficiently weakened the country to entice Saddam's Iraq to attack.

Simply put, Iran's army occupies Iran to keep it one piece, freeing up Iran's intelligence services to do other things abroad.

With a rich experience in policing multi-ethnic polities, Iran's intel systems are very good about locating and penetrating groups that do not fit in with their communities — particularly when those groups have a hint of Shia or Persian about them. Iran then turns these groups against the local state in order to keep the entire area at a low simmer: Hezbollah in Lebanon, Shia in Bahrain, Hamas in the Palestinian Territories, Houthis in Yemen, Kurds in Turkey.

As the Iranian-Saudi war heats up, that skill set will see immense use among Saudi Arabia's minorities, the most strategic of which are the Saudi Shia who live on top of Saudi Arabia's oil production, processing, and export facilities. Saudi Arabia's eastern Shia zone is home to none other than the Ghawar superfield (the world's largest), the Ras Tanura tanker loading facility (the world's largest), and several major refineries (including a few of the world's largest). Perhaps the single most sensitive spot is the Abqaiq oil processing facility (the world's largest), which gathers, handles, and transships more than 5mbpd of Saudi crude. Abqaiq is not just the central point in the Saudi energy network, it also is arguably the single-most important piece of energy infrastructure on the planet.

That said, the Saudis guard Abqaiq as if were, well, the single most important piece of energy infrastructure on the planet. Abqaiq's industrial infrastructure occupies some two square miles of territory plus another mile of military-secured stand-off distance. The insulation granted by such sheer size aside, it is very important to note that Abqaiq handles raw crude, not refined productions. Crude oil is *not* flammable, much less explosive, under normal conditions. Between the relative chemical inertness of raw crude and the sheer size of Abqaiq, taking it out in one go would require a mid-sized nuke.

An easier, cheaper, more likely, and less blammo way to shut the facility down would involve a really, really, *really* big riot. Abqaiq is right on the edge of Saudi Arabia's greatest Shia population centers. A Shia insurrection here undoubtedly would damage the various pipes that send crude to and from Abqaiq, hobbling the Saudi system nearly as much as a shutdown of Persian Gulf shipping would hobble the Iranian system.

The Ghawar-Abqaiq-Ras Tanura region is one that Iranian intelligence assets have been targeting fast and furious for years. One of their principle allies/agents in the area was a Shia cleric by the name of Nimr al-Nimr, who advocated rebellion against the Saudi royal family. I say "was" because the Saudi authorities executed him for sedition in January 2016. The diplomatic tit-for-tat that immediately followed resulted in the burning of the Saudi embassy in Tehran and the severing of diplomatic relations.

Of course the Saudis would not take that sort of dagger to the heart lying down. Iran has many minorities — recall that fully half of Iran's population is not Persian — many of whom live in strategically sensitive spots. Four are worthy of call-out:

- The first are members of Iran's 3-million-strong Ahwazi **Arab** community, which almost all live in the country's extreme southwest province of Khuzestan. Khuzestan is notable for several reasons. It is the only plains region in the country and is home to a great deal of the country's agricultural output. It is directly adjacent to the Shia-majority portions of Iraq, making it crucial for Iran's efforts to project power into its neighbor. It is home to Iran's largest refinery: Abadan. But more important, all but 800kbpd in oil production of Iran's nameplate 4mbpd is produced in Khuzestan. The fall of Khuzestan to civil unrest could be far worse for Iran than even the fall of Abqaiq would be to Saudi Arabia. While Abqaiq is adjacent to population centers, it is in the desert, as are most of the fields that supply it with crude. Establishing a cordon sanitaire around Abqaiq — or even the entire Ghawar region — to facilitate repair and reconstruction would be fairly easy. In contrast, *all* of Khuzestan — oil fields and all — is populated. Should Khuzestan's facilities burn, only a massive military occupation would enable a rebuilding effort to begin. Iranian crude would be offline for years.

- The second are the **Azeris**, one of many minorities that agitated for in-dependence in the chaos following the fall of the Shah. That would have been more than enough to earn the leery eye of the ayatollahs. Making matters worse, the Azeris are ethnically and religiously identical to the Azerbaijanis of next-door Azerbaijan — in fact there are more Iranian Azeris than there are Azerbaijani Azerbaijanis. That made a fun little academic discussion when Azerbaijan was an internal province of the Soviet Union, and was elevated to the rank of top-tier strategic discus-sions once Azerbaijan became independent in late-1991 and started roll-ing in petro-dollars by the mid-2000s. Making matters much worse, the Turks — who are as technically superior to Iran in all the same ways that Iran is superior to Saudi Arabia, see both Azeris and Azerbaijanis as their ethnic kin. Making matters much, much worse is that the Azeris are Iran's largest minority: Fully one in *four* Iranian citizens are Azeris. Even a mild rebellion among Iranian Azeris could shatter the state. Any Saudi agitation would force the Iranians to divert additional army forces to their country's northwest.

Tehran has done a great deal in recent decades to sand down some of the rougher aspects of the culture clash among Persians, Arabs, and Azeris. The Ahwazi Arabs are not a majority within Khuzestan, and so heavy Iranification efforts — helped by the fact that these Arabs are Shia and so not instinctively pro-Saudi — help dilute the threat to the oil fields. Similar efforts among the Azeris — who are also Shia — has smoothed their en-trance into the Iranian mainstream to the point that most do not consider themselves an overly-persecuted minority. Both remain threats, but both are containable without deep foreign agitation. Unfortunately for Tehran, not only is that agitation inevitable, but it already is far advanced with the two other groups:

- Textbook mountain people, the **Kurds** are a mix of many things: Sunni and Shia (so Tehran considers them apostates). The Kurds live not just in Iran, but also in Turkey, Syria, and Iraq (so Tehran sees them as disloyal). The Kurds know their way around guns and are fighting heavily in the Iraqi and Syrian civil wars (so Tehran fears that expertise will be used against Iran soon). The Kurds are good at skirting authority across four states (and so are spectacular smugglers in a country with a spectacular narcotics problem, *and* they can self-finance). In the past 30 years Iran's Kurds have had excellent relations with the United States, Saddam's Iraq, the Soviet Union, Turkey, and Israel (so Tehran sees Saudi Arabia as their Kurds' likely new source of money and weapons).

- The **Baloch** are perhaps the Iranian government's stickiest sectarian problem. Fiercely Sunni, fiercely tribal, and fiercely anti-Persian, the Baloch have no problem accepting financial and military assistance from any-where — Pakistan, the United States, the Taliban, and Saudi Arabia have all chipped in at times. The Baloch even have their own resistance group, Jundullah, which has a nasty habit of killing Iranian soldiers and then jumping the border into Pakistan. Iran tends to respond to such hit-and-run attacks with hot pursuit and/or artillery, neither of which does much to improve Islamabad-Tehran relations. With the right mix of weapons, intelligence, and timing, the Baloch could even target Iranian oil shipments *after* they've exited Hormuz.

Phase 3: Invasion

While an Iranian effort to missile Saudi cargos and spark rebellions will certainly be cause for concern, such actions are unlikely to induce Riyadh to ask for terms, much less capitulate. Ending the Saudi threat will require Iran to be far more … forceful.

At first glance it would seem that Iran would jump right to invasion. Even considering the civil control role of the Iranian army, a million-man organization would seem more than enough troops to conquer a country as open and horribly defended as Saudi Arabia. Yet while Iran would savor the opportunity to subjugate Saudi Arabia and execute the entire House of Saud, it is well aware of five major obstacles that stand between it and victory in a land war.

First, there is an infrastructure problem. Iran is *not* a naval country, so its troops must get to Saudi Arabia the old-fashioned way. The first major obstacle of note is the Shat-al-Arab riverway of southern Iraq. While there are two narrow bridges in the southern Iraqi city of Basra, both are pontoon bridges and cannot take the sort of heavy traffic required by a multi-division infantry force and its supply lines. The southernmost *real* bridge across the river is almost 50 miles north of Basra, adding a 100-mile detour to the Iranians' 500-mile march to the Saudi oil fields.

Second, because of that infrastructure problem, there is no way to avoid marching directly through populated Iraq. The Iranians will have no choice but to formally conquer Basra, a sprawling metropolis of 1.5 million. While the Basrans are Shia and so are broadly inclined to favor the Iranians, there's a big difference between inclination to favor and submission to occupation. Should even a small percentage of Basrans rebel, Iran would face a war of urban occupation on its way to its target. That distraction could prove crippling, particularly when you consider the entire Iranian effort will be dependent upon one road and one bridge. For oil markets, this too would be disastrous: of Iraq's roughly 4mbpd of oil production, three-quarters of it is near Basra and reaches the world via pipes and Gulf loading platforms that the Iranians would have to occupy as a matter of course on their way to Arabia.

Taking the remainder of Iraq's southern oil output offline increases the total disruption by another 1.5mbpd, for a new total disruption of 8.2mbpd.

Third, there is similarly no way to avoid the oil-producing regions or population centers of Kuwait. All are within a short hop of the coast, and the access corridor to Arabia runs right through Kuwait City. It isn't that Kuwait is exactly militarily intimidating — even with its post-liberation military build-out it has no strategic depth and so could be conquered (again) in hours to days. It's that Kuwait will likely have at least a partial defensive agreement with whichever country is helping convoy its oil cargos, so the Iranians will now be crossing swords with at least four players: the Saudi, the Iraqis, the Kuwaitis, and the Kuwaitis' new friends. If that new friend is a country like Korea or Taiwan (which both have limited offensive reach and bigger concerns close to home) that is one thing, but if it is a country like Japan or China bristling with sharable weapons systems, it would mean something entirely different.

Taking the remainder of Kuwait's production, refining, and export capacity offline increases the shortage by another 1.0mbpd of crude and 0.37mbpd of refined product. The total disruption to this point is now 9.2mbpd of crude and 2.3mbpd of refined product.

Fourth, after leaving southern Kuwait a series of small Saudi towns dot the desert coast, but really there is *nothing* on the road between Ghawar and Abqaiq that the Iranians can use to resupply. Iran will have to transport not just a couple hundred thousand troops, but all of the gear and food and water required to support them on a desert march hundreds of miles long.

This is as hard as it sounds, and it isn't something the Iranian army was designed to handle. Considering the Iranian army's domestic control role, it doesn't even have much in the way of support units that a normal army would have as a matter of course. Iran's tanks — what few there are — date back to before the beginning of the Iran-Iraq war in 1981. Its air force is similarly outdated, having no appreciable new aircraft added since the Shah's time. It is probably — at best — one-third its listed strength because so many craft have been cannibalized to keep any of them flying. Air defense is a somewhat better courtesy of on-again, off-again equipment purchases from the Russians, but such anti-air batteries are designed for site-defense, not mobile-defense. Iran can reposition aircraft and anti-air assets to occupied Kuwait, but then those forces cannot be operating at Hormuz. Iran just doesn't have the equipment to operate at strength in multiple theaters. Even simple things like personnel carriers and unarmored trucks are in limited supply.

Iran's odd mix of military features — stationary air defense, its trademark mountains, endless swarms of troops — make it eminently prepared *to be invaded*, but it is horribly prepared at present to *do the invading*. Such

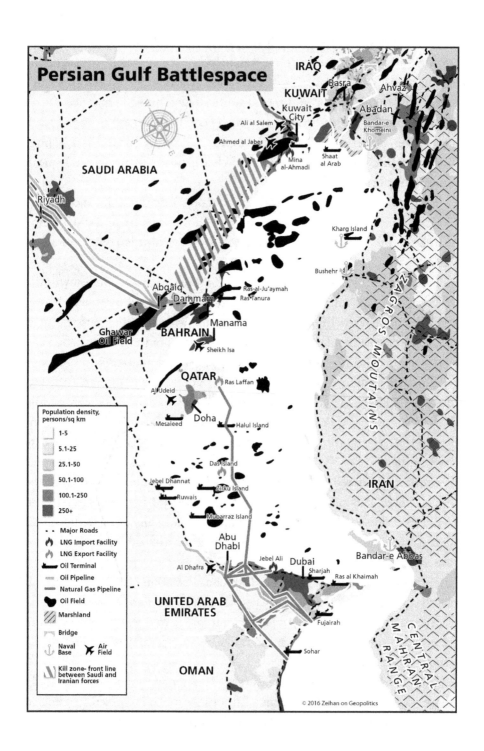

Persian Gulf Battlespace

IRAQ
KUWAIT
Basra
Ahvaz
Kuwait City
Abadan
Ali al Salem
Bandar-e Khomeini
Ahmed al Jaber
SAUDI ARABIA
Shaat al Arab
Mina al-Ahmadi

Riyadh

Kharg Island

Bushehr

Ras-al-Ju'aymah
Abqaiq
Ras Tanura
Dammam
Manama
Ghawar Oil Field
BAHRAIN
Sheikh Isa

QATAR
Ras Laffan
Al Udeid
Doha
Mesaieed
Halul Island

Das Island

Jebel Dhannat
Zirku Island
Ruwais
IRAN
Mubarraz Island

Abu Dhabi
Jebel Ali
Dubai
Al Dhafra
Sharjah
Ras al Khaimah
Bandar-e Abbas

UNITED ARAB EMIRATES
Fujairah

OMAN
Sohar

ZAGROS MOUNTAINS

CENTRAL MAHRAN RANGE

Population density, persons/sq km
- 1-5
- 5.1-25
- 25.1-50
- 50.1-100
- 100.1-250
- 250+

- Major Roads
- LNG Import Facility
- LNG Export Facility
- Oil Terminal
- Oil Pipeline
- Natural Gas Pipeline
- Oil Field
- Marshland
- Bridge
- Naval Base / Air Field
- Kill zone- front line between Saudi and Iranian forces

© 2016 Zeihan on Geopolitics

a manpower-heavy army may be of some use versus an adjacent country like Iraq, but the 350-mile desert trek from Kuwait City to the Saudi oil fields would stretch every aspect of the Iranian military logistic chain to the breaking point.

That march would be horrid in its casualties. Iran's ability to provide air cover would be at most, limited. More important, defending this stretch of open desert is something for which the Saudis have been preparing.

Many have criticized the Saudi military for its prosecution of the war in Yemen. The critics have some solid points: the Saudis are attempting to use as few troops as possible, in essence fighting an insurgency campaign with airpower only. Since the only way to root out insurgents are (lots of) on-ground patrols, the Saudi strategy seems positively silly.

It is not. Destroying the Houthi resistance isn't the Saudis' primary goal. Instead the goal is to get the Saudi air force ready for extended high-sortie-rate strike campaigns, work the kinks out of the logistics of air support, and gain expertise in leading a multi-national coalition in a fire zone.

Don't think of Yemen as a war. Think of it as practice.

When Iran's war machine comes for Saudi Arabia, the Saudis want to be able to turn their northern deserts into a gigantic kill zone.

Luckily for the Iranians, if they can reach the line that connects Abqaiq and Ras Tanura they will have taken over the bulk of Saudi Arabia's Shia zone, most of Saudi Arabia's refining capacity, all of its Persian Gulf loading facilities, and the ability of Saudi Arabia to gather and distribute crude from over three-quarters of its oil production sites. More important, the Iranians would have successfully crossed the desert barrier and could resupply their own forces as well as eliminate Saudi Arabia's forward air assets. From an economic and strategic point of view the war would be concluded.

A formal military conclusion would likely come quickly. There are no natural barriers between the Shia zones in the east and the capital of Riyadh in the center of the country. It wouldn't matter much to the Iranians whether Riyadh — with its 7 million residents — were captured or simply destroyed, but destroying the city would be quicker and easier. Riyadh is a pure desert city, so terminate the city's electricity supply and it loses air-conditioning and water. Its population would be forced to flee to the west or simply die. After that, Iran could move at its leisure toward the Hijaz cities on the Red

Sea coast, cities populated by families who bear the House of Saud no small degree of resentment. With the fall of Riyadh, organized military resistance would end.

The American Play (or Lack Thereof) in the Gulf War

Courtesy of shale the Americans already have near oil self-sufficiency. Push prices up for a few months, and shale operators will have pushed North America to full oil independence. Considering that the biggest importer of Persian Gulf crude is the (former) Bretton Woods ally of China, it is very difficult to envision the Americans getting drawn into a Saudi-Iranian blood feud to protect the sanctity, health, and stability of the Chinese economy.

Nor would American involvement likely change outcomes. If the Americans did deploy — and considering the general antipathy Americans have for all things Middle Eastern in the post-Iraq/Afghanistan era that's a big "if" — there are only two ways to participate. The first option would be to attempt to forestall the Iranian invasion at the Iraqi border. That would require the forward deployment of at least 50,000 troops into the vicinity of Basra, reintroducing a de facto American occupation of Iraq to fight off a casualty-insensitive land power on behalf of the Kingdom of Saudi Arabia. From the average American's point of view, that's three gigantic reasons to not get involved right there.

The second option would be to utilize air power — whether land-launched from Qatar or sea-launched from the carriers — to augment Saudi air force efforts in the Great Turkey Shoot between Kuwait City and Abqaiq. This would be far more in-line with evolving American battle preferences, but even this isn't a good fit. In part because it moves the United States — firmly — in the opposite direction of its strategic policy since 2007, putting it back in the Middle Eastern mix.

Strategically, a grinding desert stalemate might be the best possible outcome for the Americans. With Iran and Saudi Arabia locked in a years-long struggle, neither power could dominate the region. Locked in such a stalemate, neither power would be able to impose its tender version of morality on anyone outside of Middle East. The best national security policy for the Americans might well be to pop some corn.

But more important, what would U.S. involvement change?

The most likely outcome of American *non*-intervention would be a desert stalemate with Iranian forces holding Iraq and Kuwait, but unable to penetrate through Saudi Arabia's air screen to Abqaiq. The most likely outcome of American participation in the Great Turkey Shoot would be … a desert stalemate with Iranian forces holding Iraq and Kuwait, but unable to penetrate to Abqaiq. Either way, the result is a hot stalled war with a lot of ordinance being flung in the vicinity of a lot of oil assets, with Kuwaiti and Iraqi and (likely) Iranian crude exports remaining offline. The only difference is that by putting American forces in the middle of the shooting … American forces are in the middle of the shooting.

Aftermath: The Greater Persian Gulf

Once you factor geography, obstacles, the layout of the region's infrastructure, the imbalance of Saudi and Iranian military forces, and especially that open stretch of desert between Kuwait City and the Ghawar region, the chances of an outright Iranian victory are probably less than 50:50. A slightly more likely outcome would be a grinding war in which the Iranian invasion stalls in its push across the desert because of the twin factors of Saudi air power and Saudi agitation in Khuzestan, Iraq, and Kuwait. With the tip of Iran's spear chopped into bait, the conflict would settle into a pattern of lobbing explosives across the Gulf, destroying any hope of a recovery in oil exports.

Elsewhere in the region, bereft of either America's stabilizing influence of strategic overwatch, the post-World War *One* regional order will finally crack apart. In the aftermath of that war the Europeans literally got together over coffee and drew lines on the map to break up the region into zones of influence. This agreement — known as Sykes-Picot after its primary authors — was forged with little regard for population centers or ethnic settlement patterns and did so before the discovery of the world's most massive petroleum deposits. One, among many, results are all those straight-line borders throughout the region.

The Disorder changes all that. With no one with the means having a vested interest in regional stability, with global trade a thing of the past, with no external security guarantor to give meaning to those straight map-lines, with the region's two most-capable powers engaged in insurgent-on-insurgent warfare, several of the Middle Eastern countries will not simply disintegrate. They will lose so much industrial, electrical, and agricultural capacity that they will flat out decivilize. Syria, Iraq, Jordan, Yemen, and Lebanon — roughly in that order — will lose the ability to maintain populations more than one-third their current size. Unless Kuwait can succeed (again) in purchasing an ally to liberate it in short order, it will join the ranks of the hapless. The result will be roughly 60 million people who will either become refugees in Iran, Turkey, and Europe, or who will die of famine and/or thirst.[16] And should the general melee endanger the import of foodstuffs into the region — most Middle Eastern countries import more than half of their calories — the general breakdown could easily spread to more stable locations such as Egypt, Oman, Iran, UAE, Qatar, and Saudi Arabia.

Within the Gulf, everything of course depends on just how far the Iranians made it. Iranian victory over Saudi Arabia would quickly translate into Iranian dominion over the entirety of the Arabian Peninsula. With Iranian forces in the Saudi heartland, the remaining Gulf monarchies — Bahrain, Qatar, the United Arab Emirates, and Oman — would have no choice but to accede to Iranian wishes. It would be up to Tehran whether this accession would be in the form of suzerainty in which the emirates pay (very large) tribute but still manage their own affairs, or their incorporation as formal imperial provinces. The end result would be the ushering in of the next great Persian Empire, which would hold not only the Holy Cities but the world's largest petroleum complex by a factor of two.

Should the Iranian attack stall in the desert somewhere between Kuwait City and Ghawar, the picture is obviously somewhat different. Southern

---

16   The problem with helping desert refugees is that there just aren't many places they can go before they die in the desert. When services fail in Iraq, Syria and Jordan, deserts block movement to Saudi Arabia while the IDF and minefields block movement to Israel, leaving only Iran, Turkey and Europe as possible destinations.

Iraq and Kuwait would remain under occupation, while ongoing military tensions would label the Persian Gulf as a danger zone for years to come.

What is odd is how little the difference between Iranian failure and success means for most players not directly involved in the war.

Economically, the "stalled" scenario takes 12.1mbpd of crude and refined production offline indefinitely, considerably more than the worst-case scenario in the Russia-Europe war, and even that assumes the Iranians experience no success in spawning a rebellion in the Ghawar region.

An "Iranian victory" scenario would raise the possibility of supplies bit-by-bit returning to market over the following decade or so. There *would* be a near-immediate burst from undamaged Emirati and Qatari assets that would be no longer need to worry about a partially closed Hormuz, and Iran would be able to repair its Kharg Island facilities in short order. But damage to Ghawar would overshadow all such bright spots. Total disruption would breach 14mbpd.

Considering the wide range of plausible disruption scenarios, putting a specific price on global oil is difficult. Suffice to say that a functional price floor somewhere north of $150 would be the new normal. Iranian victory or Iranian stall, the result is a deep, global, energy-induced depression.

Strategically, the picture is equally dark. Victorious or defeated, exultant or desperate, Iran's invasion will force Iran's neighbors to prepare to deal with it on new terms. Pakistan will have seen Iran mobilize forces on a scale unmatched by anything Islamabad has seen in its independent history. And Pakistan's primary oil supplier — Saudi Arabia — will be either destroyed or endangered, hardwiring nuclear-armed Pakistan into strategic competition with Iran. Tehran may have previously considered its nuclear program a negotiating chip before. No more.

The Turks, who are in the process of rediscovering their Ottoman roots, can draw upon many historical examples of what happens during periods of Persian expansionism — all culminate with a Turkish-Persian war. Should the Turks find themselves sucked into conflict with Russia, the chances of conflict with the Iranians skyrocket. Without FSU oil, Turkey's only option for nearby energy will be Iraqi Kurdistan — a region that will be hard up on Iranian-occupied Iraq, making it child's play for the Iranians to cut Turkey's energy supplies. On the flip side, Turkey can intervene in Baghdad and

Turkey: Back to the Future

Considering how front-and-center Turkey often features in my work, there may be some arched eyebrows at the near absence of Turkish mentions in a chapter about a Middle Eastern war.

Yet, in a Persian-Arabian conflict, Turkey has no compelling reasons to join. It can meet its energy needs via the deals it has already cut (and implemented) with the Iraqi Kurds — a region that left to its own devices could likely increase its exports via Turkish territory from today's 500kbpd to something closer to 1mbpd — so there's no economic rationale for Turkish involvement in Baghdad or areas further south. Furthermore, any Turkish involvement would mean occupying over 30 million Iraqis and metropolitan Baghdad as a prelude to engaging either Iran or Saudi Arabia. Ankara doesn't have time for that sort of headache.

This hardly means Turkey won't play a role.

Back in the day — nearly a millennia ago — Ottoman Turkey served as the Mediterranean terminus for the spice trade between Southeast Asia and Europe. Control over the spice route enabled the Turks to levy a steep surcharge — typically paid in gold — for every speck of material that was sold on to the Europeans. This surcharge persisted until such time as the Portuguese were able to perfect deepwater navigation, sail around Africa and the Indian subcontinent, and interface with the spice producers themselves. That didn't become reliably possible until after 1600.

In the coming Disorder, a new sort of Turkish transport monopoly is shaping up. Barring Turkish involvement in a war with Russia, Turkey is the only reliable route for getting some 3mbpd of Russian, Kazakh, and Azerbaijani crude out to the wider world, a number that is likely to increase in the early stages of the Twilight War as the former Soviet states attempt to redirect their export flows away from the northern war zones.

Which means that without firing a shot, or even brandishing a gun, the Turks can slap on whatever sort of transit fee they feel the markets will support. Considering that in the good-ole-spice days that tariff could reach as high as 100%, this could be quite the moneymaker. Technically, Turkey must unilaterally abrogate the post-WWI Lausanne Treaty, which codifies freedom of navigation through the Turkish Straits. But considering the Turks have felt umbrage at that treaty for a century, and the superpower that has maintained the freedom of global navigation for the past 70 years has abandoned that role, consider the treaty nullified.

And that's only half the picture.

As much as Russia and Ukraine and Iran and Saudi Arabia would like for the Turks to join their wars on their side, neither Russia nor Ukraine nor Iran nor Saudi Arabia dare do anything that would nudge the Turks to join their wars on the *other* side. Of these four powers, only Saudi Arabia can offer positive incentive — in essence by offering to pay the Turks protection money for the guarding of Saudi oil shipments from Yanbu on the Red Sea through Suez to southern Europe. Or perhaps put more accurately, adding a line item for said protection money to what the Saudis charge the Europeans for their oil.

In doing so the Saudis give the Turks an economic reason to not take up arms against Riyadh, not to mention making the Iranians think real hard about whether the Saudis and Turks have any other understandings. The Europeans will undoubtedly not appreciate the move, but since they will have better things to do with their militaries than engage in extremity-measuring contests with the Turks in the Eastern Mediterranean, the likely outcome will be to scowl and bear it. Just like they did with the spice trade.

---

threaten Iran's entire invasion line from Iran proper to Basra, Kuwait, and Saudi Arabia. Even if the Iranians scrupulously avoid putting troops north of Baghdad, even if the Turks never put troops in Iraqi Kurdistan, even if both Ankara and Tehran go out of their way to reassure the other, strategic paranoia on both sides will prove unavoidable.

But perhaps the greatest outcome would be the global realignment of expectations. The absence of the Americans from the Persian Gulf conflict will be the final break in the wall of belief that the Yanks will ride to the rescue. Every geopolitical relationship — political, military, and economic — will be re-evaluated in the new environment. Even in the best-case scenario, the disruption and destruction of Persian Gulf oil production and export capacity will be more than enough to trigger a global depression lasting years — and that assumes there is no fighting elsewhere in the world over what are now sharply circumscribed energy supplies.

And there will be more fighting.

CHAPTER 8

The Tanker War

No matter how things shake out between Europe and Russia or Iran and Saudi Arabia, there is going to be an absolute reduction in the volume of crude that is physically available for purchase. Even the best-case scenario involving Russia — that only the Scandinavians and Brits become involved — still results in 3.0mbpd of crude and refined product going offline. The worst-case in the two conflicts — with natural gas disruptions included — would push the global shortage to eight times that.

The pain will not be felt equally. Instead of the unified global pricing of the Bretton Woods era, the world will labor under a messy, four-piece price structure.

First comes North America. American and Canadian crude resources are not only ample for North American demands, they mostly are contained within the continent. Nearly all Lower-48 crude is produced between the Rocky and Appalachian mountain chains, while nearly all Albertan crude is hardpiped into the American Midwest. North American prices will certainly rise as global shortages deepen, but the primary interconnect between North American and global energy markets will be in the form of American refined product exports. In 2015, U.S. refiners exported about 2.5mbpd (gross) of fuel oil, gasoline, jet fuel, and other distillates. That volume will rise. But the lack of connections between crude oil markets will lead to a sharp price split in the Disorder, with North American prices consistently being one-third (or less) that of global prices. Instead, North American prices will largely take their cue from full-cycle break-even prices in the shale fields. As of late 2016, that level is in the vicinity of $40 a barrel. Were a global break to happen in the 2016 environment, it is difficult to envision North American prices going above $75 on a sustained basis even as global prices skyrocket. Shale producers would be able to quickly ramp up output — and then would have to hit the brakes as their new supplies reached the level of total North American demand. There are now very clear markers in North America for both minimum and maximum supply levels, and prices will quickly (perhaps sometimes brutally) force shale producers to stay between the goalposts. So price volatility, yes, but within a fairly narrow range — and because of shale's rapid drilling and decline cycles — with fairly quick shifts between high and low.

The Europeans will be the second-least impacted, even if part of the global supply breakdown is Russia-centric. The belt of Central European countries from Poland to Romania will feel considerable pain, both because they are at least in part targets of Russian aggression and because their entire industrial complexes were designed to import and process Russian crude grades. None have sufficient alternative infrastructure in place to make the transition to other sources cheaply, quickly, or easily. Yet the countries on the direct Russian periphery — Poland, Hungary, Slovakia, and Romania — together import only 1mbpd, a volume small enough to allow for their direct supply with imported refined product. For these countries the question isn't so much availability, it is logistics and cost.

And while the Western Europeans are a bit out of practice, they retain remnants of their old imperial architecture — massive internationalized energy companies, mid-to-long-reach militaries, old colonial relationships that could be revitalized — that would allow them to make up for Russian crude from other sources. This is great for them and their citizens, but not so great for former colonies that could well soon be colonies once more. The Europeans will be particularly interested in places where oil infrastructure is already in place but local government is somewhat lacking. France will reprise its colonial role in West Africa, the United Kingdom will eye a "partnership" with Nigeria, particularly desperate countries might find themselves invading Libya, and so on. Prices will certainly rise — hugely — but there is a big difference between having to pay through the nose for energy, and having to pay through the nose and still not get what you need.

Third are the world's energy importers that do not live in the immediate vicinity of one of the war zones. This list runs the gamut of everyone from Cuba to Uruguay to Portugal to Mozambique to Ethiopia to Kyrgyzstan. These states are eyeing the possibility of outright economic catastrophe as oil prices quadruple (or more). For any of them to survive, they will need to strike supply deals that are better than what the naked market would normally allow. Central America will become wholly dependent upon refined product from the United States, which at least should be slightly cheaper than global norms, both because they are near the source and because there are no transport security issues so close to the American heartland. African states might find themselves forced to seek out a neocolonial relationship with their former European neighbors in exchange for preferential treatment. Spain and Portugal might find their old colonial relationships reversed as they go hat-in-hand to places like Mexico or Angola. Yet for the most part these countries will still be able to access supplies on most days, even if they cannot afford the prices that supplies require.

The fourth and final group are the Northeast Asian importers of Japan, China, South Korea, and Taiwan (NEA4), which collectively import 15mbpd (net). They sit at the very end of current global supply chains, 5,000 to 7,000 miles from the Persian Gulf. These unlucky countries will not only have to pay more than everyone else, but there simply will not be enough crude remaining by the time what is left of global supplies reach them. With the Americans no longer ensuring regional stability in Europe and the Persian Gulf — much less on the long-haul sea lanes between the Gulf and Northeast Asia — the entire development strategy of the NE4 will fail. A change of strategy is required.

They only way the Japanese, Chinese, South Koreans, and Taiwanese will be able to keep their systems fueled will be to sail thousands of miles to the Persian Gulf, take sides in a Middle Eastern knife fight in order to access to crude at the source, and physically escort the crude all the way home — or steal it from one another en route.

This is the East Asian Tanker War.

Japan's Surprising Strength

One of the great examples of conventional wisdom being misinformed is the idea that Japan is a major trading power. This certainly was true in the 1980s, when some 10 percent of global merchandise trade started in a Japanese workshop, but those heady days are long over. The 1990s brought a near-collapse in the banking sector that would have been so total that rather than attempt a repair that would have guaranteed a complete Depression-style collapse (in the best-case scenario) Tokyo instead smothered the entire system in a never-ending flood of printed money. Armageddon was avoided, but the cost was all of Japan's long-term dynamism.

After a quarter-century of economic growth averaging below 1 percent, Japan's population has become so accustomed to stagnation that it has stopped consuming, causing a slow-motion deflationary debt spiral every bit as lethal in the long term as the financial catastrophe the Japanese narrowly avoided. The funk is now so deep that most Japanese aren't even having children, making Japan the first country in the world to age past any hope of demographic recovery.[1] Unsurprisingly, Japan now suffers under the economic weight of supporting the world's oldest population: Japanese labor costs — the highest in Asia and among the highest in the world — nudge up a bit higher every year and the country now purchases more diapers for adults than for children. Combined, these intermingled crises have manifested as seven recessions in under 25 years. Perhaps most galling to the Japanese citizenry is that with every blow suffered, the technological gap between Japan and the rest of the world — and particularly among it and its Asian competitors in Korea, Taiwan, and China — has narrowed.

Such sky-high (and rising) labor costs have forced bit after bit of Japanese industry to move away, either to locate in lower-wage countries, closer to end markets, or both. Far from being a major force in world trade as it was in the 1980s, Japan in 2016 is the third least integrated major economy in the world. Japanese domestic production is now almost wholly focused not

---

1   Japan's child-per-woman figure is but 1.4.

on further shores, but instead upon the domestic market.[2] Looking forward, it is difficult to muster the optimism that this will all end well.

But never confuse "irrecoverable" or "doomed" or "decline" with "broken" or "irrelevant" or "powerless." Even if Japanese labor costs double from today's high levels, even if Japan outsources the entirety of its export industry, even if the Koreans manage to achieve their quietly-held dream of matching and then surpassing the Japanese in technical skill, Japan still matters hugely.

In fact, Japan's future strength and relevance comes directly from today's weakness.

Of what's left of Japan's trade portfolio, by far the biggest piece isn't even any specific export category at all, but energy imports. And therein lies Japan's power over the future. For while the Japanese import almost every molecule of the oil, natural gas, uranium, and coal they need, they also have a military capable of going to anywhere in the world to get it.

At the end of World War II, the Japanese signed an unconditional surrender with the Americans, who proceeded to write the new Japanese constitution. One of the key provisions was Article 9, which commits the Japan Self-Defense Forces to be just that, defensive. A complete inability to deploy its military forces to any sort of combat mission was hardwired into the Japanese system, and the Japanese navy more or less functioned as a local adjunct of the American navy. As the decades ticked by, what initially was a strategic straightjacket filtered into Japanese society, with Japanese military personnel largely seen as underachievers, unintelligent and slightly … dirty.[3]

Of course there's a big difference between perception and reality. By 1990 the Japanese navy surpassed the British navy to become the world's second most powerful. And while the Japanese and American navies work together splendidly, it isn't like the Japanese don't know how to function alone.

The spirit of constitutional law has already been pretzeled to serve current (geo)political needs.

Article 9 makes a great deal of sense in a world where Japan lives under the American nuclear and carrier umbrella and has a larger economy and

---

2   One that despite its stagnation is still the world's third-largest.

3   In hyper status-conscious Japan, that is no small point of social separation.

navy than the rest of Asia combined. Less so in the aftermath of China's rise and with an American retrenchment underway.

Consequently, successive Japanese governments have steadily weakened (the formal term is "reinterpreted") Article 9 in order to make Japan a more "normal" country. First to assist with U.N. operations in places like Cambodia. Second to allow Tokyo to deploy troops to assist with the occupation of Iraq. Third to enable anti-piracy operations off Somalia. Article 9's reinterpretation now enjoys such a deep well of support within Japan's governing elite that any media who question the mechanics of the reinterpretation process — you don't even need to challenge the merits — tend to find themselves on the receiving end of informal gag orders. A sharp international crisis would likely be all that is required for both a more formal change to the constitutional provision, as well as generate a cultural shift to celebrate rather than denigrate the military.

And a steely-eyed military it is. The Japan Maritime Self-Defense Force (JMSDF) boasts some of the best anti-mine and anti-submarine capabilities in the world. Its helicopter carriers, aircraft and Aegis radar systems not only help patrol and secure Japanese waters, but are well-suited to delivering a punishing response to any uninvited submarines or ships that would threaten the home islands. But in true Japanese fashion, the JMSDF also maintains excellent offensive capabilities via its cruise-missile-capable submarine systems and fleet of swift, well-armed destroyers.

And never make the mistake of considering Japan's order of battle the final word. Japan has been a technological and industrial superpower for centuries, particularly when it comes to anything involving the ocean. Japan floated the world's first purpose-built aircraft carrier as early as 1922 — over a decade before the Americans managed one. As the Americans step back from the world writ large, they will not only leave Northeast Asia with a very clear regional naval superpower — but they will leave that superpower with the means and need to expand its fleets. For example, Japan's Izumo-class helicopter carriers were designed with the idea of easy conversion to full jet carriers[4]. Once the order is given, Japan's navy could quickly become powerful enough to even challenge a major U.S. fleet.

And that's before you consider the tiny little issue of Northeast Asia's regional geography.

Most obviously, Japan is an island nation, and its people and military are quite at home on the ocean. But there is more to Japan's strength than simply having a capable navy — the physical location of Japan makes it far more likely to be able to wield even a moderate-sized navy with outsized capability. It all comes down to where Japan is physically positioned.

First, the gap between Japan and the Asian mainland is eight times the width of the English Channel between Great Britain and Europe. And that's just the closest point of contact to Japan's southernmost island of Kyushu, not the one that would truly matter.

The island of Honshu — home to four-fifths of Japanese — is the real deal. Not only is the island itself further east and north, but the shape of the island matters greatly: it bows out eastward into the Pacific, with the Tokyo-Yokohama-Chiba population/industrial core nestled nearly on the easternmost point. Adding in one more layer, nearly the entirety of the Japanese population lives on the Pacific side of the Home Islands rather than the Asia-facing side. This not only grants Japan's true core a bit more standoff distance, but also places a mountain chain between them and any mainland assault.

But even this belies Japan's true strategic insulation, for on the Asian side of this crossing is not the country most likely to emerge as a wartime foe — China — but instead Korea, a country desperate to not pick sides in any Japanese-Chinese throwdown. (More on Korea in a minute.)

Add in the westward bow of the Asian shoreline opposite Japan and the real distance between China's projection capability and anything truly important in Japan is more like 750 miles and buffered by the presence of Korea. While that may hardly insurmountable considering the reach of modern military aircraft, it is more than enough to grant the Japanese

---

4 For political reasons the Japanese refer to the Izumo-class as "destroyers." Yet with a deck length of 248 meters, the Izumos are larger than any military ships afloat save the American supercarriers. (An American Nimitz class' length is 333 meters.) Japan currently has one Izumo in full service with a second undergoing sea trials.

all the alert time they need to mount a layered defense. No wonder that Japanese home islands have never been successfully invaded.

Combine the Pacific-facing nature of Japan's cities with the ruggedness of the Japanese islands and you get one more factor arguing for Japanese insulation: its fractured nature. I'm not referring here to the fact that Japan's population and infrastructure are split among five major islands, but instead that the ruggedness of those islands makes Japan's population centers islands in their own right. Infrastructure among them is so thin that from a con-

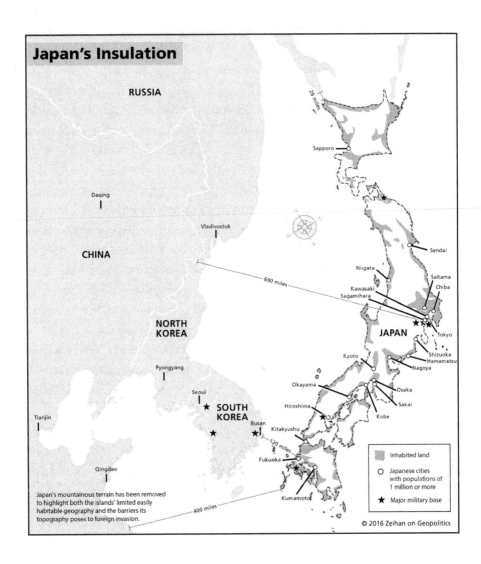

Japan's Insulation

RUSSIA

26 miles

Sapporo

Daqing

Vladivostok

CHINA

Sendai

Niigata

Saitama

690 miles

Kawasaki

Chiba

Sagamihara

NORTH
KOREA

JAPAN

Tokyo

Kyoto

Shizuoka

Pyongyang

Hamamatsu

Nagoya

Okayama

Osaka

Seoul

★ SOUTH
KOREA

Hiroshima

Sakai

Tianjin

Busan

Kobe

Kitakyushu

120 miles

Qingdao

Fukuoka

Japan's mountainous terrain has been removed
to highlight both the islands' limited easily
habitable geography and the barriers its
topography poses to foreign invasion.

Kumamoto

400 miles

Inhabited land

O   Japanese cities
     with populations of
     1 million or more

★   Major military base

© 2016 Zeihan on Geopolitics

nectivity point of view Japan's cities function like small countries, each with their own independent road, rail, power, and pipe networks.

From most perspectives this is a horrible state of affairs. Any infrastructure — whether road, rail, pipe, school, hospital, powerline, or governmental service — that serves one area cannot be leveraged to assist another. Economies of scale in physical development are largely absent. And if one of these enclave cities were to suffer catastrophic failure, there isn't all that much its physically-removed neighbors could do to render assistance. But there are perks too: were such a catastrophic failure to occur, the damage suffered from one city would not reverberate. Independent, sequestered infrastructure means that each city largely is self-sufficient. Even large-scale damage to one city would have but minimal cascade effects.

Think of what happened in the United States in the aftermath of Hurricanes Katrina and Rita in 2005: much of America's refining capacity is concentrated on the banks of the lower Mississippi in southern Louisiana and the coastal regions of eastern Texas, while a goodly portion of the country's oil and natural gas production (in pre-shale 2005) was in the Gulf of Mexico offshore. Because of storm damage — primarily from storm surges — a fair amount of U.S. petroleum production and import and refining capacity went offline all at the same time. Southern Louisiana is connected to Texas, the Midwest, the Southeast, and the Northeast not simply by the world's thickest concentration of raw and refined petroleum pipelines, but also by network of road and rail systems. Normally such an integrated system is a boon, but the hurricane-induced disruptions in the Southern Louisiana energy systems generated cascade effects, resulting in record energy prices throughout the United States and dangerously low stocks of everything from natural gas to gasoline. If not for emergency European shipments of huge volumes of refined product, the Americans may have faced outright shortages.

That simply cannot happen in Japan. There are no broad flat areas around the major Japanese coastal cities, but instead belts of steep mountains (of which Mount Fuji is merely representative). Steep mountains mean little land-based infrastructure. LNG imports to one port do not typically serve others. Oil pipeline connections between regions are non-existent, and natgas pipe systems only serve localities.[5] Because electricity interconnections are few and small, power plants serve their cities, and pretty much only their cities. There is no national grid — many portions of the country actually run on current that cannot be used by other portions. The sequestration created by Japanese topography means that an energy crisis in Osaka — or Sendai or Fukuyama or Kitakyushua or Niigata or Hamamatsu or Nagoya — is largely a local problem.

And it wouldn't even remain a local problem for long. Because of the split nature of the Japanese topography and the archipelago's utter lack of local energy resources, Japan's regions have long been forced to adapt to the mercurial nature of international energy supplies. At the time of this writing, Japan almost exclusively uses imported LNG to produce its electricity; but don't confuse current consumption patterns with a dependency. Japan has known for decades that dependence upon a single energy source or type is madness, so down to the municipal level Japan sports a vast array of mothballed coal-burning, oil-burning, and natgas-burning electricity-generating facilities.

The quintessential example of how quickly — and thoroughly — Japan can switch gears is the Fukushima nuclear disaster of March 2011. A marine earthquake triggered a tsunami that drowned a nuclear power plant, causing the world's worst nuclear disaster in a generation. A combination of legitimate concern over the stability of the Japanese nuclear power generation infrastructure and simple fear prompted the Japanese authorities to shut down the entirety of the Japanese nuclear infrastructure. The day before the tsunami hit, 51 nuclear power reactors provided Japan with 30 percent of its electricity. One month later all but 15 were shut down completely, with the remainder all offline by May 2012.[6]

Anywhere else in the world that would have been a stability-rocking experience, but in Japan things were downright placid. Japan brought natural gas, coal, and even oil-burning power plants on-line to replace the entirety

---

5   The entire country has only 3,000 miles of natural gas transmission lines (Utah or Wisconsin have more).

6   For the most part they remain offline today. As of October 2016, Japan gets less than 1 percent of its electricity from nuclear power.

of the nuclear fleet, and did so in a few weeks. Aside from some logistical juggling — such as temporarily shunting some industrial production into the night hours when electricity demand was lower — Japan absorbed the world's second-largest nuclear disaster and a catastrophic interruption to its power systems with no more than a few mild disruptions.

This sourcing flexibility gives Japan enormous strategic flexibility — even during short-term crises — to source its energy from whoever happens to be able to supply whatever, rather than being dependent upon a specific product or partner. And nearly all of Japan's major infrastructure — energy or otherwise — is on the archipelago's eastern coast. In everything from LNG imports to naval deployments, continental Asian powers just do not have the direct access required to easily disrupt Japan's operations.

Japan even has a local ace in the hole: the Russian energy-producing region of Sakhalin, an island in the Russian Far East just north of the Japanese home islands. In the 1990s several major oil firms — including supermajors ExxonMobil and Royal Dutch/Shell — convinced the Russian government to establish a completely separate contract model for energy projects on the island for firms who were unwilling to risk the Wild West style of business for which Russia had become known. The result was both some of the highest-capital and highest-technology intensive energy projects in the world.

At only 30 miles away, Sakhalin's southern coast is nearly in sight of the northern coast of the Japanese home island of Hokkaido, and Sakhalin's outputs are enough to supply one-fifth of Japan's oil and natgas needs.[7] Considering the Japanese will be willing to pay for Sakhalin energy, and that Japanese firms Mitsu and Mitsubishi are founding members of the Sakhalin consortia, it's hard to imagine that the Russians would have a problem selling Tokyo the entirety of Sakhalin output. And should the two countries fail to come to a commercial arrangement, Japan has more than enough military capability to hive the island off from Russian control.[8]

---

7   650kbpd of oil and 2bcf/d of natgas.

8   Incidentally, Sakhalin used to belong to the Japanese, so there is a not-small strain in Japanese political thinking that believes Sakhalin needs to return to the fold anyway.

In a world when naval supremacy and proximate access to energy is everything, Japan is in shockingly good shape for a country that imports all its energy.

Japan's true vulnerability isn't a direct physical one, but instead an indirect one. Any foe must be able to sever Japan's supply lines. The problem with such a strategy is that Japan's navy is both strong enough to establish and maintain deep-sea supply routes that go well out of reach of any Asian rivals, while its home ports enjoy enough strategic insulation to themselves be largely impervious to attack by anything but a vastly superior naval force. The Japanese are only truly vulnerable to another major naval power — one that could assault the country from the east and so do so without land-based air support.

That is most certainly not China.

China: A Study in Vulnerability

At a glance it seems that China is actually in a better position than Japan. Its southern coast is a cool 2,000 miles closer to the Persian Gulf than Japan, seemingly simplifying its maritime supply logistics. China also sports the advantage of having continental suppliers in the former Soviet Union. Kazakhstan and Russia both have pipelines that ship crude directly into Chinese territory; about 110kbpd of Kazakh crude enters China's Xinjiang region in the far northwest, while a transport corridor expansion scheduled to be upgraded by late 2017 will be able to deliver some 600kbpd of Russian crude directly to the Daqing refining center in China's northeast. A particularly bold Japanese strike might be able to disrupt the Russian pipe, but the Kazakh pipe — not to mention a bevy of rail connections to both former Soviet states that could probably supply another 500kbpd — is simply too deep in the Chinese interior to be vulnerable. Unlike Japan, China has domestic oil production as well. Simply put, China "only" needs to import about 40 percent of its oil needs via the water, compared to Japan's near 100-percent reliance on maritime imports.

That, unfortunately for the Chinese, is where the good news stops.

First, there's the inconvenient fact that relative vulnerability, absolute vulnerability, relative needs and absolute needs are four very different things. Japan is nearly 100 percent dependent (relative) on oil imports for its roughly 4mbpd (absolute) in oil needs, while China is 65 percent dependent (relative) on oil imports for its roughly 12mbpd of demand. So while China's relative dependence is considerably lower, at nearly 8mbpd its absolute dependency is double. No wonder that the Chinese are engaged in a mammoth infrastructure build-out campaign to tap Kazakh petroleum, as well as providing thousands of technicians to Iran to help expand Iranian oil output. Anything to increase sourcing opportunities.

Second, the Chinese system is far more dependent upon open sea lanes and markets than the Japanese market. Based on who is doing the math, somewhere between 40 percent and 50 percent of the Chinese economy is directly involved in international commerce. International links don't "just" let China keep the lights on, they are the basis for the Chinese system. This system requires a large-scale export industry not simply to generate economic growth, but to generate mass employment to maintain social and political stability. Japan used to look like this before the 1990 crash, but in the 25 years since Japan hasn't just become far more efficient in its use of raw materials and energy, it also has forward-positioned much of its industrial base in other countries to reduce labor expenditures, political friction and currency risk. Today, Japan's overall exposure to all things international is less than one-third that of China. When the Americans cease making the global sea lanes safe for all, triggering the global Disorder and the trade breakdown that comes with it, Japan will suffer a painful multi-year recession.

China will lose economic and political coherence.

Third, China (unlike Japan) lacks the tools and placement to grope its way through the Disorder. Free trade works because the Americans have sublimated their direct economic interests in favor of a global security system; the Americans indirectly subsidize the entire world by putting the American navy at the service of the global commons while keeping their markets open and running unfathomably large trade deficits. China has less than zero interest in taking the Americans' place in this way. Yes, Beijing wants the power the Americans' wield, but it certainly has no desire to subsidize the rest of the planet. If anything, Beijing wants the opposite.

Fourth, even if the Chinese were willing to put dozens of countries' economic well-being above their own, they utterly lack the military capacity — or even potential — to craft, impose, or maintain a replacement system. China isn't a maritime power like Japan or the United States, but instead a continental power, meaning it must maintain a military that is actually concerned with countering other land forces. The vast majority of Chinese history has been characterized by conflict — whether from internal warfare or invasion and occupation by outsiders. This far-from-minor-consideration gobbles up enough resources to prevent the Chinese from putting their back into a naval buildout.

Additionally, most — within and beyond China — drastically underestimate just how big of a buildout the Chinese would need to execute if they were to secure regional sea lanes for themselves.

To begin, China is in a box. Roughly paralleling the Chinese coasts are a series of archipelagic countries — Japan, Taiwan, the Philippines, Indonesia, Malaysia, and Singapore. Navies are expensive, but in comparison jets and missiles that can sink ships are cheap. Even if the Chinese navy were a match for the Japanese navy — and even if the Japanese navy were stupid enough to engage the Chinese within range of the Chinese mainland's air support — locking the Chinese within this first island chain isn't all that hard.

Next, keep in mind that it isn't enough for the Chinese navy to achieve breakout, but instead the Chinese would need to achieve permanent breakout — China dares not risk blasting open a door through the first island chain only to have that door slam shut right after its navy sails through. That would trap the Chinese fleet on the wrong side of the island chain, far from its bases, supplies, and air support. Permanent breakout means preventing the island chain from hosting any hostile forces, whether those forces be local or from far-abroad foes. That in turn would not only require the sinking of all local navies, but the neutralization of all local political authorities either through mass intimidation or outright occupation. Such neutralization would need to be thorough: China doesn't just need regular safe transit for its hardened military vessels, but for the unarmed merchant marine as well.

Finally, China could not stop with "just" the first island chain. While the economies of Japan and Southeast Asia are certainly sizable, nearly all are raw materials importers as well. They simply lack the inputs and consumer heft to support a behemoth as large as China. Doubly so if the Chinese are occupying them and sucking them dry to service their home economy.

This third requirement makes breakout impossible. China doesn't just need to be able to secure the first island chain, it must also be able to sail without molestation to commodity suppliers in the Middle East, Africa and Latin America, as well as to end markets in Western Europe and North America. Unlike the American-dominated maritime system, which functions because the Americans have no economic skin in the game and so their allies have a vested interest in cooperating, any Chinese-dominated maritime system would be based upon, well, Chinese domination: the forced occupation of the first island chain, the militarization of trade to and from East Asia, the denial of competitors from accessing a variety of energy and resources supplies, the forcing open of end markets at the point of a gun.

Chinese "success" would require a commitment to foreign military occupation far in excess of what the Germans and Japanese combined achieved during World War II at a reach in excess of what the Americans achieved during the Cold War.

And that's only the external problem. In many ways China's internal crisis is even more extreme.

In *The Accidental Superpower*, I dealt at length with the cultural and even linguistic differences between various Chinese regions, all rooted deeply in the country's physical geography. A quick refresher:

• Northern China is a broad, open plain that enabled early cultural unification of the Han ethnicity. However, its size and lack of internal barriers made it a terrifying real-life version of the board game Risk, resulting in millennia of war and ethnic cleansing among constantly competing political authorities. There is nothing unique about the rule of the current group at the top of the heap — the Communist Party — which also means you should not expect that rule to be permanent. As of 2016 that plain is home to about 500 million people, most of whom do not live on the coast.

- The belt of cities from Shanghai to Hong Kong is radically different. Unlike the deep interior of the North China Plain, the southern cities squat on smallish pockets of land with their backs to rugged and often subtropical hills and mountains. They have no hinterland to speak of and all face the sea. Survival — much less economic success — means working with whoever can reach them, and the most common way to reach these cities is by boat. Since these cities are dependent upon food from elsewhere, they've not tended to be too picky about who brings it — which historically has meant foreigners instead of northern Chinese.

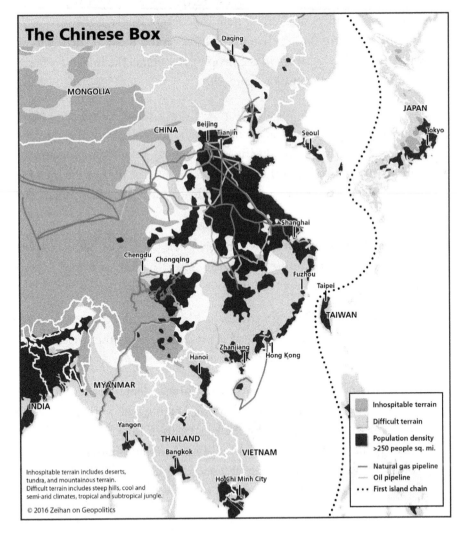

The Chinese Box

Inhospitable terrain includes deserts, tundra, and mountainous terrain.
Difficult terrain includes steep hills, cool and semi-arid climates, tropical and subtropical jungle.

© 2016 Zeihan on Geopolitics

Inhospitable terrain

Difficult terrain

Population density >250 people sq. mi.

— Natural gas pipeline
— Oil pipeline
••• First island chain

Unsurprisingly, during China's 20th century inward-looking period under the tender mercies of the Mao regime, the normally cosmopolitan southern Chinese cities endured some of the most crippling conditions in their history — complete with crushing poverty and famine. Some 200 million Chinese live in this belt of southern coastal cities.

• Then there is the interior, which in most cases begins less than 300 miles from the coast. With a few notable exceptions like the littoral cities of the Yangtze and the region of Sichuan at the Yangtze's head of navigation, the vast swathes of internal Chinese territories are physically isolated and thus painfully poor. Adding political complications to the mix, most of China's minority groups live in the interior and most of them are not exactly thrilled to be living in the People's Republic. The interior is home to the remaining 600 million Chinese.

Making matters worse for all Chinese is that China's energy geography is even more fractured than the country's economic and political geography.

China's primary energy-producing zone long has been the region around the refinery city of Daqing at the northernmost extreme of the North China Plain. Daqing's fortunes are a window into the strategic thinking of the Politburo itself:

• In the 1950s, Daqing output was barely a trickle; China had to import crude from its Communist ally in the Soviet Union, and in doing so found itself forced to be a Stalinist foot soldier in the Korean War.

• By the early-1960s, Daqing's trickle had become a flood and China became oil self-sufficient. China had achieved the economic wherewithal to initiate, and survive, the Sino-Soviet split.

• The 1979 economic opening expanded Chinese economic growth, and with it oil energy demand, overwhelming Daqing's capacity and necessitating large-scale oil imports by the late 1980s. China found itself with no choice but to remain neutral in all international politics (save those involving Taiwan) for the next two decades, lest it rock the boat and offend potential import sources.

- By 2005, declining Daqing output — and rising Chinese demand — forced another evolution: an economic partnership with the Russians, who in 2010 constructed a pipeline to supply Daqing's increasingly-idling refineries with Russian crude.

China's second-largest energy province is the Tarim Basin, a remote and barren desert region in China's far west. First meaningful production is barely a decade and a half old, yet Tarim shows considerable promise. It is (highly) unlikely to ever match the long-term grandeur of Daqing, but its output has proven sufficiently large and reliable to prompt the Chinese to build a bundle of pipelines as part of their West-East network. As Central Asia opened to Chinese investment in the late 2000s, cross-border links have brought Kazakh, Uzbek and even Turkmen oil and natural gas into the same West-East system.

The common thread in the Daqing and Tarim stories is the end-market story. Considering Daqing's location at the northern extreme of the North China Plain, the large population base of northern China, and the presence of the Politburo and military core in northern China, every drop of Daqing crude processed in the past quarter-century has been consumed in the north. Tarim (and Central Asian) energy flows through what is the world's second-longest pipeline system, a system expressly designed to service Beijing and the North China Plain. Though a bit of these energy flows do reach Shanghai (at the plain's southeastern extreme), all the meaningful energy provinces in the country — and all of the land-based energy imports — service the political core in the north rather than the economically dynamic urban arc in the south.

Consequently, the southern coastal cities from Hong Kong to Shanghai have a Japanese level of dependence upon maritime petroleum imports — over 4mbpd needed and nearly 100 percent imported. Worse yet, more than 80 percent of such supplies tends to come from the Middle East.

Which means China is set up for the worst of falls.

China lacks the internal production capacity to cover more than one-third its energy needs. Its navy is utterly incapable of day-in, day-out, sustained long-range power projection that might enable it to solve its energy weaknesses. Its political core hordes energy locally, because to do otherwise would risk breakdown in the seething heartland. The part of the country that is economically dynamic and most dependent upon foreign energy also is the part of the country that is the hardest to control and is the most comfortable working with foreigners.

In the current era, the southern Chinese in many ways have the best of both worlds: they can access international markets and capital while benefiting from the economies of scale that membership in the broader Chinese system grants. But introduce a global security and energy crisis, and this logic turns on its ear. Northern China has a good portion of what it needs locally regarding energy, and any effort to use military tactics to secure supplies for southern China brings the Chinese directly into conflict with the very powers whose cooperation the southern Chinese need to achieve local economic stability. Simply put, the southern Chinese cities need a partnership with foreign powers if they are to be successful, and the northern Chinese core needs hostility with those same powers in order to maintain Chinese unity.

Anything that drives a wedge between North and South — and energy shortages would do that in spades — would force the South to either accept destitution or seek partnership with outside powers that could help them keep the lights on. Since these southern cities — even under the centralized, north-dominated system — are the only provinces that are truly wired into international supply chains, it wouldn't take more than a small crisis to get the ball rolling. And a convoy war of a length measured in the thousands of miles would be far more than a small crisis.

Furthermore, China lacks Japan's excess capacity in terms of power generation of fuel supply. Just as Japan's enclavic geography and utter lack of domestic energy supplies has forced it to develop power-generation redundancy and fuel flexibility, China's own geography has led its power sector along a radically different road. China has a local fuel — brown coal — and has it in abundance. Consequently, in most of the past 20 years, China has added more coal-burning capacity than most of the rest of the world combined despite lip service to international climate goals and rising domestic dissatisfaction with pollution levels. Additionally, Chinese economic growth means that power demand has risen relentlessly for a generation. In a crisis, China simply cannot bring spare capacity on-line, because electricity has often been a limiting factor in development. In contrast, the Japanese economy has in effect stalled since 1990 and so has oodles of spare power generation facilities.

Finally, and perhaps most important from Beijing's point of view, China knows it lacks the naval capacity to force open (and the good reputation to garner cooperation in) supply lines should the international environment sour. It dare not increase its dependence upon foreign energy with war looming. China must rely upon electricity-generating fuels that can be supplied domestically and/or are relatively close by whenever possible. For China, coal is the only answer.

The Taiwanese Pry Bar

There is an exceedingly long list of reasons why China will be in an exceedingly worse position vis-à-vis Japan in the struggle to access global energy, but perhaps the most critical reason is Taiwan. Some of the horrors of China's participation in WWII had nothing to do with foreigners, but were instead homegrown. During the war, the Chinese were engaged in a parallel — and more brutal — conflict: a civil war between the Communist forces of Mao Zedong and the Nationalist forces of Chiang Kai-Shek that claimed nearly 10 million lives.[9] In the end, Mao proved victorious, with Chiang's forces retreating to the island of Formosa in December 1949. There, they established a sort of government-in-exile that formally claims to be the true government of all of China. Technically the country is known as the Republic of China — in contrast to the People's Republic on the mainland. These days, everyone who isn't Chinese simply calls it Taiwan.

Tensions between the two Chinas have ebbed and flowed in the decades since, but ironically the two countries' competing claims to be the sole government of all of China have provided a degree of built-in stability. So long as Taiwan doesn't claim to be a separate entity, Beijing can beat the nationalist drum without having to go to war. Should Taiwan formally end

9   That's a fairly conservative estimate that covers the entirety of the conflict from the first series Communist uprisings in 1927 to the nationalists' defeat in 1949.

the fiction that Formosa and the mainland are one people, then red China might find itself forced to launch the world's largest amphibious assault since the Korean War. That's exactly the sort of military operation the Chinese military is not prepared for, and one that could turn the nationalism that the Politburo so likes to whip up against them. For the Taiwanese, the concern is much more direct: so long as the mainland claims that Taiwan is a wayward province, the Taiwanese face the specter of war with the world's largest army and air force.

And so the Taiwanese shape their foreign and security policies accordingly. Taiwan is one of the United States' most enthusiastic allies — although Washington's formal subscription to the one-China fiction makes Taiwan's ally status decidedly unofficial. Taiwan also has taken great pains to cozy up to all things Japanese, and is probably the only Asian country that views Japan's recent moves to build out its military's deployment and technical capacity — and its political shifts away from pacifism — as an unmitigated positive.[10]

It's a quick and easy match up. The Japanese island chain doesn't end at Okinawa — about 400 miles from Taipei — but extends all the way to Yonaguni-shima, which is only 100 miles away. Japan can provide air force cover for the bulk of Taiwan without even deploying to Taiwan itself. And as the center and largest piece of the first island chain, Taiwan is the (absolutely willing) centerpiece of any effort to keep China bottled up.

When global energy shortages manifest, expect the Taiwanese to partner up with the Japanese on Day One — which is an utter disaster for the mainland Chinese.

First, most of China loses the ability to reliably import or export anything by water — oil included. Using Taiwan as a southern anchor, the Japanese islands block all direct access to all Chinese ports north of Fujian. That's roughly three-quarters of the Chinese population and two-thirds of Chinese export capacity that it becomes locked out of what remains of the international system. At that point, the only route through which Fujian and

---

10   Other Asian states might welcome Japan as a counter against China, but many have memories of Japan from WWII that force them to view Japan's return with a bit of trepidation mixed in.

areas north can "access" the wider world is the 100-mile-wide Taiwan Strait itself — all of which lies in easy range of Taiwanese air power.

Second, aircraft based on or near Taiwan could reach shipping not just in that Strait, but easily as far south as the greater Hong Kong region. And while Taiwan could hardly launch a hermetically-sealed embargo, Taiwanese forces backed by Japanese forces could consistently harass southern Chinese shipping out of range of Chinese land-based aircraft. The Chinese can — and will — hurl hundreds of ballistic missiles at Taiwan and inflict considerable damage. But bereft of the ability to launch a sustained amphibious assault, China can only blunt the pain that Taiwan can inflict.

Third, and perhaps of most concern to the political bosses in Beijing, in a war scenario Taiwan has intelligence and linguistic access to the belt of China's southern coastal cities that already would be smarting under energy shortages. Taiwan could allow select cargos to come and go unmolested to select cities, using global trade and energy access to peel these cities out of the People's Republic. Taiwan becoming the true Chinese government is a dream several (dozen) steps removed from reality, but that doesn't mean Taiwan can't nudge the mainland into a political breakup.

Korea's Day in the Sun

The key player in this — in everything from the Chinese-Japanese rivalry to internal Chinese politicking — isn't Taipei or Beijing or even Tokyo, but Seoul.

Korea's history was a painful one long before rival superpowers carved it into spheres of influence after World War II and devastated it in an unprecedented civil war with global involvement.

Korea's difficulty begins with the peninsula's geography. The most important thing to understand is that Korea is far less than what it looks like on a map. About the same size as Kansas, the combined Korean peninsula should, in theory, be a reasonably potent middle power. Unfortunately, roughly 70 percent of the country is steep hill and mountain. Most of the country's flattish land runs down the western coast, but there is enough steep terrain interspersed even here to break up populations, giving Korea's identity a distinctively broken, clannish feel. All told, the Koreans only have an amount of useful land a little larger than the U.S. state of Maryland, with South Korea's portion only just a touch bigger than Connecticut.

Zoom out and the regional geography doesn't help a bit. To Korea's east is the nearby Japanese archipelago, home to a people eminently at home on the ocean and capable of choosing the time and scope of their conflicts with peoples near and far. As Japan's closest neighbors, the Koreans have often felt the sting of Japanese raids and the pain of Japanese occupations. While Japanese actions in places like Nanking and Bataan and Pearl Harbor hold a tighter grip on the global mind, Japan flat out occupied all of Korea 35 years before World War II involved Western powers, and maintained its hold on every scrap of Korean territory right up unto its surrender.

To the west and north is a power less predatory from the Korean point of view, but every bit as omnipresent. In times of internal strength, the Chinese have always found the Koreans the easiest neighbor to invade. In those rare times that the northern Chinese manage to float a navy, Korea is the first stop. In times of internal weakness, the Koreans often find themselves sucked into China's chaos. It's a tough neighborhood, and Korea has traditionally been on the receiving end.

Not this time.

Bretton Woods removed Japan from the board and granted the Koreans access to international markets. Add in an American military presence as part of the Cold War alliance structure, and today's Korea has little in common with the Korea of ages past. Today's South Korea is a highly advanced technocracy with top-notch infrastructure, one of the world's most capable military complexes, and a strong enough technical and industrial base that it could go nuclear during a staff meeting. Today's North Korea is already nuclear and sports a million-man army. Both Koreas, in part because they have faced off these past seven decades, punch well above their weights. And even though they are still the neighborhood runts, no one can simply roll over them as in ages past. Moreover, their physical location vis-à-vis their neighbors — triply so in the case of South Korea — makes them the key to the East Asian energy contest.

While South Korea does have a capable navy, long-range deployments to the Persian Gulf with the intent of bringing back a supertanker of crude daily are simply beyond its sustainable solo capacity. Even with a strict energy diet, the South Koreans will have no choice but to throw their lot in with one of their bigger neighbors.

Which way they go will be paramount.

A pro-China South Korea grants northern China something it has rarely had: strategic depth versus Japan. Korean partnership with China would make the Yellow Sea a no-go zone for the Japanese navy and protect the bulk of North and Central Chinese waters. With Korean assistance, Chinese power projection could reasonably threaten all Japanese population and industrial centers as well, forcing the Japanese to massively expand their combat envelope to include not simply the Northwest Pacific, but all the home islands. Efforts spent that far north would immeasurably weaken Japan's ability to reach all the way to the Persian Gulf in a consistent manner.

Conversely, a pro-Japan South Korea would be damning for the Chinese. Japanese air assets could threaten the entirety of the Chinese coastal shipping, including all northern Chinese coastal cities themselves. With northern China under direct threat, the needs and interests of the southern Chinese cities would seem a far less present concern — greatly hastening southern Chinese secessionist efforts. Korea's leaning toward Tokyo would instantly put China on the defensive not simply internationally, but domestically. China would find itself firmly pushed in the direction of yet another brutal internal conflict.

The question is, who do the Koreans side with?

Looking at current geopolitical alignments, it would seem that China wouldn't even be considered. With the singular exception of Sri Lanka — a country whose loyalty China flat out purchased — nearly every country between the Chinese coast and Pakistan has become paranoid about China's rise. China's navy may have the ability to cruise-missile its way beyond the first island chain, but then what? The bulk of its forces lack the ability to sustain operations over the 10,000-mile-plus round trip required to fetch Persian Gulf oil without a couple of stops on the way out and the way back. Even assuming the Indians do not do something about Sri Lanka's strategic realignments (which is in itself a laughable assumption), China must strike a deal with — or more likely coerce or invade — at least a couple additional countries along the way. And, even if China succeeded against Japan (and

Taiwan and Korea), it wouldn't give the Chinese the freedom of movement that they need. The Chinese economy also needs unrestricted access to end markets. Blindly firing waves of cruise missiles as part of the process to secure your energy supplies is a piss-poor way to ensure that your end markets want to buy your wares. And the Koreans know it.

It seems that Japan would be the obvious choice. Japan has the far more powerful and experienced navy, which is easily capable of operating well beyond China's first island chain. Its fleet has the ships and the reach to cover the distances in question without need of bases along the way, yet it also can offer big dollops of financial and technical add to en-route countries should the need arise. It has a strong record of paying for things in cash and up front, and has a seven-decade track record for not taking sides in other people's politics. Of the four Northeast Asian powers, it is the one the Saudis and Iranians are most likely to perceive as broker both honest and capable. In part because of these factors, and in part because Beijing wants to fly its flag above Taipei, the Taiwanese will clearly and quickly side with the Japanese in all things relating to energy convoys. Its seems the Koreans should just go with the obvious.

But for the Koreans the issue just isn't that simple.

As the NEA4 takes matters into their own hands as regards sea-lane access and energy supplies, they actually will be shooting at each other on the open water. Bretton Woods-era American strategy is absolute freedom of the seas — seeing allies and rivals alike aggressively disregarding that precept will prompt the Americans to wash their hands of the whole region. The end result isn't just a pull-back of U.S. naval forces, but also an end to America's strategic overwatch of and American troop presence in South Korea. South Korea is simply too deep in the regional mess — and needs excessively high volumes of imported energy — to make a compelling case for ongoing American intervention. On the flip side, it means that American preferences for who the South Koreans should partner with in the Tanker War don't even fill a bucket of spit.

Leaving the decision to purely domestic issues, Japan is far from the Koreans' favorite regional power. To the Koreans, Japan's 1910-1945 occupation of the Korean peninsula was nothing less than an attempted genocide, and Japan's ongoing inability to come to terms with its role in World

War II in general and the Korean occupation in specific constantly keeps Japanese-Korean relations from being more than a cold partnership. Tokyo's December 2015 admittance of guilt for forcing Korean women into prostitution during the war was made with healing this rift in mind, but from most Koreans' point of view that admittance came 60 years too late.

Economically, Japan and Korea are far from natural partners. Both countries' demographic declines are far advanced, well beyond the point of possible recovery, and so both represent rapidly shrinking markets that rely upon protectionism to husband economic strength. Korea also has advanced to a point that it regularly is competing with top-notch Japanese products in everything from automotive to cellular to household appliances. Korean competition with the Chinese is also fierce, but the tech gap between Korea and China is wider while the Chinese market is both somewhat less pro-

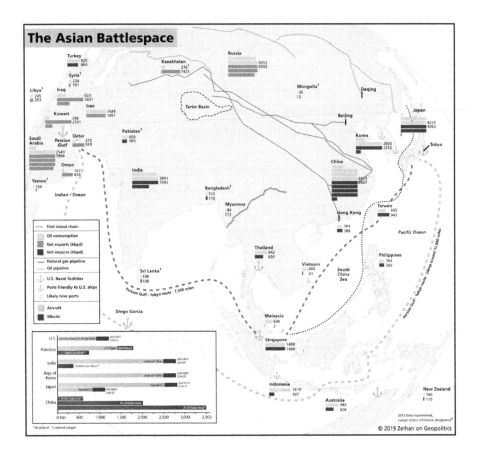

tected and larger than Japan's. If we are moving into a world where market access is hard to come by, China simply has more to offer the Koreans than the Japanese — and with less emotional baggage. And there is the niggling problem of if Korea does side with Japan, what does Japan — now with a navy that is potent and battle-hardened — do once China is thrown down?

The Koreans have long lived in the shadow of their more powerful neighbors, and have longed to have their day in the sun. They're about to get their wish, good and hard.

Enemy at the Gates:
Vietnam, the Philippines, and Malaysia

And that's just the war's beginning. The next stage of the conflict will rage around the southeastern extremities of the Asian continent. This region is no stranger to trade or naval warfare. In the Middle Ages it was the origin of the spice trade. In more recent times the Strait of Malacca became the world's busiest trade artery. But disrupt Hormuz and the picture shifts drastically. The NEA4 will be competing not only for those much-reduced energy supplies but also crucial naval basing rights in order to secure the routes themselves.

While the Northeast Asians will be desperate, all have a few options as to how they can meet their needs. Taiwan and Korea have the luxury of being able to pick sides. Japan has access to Sakhalin, deep-ocean routes, and the Pacific Basin. All three can — to a degree — be flexible in the energy inputs they use, and so all three can be somewhat flexible and patient in their efforts.

But not China. Japan and Taiwan completely block all northern and eastern options, so China has no choice but to sail south. China lacks fuel-switching capacity. It must secure oil. The result will be a redux of the bloody campaigns waged in WWII for control of the region's waterways, with Japan and China the primary competitors in a game to secure basing rights among the islands and littoral waterways of archipelagic Southeast Asia.

The first phase of the East Asian Tanker War will be fought in the South China Sea, with the flanking countries of Vietnam, the Philippines, and Malaysia being the first in the crosshairs.

First comes the long, coastal state of **Vietnam**. Think of the country like a barbell — wide on the ends and narrow in the middle. The northern and southern "bells" are home to the sprawling metropolises of Hanoi and Ho Chi Minh City (formerly Saigon), the headquarters for the two sides in Vietnam War of 1946-1975.[11] The former North's ongoing efforts to grind away any opposition from the former South is a generational process that has at least another couple of decades to run. The result is a young and dynamic economy aching to use the country's agricultural, mineral, and labor wealth to take the country into the future, ruled by a gerontocratic cabal more comfortable with hero projects and wood shampoos.

Vietnam's long coastline along the South China Sea will be its most strategic asset and greatest liability. On the asset side, Vietnam has found a series of moderate oil deposits in its offshore, most notably the Nam Con Son Basin off the Mekong Delta, which have increased the country's reserves by a nearly factor of six since 1995 to 4.4 billion barrels. Long dependent upon its Soviet ally for all its fuels, Vietnam now has a diversified energy import base and actually (net) exports a small volume of crude despite its rapidly growing domestic demand. Maintaining that position requires steady international investment into projects that Vietnam cannot operate itself.

On the liability side, these deposits are in the South China Sea. One of the best-performing economic sectors in the country's recent history — and one of the few that Vietnam's aging generals and apparatchiks don't suspect of being seditious — Vietnam's oil industry lies along the path of would-be Chinese militarized oil shipments.

Vietnam's leaders also fear — and likely are correct — that the Chinese will come for them. For starters, the Vietnamese and Chinese loathe each other. Every time Southern China has been involved in empire, its sights have turned to the Red River region of northern Vietnam. Sometimes the result is tribute, sometimes occupation, but always war. The last Chinese

---

11   This date range includes the Vietnamese liberation war from the French, as well as the subsequent civil war and American involvement.

invasion is more recent than most think, occurring on the heels of the American withdrawal (1974-1975).[12]

Then there's simple strategy: some 2,000 miles of Vietnam's coastline directly parallels what the Chinese will consider a national security zone. Making matters worse, one of the world's best deepwater ports, Cam Ranh Bay, lies at an ideal jumping-off point from the South China Sea into the Natuna Sea and Gulf of Thailand, making it a superb location for a naval base for either the Chinese seeking to project power throughout the region, for the Japanese seeking to deny the Chinese sea access, or for the Americans seeking high leverage at a low cost.

Directly opposite the sea from Cam Ranh is Subic, an equally good port in the **Philippines** that was one of the Americans' largest naval facilities throughout the Cold War.

---

12   The Vietnamese treated the Chinese to the same sort of hospitality they extended to the Americans, with more or less the same results.

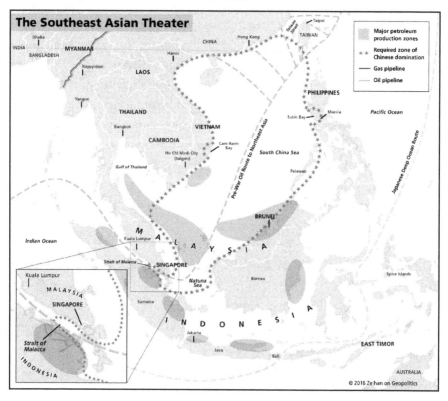

The Southeast Asian Theater

The archipelago of the Philippines has served as the crossroads of Europe, the Islamic world, East Asia, and even the United States for the past millennia. What the Philippines never could do, however, is stand on its own. Outsiders have found playing the Philippines' 20 "primary" ethnolinguistic groups and dozens of "major" islands against each other child's play, just as they've found those islands' location between Southeast Asia, Northeast Asia, and the Central Pacific critical. (Manipulation and conquering are, of course, completely different from occupation. Many powers have found it easy to sail into the Philippines and conquer a bit of it. No one has particularly enjoyed what comes next.)

The people of the Philippines, as one might surmise, have been disunified and weak for almost the entirety of their history. The lack of unity and the separated nature of all those islands also made them poor: no central authority local to the islands could ever raise the resources required to build basic infrastructure, much less develop the area into anything greater. Only with the onset of Bretton Woods and the elimination of all the imperial navies did the Philippines get its first true taste of unity and independence (albeit as an American client state).

Which means that the Philippines faces a bleak future indeed. America's first steps away from its Bretton Woods global engagement were taken in the Philippines with the 1992 Subic Bay closure. Since then American involvement and interest in all things Filipino has been thin at the best of times. Particularly in the coming Disorder, the Philippines is just too exposed and too poor for a forward-positioned military asset — no matter how nice a spot Subic is. Unsurprisingly, it is Manila that has been shrieking the loudest since 1992 about Chinese imperialism.

Though Japan would certainly like to hold both Cam Ranh and Subic, and though both Vietnam and the Philippines would choose Japanese largess over Chinese domination, the simple fact is that China cannot tolerate a foreign presence in either, while the Japanese (and the Americans) have other options. Unfortunately for the Chinese, the only way to keep both premier ports out of enemy hands is to make those ports utterly unattractive.

Disrupting the Philippines will require a lower outlay of effort. The "country" is unstable in the best of times, and with the breakdown of the global trade order and sharp rises in energy prices it will not require much pushing to make it fall apart. China can "simply" play the various ethnic groups and islands against each other, spawning a raft of new secessionist movements to complement those that Manila never really got under control. The archipelago will devolve into a series of shifting skirmishes as various local authorities adapt to the falling power of Manila and the rising Japanese-Chinese rivalry for their loyalty. Remember, China doesn't need to occupy the whole country, it just needs to keep Subic out of the game and prevent any foreign air force from basing on the island of Palawan, a long, thin strip of land that roughly parallels China's would-be tanker routes.

Vietnam will be harder. Unlike Subic, which would grant strategic advantage, Cam Ranh is a strategic necessity since the eastern bulge in the Vietnamese coastline puts the bay at the halfway point between southern China and the Strait of Malacca. Control of the Cam Ranh would enable China to efficiently and effectively project power 1,000 miles further south of the Chinese coast as well as grant Chinese naval forces air cover all the way to Singapore. That means the Chinese actually have to invade and hold a spot of land roughly halfway down the coast of Vietnam, forcing the Chinese into an open-ended occupation against a people who have millennia of expertise in fighting as guerrillas, and who tend to celebrate their hatred of all things Chinese.

Next down the line, **Malaysia** enters the new era in a somewhat more favorable position. Malaysia enjoys the best educational, civil, power, and transport infrastructure in the region after Singapore. Its economy is well-diversified among everything from primary commodities like timber and rubber to advanced manufacturing into electronics and heavy chemicals.

It also sports — by far — the region's most sophisticated energy firm. State oil company Petronas excels not only in refining and transport, but also makes a name for itself in shallow offshore production. Petronas' success rests on two pillars: the country's diversified and sophisticated economy enables it to master many technologies, and it hasn't let this success go to its head — for things Petronas cannot do it is very willing to partner with foreign firms. Despite having old fields and rapidly growing local demand,

Malaysia's total oil deficit is only about 150kbpd[13] and it is one of the world's largest LNG exporters.

Shift to the new strategic environment and expect outside firms to flood in to leverage what is at heart a technologically and culturally savvy country with a technologically and culturally savvy Petronas. Malaysia's modest oil deficit could become a modest surplus in a few short years, and as Malaysia already possesses the region's second-largest refining and oil/product storage facilities, it stands to make massive profits selling to everyone who needs energy. With such perfect pre-positioning, all that remains is for the Malaysians to hope that the convoy wars pass them by.

No such luck.

That's because long before supertankers were a regular sight in the Malacca Strait, there were Chinese. Sprinkled throughout the region by silk and spice trading links that date back to antiquity, (southern) Chinese exist in urban pockets all along the sea lanes that link the Indian subcontinent to China itself. The easy familial and ethnic links among these pockets make Southeast Asia's Chinese the region's natural bankers and traders.[14] By far their most politically and economically significant concentration is in contemporary Malaysia where they account for a quarter of the 30-million-strong citizenry — and apocryphally generate at least two-thirds of its economy, relegating the majority Malays to society's lower rungs.

China will undoubtedly attempt to utilize Malaysia's Chinese minority as a fifth column either to help the Chinese get basing rights (if Malaysia tilts toward China) or to destabilize the government (if Malaysia does anything else).

The ruling Malays are well aware of Chinese power, both at home and abroad, and that fear shapes the Malaysian political space. The country's ethnic Malays have determinedly — almost desperately — maintained full ethnic Malay control over all aspects of the police, judiciary, military, and internal security services. And if push comes to shove, the (almost exclusively Malay) authorities in Kuala Lumpur are more than willing to sacrifice

---

13   666kbpd production versus 814kbpd demand.

14   Locals often refer to them as the "Jews of Asia," with all the connotations and implications that the reference implies.

some of the country's economic dynamism if it means the Malays stay atop the heap.

As for the East Asian Tanker War, it's highly unlikely Malaysia will catch a break. Even in the unlikely possibility that Kuala Lumpur can cast itself as fully neutral in the conflict, the fact remains that nearly all of Malaysia's domestic oil production is in the Natuna Sea — a body of water transected by all those trade routes between the Malacca Strait and the South China Sea. No matter how well the Malaysians try to keep their heads down, the most visceral part of the Tanker War will be fought right in the middle of their most important territory.

Vietnam. The Philippines. Malaysia. China must bring these three countries to heel. Failure to do so will shut off China's only maritime supply route, end the Tanker War before it begins, and result in breakdown of the Chinese economic system and/or the immediate breakup of Chinese political unity.

No wonder the Chinese are attempting to create military fortifications in the region. Since 2014 the Chinese military has been working to build islands of sufficient size to serve as air bases and forward naval supply centers. Vietnam, the Philippines, and Malaysia's own navies can do little to counter such Chinese efforts without outside assistance, and China's actions are specifically tailored to intimidate the trio of littoral states into acquiescing to Chinese authority in the region.

It hasn't worked, and I'm not referring to the 2016 ruling by the International Tribunal for the Law of the Sea that China's claims to the region are legally null and void. Vietnam, the Philippines, and Malaysia have all reached out to any (other) power who is willing to help them. The United States has given lip service to freedom of navigation but has remained largely absent. Japan, not so much. And in a hot war these Chinese "island" bases, far beyond Chinese land-based air support, would not last more than a few minutes against the power and reach of the Japanese navy.

War is Good for Business:
Singapore, Indonesia, Thailand, and Myanmar

Beyond Malaysia the competition takes on a very different tone. The countries involved have deeper roots, stronger capabilities, more strategic insulation, and better and more capable allies. The Chinese (and Japanese) cannot simply brute-force bully their way through. Bullets must give way to negotiations, flotillas to diplomats. While the northern trio of Vietnam, the Philippines, and Malaysia are likely to suffer from being in the firing line, the southern trio of Singapore, Indonesia, and Thailand are likely to profit hugely.

Located at the southernmost tip of the peninsula occupied by Thailand and Malaysia, the city-state of **Singapore** is an economic powerhouse. A good example of how technology and chutzpah[15] can transform a chunk of land, the city-country has transformed itself from a site of low-end manufacturing to high-tech development, a key transshipment and refining hub, and global banking and insurance giant.

In the world soon-to-be, Singapore simultaneously faces disaster and success.

Disaster in that the city-country's entire development plan has been to make the most of the Bretton Woods world by leveraging its physical location atop the Strait of Malacca to the utmost. End Bretton Woods and the world's thickest, richest trade route becomes something less impressive — and so does Singapore.

Singapore still has five trump cards to play:

- Part of Singapore's security strategy these past 50 years since independence been to be indispensable to countries well beyond the region. Part of that plan has been to build the world's largest refined products storage capacity so that any vessel from anywhere can load up with anything at any time. In a world in which energy reliability will command a premium, Singapore is already head and shoulders above the competition, and is

---

15   Along with an authoritarian single-party regime.

still located in precisely the right spot. The size of Singapore's bunkering operations still makes them a natural end market for Persian Gulf exporters who dare not risk their own ships in East Asia, and since Singapore is the last safe-ish stop before entering the zone of heavy, direct Japanese/ Chinese/Korean/Taiwanese competition — it is a safe end market.

- The NEA4 view Singapore in almost an identical light. Any supplies they can source from Singapore are supplies they have to ship only half as far. This is triply true for the Chinese, who will lack the Japanese's option of deep ocean routes.

- No one sees Singapore as a problem country. The country has only 5.4 million people, and with a per capita income of $57,000 has more money than God. No one is worried about Singapore invading them. Or paying late.

- For all that, the country is no military pushover. All that income and technological skill has prompted Singapore to maintain close training relationships with the United Kingdom and United States, as well as maintaining some of the most advanced and capable military equipment in the world, let alone the region. Moreover, the ultra-valuable strategic real estate makes Singapore one of only a handful of locations around the world where the Americans are likely to remain engaged. That alone will make Beijing or Tokyo think twice — or more — about threatening the city-island.

- But perhaps most of all, from the NEA4's points of view, you cannot leverage Singapore's advantages without Singapore being in charge of Singapore. Direct control of its storage tanks are of no use to Chinese occupiers because Japan would destroy them. Direct control of its piers are of no use to Japanese occupiers because China would destroy them. Should Singapore become a wholly-owned piece of any of the NEA4's supply chains, the others would have a vested interest in breaking that chain. Singapore's usefulness is in its neutrality.

Neutrality doesn't mean that the city-country faces no threats, just that those threats originate from inside the region; Malaysia and Indonesia have long had ambitions of taking over the city-island and making its riches and infrastructure their own. As energy prices rise, as the Americans step back, and as Singapore becomes invasion-proof to the Chinese and Japanese in part because of its energy-brokering capacity, both neighbors are likely to re-evaluate just how badly they want/need the city-island.

In 2016 **Indonesia's** 260-million-strong population took it within a hair's width of being a trillion-dollar economy, but it is an odd beast of an economy. Mineral-rich in pretty much everything, the common practice is to pull raw commodities out of its many islands' often-mountainous or jungle (or both) interiors, drag them to the coast and then ship them far over the horizon. It's a pattern first established during the medieval spice trade — contemporary Eastern Indonesia was the source for most of the world's mace, cumin, cinnamon, and pepper, just to name a few — and has kept up right until the current day with copper ore and in particular coal being shipped out primarily to China and India. But while Indonesia has always sported a very high degree of involvement in international maritime shipping, it has never been able to develop local supply chains.

It hasn't helped that roughly half of the population is crammed on the island of Java while most of the resources are elsewhere. One — among many — results is a built-in semi-instability that Indonesia can never really shake. In the past it has manifested as anti-Communist, or anti-Chinese or anti-Javanese. Sometimes it's even Islamic. But as in all things the physical separation between most of Indonesia's many people tends to keep "extremism" mild and local. For example, the form of Islam practiced in Indonesia is a much more laid back, gentle variant than seen in much of the Middle East or South Asia (or North Africa, or West Africa, or East Africa, or Western Europe).[16]

The rule holds true in the energy industry as well. The lowlands of eastern Sumatra and southern/eastern Borneo — regions packed with minorities — hold the bulk of oil and gas production as well as coal and oil palms. Local firms are technological laggards, and Jakarta's desire to change that has led it to impose conditions on foreigners that make them less willing to even participate. About half of Indonesia's oil production comes from two large, old,

---

16   Or Toronto.

fields on Sumatra — fields that local state energy firm Pertamina couldn't operate without American energy supermajor Chevron. Complicating matters is that since 2000, Indonesia has experienced an echo boom, benefiting from China's economic surge. The result has been sufficient growth to send local oil demand spiraling by 40 percent (to 1.6mbpd) even as output fell by a like proportion to (825kbpd).

Put another way, while Indonesia has often been able to grow, it has never really been able to develop, and events of the past decade that have pushed a lot of investment into a lot of poor places around the world just haven't had much of an impact on Indonesia.

That all may be about to change.

First and most notably, high energy prices will force the supermajors to take a second (and third)[17] look at Indonesia. Even if Indonesia keeps subsidizing domestic energy consumption, even if the country only exports the odd oil cargo, even if Jakarta simply reshuffles its LNG production internally rather than export it, the new price environment will still attract interest where there was little before.

Second, Americans are likely to see Southeast Asia as a favored region and Indonesia specifically as a favored ally — in no small part because the Australians are so committed to a unified, stable Indonesia in order to protect their own interests that they consistently put the Indonesia topic at the top of their agenda with American officials. Between American "commitments" and Indonesia's largely on-shore and difficult energy patch, Northeast Asians are unlikely to think a fight with giant Indonesia (backed by LNG-exporting Australians and by even more giant America) is worth it. Start militarizing supply chains and Jakarta becomes both a capital you dare not offend and a potential partner with nearly unparalleled experience in handling short- and medium-haul transport in sketchy areas.

Third, due to the convoy war, transport costs will go up sharply. That's obviously a huge negative for everyone, but for Indonesia there is a very silver lining. For the first time in Indonesian history, it might actually make sense for at least some of its resources to be processed locally, rather than shipping them far abroad into the teeth of a naval conflict. Industrialization

---

17   And fourth.

just may be about to happen, and unlike most countries, Indonesia has most of the inputs at home (just on a different island from where they are needed). Indonesia may be about to enjoy a golden age.

Jakarta's biggest complication regarding the East Asian Tanker war is likely to be its diplomacy. No matter how deep-sea the Japanese re-route their oil shipments, they must run their tanker lines through the Indonesian archipelago, most likely in the vicinity of the Spice Islands and Bali. Similarly, no matter how successful China is in browbeating countries like Vietnam and Malaysia, Chinese supplies must continue to flow through Malacca. Unique among the Southeast Asian states, Indonesia will be dealing with both major Northeast Asian states from a position of strength because both need Indonesia to not give in to the other — to do so would both risk their energy supply links and rouse the Australians and Americans against them. Expect the Indonesians to cooperate with both enthusiastically — in part for the strategic cover, in part for the investment, in part for the bribes.[18] Both China and Japan will resent Indonesia for the double dealing, and both will seek to destabilize islands in the vicinity of the other's selected shipping routes, but both know they cannot go too far lest they create an enemy where they cannot afford one.

The physical location of **Thailand**, tucked up and away from the major shipping routes on the far side of the Gulf of Thailand, makes it uniquely positioned to make the most of the Tanker War. Any third parties brave enough to sail the South China and Natuna Seas during the conflict will be able to sidestep out of harm's way and find safe port in the Gulf.

This is doubly convenient for the Thais. Not only will it earn them kudos (and cash) from non-belligerents near and far, the Thais' anything-goes tourism reputation carries over to the country's refining industry. Thailand imports some 820kbpd of crude but exports some 290kbpd of refined production, making it critical to regional fueling efforts. Much of the shipping that will be seeking safe harbor will be Northeast Asian. In essence the Thais will be able to war-profiteer, selling their refined product to whoever shows up with an armed convoy. Think of it as the Thai equivalent of the cash-carry program that the Americans used to supply their allies in the

---

18   OK, especially for the bribes.

What About ASEAN?

Those with a passing familiarity with Southeast Asia are likely perplexed by this chapter's lack of attention to the region's dominant grouping: the Association of Southeast Asian Nations (ASEAN).

Formally, the group deals with disputes among its 10 members — Myanmar, Laos, Cambodia, Thailand, the Philippines, Vietnam, Indonesia, Malaysia, Brunei, and Singapore — as well as presents a united front in order to punch above their weight. It would seem that with the Tanker War being fought in the middle of ASEAN's collective sea territory that the organization would be highly relevant.

Nope. ASEAN's founding principles are non-interference and agreement. The non-interference part means the grouping tolerates everything that happens in every member, up to and including military coups. The agreement part means that if even one member for whatever reason disagrees with anything that the other nine would like to do, everything is put on hold. Tokyo and Beijing both have ample strategic reasons and sufficiently deep pockets to peel a member out of any budding consensus that would threaten their interests. (China did this in 2016 by leveraging its relationship with Cambodia to prevent ASEAN from getting diplomatically involved in the South China Sea issue, despite the fact that Vietnam, the Philippines, Malaysia, Brunei, and Indonesia all are resisting Chinese maritime encroachment.)

In the Tanker War one of two things will happen to ASEAN: Either the organization will unofficially suspend itself until the war's conclusion, reducing it to something less than the value of its stationary, or any attempt to forge a common strategic policy will destroy the grouping in its current form.

early stages of the Second World War, but potentially applying to all belligerents. With some savvy diplomacy, Thailand may even be able to convince the belligerents to exchange use of its refining capacity for safe passage through the Natuna Sea and beyond, enabling Thailand to continue its role in regional automobile and electronics manufacturing.

One final Southeast Asian country is worthy of mention: **Myanmar.**

Myanmar's geography is defined by the contrast between the jungle mountains that define its borders with China and India, and the Irrawaddy River valley and drainage basin that bisects the lowlands. The highlands are host to a variety of tribal groups and ethnic minorities that have long fought against the dominant Burmese ethnic group that inhabits the Irrawaddy River basin since time immemorial, and a recent Burmese attempt to control such rebellious groups led to the rise of a military junta whose tactics and policies made Myanmar an outcast to the wider world — with the notable exception of China, who didn't care a whit.

China has invested at least $5 billion in Myanmar's energy infrastructure — that's their data, a more realistic figure is probably over triple that — to pipe natural gas and oil up and across the Myanmarese jungle highlands and into southwestern China. The idea was in part to avoid Malacca, and in part because southwestern China lies closer to Myanmar's ports than it does to Chinese ports. Unfortunately for the Chinese, all this investment will prove for naught. Just as the pipes were starting to come on-line, Myanmar started liberalizing both economically and politically, breaking free of Chinese exclusivity. At the time of this writing, Myanmar has its first democratically-elected majority government in decades — and this government holds arctic feelings toward Beijing for China's role in backing the military junta. Reform is lurching, but the Myanmarese have shown few signs of backtracking on their way toward reintegration with the wider world. Simply put, China has lost its client state — and the energy perks that go with it likely will soon be revoked.

But even should Naypyidaw continue to honor its pipe transit agreements, and even should Myanmar's many restive mountain peoples not endanger the pipelines, there's still the Japanese (and Taiwanese). The Japanese (or Taiwanese) will simply blow up the loading terminal at Kyaukphyu and negate the entire investment in a day. Which means that Myanmar's primary contribution to the regional energy dynamic will be to supply Thailand and Singapore with oil and natgas, giving both regional refining heavyweights that much more flexibility in dealing with the NEA4.

Flipping Roles in South Asia

Pakistan and India's rivalry is cultural, economic, political, and strategic — and filled with as much vitriol as the Saudi-Iran enmity. Free trade or no, energy crisis or no, Islamabad and New Delhi aren't about to bury the hatchet. Instead their smoldering conflict will add its own painful twist to the global energy crisis.

A leading problem in the relationship is that there just isn't a meaningful buffer between the two countries. The Pakistan core is the Five Rivers region where five ... rivers flow southwest from the Himalayas before merging to form the Indus, the backbone of Pakistan. The eastern extreme of Five Rivers is a low saddle of land that is part of the uplands of the extreme western edge of the Ganges River Basin — the central core of India. Complicating matters, the same ethnolinguistic group — the Punjabi — dominate both Five Rivers and the upper Ganges.[19] In a quirk of post-colonial military retreat, the political boundary between the two regions is anything but a clean cut. The southeastern third of Five Rivers lies on the Indian side of the contemporary border, and the rioting that accompanied the partition of the Punjabi people into separate Indian and Pakistani sections in 1947 killed upward of 1 million people.

With nothing but a broad sweep of open farmland between the two countries' population cores, any conventional military contest wouldn't be much of a contest at all. Faced with no option but utter defeat, the Pakistani government has struck upon a three-part strategy to change the game:

• Use Islam to turn Pakistan's own rebellious regions against India, and encourage on-again, off-again attacks into Indian Kashmir to keep the Indian military off-balance.

• Develop a nuclear option so the Pakistani state can at least partially rely upon deterrence to dissuade Indian adventurism.

• Seek outside allies to bolster Pakistan against India, a power too big to seriously consider subordinating itself to an outside power (and thus get its own great power backing). During the Cold War the Pakistanis sought both Chinese and American sponsorship, often at the same time.

---

19 For more proof that not only white people lack name creativity, Punjabi is Persian for five (panj) river (ab).

The Chinese see the Pakistanis in much the same light as the Pakistanis see their own mountain people — as a means to unbalance India — and so have assisted them with everything from infrastructure to their nuclear program. The Americans are similarly disenchanted by Pakistan except as a means to an end, in their case it was all about using Pakistan as a conduit to fight the Soviets in Afghanistan in the 1980s, and more recently to fight their own Afghan war in the aftermath of the 9/11 attacks.

It's a more recent incarnation of this third strategy that brings us back to the energy question. Considering the strategic imbalance with India, Pakistan will play whatever card it can to secure whatever assistance it can.

It all comes down to the Saudi work ethic, namely that the Saudis don't have one. As such the Saudis import scads of laborers from South and Southeast Asia to do everything from construction to home servicing. The Saudis quickly discovered that unlike other sources of workers, there was more to Pakistan than simply a source of cheap labor. Pakistan's decades-long military standoff with India has left it not just armed to the teeth, but with the expertise to make the most of the weapons it has. Pakistanis now comprise the bulk of the Saudi Air Force's pilot corps. And all for the mere cost of about 100kbpd of discounted crude oil. In sum, the relationship may have started with a simple desire for round-the-clock maid service, but is now a fully-fledged mutually-beneficial association comprising military, economic, energy, and strategic links.

In the era to come, this de facto alliance will blossom as both face common challenges. While the Pakistanis do not have the same harsh hatred for Iran that the Saudis sport, Islamabad and Tehran have long been at odds over the minorities on both sides of their common border as well as the shape of governance in Afghanistan. The two are not itching to fight a land war, but Saudi entreaties for bits of Pakistan's military to forward position on the Iranian border to at least partially diffuse Iran's focus on the Arab states of the Gulf will likely be answered favorably.

In addition, Saudi Arabia will want as many of its oil shipments as possible — and as few of Iran's as possible — to make it as far along the Northeast Asian tanker trail as is possible. Pakistan has the air and sea capacity to at least help Saudi and Emirati (and perhaps some lucky Qatari and Kuwaiti) shipments start along their way, providing friendly waters and ports for the first step of the long voyage to Northeast Asia. This makes Pakistan one of the very few countries that will be taking proactive steps to encourage international economic stability in a dangerous time and area. Pakistan could well become one of the few bright spots of international safety and stability in the new era.[20]

The same cannot be said about India, which tends to trade on its own merits.

The Indian geography is a complex one, riddled with river valleys, deserts, plains, mountains, hills, swamp, and a mix of coastline styles. But one feature always stands out: the Ganges Basin. Set in the oddity of a temperate zone that knows no true winter, the plain's outstanding fertility and multiple potential growing seasons generates the largest volume of calories per acre per year of anywhere in the world. However, the Ganges itself is not navigable. The result is fantastically high rates of population growth, but fantastically low capital generation per capita. Massive populations, but crushing poverty.

Forever.

That simple fact smothers the significance out of every other feature of the Indian system. The sort of economic development that makes a country wealthy, secure, and powerful simply does not happen in India. Pick your measure: rail reliability, road conditions, educational depth, electricity availability, quality of governance. In all cases India's performance is pitiable and inconsistent. India is home to nearly as many people in poverty than the rest of Asia combined. And that isn't going to change.

Which is *not* to say that India is irrelevant. First off, any place with 1.3 billion people is at a minimum going to matter locally, and India is hardly an exception. It is the undisputed first-power of the Subcontinent and all its regional neighbors define the bulk of their identity and strategic policies wholly in the context of — or in the case of Pakistan, direct opposition to — India. Second, India's top 1 percent is still 13 *million* people, so the

---

20   Believe me I feel as weird saying this as you feel reading it. And to be perfectly clear, this "stability" only refers to maritime energy shipments flowing through Pakistani waters. From a domestic militancy and terrorism point of view, Pakistan will still be a reliably hot mess.

exceptions to the rules of education and wealth and reach are still a bigger elite dripping with skills and money than that of any European country.

Third and most important, while India might not ever be *wealthy*, it will always be *stable* — particularly since much of the world convulses around it.

One of the political side effects of having so many people living without the basics is that politics in India tilt decidedly in the populist/socialist direction; although formally non-aligned, New Delhi preferenced the Soviet Union during the Cold War. India's status as a former British colony got the country into the Bretton Woods framework, but its anti-American leanings combined with the absolute dearth of local capital supplies prevented India from ever really capitalizing on free trade. India's per capita GDP "only" increased by a factor of three between 1960 and 2000. Compare that to China's which almost increased by a factor of 10 — with most of that improvement after 1980. While this could be perceived as unconscionable from a governmental perspective — the Bretton Woods era was the greatest explosion of economic growth in history and India largely missed out — the lack of growth actually positions India very well in the crises to come. Since India never got into globalized manufacturing supply chains, when free trade collapses India doesn't have far to fall.

What international links India *does* have falls into two buckets: services (which are likely to suffer less from the Disorder's trade breakdown than goods) and oil imports (which India can do something about).

As you might guess from an anti-capitalist, populist country of 1.3 billion people, oil production in India is insufficient to the country's needs, forcing the country to import roughly 80 percent of the 4.3mbpd it uses. One, among many, results is that India has had to pay through the teeth to import crude — railing against the hated Asian Premium is probably the country's third most favorite topic after curry and cricket.

India will still need oil. What India is unlikely to be able to do, however, is *afford* oil. A good rule of thumb is that when total energy costs breach about 8 percent a year, a recession is all-but-inevitable. India's costs for oil alone run it about $76 billion a year at $50 a barrel. That's about 3.7 percent of GDP (America's total oil bill is about half that proportion). Once the global price split happens, Americans' relative costs will remain fairly static, while India's can be relied upon to at least triple. Economic growth — much less any meaningful economic development — in India becomes impossible because Indians simply won't be able to pay the sharply higher costs to import the oil.

Which means they must take it — and India's geographic location grants it any number of options to do so.

First and most obvious, the subcontinent's jutting out into the Indian Ocean forces any oil tankers originating in Persia or Arabia to navigate Indian waters, granting India a wealth of opportunities to intercept cargos. While I'm not overly impressed by anything the Indian navy has afloat, everything they patrol with is faster than a supertanker and the Indian navy's operational range is more than sufficient to force unarmed civilian tankers to make port.

Second, India need not even use its navy. India could dust off the old British strategy of privateering, granting commissions to private interests — which need not even be Indian-flagged — to, in essence, pirate in the name of India. The Somalis have shown us — vividly — that it doesn't take a particularly robust ship to capture large merchant vessels; they've captured and ransomed four fully-loaded VLCCs in recent years.

Third, India could well coerce others to simply give them crude. Avoiding India outright is very difficult, but confronting India several thousand miles from home would be a bit of a challenge for even significant naval powers — especially if your goal was to establish a long-term supply line through India's sphere of influence. It's not so much that India's navy is a military impediment — in a fair fight Taiwan's navy could probably sink everything the Indians have. Instead it is the Indian air force that is quite competent. Any NEA4 power that found itself in a brawl with the Indians would find themselves facing a wall of hostile land-based air power. It might prove easiest to simply buy India off one cargo at a time, triply so for China, who lacks the Japanese option of deep-sea routes.

Well played, India might end up spending *less* money on crude oil in the world-to-come because it will have extorted out the difference. Sum it up and the best hope for global energy security may be … Pakistan.

Aftermath: The Asian Rim and Beyond

With so many moving parts, there are any number of ways these conflicts and rearrangements can go — and any number of ways everything can go hideously wrong. But here are a few clear outcomes for the wider world.

First, the oil price split between North America and the wider world is just the beginning of the confusion and volatility that will soon rule energy markets. Having the NEA4 duke it out across the breadth and width of the East, Southeast, and South Asian rim will drastically increase import prices for all four with regard to global average prices. Add in the high likelihood that the Indians will take supply matters into their own hands, and the price gap between Northeast Asia and everyone else could be massive. Putting specific numbers to oil price forecasts is always a dangerous action, but considering insufficient supplies, state-piracy, and roving warfare where oil tankers are both target and goal, at least $50 a barrel premium for Northeast Asia seems reasonable.

There's no way that this is anything but horrible for the NEA4, but the pain would not be felt equally. Japan, to put it simply, has options. Japan can fuel-switch and so somewhat limit its need for oil, and even for LNG. Japan's navy begins with strategic freedom: its home bases are under lesser threat than the rest of the NEA4, and the navy doesn't have to achieve immediate breakout from something like the first-island chain. Most important Japan's navy is powerful enough that it can sail the long way, arcing widely out into the Pacific, taking deep-ocean routes to keep its tankers well out of range of Chinese or Indian military assets. Japan has more than enough income and technology to purchase cooperation from Thailand, Indonesia, and Singapore. In addition, between its money and its naval reach, Tokyo could help the Philippines, Vietnam, and Malaysia stand up to the Chinese. Finally, Japan's huge distance from the Persian Gulf also ironically means it is the closest to potential *Western* Hemispheric sources: crude from Ecuador or Colombia or Peru or Alaska or Argentina, as well as refined product from the continental United States. Given current anti-Chinese trends in American politics, it is fairly safe to say the Americans would be quite happy to provide Japan (and its chosen allies) with vast varieties and at least moderate volumes of refined products and ordinance to assist their war efforts.

China can count on none of this. Its ports and coastal refineries are all exposed. Taiwan is implacable and likely to buddy up with Japan immediately, turning that exposure into a chronic vulnerability. Each of the maritime Southeast Asian littoral countries have sought out Japanese (and American) partnership as early as 2013 to mitigate an increasingly bellicose China — and that in an era before the Chinese get violent. Japan's geography and naval reach enable it to source a bit of crude and refined product from Western Hemispheric sources while preventing China from doing the same.

China's only not-horrible option is to expand its land-shipped imports, but even this is no guarantee. Russian shipments could be disrupted by Japan — or alternatively Japan could simply bribe the Russians to send the crude direct to the Pacific along an already-operational pipe that terminates near Vladivostok. Supplies from Kazakhstan might prove stable, but increasing those supplies from today's level of 110kbpd to something that is strategically significant would require deep Chinese political, technical, and financial investment in a 4,000-mile corridor to connect eastern China to the oil provinces of Kazakhstan's Caspian region. Russia would certainly view that as a bid for outright control of its backyard, and move aggressively to counter. That just leaves the new pipe through Myanmar, which will *certainly* be cut should the Chinese not manage their relationship with Naypyidaw perfectly — and even if they do, Japan will simply bomb the loading port.

The Tanker War will neither be easy nor kind for the Chinese, who will face the double indemnity of needing the most energy while suffering from the greatest strategic vulnerability. Even if they can forge partnerships with the Koreans and Malaysians, there are simply too many hostiles on too many horizons for them to have a hope of surviving, much less winning.

Which brings us to the second outcome: China is finished.

Beijing's maritime periphery is surrounded by hostile powers, and ultimately there is very little China will be able to do to reverse the geographic realities that limit its naval capabilities. This is hardly a new turn of events. The Japanese have been plying the Pacific, trading with the entire East

Asian rim for centuries[21], while China has struggled simply to unify. Only under Bretton Woods was China finally able to fully consolidate and interact with the world on its own terms. Destroy global free trade, unleash the Japanese, and the end of China is nigh.

But don't expect China to go down easy or without a fight. While Japan is set to ultimately prevail, and most likely replace the United States as the region's dominant regional naval power, Chinese aggression in some form or another will be part of Asia's new emerging reality. In the first part of the conflict, global perceptions of China will shift from China as a proud juggernaut to China as a desperate has-been, clinging to the remnants of a fallen empire and lashing out at its neighbors in the hopes of some crumbs to aid in its survival. Such lashes will generate panic throughout East Asia, and that fear will be precisely what the Japanese need to forge the region into a new sphere of influence. In an ironic twist of fate, the once-conqueror of Southeast Asia will emerge as a somewhat feudal guarantor of its security, and a ready importer of its resources. None will accept this relationship as happily as the Philippines, which will eagerly seek out Japan as a source of security, investment, and remittances.

The country nursing the largest concerns — economically, demographically and militarily — will be Korea. Whether Seoul chooses to join with Beijing or Tokyo, it will be Japan that is in a state of de facto alliance with every country that straddles the sea lanes that supply Korea with all its energy, raw materials and market access. If the Koreans fail to play their hand well, the East Asian Tanker War could have a brief sequel in which Japan — again — snuffs out Korean dreams. And even that winceful forecast assumes that nothing untoward boils out of North Korea.

The economic reverberations of China's fall are the third major outcome, and they will be most heavily felt within the rest of Northeast Asia. Simply put, the days of China Inc. and Factory Asia are over. The Japanese, Korean, Taiwanese, and Chinese economic miracles were predicated on cheap capital, absolute freedom of the seas, and open markets — particularly where the United States was concerned. All those factors are in the process of collapsing even before the Tanker War commences. Soon the NEA4 will find

---

21   Critics would prefer a term somewhat harsher than "trading with."

themselves forced to expend capital and military assets simply to access a much-reduced supply of imported oil — a task that until now has cost them zero. By definition not all will succeed; there simply will not be enough crude to go around. Whether due to inability, instability, or hostility, the final piece of Northeast Asia's success — mutual integration to maximize exports — will collapse.

Beyond Northeast Asia the world will suffer from a massive — and very sudden — decrease in the size of the global manufactures market, as well as a massive decrease in all of the things that service that market. Cement, iron ore, copper, zinc, and aluminum — just to name a few — will see outright collapses in demand. And that's just the *input* side.

On the *output* side the disruption will be even grander. Pre-World War II, most manufacturing happened in large complexes. Inputs were imported, processed by local labor and infrastructure into finished products and then exported elsewhere for consumption. Bretton Woods changed all that by making international transport safe and cheap. The holistic production processes of those large complexes were broken up, scattered to myriad facilities who would pound out whichever piece of the process they excelled at. Single-point manufacturing gave way to gangly supply chains with dozens, even thousands, of steps.

Roughly half of the world's manufacturing supply chain steps are in East Asia. The Tanker War will sink far more than "just" the global energy market.

In many ways the rise of Northeast Asia — and in particular, China — is the ultimate expression of the success of Bretton Woods. Countries devastated by war, impoverished for centuries and largely devoid of industrial resources could transform into stable, secure, advanced powers with global reach.

But the converse is true as well. As the Bretton Woods system ends, not only is Northeast Asia the region with the most to lose and the furthest to fall, it is also the region most certain to devolve into internecine warfare marked by desperate efforts to secure the resources Bretton Woods allowed access to. For the most part, the region will not only fail in those efforts, the war itself will delay the emergence of a new global equilibrium by years. When the rebalancing does finally occur, it will not be based on factors or powers within Northeast Asia. Instead, an entirely new — or based on your perspective, old — constellation of countries will determine what order manages to rise from within the Disorder.

CHAPTER 9

The Sweet Sixteen

Blockades on the Baltic Sea. Oil fields attacked in the Persian Gulf. Tankers targeted from Hormuz to Osaka. Very soon the world will face global energy shortages unheard of in the modern age. In the *least* involved versions of the Twilight and Gulf Wars, and assuming no Tanker War, that's still 14mboed that goes offline.

In the low case that's as if Kuwait and Norway and Colombia and Egypt and the United Kingdom and Angola and Algeria and Nigeria went offline at the same time, a shortage enough to starve out India and Mexico. In the high case that's roughly the production of Saudi Arabia, Iran, and Russia combined, and the shortage would be enough to deny *all* the crude used by China and Japan and Taiwan and Korea and Germany and France and Italy. And *that* before the Northeast Asian Tanker War even begins. Global energy prices will skyrocket.

That is not the end of the bad news — and once again you can blame shale.

Between 2007 and 2015 the transformation of the American energy complex reduced the country's oil imports by 7mbpd, in large part because of increased production of high-quality shale crudes. Those shale crudes in particular cut into American imports of similarly high-quality crude from African producers, who had to find new customers — at lower price points. Hardest hit were African producers, who lost at least 2.3mbpd in exports to the United States. This substitution and redirection was in large part responsible for the weakening of prices in 2014 even before the Saudi price war started.

Even without the wars, for the world to come, low prices are a monumental problem. There's a maxim in the energy sector: the cure for high prices is high prices, the cure for low prices is low prices. The concept behind the maxim is simple: if prices stay high for a long while, firms invest in new technologies and new fields and new infrastructure and bring new oil production on-line. The surge of new oil then overwhelms demand and triggers a price crash. If prices stay low for a long while, firms cease investing in technology and fields and infrastructure. Production falls off in an ever-steepening curve until it screams past demand. The imbalance then shifts to too little crude, leading to rocketing prices.

The world entered a period of non-investment in early 2015, and by the end of 2016 energy companies around the world had reduced their capital expenditure plans by a cool $1 trillion. The only real exceptions are the Saudi-led Arab producers in the Persian Gulf, who are the ones fighting a price war. Everywhere else we're already deep into the decline curves. Output has already started to stall — and fall — in some of the more politically persnickety, technically difficult, or geographically isolated of the world's energy plays. Australia, Azerbaijan, Brazil, Iraq, Kazakhstan, Nigeria, Norway, Russia, Venezuela, Vietnam, and Yemen all come to mind.[1]

And that's "just" production. Searching for new crude has all but stopped. Globally just 2.7 billion barrels of new supply were discovered in 2015. Sound like a lot? Keep in mind that demand for that year totaled thirty-five billion barrels. That 2.7 billion figure is the smallest volume of new supply discoveries made since 1947.

This is part and parcel of the normal price cycle, but the timing of this price trough is particularly unnerving because it is happening just as the previous American-led global system is unravelling. When prices next skyrocket because of Russia or Iran/Saudi Arabia or the Northeast Asians, there

---

1   Iran would be on this list if not for the 2016 rebound in output as the country recovered from the sanctions regime. Under normal circumstances Canadian output would fall as well, but so many greenfield projects that were a decade in the making reach completion in 2016-2017. That means Albertan output won't fall in a sustained way until late-2017 at the earliest — which of course only deepens the glut and defers future investments for everyone.

Pre-Conflict Persian Gulf Petroleum Production and Exports

	Total Crude Production (kbpd)	Total Crude Oil Exports (kbpd)	Total Products Exports (kbpd)	Total LNG Exports (mcf/d)
Iran	3150	1100	510	
Iraq (Basra)	3500	3000	15	
Kuwait	2900	2000	740	
Qatar	656	500	520	10300
Saudi Arabia	10200	7200	1200	
UAE	2990	2400	950	730
Total:	23396	16200	3935	11030

Petroleum Exports disrupted by the Gulf War

	Crude Oil Exports Disrupted by Conflict (kbpd)			Refined Products Disrupted by Conflict (kbpd)			LNG Exports Disrupted by Conflict (mcf/d)		
	Phase I	Phase II	Phase III	Phase I	Phase II	Phase III	Phase I	Phase II	Phase III
Iran	550	550		260	260	15			
Iraq (Basra)	1500	3000	3000	8	15	15			
Kuwait	1000	2000	2000	370	740	740			
Qatar	250	250		260	260		5150	5150	
Saudi Arabia	2200	2200	7200	600	600	1200			
UAE	1200	1200		470	470		365	365	
Total:	6700	9200	12200	1968	2345	1955	5515	5515	

Source: OPEC, BP, JODI

Phase I: Saudi Arabia and Iran Target Each Others' Exports; Phase II: Iran Invades Southern Iraq and Kuwait; Phase III: Saudi Arabia's Defeat; Other Gulf States Surrender

Pre-Conflict Russian and Periphery Petroleum Production and Exports

	Total Crude Production (kbpd)	Total Crude Oil Exports (kbpd)	Total Products Exports (kbpd)	Total NatGas Exports (mcf/d)
Russia	10980	4900	2270	20100
Kazakhstan	1669	1400	15	1100
Azerbaijan	841	665	46	735
Total:	13490	6965	2331	21935

Petroleum Exports disrupted by the Twilight War

	Crude Oil Exports Disrupted by Conflict (kbpd)			Refined Products Disrupted by Conflict (kbpd)			NatGas Exports Disrupted by Conflict (mcf/d)		
	Phase I	Phase II	Phase III	Phase I	Phase II	Phase III	Phase I	Phase II	Phase III
Russia	1500	3100	5000	1500	1500	1500		7000	15500
Kazakhstan			950						
Azerbaijan			740						735
Total:	1500	3100	6690	1500	1500	1500		7000	9335

Source: OPEC, BP, JODI, Gazprom

Phase I: Seaborne Exports via Baltic Sea Halted; Phase II: Northern Pipeline Exports Affected; Phase III: Southern Exports via Ukraine, Caucuses Halted

will be *no* conventional projects anywhere in the world that will be able to suddenly ramp up output. Most of the new output-in-progress the Gulfies are working on will be blocked-in by the war there. The world is set up for a price transition in which normal market corrections will sloppily overlap with geopolitically triggered shortages on an unprecedented scale.

In short, the world will transition almost immediately from a world of hilariously-reliable sub-$50 oil to a world in which $150 oil feels cheap and price gyrations take on a decidedly Turkish-belly-dancer flare.

And Now For a Bit of Good News

There is, however, a bit of room for a very small amount of hope. There are a few places in the world that boast sufficiently lucky geography and geology that they theoretically could increase output in less than five years. These places are all insulated from the Disorder's wars, *and* have energy sectors that are oil-heavy, *and* face few problems getting any crude production to port if they have a bit of financial and technical assistance. Their collective output still isn't (nearly) enough to compensate for what will be lost from the former Soviet space or the Persian Gulf, but these players just might prove capable of smoothing out some of the price volatility and perhaps even drop global price levels by as much as a third. Still, most of them are anything but sure bets.

Nigeria is undoubtedly the only country in the world that could bring a large volume of crude on-line quickly, largely because there are so many places to work. The southern onshore is riddled with thousands of wells, some dating back a half-century or more. The offshore has a score of production areas, some near the coast, some far, some in shallow water, some in deep. Nigeria's sheer abundance of production zones means every energy operator in the world with international experience potentially can play, whether they specialize in greenfield or brownfield or enhanced recovery or new exploration. The country even has a (massive) LNG export program, so even expanding what is typically a long-term, high-dollar program wouldn't be from a standing start. The only challenge is, well, Nigeria. The country's political factions often are willing to hold the entirety of the energy sector hostage in order to further their domestic agenda, which typically revolves around who gets the presidency. The next presidential campaign starts in 2018, with elections in 2019.

Nearly all of **Angola**'s oil production is offshore, making it largely immune to the Angolan government's ongoing ethnic cleansing campaign. Unfortunately, Angola's decline curves are much steeper than industry norms, requiring more drilling simply to keep production steady. That nudges Angola's position out of the first few pages of any investor's little black book, and that before one considers the country's OPEC membership dampens interest — particularly at low prices. A high-price environment, of course, will wipe such concerns away. But it will take at least a year to arrest the country's ongoing output declines before moderate, if steady, increases can be attained.

The 1990s were good to **Equatorial Guinea** (EG). Offshore oil exploration saw a boom in output and exports, leaving the tiny country continental Africa's wealthiest in terms of GDP per capita. Yet the country's limited offshore acreage has presented few opportunities to offset the decline of fields that have been under operation for the past two decades. Output peaked in 2005, and has been steadily declining since. It's unlikely that — short of a miracle — export volumes will top 300kbpd ever again. The country's president is the longest-serving dicta—leader in Africa, and has dedicated much of EG's oil wealth to building a new capital on the mainland. Things have recently become a bit dicier because of ... shale. Initially nearly a third of Equatorial Guinea's oil went to the United States, and so there were some lines the government would hesitate crossing in terms of oppression and corruption. Shale then took away Equatorial Guinea's entire American market. China now is the country's top market, and Beijing is the government's primary lender. The ... propriety for which Equatorial Guinea was once known is long gone, and political opponents are now regularly shot in the streets.[2] In the aftermath of the Tanker War, Equatorial Guinea must find yet another market and yet another sponsor. Its coming shift matters

---

2   A sample statement from a government spokesman on Equatorial Guinean state television to drive the point home: "[The President] can decide to kill without anyone calling him to account and without going to hell because it is God himself, with whom he is in permanent contact, and who gives him this strength."

hugely. Not because it is a big player, but because it is representative of a chain of smaller offshore African producers sandwiched between Nigeria and Angola that have strong U.S. supermajor presences, strong colonial and political ties to Europe, and now strong (if recent) economic ties to China.

Gabon shares much in common with neighboring Equatorial Guinea, with the exception of its colonial master.[3] France's Total has run Gabon's offshore energy sector since the 1930s. As one of the oldest producers in the Gulf of Guinea, Gabon has some of the most mature fields currently in production. Recent investments by Total and Shell have slowed the rate of decline in recent years, but only just. Still, Gabon has traditionally competed with Equatorial Guinea and Congo-B (see below) for the title of third-largest sub-Saharan oil producer, and Gabon still boasts the largest proven oil reserves of the three. Gabon's political leadership also has developed a strong understanding of what is required to make its sector work, enacting reforms including recreating the national company in 2011, well before the price plunge. The country is still feeling its way through a new energy law (as well as recently re-joining OPEC), but triple (or more) the cost of oil and the French will have few concerns about investing en masse.

The Republic of the Congo (more commonly referred to as **Congo-B**[4]) rounds out the trifecta of smaller-yet-significant producers between Nigeria and Angola. Home to Africa's most urbanized populations, the country's economy — like its neighbors — almost entirely depends upon its offshore oil sector. Dominated by Total and ENI, Congo-B's output peaked at the start of the decade. But whereas its neighbors' problems are largely due to age, Congo-B's problems are largely due to mismanagement and its insistence that most oil jobs go to locals ... despite a complete lack of a skilled labor force. The European supers are willing to work with Equatorial Guinea, and Gabon is already moving its domestic policies in the right direction in order to facilitate investment, but Congo-B is likely to require a more direct approach if its energy sector is ever to recover. No Europeans would dream

---

3   Equatorial Guinea was colonized by the Spanish while Gabon was within the French Empire.

4   Itself short for Congo (Brazzaville), in order to differentiate it from its much larger neighbor Congo (Kinshasa).

ing the right direction in terms of producing more oil even *before* a spike in prices. The downside is that any new production will face the dual challenge of offsetting ongoing production declines *while* supplying domestic demand for a large population that may finally be able to industrialize. Indonesia may achieve self-sufficiency, but significant exports are an unlikely outcome. Nonetheless, Indonesia's potential is sufficient to attract the likes of Chevron and ExxonMobil, with other supermajors playing supporting roles throughout the energy complex.

In a bit of an ironic twist, **Malaysia** lags Indonesia in oil production despite similar oil reserves, but the country absolutely beats out Indonesia in terms of natural gas exports (primarily LNG — Malaysia is the world's third-largest supplier), and that despite smaller natural gas reserves. With only 12 percent of Indonesia's overall population and an already-industrialized economy, any new output is unlikely to be gobbled up by steep rises in domestic demand. Unlike Indonesia, Malaysia's hydrocarbon sector is almost entirely offshore, but state energy firm Petronas is one of the world's best national firms at handling shallow-to-medium offshore production. With a long history of working well with others (including ExxonMobil and Shell, the country's largest foreign producers of oil and natgas), Malaysia will be a first-stop not only for the supermajors (the ones that can get there, anyway) but also the navies of Northeast Asian countries hungry for crude oil.

Technically, **Venezuela** sports a nearly unparalleled volume of crude oil reserves, but the vast majority are a type of tar deep in the interior. As global output and transport wither, Venezuela's difficult deposits can and will be developed, but the infrastructure requirements saddle the country with some of the highest upfront capital costs and longest lead times in the industry. In the shorter term, it is only the rehabilitation of Venezuela's older producing regions — such as those in the vicinity of Lake Maracaibo — that are likely to contribute to export volumes in the next few years. And before *that* can happen, Venezuela must sort through its internal political mess as well as restore rule of law to Maracaibo, a region where pirates now hold sway.

The future of the oil industry of **Brazil** is locked within its pre-salt deposits. Named that way because of their geological position under a layer of salt, such oils are among the world's most difficult to exploit and process —

and that before one considers that they *also* happen to be under a mile of ocean. You can count the number of companies who could attempt such feats on one hand. Brazil's state oil company, Petrobras, is one of them, and in 2008 it launched a monumental effort to bring the pre-salt on-line. As of 2016 that effort has stalled almost completely. In part, the backsliding is part and parcel of the back-burnering of high-cost oil that has wracked oil plays around the world. It is difficult to see the pre-salt being profitable at anything less than $80 a barrel. But Brazil is also a *very* young country. Its currency, constitution, and governing system are not even 30 years old, and in 2015 its adolescent government slammed into its first true legitimacy crisis: a bribery scandal with Petrobras itself at its heart. At the time of this writing, corruption indictments are pending against a vast raft of officials, have already claimed the sitting president, and may even result in the jailing of her immediate predecessor. Between political outrage at home and hostile financial conditions abroad, everything associated with Petrobras has become toxic to investors regardless of from where they hail. The retrenchment has been so all-encompassing that Brazil will be one of the last beneficiaries from a future high-price environment, and even that assumes it can straighten out its politics. Will Brazil play a role in the oil markets of the future? Certainly, but any early contributions from Petrobras will come from its operations in other Atlantic basin energy plays long before those in Brazil itself.

Literally *the* textbook example of how to not run a successful economy, **Argentina** has had a terrible track record of nationalizing assets held by foreign investors — most recently nationalizing the country's largest oil company YPF, previously held by Spain's Repsol. National elections in late-2015 generated a new, more market-friendly government, but would-be investors are understandably a bit nervous about trusting a country that has spent the last 15 years dreaming up ways to take things from businesses of all stripes. The most promising geology in the country are its shale fields, which incidentally are the most technically attractive shale fields in the world outside the United States. Their development will require the importation — or local fostering — of dozens of shale operators. As the United States' second language is Spanish, and its speaking is heavy in the top shale state of Texas, this workforce *is* available and its partial transfer to

Argentina *will* happen. But it will take time for momentum — and trust in the new government — to build.

In 2013 **Mexico** finally made it legal for someone other than the Mexican government to own discrete pieces of the country's oil complex ... just in time for the global oil price collapse. So while the first rounds of auctions have already been held, no one is planning any meaningful large-scale investment until prices rebound. Once they do, fabulous. But even if the Mexicans — who have never collaborated with any private company in their offshore operations — get everything perfect on their first try, every offshore project is a completely virgin zone necessitating tens of billions of dollars into exploration, drilling, and connecting infrastructure. The biggest obstacle likely will be Mexico's inexperience — not so much with deep offshore work, but with the nuts and bolts of auctions and contracting and financial transfers and production sharing. The Mexican oil renaissance is coming, and it will be big, but it won't happen overnight or without bumps along the way.

Colombia is an old hand in the energy business. Not just in the duration of its participation — its first fields came on-line over a century ago — but instead because of the smooth confidence that pervades every stage of its production and refining complex. Its national oil firm, Ecopetrol, boasts an exceedingly rare combination of technical capability to handle most projects, and sufficient humility to know when it needs to seek outside help or capital. The result is both a thriving, steadily advancing local energy industry *and* excellent relations with a host of foreign firms, most notably the American (super)majors. Spurring Colombia's energy plays on to new heights is the fact that the country's multi-generation civil war is finally winding down. The only downside, and it's a doozy, is that many of Colombia's oil fields have been in operation since 1918 and all are far past maturity. Only cutting-edge (read: expensive foreign) technologies can enhance output sufficiently to stave-off rapid declines. Investment will come — indeed much is already there — but there is only so much oil that can be squeezed out of such aged projects.

The problem in **Canada** isn't so much potential or technology or even capital availability, but price. So long as the Americans have shale and the Albertans lack alternate markets, Alberta's heavy/sour crude has to sell into the world's most supersaturated market. There are only two ways of address-ing this problem. The first is to run a pipe to the Canadian coast, but that would require overcoming local politics in the other Canadian provinces — something that to date has proven utterly impossible. The second is to sig-nificantly expand the pipe infrastructure between the two countries so that Albertan crude can be mixed with shale crude throughout the American refining network. The third is for Alberta to build its own refineries and then export the product to places beyond North America, an investment project that would cost at least in the high tens of billions — and that in a time when investment funds are scarce. If the order were given as you read these words, the first income from any of the three options would not manifest within four years. Complicating matters hugely is the unfortunate fact that in 2016 wildfires devastated the Fort McMurray region, Alberta's oils sands production center. Unlike conventional oil production, oil sands product must be mined and processed before it can be piped or railed. This is not just capital intensive, but labor-intensive. Until Fort McMurray can re-build, all of the related support businesses that make the Albertan oil sands sector function cannot operate at full capacity. That will retard Albertans' contribution to global oil for years, encouraging American shale operators to eat into Alberta's market share.

The Long Road Back

Buried within all of this detail are three critical conclusions.

First, any meaningful price recovery that is global in scope will take a *decade,* and simply getting global energy production on an upward track will require a *minimum* of three years. Ignoring demographics, ignoring America's withdrawal from the trade system, ignoring the chaos and wars of the Disorder, this energy shock alone will cause an energy-induced de-pression that is nearly global in scope.

Second, the United States will not be caught in the global trap. While it will take a minimum of three years before the world can begin any sort of meaningful production and price recovery, it will only take the United States three *months.* A fairly complex shale well can be brought on-line in as little as six weeks for a few million dollars. And that's for *new* projects. There are plenty of ways to get to low-hanging fruit without even engaging in greenfields projects: Exploit the fracklog, complete operations at wells that have only had one stage fracked in order to fill up gathering infrastructure, apply new technologies to old wells, go back through well inventories and indrill. None of these steps require new exploration or new leasing or new infrastructure, and all this and more would likely add up to more than 1mbpd in new and restored output in less than a year. A total output rise of 2.5mbpd within 24 months is easily feasible, more than sufficient to bring North America to zero net oil imports. Such independence likely will limit U.S. oil prices to a ceiling of around $60-$70 — the point at which most shale oil projects are profitable — and trigger a full price break with the rest of the world.

Third, what all those 16 non-American production zones have in common is that none are cheap or easy. They will (each) require mammoth applications of technical capacity, skilled labor, and above all, money. Especially if the goal is to bring new output on-line in a hurry.

In a word, success in any of them will require the supermajors.

The California Exception

Just as the United States is becoming the exception to global energy prices, California is becoming the exception to American energy prices. While California boasts a promising shale field in its Monterrey formation and while California has consistently ranked as the second-largest oil user in the United States, state-level regulations have equally consistently prevented a shale industry from arising within the state.

This decision has a cost: California is nearly separate from the American energy complex. There are no oil pipelines that cross the Rockies from the Greater Midwest and Texas. There aren't even smallish pipelines that come in from Canada. Any crude produced in North Dakota (or Canada) that is shipped to California must come by rail (or a combination of rail to and then barge from the Pacific Northwest).

In a globalized world of open borders this is deserving of little more than the occasional comment or quiet snicker (the sounds from Texas are probably more guffawlike). After all, the Californians are quite capable of importing crude from elsewhere in the world to make up for what they refuse to produce locally, and an extra buck per gallon of gasoline is a price they are willing to pay for their politics.

But that price is about to increase substantially. Most of the oil "imported" into California comes from three locations, the first of which is Alaska. A quirk of American law allows petroleum produced in Alaska to be exported to the wider world independent of other laws that sometimes bar domestic energy exports. This will allow Alaskan crude oil to flow to what soon will be the highest-paying end-market in the world: Japan. Imports from the second source, Latin America, are likely to follow a similar logic. California will have to replace all these supplies from elsewhere.

That elsewhere is likely to be the remaining major current source of California's imports: the Persian Gulf. At the time of this writing, California imports 450kbpd from the region, nearly as much as the 550kbpd it produces locally. When Iran and Saudi Arabia's conflict erupts, California will suffer nearly as much as the East Asian states do in terms of supply disruptions and price. American shale will kick into overdrive, eliminating extra-hemispheric oil imports ... except those to California. The state will now be importing more Persian Gulf crude than the rest of the country combined. The spread between

California gasoline prices and other Lower-48 prices can be counted upon to increase from today's $1 barrel to something in the $5-$9 range — easily enough to hurl California into a protracted energy-induced depression.

But it isn't a depression without escape. The Californians have everything they need within their own state to fix the situation.

Nearly all of California's oil and natural gas production lies in a single county: Kern. Kern County also is home to the Monterrey shale. Though the Monterrey has been massively underexplored and underutilized, the lack of activity is not wholly due to regulations and restrictions out of Sacramento. The Monterrey's geology is tangled; it's a series of stacked layers crisscrossed by a multitude of fault lines. While locals may grind on about Sacramento's limiting of local industry, even if the Monterrey were in Texas it wouldn't have been considered a world-class energy play.

Or at least it wouldn't have until recently. The Texans and Pennsylvanians and North Dakotans have been unlocking shale's secrets bit by bit during the past decade, but it wasn't until 2016 that true best practices started to form up. The same complex, stacked features that made the Monterrey difficult-to-impossible to develop in 2014 make it a mouth-watering play now. Microseismic and especially multilateral drilling are turning similarly complex shales like the Permian and the Marcellus into fabulous production zones. Kern may be late to the party, but it will enjoy a distinct second-mover advantage.

Kern already has the capital, infrastructure, local regulatory structure, and workforce required to transform the Monterrey. Double (or more) the price of energy in California, change Sacramento's view of Kern — and more important Sacramento's *regulation* of Kern — and a California shale boom will happen almost overnight. The United States' Big4 shale plays are about to become the Big5.

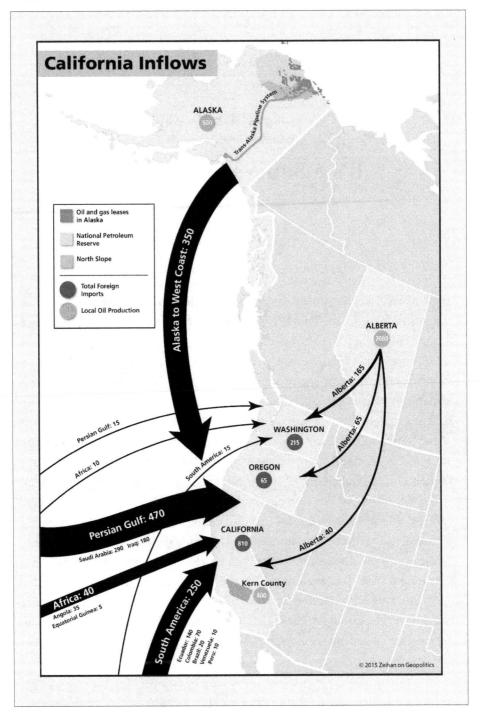

California Inflows

ALASKA
500

Trans-Alaska Pipeline System

Oil and gas leases
in Alaska

National Petroleum
Reserve

North Slope

Total Foreign
Imports

Local Oil Production

Alaska to West Coast: 350

ALBERTA
2080

Alberta: 165

Alberta: 65

Persian Gulf: 15

Africa: 10

South America: 15

WASHINGTON
215

OREGON
65

Persian Gulf: 470

Saudi Arabia: 290   Iraq: 180

CALIFORNIA
810

Alberta: 40

Kern County
400

Africa: 40
Angola: 35
Equatorial Guinea: 5

South America: 250
Ecuador: 140
Colombia: 70
Brazil: 20
Venezuela: 10
Peru: 10

© 2015 Zeihan on Geopolitics

CHAPTER 10

It's a Supermajor World

The supermajors, as you might guess from the name, are the big boys on the block. Back in the late 1990s before the massive wave of mergers that formed them, they were *already* the world's largest private companies. They then proceeded to pair up (or in some cases triple and quadruple up) to form the truly massive entities they are today. In the immediate post-merger names you can get a pretty clear idea of what happened: ExxonMobil, BPAmocoArco, TotalFinaElf, ConocoPhillips, ChevronTexaco.[1]

The supermajors think big. They have the resource base and technical skills of not-so-small countries, and are after energy projects that can quite literally shift global chains of events. In doing so they want huge, fat expensive projects that no one else can do. Fields so difficult that not only can no one else attempt them, but no one else can even develop the technologies required to try. Places so remote that the price tag for just the extraction pipeline is more than other firms' annual revenues. Projects so expensive that no one else dare even apply for the financing required to handle the feasibility study. Production horizons whose commencements are so distant that no one else could handle the risk or the years of negative cash flow that are a matter of course. In short, they want to work in basins where only a few

---

1   The final supermajor is Italy's ENI, which has long been a de facto holding company for the Italian state. It didn't bother with a name change during the 1990s mergermania.

firms — seven to be specific — would even dream of operating. Because if one of those seven firms does bring one of those expensive, difficult, remote, long-term fields on-line, the profits will be fat and last for decades.

First, however, it is important to understand what they are after.

The State of American Energy

There has been much (legitimate) criticism in years and decades past of the United States' lack of an energy policy; in fact, the United States often goes years without even having an energy bill pass through Congress. The last moderately serious one was adopted in 2008. This reality is compounded by the United States' until-recent status as the world's largest energy importer, with many of its imports being sourced from countries like Saudi Arabia (with questionable agendas for American interests) or Venezuela (who views Washington with downright hostility). If the Americans cannot cobble to-gether an energy strategy when there is a clear and present national strategic and economic need, imagine the lack of interest in a national energy policy when the average American realizes that North American energy indepen-dence isn't simply possible, but already is a done deal.

This casual disinterest in energy security from a public policy point of view is just half the picture.

One of the greatest misconceptions in modern energy politics is that the U.S. supermajors are the driving force in U.S. energy politics and policies. Liberals condemn them as massive polluters, conservatives laud them as eco-nomic pillars, and to the average citizen their names are ever-present with the weekly ritual of a trip to the filling station. The reality isn't nearly as sexy. Smaller independent energy companies have long been chewing away at the supermajors' collective market share, and the independents' ownership of the shale revolution has largely sidelined the American supers in their home market. We stand on the cusp of a near-complete divorce in terms of the structure of American firms, and it all has to do with the technical aspects of shale production — particularly as viewed through a supermajor lens.

The American supermajors *loathe* shale, seeing it as the worst of all worlds.

Shale produces too little for too much: Over the entirety of their lifespans, shale oil wells produce an average of only a few hundred barrels per day — not the hundreds of thousands that the supers are after. Bringing such a small well on-line isn't worth the millions of dollars and thousands of man-hours, particularly when you factor in the specialized equipment and cutting-edge tech that is required. It's not that the supermajors can't master the techs involved — they have, and are probably better at them than almost all shale operators — instead shale economics just don't work for the supermajors' business models.[2]

Shale is the crucible of *competition*: In 2014, there were more than 500 operators in the American shale fields, all of whom were willing to undercut one another — or overpay suppliers — to get everything from land leases to pipe supplies to frac crews to sand. Such cutthroat competition is anathema to the cozy world of the supermajors. When there are only seven players and those players often must partner with each other or with government firms, a certain degree of collaboration — critics would say collusion — is par for the course.

Shale has since become the catalyst of *cooperation*: Because of the price collapse, the surviving shale firms are pooling their technologies and expertise, building toward a complete suite of operational and regulatory best practices. This not only drives operating margins down even more, it spreads the expertise over a wide swathe of the industry — hugely diluting what used to make the supermajors so special.

Shale has damaged U.S. *refining* margins: Because the world *knew* as of 1990 that all of the world's easy high-quality oil had already been tapped, the American supermajors invested some $100 billion in upgrading the U.S. refining complex, particularly along the Gulf Coast, where most imports were heavy and sour crudes from abroad. The result was a massive technical advantage for U.S. refineries, which could transform the world's crappiest

---

2   As of late 2016, some of the supermajors have started buying up shale acreage in the United States. It appears they are beginning to consider that the shift in energy markets in favor of shale may be long-term and so are repositioning somewhat. But even if this proves to be the beginning of a very serious effort, it still will be well over a decade before the supermajors get anywhere near where they used to be in terms of their centrality to the U.S. energy complex.

crude grades into high-quality products like gasoline. Then shale came along and wrecked everything. Shale crude is light/sweet and is a technical breeze to refine. With shale crude flooding the U.S. networks, the *less* advanced, *less* technically skilled, and *less* expensive older refineries now have a competitive advantage over the high-end supermajor refineries.

Shale has destroyed North American *natural gas* markets: As a rule, shale drillers are after the easily-transportable oil rather than the more difficult-to-transport natural gas, and so often sell associated natural gas into the pipe network at below-market values. This has not only driven U.S. natgas prices down to stable lows since 2009 — so far the bottom has been $1.68

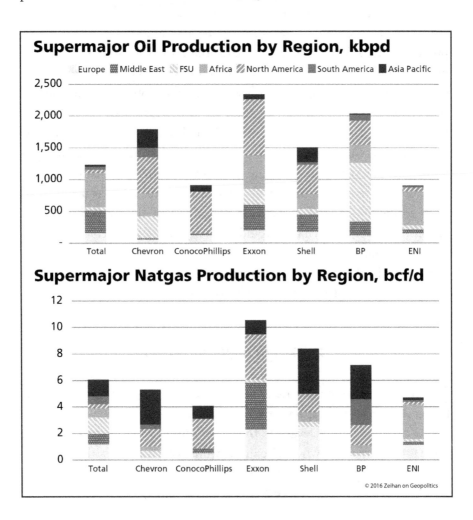

per 1,000 cubic feet — oftentimes shale gas' *selling* price is now roughly half the *production* cost for most of the supermajors' legacy natgas production.

North America itself has become *hostile* to the supermajors: Not so much because of regulations or court cases or environmentalists or NIMBY campaigners or aging demographics or green technologies, but because shale is putting the supers' local operations out of business. Oil output in northern Alaska is falling so fast that the TransAlaska pipeline is in danger of closing because of insufficient flows.[3] Natgas output from a multitude of shale zones rose so fast to knock the Gulf of Mexico from the No. 2 slot for U.S. natgas production to No. 7. Independent refining firms are expanding like mad while the supermajors are lucky to stagnate.

Of the roughly 14mbpd of oil and condensate and the 74bcf/d of natgas produced in the United States in 2015, the American supers collectively produced only about one-eighth. ConocoPhillips gets fully one-third of its output from beyond North America. For ExxonMobil and Chevron, the proportion is over two-thirds. Instead, the U.S. supers have moved abroad to focus primarily on locations where their skill sets generate the biggest financial gain. And as oil production (and consumption) in distant lands grew, so too did the role of the supermajors in refining and chemicals industries. They have the capital and the expertise to exist solely as downstream retail entities in many of the countries that they operate, leveraging a global supply chain with a reach that would even impress an 18th century imperial British bureaucrat.

Put bluntly, the American supermajors aren't very American anymore.

But they are most *definitely* still supermajors.

Bucking Deglobalization

The American supermajors are among the densest concentrations of capital, technology, logistical capacity, and skilled labor in the world. Just because that is becoming less relevant to the American oil patch doesn't mean the same is true for oil anywhere else in the world. In a more chaotic world, the

---

3   The pipeline's age isn't helping things, either.

size and stability of the American supermajors — combined with the high likelihood that involvement with the Americans will mean fewer security and political entanglements than similar involvement with the Europeans or God forbid the Northeast Asian Four (NEA4) — will make them *the* partners to have.

And as luck would have it, many of their recent investment decisions position them exceedingly well for the Disorder to come.

- All are heavily present in Latin America, an area struggling with the 2014 price collapse but that will roar back in the coming price split. The entire region will benefit from the high global prices caused by the Eastern Hemisphere's degradation, while the combination of strategic distance and America's ongoing interest in its own backyard will insulate the broader region from the rolling security crises that will plague competing energy exporters in the Eastern Hemisphere.

- All three American supers already have made it clear they intend to be first-among-equals in the Mexican energy patch as soon as the Mexicans operationalize their opening. The three's dominance in the U.S. sector of the Gulf of Mexico will soon be extended into the Mexican sector.

- ExxonMobil and Chevron already are positioning themselves in Argentina's rapidly expanding and opening energy patch, with ExxonMobil holding production leases on nearly a million acres in the Vaca Muerta shale field.

- All three American supers are significant players in the North Sea. ExxonMobil is the second-largest oil producer in the Norwegian sector.

- All are major players throughout Southeast Asia, particularly in the offshore.

- ExxonMobil and ConocoPhillips are major producers in northern Europe, with ExxonMobil holding a 30 percent stake in the Netherlands' Groningen field, continental Europe's largest natgas project.

- ExxonMobil is a dominant producer in sub-Saharan Africa, especially Equatorial Guinea and Angola, where its projects produce 0.3mbpd and 1.0mbpd, respectively. ExxonMobil also is a significant producer in Nigeria.

- With Middle Eastern supplies becoming locked in the Persian Gulf and Russian piped natural gas exports being shut in because of military conflict, other LNG exporters will do a mad business. The biggest beneficiary by far will be Australia, soon to be far and away the world's largest exporter — and ExxonMobil and Chevron are among the two largest Western firms involved in the Aussie LNG industry. Other sweet spots include Chevron's LNG operations in Nigeria and ExxonMobil's in Malaysia.

- Chevron makes a habit of being *the* player in particular markets — it is the largest producer of energy in Bangladesh, California, Colombia, Indonesia, Kazakhstan, the Kuwait-Saudi neutral zone, and Thailand — entitling it to special political treatment almost everywhere it does business.

- Unlike the European supers, the U.S. equivalents have largely eschewed the Persian Gulf. Only ExxonMobil is really present, and its investments in places like Iraqi Kurdistan are in reality little more than disposable toeholds. When the Persian Gulf becomes a warzone, there isn't much to be lost in terms of assets, and there are massive upside gains to be had from the increase in global prices.

Taken together, the American supermajors will be far more willing to go into risky areas nowhere near the United States, for they will not be nearly as desperate to maintain day-in, day-out flows of precisely the right kinds of crude. Such flexibility will prove a huge boon since the supermajors will be able to play the arbitrage game and invest in projects far from (what is left of) their home market. Additionally, and somewhat counterintuitively, they will be able to do something that most businesses find difficult: walk away. There always will be issues of sunk investments, but the American supermajors are driven by business needs and board meetings and shareholder demands, not national needs and the joint chiefs. So should an American super's threshold be surpassed as regards violence levels or government regulation or shipping security or corruption, there is nothing but its bottom line keeping it engaged. For countries seeking to maximize their energy production and income with a minimum of strings attached, the U.S. supers will be far more attractive partners than European supers or the state-owned companies of other countries, which will have core national interests at heart. Simply put, the American domestic energy boom means the U.S. supers will favor allowing countries to sell their crude to the highest bidder rather than forcing tanker ships to pre-determined markets.

This does not suggest that the U.S. supers are going to completely escape global carnage. Industrial patterns may be shifting to fewer and less gangly supply chains with production and consumption increasingly co-located, but non-North American oil will still need to be hauled long distances. While that certainly raises possibilities of profits that border on the extreme, many of the American supers' operations are in locations that will interest players who are organized, desperate ... and militarized.

• ExxonMobil is the operator of the Sakhalin-1 oil and natgas project in the Russian Far East, a facility that likely will see all its output redirected to Japan. In essence, on Day One ExxonMobil will have already chosen sides in the Tanker War. This is of far more than academic concern. In addition to the Chinese likely viewing ExxonMobil's operations and assets as legitimate targets, the American super has a wealth of other assets elsewhere in the Asian conflict zone. Of greatest focus will be Malaysia, where ExxonMobil already is the largest foreign natgas producer. Unfortunately, Malaysia exports most its natgas as LNG, and that LNG capacity will be at ground zero of the Tanker War.

• Both ExxonMobil and Chevron have significant operations in the former Soviet space. ExxonMobil has a score of major joint ventures with Russian state firm Rosneft, while Chevron's Tengiz project in Kazakhstan produces roughly 1.3mbpd for shipment through Russia to the Black and Mediterranean Seas. Once the shooting on Russia's western periphery escalates into the Twilight War, both firms risk losing everything without some very fancy footwork. One possible solution is to prioritize alternative shipping routes via locations such as Azerbaijan and Georgia, Iran or China — all of which bear their own carousel of geopolitical baggage and could place the supers in the targeting sites of an entirely new list of belligerents.

- It will prove impossible for France, Italy, the United Kingdom, and the other European states to maintain supplies to the European continent without full commitment from the American supers' African production volumes. Mild corporate disputes about shipping contracts and facility access for the American supers are issues of hard national interests for the Europeans. The pressure will be extreme for the American supers not simply to accede to European demands on redirecting all African oil exports to Europe, but actually to sell those assets wholesale to European firms/governments. A friendly way forward would be outright asset swaps, with the Europeans getting what they so urgently need in Africa while the Americans walk away with choice bits of Southeast Asian and Western Hemispheric holdings. A less friendly approach would be for the Europeans to reprise some colonial-era habits of turning local populations and governments against opposing interests, starting a not entirely cold war with the American supermajors.

Regardless of which way things go, the American supers can*not* count on significant support from Washington. With North America outright energy independent, disputes between, say, ExxonMobil and Luanda don't exactly capture Washington's (to say nothing of the American citizenry's) imagination — especially when one considers that companies like Chevron are far more important to Dhaka than they are to the Dakotas. The American supermajors will be on their own.

That is *not* how things will roll in Europe.

The State of European Energy

The Europeans will need state influence — some might even call it control — over their energy sectors because for them the energy supplies are critical to national functioning, even survival depending on how the war with Russia spreads. They *need* to reboot their old empires in order to maintain national coherence at home. The result will be pushes into very specific locations where the Europeans must lock down very specific crude streams to supply very specific refining facilities back in Europe. The European supermajors will form the economic, financial, logistical, and technical backbone of this effort, but the broad array of government prerogatives ranging from diplomacy to military capability can and will be applied to whatever opportunities and problems happen to crop up. The European supermajors will — again — become tools of governance. Tools of empire. Should a *European* super's threshold be surpassed regarding violence levels or government regulation or shipping security, a foreign minister or special forces squad and/or some 500-pound bombs are likely to come a-callin'.

The breakpoint for most European decision-making regarding energy will be Russian actions on their eastern frontier. When the Russians move, the Europeans will be faced with four simultaneous harsh realities.

First, their energy sectors — all of them — are in steep terminal decline. First oil was produced in Europe over a century ago, and in most cases production maxed out *before* World War II. Of the handful that didn't, only five — Denmark, the Netherlands, Norway, the United Kingdom, and Romania — sported output that didn't decline until a couple of decades ago. But with the notable exception of Norway, these have since entered terminal decline, and overall European oil and natgas output is roughly one-third below where it was a mere decade ago. In fact, there is only one new oil and natgas province that has been cultivated since 1950.

That province — the North Sea — is the second harsh reality. The North Sea was brought on-line in the 1970s in reaction to the Arab Oil Embargo of 1973, and it — nearly by itself — prevented a Europe-wide energy recession from turning into something far uglier. It soon supplied over one-third of Europe's oil. But everyone always knew that the North Sea, while a godsend, was no Saudi Arabia. For three decades, aggressive exploration and the ongoing application of the best technology available stretched out the North Sea's decline curve, but production finally slipped off the long-predicted cliff in 2005. In that year the Norwegian/U.K./Danish endeavors in the sea pumped out 5.2mbpd. By 2015 that figure had fallen to 3.0mbpd. New fields are still being found, and they are being linked into the existing infrastructure, but with some notable exceptions in the Norwegian sector those fields are progressively smaller and in progressively deeper waters, further from shore.

To mitigate the impact of the North Sea and onshore declines, the Europeans were forced to find alternate supplies, which brings us to the third harsh reality: in almost all cases those alternate supplies come from the Russian sphere of influence, with the lion's share coming from Russia itself. In 2014 some 4.3mbpd of FSU oil and refined product, 3.1mbpd of which came from Russia direct, fueled Europe.[4] Russia in peacetime has regularly used "safety inspections" to shut down lines for years when Russia's geopolitical needs are not addressed. Expect something far more aggressive during wartime. Between disruptions intentional or otherwise, nearly half of Europe's imports could disappear. There could be plenty of collateral damage as well. Europe isn't the only destination for the former Soviet Union's west-flowing energy exports. An *additional* 3.9mbpd transits Europe's soon-to-be conflict zones en route to the wider world.

Fourth, the *belligerents* will control what is left of Europe's oil production. The Russian piece of this is obvious, but the *European* powers most likely to become involved in the war control the entirety of the North Sea: The United Kingdom, Norway, and Denmark are Europe's three largest petroleum producers. The war will certainly force the end of all Russian energy exports via the Baltic Sea, while demand within the Scandinavian alliance will require every drop of available North Sea crude. North Sea redirections takes away another 750kbpd crude that used to go elsewhere in Europe. And that is without the war spreading to Germany and Poland or beyond.

Even in the "minor disruption" scenarios, an additional 3.0mbpd of oil and refined product imports will need to be sourced from outside of Europe, and as local European output continues to fall, that figure will go up every year. Which means the Europeans — *especially* the ones *not* fighting the Russians — will have to utilize their old colonial networks.

After 70 years of the Americans taking care of resource access and capital flows and physical security and trade accessibility, the Europeans are a bit out of practice at running empires — but empires are what they will need. Luckily for some of the Europeans, there are still a few remnants of their

---

4   Along with 0.50mbpd from Azerbaijan and 0.67mbpd from Kazakhstan.

old imperial networks — some of which have links that are still global in scope. Those networks are Europe's energy supermajors, and they are about to be called back to government service.

France: Retour à l'empire

In the early days of the Bretton Woods system, Paris interpreted the free trade regime as the United States making the world safe for European empires. That, obviously, was not Washington's intention. The Americans intended for *all* empires to be dismembered, and had little patience for French and British attempts to simply pick up with their imperial ambitions where they had left off in 1939. When an Anglo-French task force seized control of the Suez Canal in 1956, the Americans let it be known — publicly — that unless all forces were removed the Americans would not only revoke trade access and cancel WWII reconstruction loans, but they would actually consider leading a multi-national military force to eject British and French forces from Egypt. The result was a withdrawal that was as humiliating as it was rapid. The British takeaway was to never again be on the wrong side of the Americans; London started formally integrating all aspects of its diplomatic, economic, and military strategies with Washington's.

The French takeaway was never again to be *dependent* upon the Americans, and so Paris started laying the groundwork to be a functionally independent pole in global affairs.

Energy instantly became a cornerstone of that policy, which ironically encouraged France to hang on to its imperial legacy even more tightly. Of heavy concern was the open rebellion in Algeria, a territory that wasn't even technically a colony but a constitutionally incorporated French province. Oil was discovered in 1956 — the same year as the Suez Crisis — and the French began large-scale production in 1958 in the teeth of an increasingly brutal independence war. French troops were completely ousted in 1962.

France found itself in a precarious position a decade later when the Arab Oil Embargo struck. Energy prices quadrupled, and France lacked dedicated supplies. Paris' solution was to limit the use of oil and natgas to processes for which there were absolutely no substitutes. France writ large moved its economy away from most heavy industry. It instituted the world's most advanced mass transit system, which for the most part was electrified rather than diesel-powered. It installed so many nuclear reactors that by the mid-1980s France obtained over three-quarters of its electricity from them, and had enough to spare that much of Western Europe remains dependent upon French nuke power to the current day.

But no matter how much you substitute, there are still things that can only be done with oil and natgas. The French knew full well that their independent-minded foreign policy requires a national energy firm, and so they have one of the best — Total — and in true French fashion it is active in nearly every energy-producing region in the world.

This diversification provides the French with some interesting opportunities in the coming Disorder. France is not directly threatened by any of the world's major brewing crises. France isn't a border state with Russia's perceived sphere of influence — it doesn't even border a border state — so Paris will not feel the need to respond to Russia's aggressive insecurity. France's traditionally independent diplomatic efforts even make France one of the very few powers that has passably good relations with *both* Saudi Arabia and Iran. And despite being a European power, China and France are each other's third- and fourth-largest trading partners, respectively, giving France a handhold in supply chains on the opposite side of the planet.

As the world (d)evolves into something more like 1910 than 2010, France already has much of the institutional, diplomatic, military, and cultural infrastructure in place to do fairly well — and Total is a key part of that infrastructure:

- Total has production assets all over the North Sea and will prove critical to indirectly fueling the Anglo-Scandinavian war effort.

- Total is one of the largest foreign players in some of Russia, Kazakhstan, and Azerbaijan's most technically complex energy projects. Its holdings here certainly will not be safe, but as France is likely to be a non-belligerent in the Twilight War, Total may be the only Western firm of size to be able to continue any meaningful operations.

- Total is one of the of the largest foreign energy producers in the Persian Gulf. If any foreign firm can get both Iranian and Arab permission to broker passage of either Iranian or Arab crude out of the region, it will be Total. Should diplomacy fail, France is the only European country with both the naval capacity and strategic freedom to consider convoying crude out of the Persian Gulf. And unlike the Northeast Asians, who would have to escort any such supplies all the way home, the French navy would only need to get them clear of Persia and Arabia and so could shuttle far more shipments at far less a cost. That will make Total/France a sought-out partner for all of the Northeast Asians as well — something that will serve as quite the cap-feather as far as Paris is concerned.

- Total might not be quite as good at deepwater operations as either Exxon-Mobil or Petrobras — and it might have a (very well-earned) reputation for stealing its partners' technological tricks[5] — but its holdings in the Brazilian and Angolan offshore are likely to prove some of the least po-litically-complicated future production zones. All that crude can be used to keep France's European neighbors running, belligerents or not. For a price of course.

- The biggest share of Total's oil production is Africa, particularly the African energy superpowers of Angola and Nigeria. Nigeria is the only country in the coming Disorder that has a) the existing on-shore infra-structure where a new price regime would justify the sort of investments that would result in rapid output increases, *and* b) an existing offshore infrastructure that could be expanded without new investments mea-suring in the hundreds of billions, *and* c) a pre-existing and stable LNG export system, *and* d) a suitably corrupt government that plays to France's … independent style of doing business.

- Total even has a modest asset list in Southeast Asia and Australia that could be used to sell into the ultra top-dollar Northeast Asian markets,

---

5   Former U.S. Defense Secretary Robert Gates didn't hold back when he named France as the second-biggest cyber threat to American technological secrets in a 2014 interview.

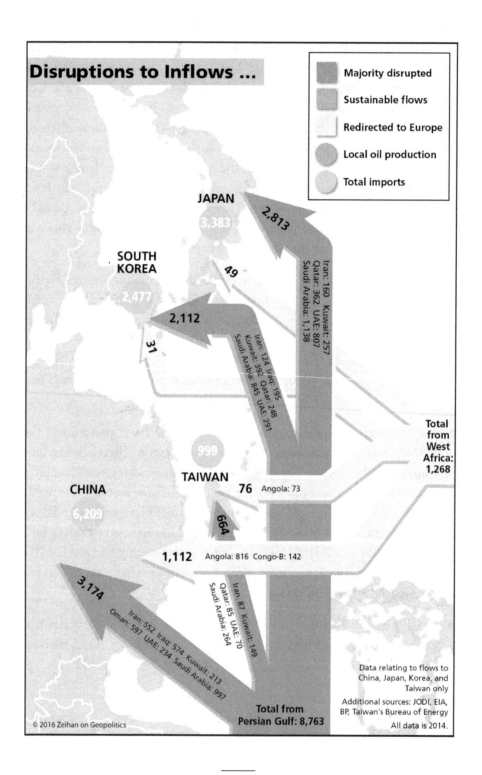

Disruptions to Inflows ...

Legend:
- Majority disrupted
- Sustainable flows
- Redirected to Europe
- Local oil production
- Total imports

JAPAN 3,383

2,813

Iran: 160 Kuwait: 257
Qatar: 362 UAE: 807
Saudi Arabia: 1,138

SOUTH KOREA 2,477

49

2,112

Iran: 124 Iraq: 195
Kuwait: 392 Qatar: 248
Saudi Arabia: 845 UAE: 291

31

CHINA 6,209

999

TAIWAN 76 Angola: 73

Total from West Africa: 1,268

664

1,112 Angola: 816 Congo-B: 142

3,174

Iran: 552 Iraq: 574 Kuwait: 213
Oman: 597 UAE: 234 Saudi Arabia: 997

Qatar: 85 Kuwait: 70
Iran: 87 UAE: 70
Saudi Arabia: 264

Data relating to flows to China, Japan, Korea, and Taiwan only

Additional sources: JODI, EIA, BP, Taiwan's Bureau of Energy

All data is 2014.

Total from Persian Gulf: 8,763

© 2016 Zeihan on Geopolitics

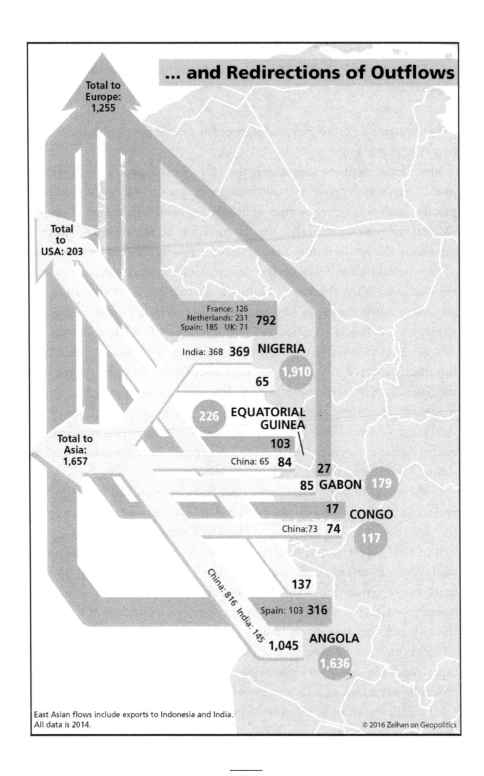

... and Redirections of Outflows

Total to Europe: 1,255

Total to USA: 203

Total to Asia: 1,657

France: 126
Netherlands: 231
Spain: 185 UK: 71 **792**

India: 368 **369** NIGERIA **1,910**

65

226 EQUATORIAL GUINEA

103

China: 65 **84** **27**

85 GABON **179**

17 CONGO

China:73 **74** **117**

China: 816 India: 145

137

Spain: 103 **316**

1,045 ANGOLA **1,636**

East Asian flows include exports to Indonesia and India.
All data is 2014.

© 2016 Zeihan on Geopolitics

that could be used to trade favors with the Chinese throughout the region, or that could be swapped for Atlantic assets of more use at the European poker table.

In the coming Disorder France is exceedingly well positioned, but it faces two critical challenges.

First, Total's refineries are among the *least* sophisticated in the developed world. France is dependent upon the highest-quality crudes the world can provide, with over three-quarters of its imports being light/sweet. As global pickings become slim, France will be forced to be far more aggressive at protecting the production and transport of very specific crude grades.

The second problem will be the Asians. Unlike the American financial crisis of 2007-2009, the European financial crisis began a year earlier and (as of late-2016) shows no sign of resolution. Overall European economic activity has barely returned to 2006 levels, and in such economic doldrums energy demand has steadily fallen. Instead of supplying their former European masters with energy supplies, most of the African states now send the lion's share of their output to East Asia. And of course, much of the oil production from these players is precisely the light/sweet grades upon which the French depend. West African energy exports traditionally satisfied U.S. energy demand, but in recent years the American shale boom has freed up this oil for other markets.

In the world to come the Asians need this oil — *all* this oil — to flow to Asia to compensate for the lack of Persian Gulf supplies. The Europeans will need this oil — *all* this oil — to flow to Europe to compensate for the lack of FSU supplies. Left to their own devices, the West Africans would vastly prefer to sell to Asia — the premium is bigger and there is no emotional baggage from the colonial era. But Asian military forces — whether Japanese or Chinese or Indian — are simply on the wrong side of the planet and will lack the strategic freedom to sail 12,000 miles to secure African oil for themselves. In contrast, the French have a military with centuries of experience in colonial operations, the strategic freedom to use it, and the proximity to make it all relatively easy. Combine that military capacity with Total's ability to run the region's offshore energy production and you have the makings of a neoimperial system that serves as a broker for European needs, all run from Paris. "All" France has to do is cut out the Asians.

The United Kingdom: Fueling a War

Between its own sector of the North Sea and extensive infrastructure that enables Great Britain to import energy from the sea's Norwegian sector, the United Kingdom does not face any real risk of domestic energy disruption. But this isn't about just the United Kingdom. London will be part of a multinational coalition that is certain to be doing battle with the Russians, and all those countries will need to be supported economically, financially, militarily, and (of course) with energy. The North Sea has (just barely) enough oil to keep the Scandinavian alliance operational, but the United Kingdom will need to venture abroad for energy for three reasons.

First, wars use a *lot* of fuel. A leading reason that Europe has traditionally used less petroleum than the United States is that the Europeans have for decades contracted out their defense oversight to the U.S. military. When the American retrenchment occurs, the Europeans will have no choice but to ramp up their military activities, which in turn will necessitate more petroleum consumption. Courtesy of tech upgrades in the U.S. military that monitor this sort of thing, we've got a good idea of just *how* much more. An Army heavy division under operations uses some 600,000 gallons of fuel a day, which requires about 15kbpd of raw crude to produce. The U.S. Air Force alone uses over 150kbpd of fuel a day as part and parcel of normal *peace*time operations. Since Anglo-Scandinavian forces are heavy on air and naval power, expect their fuel usage to be well above global averages.

Second, Russian attempts to scramble Anglo-Scandinavian logistics will be par for the course. The United Kingdom simply cannot assume that its mastery of the waves will enable every shipment to make it to where it needs to go. Backups will be needed.

Third, London's responsibilities during the war will be more than military and economic, but diplomatic as well. The Scandinavians are hardly slouches, and their maritime capabilities are historical echoes of the medieval Vikings, but the combined Scandinavian population is only 26 million. The Scandinavians can certainly bloody the Russians — badly — but they simply lack the demographic heft required to field an army capable of rolling back Russian advances, much less force a peace upon Moscow. And to be blunt, the United Kingdom isn't capable of fielding one either. The Brits are at home sailing the waves, not trudging through the wide Russian open. The Anglo-Scandinavian alliance will need the Germans and Poles in the fight, and it would be far easier to convince Berlin and Warsaw to join if London can keep them fueled. Considering how supplies were becoming interrupted or would shift around during the Twilight War, it would behoove the Brits to scrape up another 1mbpd of crude.

The problem facing London is that even before the war begins, the quintessential British supermajors are broken shells.

BP — formerly known as British Petroleum — is the firm that kicked off the mergermania that created today's supermajors. It laid out extensive volumes of capital to expand to every corner of the world. A quarter-century on a series of strategic miscalculations, poor judgement, and outright bad luck have gutted the firm of its capital, its best staff, and many of its most promising production zones.

Two particularly bad corporate crises illustrate the point. BP was the supermajor that most aggressively pushed into the former Soviet space, going so far as to partner with a trio of Russian oligarchs in 2003 to form a subsidiary known as TNK-BP. Those oligarchs used their Kremlin connections to manipulate the Russian legal and judicial systems to, in essence, rob BP at every opportunity. In an attempt to maintain its position as one of the world's largest energy firms, BP continually sent good money after bad, to the point of actually transferring some of its non-FSU assets to the TNK-BP tie up. This strategy reached its absurd conclusion in 2013, when Moscow forced the majority sale of TNK-BP to Russian state oil monopoly Rosneft, denying BP the ability to even direct investment decisions for its Russian operations. And when hostilities in Central Europe get serious, expect Rosneft/Moscow to simply take all of BP's Russian holdings outright.

Concurrently, many of BP's operations around the world picked up a whiff of desperation from the souring of such large investments into the FSU and started to prioritize maximum production rates over all other concerns. Such as safety. The exemplar was the Deepwater Horizon oil rig disaster in the U.S. sector of the Gulf of Mexico in 2010. Despite a series of rising technical warnings, BP personnel pushed production efforts in order to meet time schedules and production goals. The result was a fire, explosion, 11 deaths, heavy damage to the rig's subsea infrastructure, and a massive oil outflow that required weeks to seal. By the time all was said and done, nearly 5 million barrels of crude had leaked into the gulf, BP faced a temporary ban from all U.S. government contracts, more than $50 billion in fines and settlements had been paid out — an amount greater than BP's typical annual profits — and Mark Wahlberg starred in a major motion picture showcasing the entire fiasco.

As of 2016, BP is simply in the wrong places. It is a negligible player in Southeast Asia, Nigeria, Venezuela, Argentina, Mexico, and even its Canadian operations are too little, too late. It is part of more than 20 promising (very long-term) plays in Brazil, but it is the operator in only two and so cannot steer the projects in the directions that it — or London — so desperately needs. Yet BP has committed nearly $20 billion to Oman, a country whose output is — at best — middling, and that could well be facing a civil war when its current Sultan — aged 75 — dies.

The 2014 price crash combined with this cavalcade of defeats has forced BP to scale back on almost all its operations that aren't in the United States or Canada. BP is working from the sound logic that servicing the only developed economy likely to experience long-term economic growth is the best strategy for a company that needs to take a more conservative business view of the world. Unfortunately, that does *not* work in the case of supermajors. The cost, labor and market structure for shale eats away at the supermajors' advantages. Even with the vast improvements of the past two years, shale is far too labor-intensive — the output per well is an order of magnitude too low — to justify the application of the supermajors' top-notch staff. The heavy role of small production firms means that competition is fierce and the market is supersaturated, so profits are small and margins thin; the supermajors are better off applying their capital elsewhere. Furthermore, the American market is simply too closed in terms of infrastructure and politics to export local output. BP's Alaska holdings may in time prove the exception, but any Alaskan production is on the wrong side of the planet to help the United Kingdom's war effort. Only BP's Angolan operations appear to offer much hope in terms of long-term sustainable, geographically-relevant output.

For London this must be supremely frustrating. Just as the United Kingdom needs its energy complex to rise to an imperial challenge, BP's fortunes have shriveled to a purely national scope. It's not like the United Kingdom will be facing electricity shortages — possible shale output locally plus a probable nuclear resurgence will address such concerns in spades — but BP just isn't capable of sealing any deals with Germany or Poland on its own.

There are two ways forward for London.

First, London can always add a layer to imminent deals it is brokering with Washington. In June 2016 the British citizenry voted to remove the United Kingdom from the European Union. Shortly thereafter London (very unofficially) began free trade talks with India, Canada, and the United States and may well end up being admitted as the fourth member of NAFTA. With close economic linkages about to become even closer, what is bad for the British economy isn't exactly great for the American economy. But it isn't all bad, and that holds true for both of the major English-speaking powers.

Courtesy of the shale revolution, the United States is now the world's largest refined product exporter and as such will have plenty of fuel to sell on to the Anglo-Scandinavian alliance (who in turn will provide it to Germany and Poland). BP's logistics system is perfect for managing the transfers. The scale of such transfers — in excess of 1mbpd of refined product — will be the largest directed fuel stream since the Second World War. However, America does not do favors for free — particularly where its former colonial master is concerned.

A good guide for how this will play out are the Anglo-American Cash-Carry and Lend-Lease deals of WWII's early years. At that time the Americans saw the strategic need to counter Nazi Germany and so provided the United Kingdom with a series of fuel, food, and military materiel deals. But the assistance came with steep costs. Before all was said and done, the British were forced to "grant" the Americans century-long leases on all but two of their Western Hemispheric military bases and accept debts that London was not able to fully discharge until the 2000s.

Expect a 21st century equivalent with BP being forced to divest itself of interests the Americans find useful to American firms, up to and including *everything* in the United States and Canada. Considering that 1mbpd of crude at $100 a barrel would wholesale for $100 million a day — with refined product selling for at least double that — BP would burn through its Western Hemispheric holdings fairly quickly. What is left of BP after such deals are initiated will likely be so small and so limited to wartime supply runs that a smaller BP might as well be nationalized and folded into the British military.

The British do have a bit of a back-up plan — another supermajor with British links — but it isn't a very good one: the Anglo-Dutch partnership that is Royal Dutch/Shell.

Royal Dutch/Shell does have international assets of more value than BP, but to a large degree it too is in the wrong places. Shell *was* able to secure some assets in post-Saddam Iraq, but the Saudi-Iranian fight in the Gulf will close the Strait of Hormuz to Iraqi crude — and an outright Iranian invasion of Saudi Arabia would have to pass through Iraq, making all that investment in southern Iraq moot anyway. Of even less use is Shell's recent decision to purchase British Gas, primarily for natgas-producing assets in the Gulf of Mexico — assets that are now largely shut down in the aftermath of the U.S. shale revolution. Some century-plus-old facilities in Malaysia and Indonesia are indeed valuable, but they are on the wrong side of the planet to be of any use to London. Their primary purpose will be for sale — or perhaps asset-swaps to get something of more use in the Atlantic Basin. The logic holds for Royal Dutch/Shell's positions in Australian LNG as well. Brazilian assets might prove a long-term solution, but first meaningful oil is highly unlikely to arrive before the Twilight War ends.

Shell still holds two extremely important asset sets, nonetheless. First, Shell is a major player in Nigeria — both onshore and off. Nigeria may not exactly reek with stability, but the sort of grinding civil unrest that is the norm in the West African country is a far cry from the mobile warfare of Ukraine or the blood feud of the Persian Gulf. Second, Shell maintains one of the world's largest refinery networks in the Netherlands. The Rotterdam region has everything that the Brits and their allies need — from storage capacity to natural gas processing to a multitude of refineries — to fuel a war effort further east.

Regardless of approach, a massive problem/opportunity looms in the United Kingdom's future.

Nigeria is where the United Kingdom's colonial legacy lies, Nigeria is where BP and Shell both have assets, and Nigeria is the one place on the planet that can potentially increase oil output rapidly. If London can manage a peaceful and constructive return to involvement in Nigerian affairs, the United Kingdom will have all the oil and natgas flows it needs both to fight its war and recruit other major countries to join on its side.

The problem is that the 180 million Nigerians disagree on almost everything, regularly engaging in internal religious, ethnic, and economic wars that often kill thousands of people a month — and much of that violence is directed toward the petroleum sector. Of the half of Nigeria's 2.4mbpd of oil output that is on shore, most of it comes from the lands of the ethnic Ijaw and Igbo — ethnicities whose rebellion often dominates national politics. (An Igbo rebellion led to a flat out civil war in 1967.) Nigeria's offshore facilities are safer, but not as safe as you might think. During the Ijaw uprisings in the 2000s, militants in speedboats regularly hijacked oil platforms 50 *miles* out to sea, kidnapping foreign oil workers for leverage in their talks with the national authorities and foreign firms. Very few tactics are considered off-limits. And even if the oil can be produced, so many people punch so many holes in so many pipelines that roughly 300kbpd of Nigeria's output is flat out *stolen*. In mid-2016, a fresh wave of attacks so damaged infrastructure that Nigeria's oil exports were down by over 40 percent for five months.

In peacetime this is series of problems that never really go away, but can be endured because there is sufficient redundancy elsewhere in global oil. In wartime this is a threat to the stability of the British economy, the sustaining of a critical alliance system, and — most important — the prosecution of a war that will determine the next half-century of European history.

The contrast between the British and French futures could not be starker. The French can dominate offshore energy production with an already-involved supermajor backed by a military that has little else to do, setting themselves up to become the dominant power in European affairs. The

British face a war of movement in the Baltic Sea and the plains of Eurasia that may well suck them into a war of occupation in the swamps of Africa that will hobble their ability to project power for decades to come.

Italy: The Geopolitics of the Business Lunch

Italians have long pursued business deals according to a slightly different set of rules compared to the rest of Europe. Or the West in general. Or anyone really.

During the Middle Ages, the Italian city states — exemplified by Venice — amassed fortunes by monopolizing the spice trade between Europe and the Islamic world. The relationship between the Italian middlemen and the Islamic world was a complicated one; Italian merchant ships from Venice, Genoa, and Pisa plied the waters of the eastern Mediterranean, but the Venetian arsenal also supplied many of the ships used by Europeans during the various crusades. (When you have a monopoly on transport, pretty much any business becomes lucrative, and normally insurmountable politics magically transform into mere budgetary line items.)

Such a mindset carried over into Italy's post-WWII reconstruction, with the formation of state energy firm ENI no exception. After Italy's world war defeat, the Fascist-era state energy major — Agip — was supposed to be dismantled. Instead the Italians expanded it hugely, in part by entering into production sharing contracts with Iran and Libya. Italy's somewhat blasé approach to politics and national interests enabled it to outmaneuver the North American and Western European "Seven Sisters"[6] in securing production rights throughout North Africa and even in the USSR. ENI found itself in a pre-eminent position in post-independence Libya's burgeoning oil and gas sector as a result of a close relationship with the pre-Gadhafi Libyan royalty, as well as being one of the most successful European majors in penetrating the notoriously difficult Algerian market.[7] It has paid off.

---

6   A term coined by then-ENI CEO Enrico Mattei to describe the leading global oil majors of the time: the Anglo-Persian Oil Company, Gulf Oil, Royal Dutch/Shell, SoCal, Esso, Socony, and Texaco.

7   The difficulty was less about technicalities than anti-European testiness, so the Italians soothed the Algerians over a few of their trademark lunches and started work the following

While most of the other players in global oil are desperate to either acquire oil from the Persian Gulf or equally desperate to acquire oil from anywhere *but* the Persian Gulf, ENI has long sourced the majority of its oil and natgas production from Africa.

For many of the same reasons that ENI has proven successful, however, recent history has not been kind to ENI. The cozy, apolitical Italian way of doing business tends to grate against the national interests of many of contemporary Italy's partners and allies, and is — in many of them — actually illegal. ENI has become tripped up by its sanctions-busting with Iran, its backroom deals in Algeria, and its outright bribes in Russia. And since in Italy everything is in the family, the scandals — and charges — go deep into the Italian government. Even within some countries in which ENI is active(ly bribing), it has run into trouble with authorities who were … overlooked. Such … concerns run particularly high in Nigeria, Gabon, and Congo-B.

But by far the biggest challenge has been the Libyan collapse. Rome, via ENI, had long been the biggest investor in Libyan energy and viewed the Anglo-French-American effort to dispatch Gadhafi with disbelieving horror. The subsequent civil war has reduced the "country" to a state of near-anarchy that will abate only should someone with a significant army go in, occupy the place, and rebuild its institutions (and increasingly of relevance, its infrastructure) from scratch.

In dealing with the Libyan shortfalls, the Italians have two things going for them.

First, ENI's (in)famous middleman mentality has enabled the Italians to source replacement supplies from a broad array of countries: Russia, Algeria, Iraq, Angola, Congo-B, Gabon, Egypt, Nigeria, and Ghana. Such import flexibility would have been impossible without ENI's long-standing policy of investing in refinery flexibility. Italy boasts Europe's second-largest refining capacity, and ENI's facilities can accept a mix of almost all crude grades that the world can offer and refine them into an equally wide set of product varietals. Should something not quite fit, Italy has no problem

week.

blending multiple raw crude streams into a Meritage perfect for this or that refining run.

Second, and much less impressive, between the country's rapidly aging demographic and the European financial crisis, the Italians have suffered through more recessionary periods than growth for 15 years. Those recessions have crimped demand of both oil and natgas. As depressing as it is to say, Europe's terminal demographics and crappy financials may well prove to be an indispensable ally in combatting future energy disruptions, and Italy is most certainly a trailblazer in the practice of how economic dysfunction need not be a total catastrophe. So while the Italians' dismay of what's happening to the south of them deepens by the day, it has not (yet) reached the stage of an economic crisis (for Italy, that is).

What's on the horizon is either perfect for the Italians ... or utter disaster.

First, the positive case: Italian military strategists[8] don't see the point of the slowly-firming European efforts to counter Russian actions on Europe's eastern periphery. In part that's because the Italians have no economic or strategic stake in any of the current (or likely future) Russian targets, but it also is due to the simple fact that Russian crude supplies have become more common in the Mediterranean region during the past 15 years. So long as the war raging in Ukraine doesn't expand to the southwest, Russia will try to redirect what oil exports it can to the Mediterranean, where ENI's refineries will giddily gobble them up.

There's a Middle Eastern angle here too. As shipments to East Asia become more problematic and the Saudis shift their primary export points from the Persian Gulf to the Red Sea, redirecting a heavy trickle of oil to southern Europe also makes more sense. Italy has excellent relations with the Egyptian government regardless of its political stripes — in part because Rome doesn't bother itself with pesky details like whose fault the Arab Spring was, or whose fault the end of the Spring was, or whose fault the killing of the people who ended the Spring was, etc. From Suez — whether via the canal or the bypass pipelines, it's a very short — and very safe — sail to ENI's refineries.

---

8   I feel more than just a bit dizzy just putting those three words together.

Flush with crude, and sporting the refining size and flexibility to make the most of it, Rome would continue its historic role of middleman, although this time with diesel and jet fuel rather than saffron and nutmeg.

Of course, there is also a worst-case scenario: Should Turkey find itself involved in the Twilight War, *all* FSU exports via *all* southern routes will end as the Turkish navy denies Russia any use of the Black Sea. In one fell swoop 3.6mbpd of crude vanishes overnight from the Mediterranean. Italy's only realistic option would be a return to Libya. That effort would require purging the militias from the country's central coast,[9] reconstructing the production infrastructure deep in the desert, and occupying the transport corridor that would bring the oil out. Though many of the demographic and topographic features of Libya argue for a lighter effort than what was required for Western occupations of places like Algeria or Iraq, Italian military organization and capabilities are, shall we say, somewhat … underwhelming.

Putting Some Order in the Disorder

The nature and tenor of global relations is about to change, and the nature and tenor of global energy cannot help but change with it. The Europeans have a few options to maintain their security and ways of life. They are ugly, gritty, violent options, but options nonetheless. The Asians not so much. And the Americans? They will be able to move from place to place, cutting deals and making money with a flexibility and ease that is sure to generate intense dislike.

In fact, what the American supermajors are about to become famous for will become the standard for how Americans react with the world. Reach without interests. Capacity without commitment. Corporate without government. For though America may be withdrawing from the world, that is a far from saying that Americans will be nowhere to be found.

---

9   As of late 2017, a local IS affiliate is the single most powerful group in that area.

PART III

The American Play

CHAPTER 11

Tools of the Trade

Geopolitics is ultimately the study of the balance between options and limitations. A country's geography determines in large part what vulnerabilities it faces and what tools it holds.

Countries with flat tracks of land — think Poland or Russia — find building infrastructure easier and so become rich faster, but also find themselves on the receiving end of invasions. This necessitates substantial standing armies, but the very act of attempting to gain a bit of security automatically triggers angst and paranoia in the neighbors.

Countries with navigable rivers — France and Argentina being premier examples — start the game with some "infrastructure" already baked in. Such ease of internal transport not only makes these countries socially unified, wealthy, and cosmopolitan, but also more than a touch self-important. They show a distressing habit of becoming overimpressed with themselves — and so tend to overreach.

Island nations enjoy security — think the United Kingdom and Japan — in part because of the physical separation from rivals, but also because they have no choice but to develop navies that help them keep others away from their shores. Armed with such tools, they find themselves actively meddling in the affairs of countries not just within arm's reach, but half a world away.

In contrast, mountain countries — Kyrgyzstan and Bolivia, to pick a pair — are so capital-poor they find even securing the basics difficult, making them largely subject to the whims of their less-mountainous neighbors.

It's the balance of these restrictions and empowerments that determine both possibilities and constraints, which from my point of view makes it straightforward to predict what most countries will do:

- The Philippines' archipelagic nature gives it the physical stand-off of islands without the navy, so in the face of a threat from a superior country it will prostrate itself before any naval power that might come to its aid.

- Chile's population center is in a single valley surrounded by mountains. Breaching those mountains is so difficult that the Chileans often find it easier to turn their back on the South American continent and interact economically with nations much further afield.

- The Netherlands benefits from a huge portion of European trade because it controls the mouth of the Rhine, so it will seek to unite the Continent economically to maximize its economic gain while bringing in an external security guarantor to minimize threats to its independence.

- Uzbekistan sits in the middle of a flat, arid pancake and so will try to expand like syrup until it reaches a barrier it cannot pass. The lack of local competition combined with regional water shortages adds a sharp, brutal aspect to its foreign policy.

- New Zealand is a temperate zone country with a huge maritime frontage beyond the edge of the world, making it both wealthy and secure — how could the Kiwis *not* be in a good mood every day?

But then there is the United States. It has the flat lands of Australia with the climate and land quality of France, the riverine characteristics of Germany with the strategic exposure of New Zealand, and the island features of Japan but with oceanic moats — and all on a scale that is quite literally continental. Such landscapes not only make it rich and secure beyond peer, but also enable its navy to be *so* powerful that America dominates the global oceans. How do you predict what a superpower flush with tools and options will do when it suffers from so few vulnerabilities and limitations?

From a certain point of view, you don't. In foreign affairs the United States tends to be a bit on the unpredictable side. Approaches that would be asinine for normal countries because of risk or cost are within the Americans' easy reach. It never occurred to the Soviets that the United States could supply a metropolitan area by *air* — by far the most expensive way to ship anything — or they wouldn't have attempted the 1948 Berlin blockade. In 1990 Saddam Hussein was convinced that the Vietnam-shy Americans wouldn't deploy the 600,000 troops required to eject his forces from Kuwait, a country with which the Americans didn't even have a treaty.

Simply the aura of U.S. power is often sufficient either to provoke actions that either seek placate the Americans or shield from a perceived threat. Libya's Muammar Gadhafi was so convinced he was on the chopping block after Hussein's fall in 2003 that he disclosed his entire WMD program without prompting. Turkmenistan's Saparmurat Niyazov was similarly terrified for his life and position, and so he (unofficially) ended his country's neutral status and sought protection from Moscow.

Luckily, American politics in the mid-2010s allow me to cheat a bit.

The pace of American military intervention in the post-Cold War era is *higher* than it was during the Cold War itself. Every year since 1998 the Americans have been involved in large-scale military operations on some part of the planet, with Serbia, Kosovo, Iraq, and Afghanistan being the big four. The Iraqi and Afghan wars have made the Americans loathe to engage in large-scale military engagements in general and deploy significant ground forces in specific. The Americans are *done* with land wars in the Middle East (for now). Of even less interest would be getting involved in an attritional land war over a 2,000-mile front with a nuclear-armed cripple that is convinced it has nothing to lose in order to defend countries that in the American mind seem unwilling to defend themselves.

The shale revolution has removed energy vulnerabilities from the (short) list of topics that necessitate American engagement with the world. Across the American political spectrum, ideological sniping and more important (from my point of view) a rising hostility toward international involvement of all types and free trade is the new norm. For a mix of largely unrelated reasons, the economic and strategic threads have been removed from the ties that bind.

This gives us a few things to keep in mind for the next decade or so.

First, the American retrenchment is deep, broad-based, and will remove the support structures that enable the international order to exist. The Twilight, Gulf, and Tanker Wars are but pieces in a world unmade which will touch nearly every aspect of the global system. Throughout the Disorder wars, famines and national breakdowns will sweep large portions of Europe, Asia, and Africa.

Second, as holistic as the American withdrawal is, it is also *temporary*. After a 20-to-30-year hiatus the United States will venture out again. Due to the intervening global breakdown, when the U.S. does again venture forth it will be far more powerful relative to the rest of the world than it is in 2016. That imbalance may well prompt it to impose some new order on a chaotic world. But this still leaves a large time block jam-packed with economic, political, and security degradation.

Third, it isn't the American *capacity* to exercise power that is in doubt, but instead American *willingness*. In part, this means that if the United States gets poked, it is entirely capable of responding. (Woe to anyone stupid enough to do the poking.) But far more important it's a question of who the actors will be. It is the American *government* that is retrenching. American *citizens* can and will choose to involve themselves in the wider world. Put simply, it isn't so much that Americans will disappear from the international scene, but instead that the actors and tools in play will seem very different to us than the post-1945 norms.

In order to play forward the American position, let's first take a good hard look at the tools that will shape Americans' options and reach.

The United States' Military Will Remain Unchallenged

As the strategic scaffolding that supports the global order falls into Disorder, countries will seek to take advantage of the resulting power vacuum and/or be forced to take their economic and physical security into their own hands. The result will be myriad conflicts, most of which will be as lethal as they are contained by regional geographies. Yes, there may be many countries and forces that are not overly fond of the United States, but exceedingly few will be willing and/or able to antagonize the Americans once they find themselves in the middle of a decidedly American-free melee.

An excellent example is the state of the Syrian civil war that began in 2011, and in particular the role of the Islamic State. IS preaches a particularly vicious form of Islam that appeals to sociopaths, and a big piece of the IS recruitment drive is to draw-in supporters from the wider world who have an interest in killing large numbers of people. This has earned IS a great deal of condemnation from a great many players, with most labelling them "terrorist." IS' public (and private) ideology strongly encourages attacks against any and all Western targets whenever opportunities arise, and there is ample evidence that IS had deployed several of its fighters abroad to foment attacks.

At the time of this writing, IS is responsible for tens of thousands of direct deaths in Syria and Iraq, about 200 each in Turkey and Western Europe, and zero in the United States.[1] Why such a spread?

It's simple geography. The territory that IS occupies is landlocked desert. Ringing IS territory is empty desert to the south, the major power of Iraq to the east, the major power of Turkey to the north, and several other factions of the Syrian civil war and Israel to the west. IS is involved in a broad-spectrum fight-to-the-death melee. Regardless of desire, regardless of planning, regardless of rage, IS simply lacks the capacity to reliably send operatives much beyond its home conflict zone. Strategically, it is bottled up. What success IS *has* had is largely limited to Turkey, which is proximate, and Western Europe, which IS operatives can at least walk to.

---

1   I realize it seems like these figures should be loads higher, but I'm only counting deaths caused by proven IS operatives, rather than people who pledged themselves incidentally to IS' ideology but have no links to the Syrian war zone. For example, there is zero evidence that the attackers in the December 2015 San Bernardino massacre had any links to Syria or Iraq (it appears one of the attackers was radicalized in Pakistan before IS was even formed, and thereafter lived in the United States and never once set foot in Syria or had contact with anyone from IS). Similarly, in the June 2016 Orlando massacre the attacker pledged loyalty not only to IS, but to other militant groups engaged in active combat *against* IS. And even should you include everyone who is "inspired" by IS to launch attacks, deaths in Europe still outnumber those in the United States by more than 4:1.

This hardly means that there will be no successful terror attacks on the U.S. mainland. Nor does it mean that the time has not come for Americans to have an open, honest, national conversation about the intersection of religion, militancy, mental illness, social media, and easily-accessible fire-arms. What it *does* mean is that as the Disorder deepens and spreads, as wars and civilizational breakdowns proliferate, that the terrorisms of the Eastern Hemisphere are remarkably self-containing. The chaos is not only half a world away, literally, it is locked down by a plethora of local military concerns.

As for more traditional rivals — say Russia or Iran or China — a much simpler logic prevails. All three may not overly care for the United States, but none of the three want to seek out conflict with the United States *in addition to* their regional foes. Such would result in catastrophic outcomes (for them). Sufficient American forces prepositioned in Poland and Romania could defeat a Russian advance before it began, dramatically accelerating Russia's decay. American air assets in Qatar could guarantee that Iran's invasion of Saudi Arabia's Ghawar region would stall in the desert. A handful of American military assets based out of Diego Garcia, Darwin, and Singapore could intercept China-bound oil tankers well beyond the effective reach of the Chinese navy. If the United States pulls back from the global system, then these three countries have a much higher chance of success. There's no conceivable reason for them to make their already difficult strategic environments any more complicated. They all have bigger fish to fry closer to home.

Such negative decisions and the non-involvement it will encourage in American strategic policy will have dramatic long-term effects.

By not becoming (directly) involved in the Twilight, Gulf, or Tanker Wars, the United States military will have the freedom to fully digest its post-Cold War experiences, in particular the lessons of the Iraq and Afghanistan wars. Over the next decade or three this will result in not simply a battle-hardened military, but one that has been able to translate battle experience into a new generation of integrated technologies and tactics. On the tech side the entire process of drone usage will be heavily overhauled with a three-part emphasis on long-duration deployment, micro-lethality, and micro-deploy-ment. Among the many new applications will be high-altitude reconnaissance drones that can remain aloft not for days, but weeks, and deploy their own munitions. Hunter-killer drones whose armaments are so precise that they can attack not so much areas or even vehicles, but individuals — with negligible collateral damage. And stealth drones so small that they can fit into a jump drive, enabling soldiers and spies to gather real-time information about precisely who or what is on the other side of a wall.

Such techs have myriad implications for any battlespace, but the sort of military operations for which they are the greatest force multiplier are not the sort of infantry-heavy deployments that the Americans have (temporarily) tired of, but instead much smaller, more precise maneuvers that be carried out beyond the view of the general public.

The first, sharpest, and most versatile of these tools are the Americans' Special Operations Forces (SOFs), a series of small, specialized teams designed for precise, intensive operations including foreign counter-insurgency, reconnaissance, counterterrorism, unconventional warfare, combat behind enemy lines, search & rescue, information & psychological operations, hostage recovery, and good old-fashioned manhunts. The United States maintains and operates a variety of SOFs, including the renowned Navy SEALs and Army Rangers as well as far-less-discussed Special Operations Group of the CIA. All are highly trained, highly competent, highly lethal, and in general people you should never, *ever* piss off. Combine skill sets that are simultaneously precise and wide-ranging with the global deployment capability of the American Navy and Air Force, and the SOFs can deploy, act, and return to base anywhere on the planet in a couple of days if need be without anyone knowing they were ever in play.

In an age of decreasing American public support for overseas military action, the SOFs are increasingly becoming the tools of choice for the American presidency. While regular troops are now less likely to be deployed abroad than at any time since before World War II, the SOFs are the reverse. In order to maximize freedom of (covert) action as the rules of the international system change (or break down), the Bush and Obama presidencies have rapidly built out all of the SOFs teams. Between 2001 and 2016 the combined SOFs combat staffing has increased from 40,000 to 70,000. Its real staffing increase is probably considerably higher. Not only has the SOFs budget increased by a factor of *five* during that time window, but this is only the declassified budget for what is at its heart a highly classified series of institutions.

We might not see these forces operating publicly in the years to come, but we will certainly see the outcomes of their actions on a regular basis.

The second tool isn't quite as versatile, as all it does is spy on and kill people: drones. Unmanned aerial vehicles got their start in the 1980s, but the first real proto-Predator — largely an intelligence platform — debuted in the 1995 Bosnian conflict. Then, in 2001, someone decided to try attaching a couple anti-armor Hellfire missiles to it. The drone era was born. Weaponized drones are now operated across the length and breadth of American (para)military activity. The Predator itself is in the process of being supplemented/replaced by the Reaper, which can fly at twice the altitude and carry *eight* times the armament. Next up is the Avenger, a stealth variant capable of operating from the carrier fleet.

Drones have already overhauled the way the American military handles counterterrorism and counterinsurgency operations. Instead of needing to sweep and secure vast swathes of territory and engage in constant house-to-house urban sweeps, a mix of signals, drone, and human intelligence informs high-in-the-sky weapons platforms to target threats with minimal risk to American soldiers and vastly reduced risk to civilians.

But — from the White House's point of view — the greatest advantage of drones is somewhat similar to the greatest advantage of the SOFs: how little of a splash they make publicly when compared to the sort of conventional deployment that would be required to achieve the same end. A president can direct and fight a war in a foreign land with few to no boots on the ground, and with little to no public awareness or interest. President Obama, whose public persona and reputation is somewhat to the left of a my-country-right-or-wrong-chest-beating-Cold-Warrior, hasn't just directed a massive expansion of the military's drone program's capabilities, but also its use. George W. Bush signed off on 50 drone strikes that killed some 300 enemy combatants. Barack Obama personally approved over 10 times that figure that killed more than 3,000.[2]

---

2 Say what you will about the man's strategic policy, he has no problem killing people.

Third and finally, the American carrier force isn't going away. There are very few weapons systems in existence not under American control that pose the carriers any meaningful threats anyway, but what do exist are in the arsenals of countries that are going to be far more interested in using them against non-American forces. The Brits and Russians are facing off. The Chinese and Japanese are facing off. That leaves the French as the only people in the world who possess the technical capacity and freedom of action required to even theoretically threaten U.S. naval supremacy.

The tools that enabled the United States to dominate the global space since 1945 are not only going to persist, they are being upgraded. The new Ford-class carriers — the first of which is due to begin full operations in 2021 — will be able to carry more jets, deploy them more quickly, and sustain higher rates of operation for longer periods of time, while requiring a 15 percent *smaller* crew and having *lower* costs of operation. Even better, the Fords have a modular design to facilitate rapid overhauls and new tech installation. For example, the Fords' power plant generates twice the electricity required by the ship's current systems operating at full demand. That way when new power-hungry techs are ready for prime time — such as offensive and defensive lasers[3] — they will be somewhat plug-and-play. Not to mention the carriers are being increasingly augmented by an ever-expanding SOFs service and ever-more-capable drones expressly designed for carrier deployment.

It isn't just that this adds up to an American military that is even *more* effective, especially when measured against most potential adversaries, who are very likely to see degradations in their military and strategic positions during the next decade or two.

It is also a reminder that the U.S. military isn't designed for the sort of wars that the United States has been fighting since 2001. The United States is a maritime nation. Its most strategically relevant military arm is its Navy. The core of American strategic doctrine has always been about controlling the oceans and using that control to shape global events to its liking. Bretton Woods took the United States somewhat out of its comfort zone because it made the United States responsible for actively managing global affairs

---

3   That's right! LASERS!!!

on *land*. In the aftermath of Iraq and Afghanistan the U.S. military is now marrying the best naval forces in history with the best in-and-out- and drone-strike capacities in the world. The result will be a new sort of warfare that the United States *already* excels at: intervening at any spot on the globe at any time — and then fading away the next day. Over-the-horizon lightning and SOFs strikes, yes. Large-scale invasions and occupations, no. It is highly likely that the United States will be involved in a far higher *number* of military operations in the years to come, but those operations will be far smaller in size and scope.

There Is More to U.S. Military Capacity than the U.S. Military

The Bretton Woods system started fraying at the edges as early as the early-1990s. In some of the darker corners of the world, conflicts that normally would have been smothered were allowed to burn, because there was no longer an overriding American security need to keep everything on lockdown. Examples include, but are not limited to, the Yugoslav War, the Somali Civil War, the Rwandan Genocide, the Ethiopian Civil War (and its daughter conflicts), and the Congolese Civil War (which lead to the Great African War). Collectively these wars claimed at least 5 million lives.

Tragedies? Certainly. But in all these conflicts the world also saw something it had not seen since before the Bretton Woods era was established: large-scale use of mercenaries. Soldiers of fortune have been part of the international system for centuries, but in the Bretton Woods era governments kept a tight grip on organized military action. Or perhaps more important, the Americans' enforcement of the security side of Bretton Woods meant few states had large militaries, and even if they did those militaries were under heavy American influence if not actual American command. Leakage of troops into the "private sector" wasn't common; any mercs were typically in smallish groups if not flying solo. And since the Americans tamped down conflicts as a matter of course, there wasn't all that much fighting for would-be mercs to engage in in the first place. But Post-Cold War the Americans steadily released their control on both global militaries and the global system. Reduced American involvement enabled mercenaries both to trickle back into the system as well as find their preferred sort of work.

Three factors turned this trickle into a flood.

First, the Soviet Union imploded. Central control of the Soviet/Russian system has always been predicated upon deep intelligence penetration throughout society. When budgets tightened, many of these intelligence personnel were cut loose, leaving them to find their own way forward in an increasingly chaotic country. In the early 1990s, the post-Soviet Russian government attempted to shift the centralized economy to free market norms, in part by launching large-scale privatizations of state assets. As people in Soviet intelligence had the best understanding about how things were run and where the good assets were, former intelligence officials tended to make out like bandits. The result was a mass transfer of state wealth to former state employees who were *very* well connected. As intelligence officials tend to live in the shadows, a great many of them worked in the grey and black markets, and more than a few extended their operations internationally.

Many quickly found themselves interfacing with governments and criminal organizations the world over. And whenever these nouveaux businessmen found themselves needing muscle, they would reach back into the former Soviet space. After all, it wasn't just the intelligence services that were downsized, but every branch of the military and paramilitary security structures. Former Spetsnaz (Russian special forces) became active in Colombia on the side of the FARC. Former Russian border forces fought in the Tajik Civil War. In one weird application of mercenary activity, Russian pilots in Russian jets found themselves dogfighting on opposite sides in the 1998-2000 Ethiopian-Eritrean War. The group that became most insinuated into global organized crime were former members of OMON forces (run by the Interior Ministry), a sort of shock troop who have had whatever part of the brain is responsible for moral decision-making scooped out with a melon baller.

Second, post-Apartheid South Africa dismantled its security system. The South African Apartheid regime required a very heavy white military component both for internal control of the country's large black population, as well as to fight (para)military conflicts throughout the whole of southern

Africa. With the end of white rule and the rise of Nelson Mandela to the South African presidency in 1994, this entire apparatus was defunded and disbanded. This left an uncomfortably large number of well-trained, battle-hardened, heavily-armed, amoral white supremacists without jobs. They quickly evolved into the ultimate soldiers of fortune, selling their skill sets to the highest bidder.

Third, the U.S. military found itself with a staffing crunch and felt forced to subcontract. The post-Cold War demobilization had cut most deeply into the Army, and the Iraqi and Afghan occupations required far more troops in far more places than the U.S. Army could supply. The result was the rise of an entire industry based on former U.S. military personnel, colloquially known as contractors, to close the gap. For much of the Iraq War more than 100,000 contractors were in-country, and for much of the Afghan War fully half of the American troop commitment was not regular troops.

The chief hallmark of the Disorder to come will be that it will be, well, Disorderly, and in that world these contractors are going to be exceedingly busy. In an era of demographic decline, troops will often need to be hired from out-of-country. In an era of high security risk, companies will often need to look out for their own security needs. Corporate activity across Latin America and East Asia will in particular seek such help. Germany, Japan, and Ukraine in particular will need to beef up their troop numbers. In an era of maritime warfare and piracy, civilian shipping will need to be armed, particularly in Southeast Asia and along the African coast. In the aftermath of the Bretton Woods era of a largely non-militarized world, militaries will need to be mustered from scratch and mercenaries are an excellent way to jumpstart the process. The most pressing need will be in countries that used to be U.S. allies and so have lots of U.S. military equipment, but are perhaps not as good as they would like to be at using it; the Philippines, Latvia, Poland, and Saudi Arabia come to mind.

These contractors/mercenaries will be drawn from an exceedingly large pool. In Iraq and Afghanistan, the American military has cycled through more than 1 million combat troops along with hundreds of thousands of military support personnel (not counting contractors). Those wars are now over. Without major land conflicts to wage, the U.S. Army has already started a multi-year downsizing effort. Between demobilization and normal staff churn, most of those million-plus troops and support personal are no longer in the military, but it isn't like they all suddenly forget the relevant skill sets.

The American Economy Won't Overly Suffer from the International Breakdown

What is most striking about the global economy in 2016 is how lopsided the balance of power is.

As a continental economy, the Americans enjoy a wide range of self-sufficiencies in their day-to-day lives. International trade accounts for but 8.25 percent of GDP for exports and 12.9 percent of GDP for imports. Factor out trade with Canada and Mexico, and both of those figures slip by about one-third. Of what's left, bilateral trade with China is by far the biggest component, accounting for about 2.8 percent of GDP of imports and 0.6 percent of GDP of exports. China is roughly four times as dependent on exports as America, Germany is five times. And that's before figuring in that most of China's export markets are not nearly as proximate as America's.

This baseline is critical to understanding the unfolding Disorder's impacts, but four additional factors are — if anything — even more central.

First come demographics. Of the world's 200(ish) countries, only 17 of them will boast the trifecta of wealth, security, and a large and growing cadre of young workers capable of engaging in large-scale and rising consumption, and the American consumer market is larger that of *all* of them combined. Of those 17, the fourth-largest on the list, Mexico, is already attached to the American system.

Of the remainder, the list must be split. The first half includes countries that are free and clear, boasting as-of-yet not-degraded demographics, access to energy, and good physical security: Australia, New Zealand, France, the Netherlands, Indonesia, Myanmar, Switzerland, Turkey, Argentina, and India[4]. The remainder are countries with good bones, but likely to get caught

---

4   Technically, all of the Central Americans are also in this category, but they are so small that even collectively they barely register statistically.

up to some degree in one of the Disorder's major wars: the United Kingdom, Denmark, Sweden, Malaysia, Philippines, and Vietnam.

And that is *everyone*.

For everyone else — and to a degree even for countries on this list — the only way to generate export-led economic growth is to gain access to the U.S. consumer. With the dissolution of Bretton Woods, such access is no longer part of the international foundation. Now it will require a separate deal with Washington, and Washington is in a nativist, protectionist, anti-trade, anti-internationalist mood. Would-be trading partners will have to come to the United States with something that the Americans *want*. And courtesy of shale and nukes and carriers and the Millennials, the United States already has damn well everything that it needs.

Second is the thorny topic of supply chains.

In the world before Bretton Woods nearly all — if not *all* — of the steps of an industrial process were located in a tight grouping of facilities, in large part to insulate a country's supply chains from foreign interruption. Inputs were shipped in, and local labor transformed those inputs into basic, intermediate, and finally finished goods — with all of the work done within the same area. In contemporary lexicon we would call it cluster manufacturing. Zones with cheap internal transport — most notably areas with navigable rivers — enjoyed massive competitive advantages because they could utilize more territory (and thus more labor and more inputs) in the same "cluster."

Bretton Woods turned this system on its ear by reducing the global chaos level and thus making global transport easy, inexpensive, and secure. Why build everything in one neighborhood if a neighborhood on the other side of the city — or country, or continent, or planet — could handle a few of the steps better? The clusters were sliced and diced and their steps distributed the world over. Most modern manufactured products now have hundreds of steps in a dozen or more countries. For example, each of the iPhone's 22 "major" components are produced in different facilities, and that doesn't touch the issue of the subcomponents or the various assembly processes. Places that once held local advantages under the old system — such as well-rivered zones — degraded; the American Steel Belt became the American Rust Belt.

The first time a tanker or container ship is shot at in either Northern Europe or the Persian Gulf or East Asia, the cost of oceanic transport will skyrocket as much as the reliability of oceanic transport will plunge. Current manufacturing norms will come to an unceremonious and catastrophic end.

But the world will still need manufactured products. What it will lack are many places that have the magic mix of factors to produce goods in the new security environment. The successful manufacturing power of the future will need to not simply secure inputs *and* production *and* consumption, but ideally *co-locate* them.

Western Europe — with some stress — can manage the production, but its lack of inputs will force the Europeans into a neocolonial framework in, at a minimum, Africa. Yet even once this is done, Europe's rapidly aging and shrinking population will put an absolute ceiling on what the Continent can consume — and that ceiling is already far *lower* than Europe's current production capacity. Too many goods and not enough consumers will trigger mass economic dislocation, mass unemployment, and a painful slide into a deflationary morass.

Southeast Asia looks much better. Young populations, local (energy) resources, and a lack of a history of large-scale warfare will enable it to collectively rise as a new hub for both production and consumption of manufactured goods. Whatever raw materials (and financial acumen) the Southeast Asians cannot supply themselves can be brought in from nearby Australia and New Zealand. *But* it will be starting from a low level. The region's future is bright — so bright it is the topic of the next chapter — yet much of this area needs to go through some basic industrialization before it can evolve into a large-scale manufacturing center.

A far larger chunk of global manufacturing will reshore to North America: the U.S. shale revolution provides ample energy, Wall Street the capital, the Western Hemisphere writ-large covers industrial inputs, NAFTA provides multi-step manufacturing supply chain systems in a favorable security environment, while the United States and Mexico are massive consumers. The biggest American problem will be (re)shuffling of once-global supply chain stages into a series of cluster-style manufacturing hubs across the continent. Considering what will be going on in Europe, the Persian Gulf and East Asia, that's a great problem to have.

Third is the issue of currency. The U.S. stock and bond markets are almost bigger than the combined totals of the rest of the world, and that is before the world gets serious about falling apart. By 2014 it was becoming clear to a wide variety of players that the European financial crisis was getting worse instead of better and the Chinese economic system was unable to reform its way out of its 25-year investment binge. In 2015 streams of capital flight that had been trickling out for years accelerated into floods. Considering that half the reason for sending your money abroad is to avoid your government, quantifiable data isn't exactly available. But there are sufficient anecdotal and leaks to suggest that three-quarters of a trillion each flowed from Europe and China to the United States.

There are a number of relevant threads here:

- The breakdown of the eurozone will force a re-nationalization of the European currency system. That is *far* more wide-ranging than it sounds. Everything from corporate loans to government bonds to credit card debt to mortgages is typically in euros. Regardless of what value relative to the euro the new national currencies take the day the euro disappears, those separate currencies will start shifting against each other the following day. For any debts owed or deposits held in other countries, the present values will shift — and Europe loses either way. Either the debts will be kept in euros, in which case the entities in weaker states will default, and so the banks who granted the loans will take massive losses; or the debts will be redenominated into the new currencies, and as those currencies fall the banks receiving payment will take massive losses. Most of the lenders are in the European core countries — most notably Germany, France, Austria, the Netherlands, and Belgium. Banks in these states are the most stable part of the European mainland's financial sector. Because of this newfound exposure, most will either go belly up, be nationalized, or both. And since bank loans are the primary means that European companies use to raise money (in the United States it is stocks) that alone heralds a continent-wide depression. Ignoring demographics. Ignoring energy shortages. Ignoring Russia. Regardless of how the specifics are managed, the flow of capital out of mainland Europe is about to increase catastrophically.

- The breakdown of the Chinese economy has been coming for a long time. A bad loan is one in which the lendee is no longer paying back the lender (the technical term is non-performing loan or NPL). Back in 2003 the best independent guesstimates pegged the total holdings of NPLs in the Chinese system in the vicinity of 40 percent of GDP in 2004, higher than the proportion that in 1990 condemned the Japanese system to a multi-decade stall. After a facelift-style reform in 2003, the Chinese declared the problem solved and asserted[5] that it did not issue a single dud loan for the next five years. Then came the financial crisis and Beijing spammed out credit like confetti. Since 2009 total Chinese financing has roughly tripled, first to offset the collapse in demand for Chinese exports in the aftermath of the global financial crisis, then to artificially generate economic activity when the country's inland-development and consumption plans failed. Aggregate debt in the Chinese system has not only surpassed Japan's (a goal no one should aspire to), it has grown at the fastest rate in the world during the past decade. Part of the Chinese anti-corruption program is to so publicly punish high-ranking officials that the rank-and-file are scared to take their money (ill-gotten or otherwise) out of the country. If anything, the fear is demonstrating a system in panic mode and so encouraging the opposite.

- The U.S. dollar is the only internationally credible store of value and so the United States is the destination of choice for those attempting to get their money out their home countries. As a rule, the higher up in a country's decision-making apparatus people are, the more likely they are to try and relocate cash to the United States because they have the deepest understanding of just how hopeless their country's situation truly is. (Chinese Communist Party officials are most likely coolly in first place.)

- There is no longer even a theoretical challenger to the U.S. dollar. The Japanese are years into a multi-decade currency manipulation effort in order to stave off an endless demographic-induced depression and so are not interested. Since 2006 the British have printed as much currency

---

5   With impressively straight faces.

relative to their economic size as the Americans, but their economy is but one-eighth that of the U.S. The Chinese inflated their money supply to one larger than the United States back in 2009 — at a point when the Chinese economy was but half the size of the Americans'. Neither the pound nor the yuan is a credible store of value compared to the USD. The next-largest currency is the Canadian dollar, and no insult intended to Ottawa but the Canadian economy just isn't big enough to hold much more capital flight than it has already taken without generating unsustainably massive distortions in the prices of everything from the value of the Canadian dollar to a flat in Vancouver.

In essence, the U.S. dollar is segueing from today's role as the ultimate store of value to a future role as the first and nearly only store of value.

Fourth and last is the oil question.

International supplies are predicated upon crude produced by state-owned companies who adjust production schedules due to factors political and strategic, and have to ship their oil thousands of miles on the open sea through conflict zones. Courtesy of the shale revolution, American supplies are produced by small firms driven by profit, who benefit from short-haul pipe and rail transport connections in territories free of tank divisions, sea-fired ordinance, and dynamite-laden suicide bombers. Consequently, global oil supplies will be erratic and expensive, while American oil supplies will be calm and relatively cheap.

This does more than make the United States largely energy independent when considered in league with its North American neighbors. This does more than give the United States a competitive advantage in any industry that is energy-intensive. This does more than make the United States largely immune to the ebb and flow of international conflict. This does more than free the United States to undertake a cold-hearted reassessment of its strategic posture.

This means that for the United States oil is no longer a vulnerability, or even a goal. Now it's a tool.

Or even a weapon.

Pool it all together and the world looks very different from today. Consider the sum total of the factors in play:

- The U.S. Navy can prevent competitors from approaching (or even arising within) countries or even regions that the United States wants to seal off from the world.

- U.S. SOFs and drone warfare can help shape any zone of competition in which the United States feels necessary to participate. This isn't limited to zones of military competition, but also economic and even political zones.

- U.S. economic exposure to global developments is limited, and in no case is the exposure strategic. Any disruptions — even disruptions caused by the United States — are not felt by the United States.

- The U.S. consumer market is the only market of size that will grow, and any country hoping to generate export-led growth must have access to it.

- The U.S. dollar is nearly the sole global currency, and nearly all peoples and countries will desire access to it.

- The United States is largely disinterested in global energy, unless one of two factors enters into play: an economic growth opportunity for an American firm or the strategic disruption of a rival.

- The country that controls the global ocean, global trade, and global energy no longer has an interest in global security.

With these evolutions, conventional conflict with the United States is becoming a losing proposition for nearly every country in the world. It isn't so much that the Americans have over-the-horizon global strike capability with a wide variety of weapons systems, or that their deployment capabilities can put large forces on any coastline in a matter of weeks, but instead that the U.S. Navy can interrupt energy shipments anywhere on the global ocean thousands of miles away from its foe. Whether that foe is an energy importer or exporter is largely irrelevant. American power can starve its target of either energy or income without engaging in battle. And because North American energy systems are de facto encapsulated within the continent, any market volatility or shortages for the most part passes by the Americans.

This enables the Americans to dabble nearly anywhere they like without fear of meaningful reprisals or consequences.

In short, the United States is the only power on the planet with global *power* and global *reach* — but it is transitioning into a power without global *interests*.

As to everything that lies shy of outright military confrontation, we've seen before how these factors can assemble into something resembling a national foreign policy, albeit in a less intense manifestation.

In the 1890s the Americans had recently emerged from the expensive and time-consuming task of the post-Civil War Reconstruction. With the transcontinental railroads operational, the initial settlement wave of the Midwest completed, and the South once again contributing economically, the Americans had a great deal of spare money to fund a different sort of expansion. So they built a navy and went out exploring. The Americans melded military strength and reach with corporate interest, backed by government loans to penetrate foreign economies.

Some version of this fusing of state, corporate, military, and financial power existed until the run up to the Second World War. While historians wisely shy away from applying a single label to any period that involved an imperialist war, a world war, the Roaring Twenties, and the Great Depression, the closest term that matches tools to description would be "dollar diplomacy," the formal foreign policy of the Taft Administration (1909-1913).

From economic and state power points of view, dollar diplomacy was wildly successful. The Americans were able to impress their interests upon the countries they visited. American investment created infrastructure and industrial plant to metabolize local labor, generating products for the host countries as well as the Americans back home. Similarly, and due to the linking of American diplomatic power with private economic interests, American products received privileged access to the targeted markets.

Such a fusing of state power with private enterprise isn't all that alien of a concept. It is, after all, how most of the world worked before Bretton Woods (and how some BW participants like China and France still work today). But that doesn't mean it is something that comes natural to Americans — or that it doesn't come with a boatload of complications.

Anytime private and government interests intertwine, normally straightforward operations can tap entirely new sets of tools. Government diplomatic directives can harness private companies to deliver messages. And threats. Private loan makers can call upon government offices to induce foreign interests to keep up payment. Military capacity becomes an arm of not just the state, but of corporate power. During past dollar diplomacy periods, U.S. military power was used on dozens of occasions to directly intervene in the internal affairs of a host of countries in order to facilitate corporate entry, block non-American competition, and, if necessary, even enforce contracts with sovereign governments.

In the coming Disorder the Americans will enter a new age of such dollar diplomacy. Once again, the past provides ample suggestions as to which areas the Americans will favor engagement.

Dollar Diplomacy in the Disorder

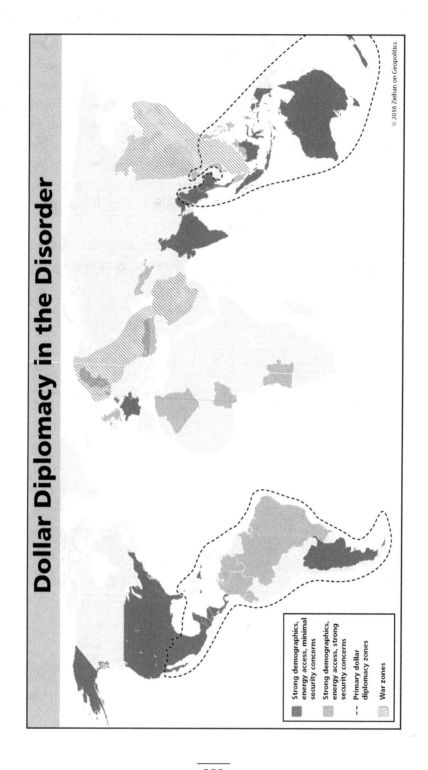

Strong demographics, energy access, minimal security concerns

Strong demographics, energy access, strong security concerns

-- Primary dollar diplomacy zones

War zones

© 2016 Zeihan on Geopolitics

CHAPTER 12

Dollar Diplomacy in Southeast Asia

Since the mid-19th century, Southeast Asia has been — at best — a bit player, not so much important for who is there, but for where it is.

Ever since there has been international trade, the region has served as a stopping point between the Western world and the East Asian rim. The Indians, Turks, Arabs, Portuguese, British, French, Dutch, Japanese, and Americans have all needed footholds here. The ebb and flow of global empires has often involved battles and occupations as one player or another has attempted to wrest control of trade routes or resources from another, whether it be Chinese porcelain, Indonesia nutmeg, or Malaysian crude oil. In modern times it is home to the world's busiest waterway — the Strait of Malacca. Yet over 90 percent of the Strait's cargo load not only neither originates nor terminates in the region, it doesn't even stop on its way through.

This is all about to change.

As the Disorder deepens the pillars of global power that have long traded through or struggled over this region — primarily Europe and Northeast Asia — will break down. The twin crises of the Twilight and Tanker Wars will make both regions obsessed with issues closer to home. The Southeast Asians are about to find themselves with something they've never had before: a bit of a say over their own future. And for a mix of factors ranging from demographics to energy to transport to sheer luck, that future looks brighter than it ever has.

Making it Big in Southeast Asia

The topography of Southeast Asia is unique, and the word "unique" is most certainly *not* synonymous with "good."

The entire region is so firmly in the tropical belt that most of archipelagic Southeast Asia doesn't even have a dry season. That's wonderful for growing a jungle — which is by far the dominant biome throughout the area — but it isn't all that great for anyone who happens to live there. Deep tropical climates plague the locals with persistent disease issues. It also largely prevents Southeast Asia from having what Westerners consider "normal" agriculture; grains like wheat and corn and rye and soy cannot ripen or dry in oppressive humidity.

Every topographical and climatological classification that impedes the formation of a unified, ethnic identity or a strong, centralized government exists here in spades. The jungles make even basic movement extraordinarily difficult. The entire region is hilly-to-mountainous, turning already-difficult infrastructure building into a nightmare. Many of those mountains come nearly all the way down the coast, denying the area's ample oceanfront the flat hinterlands required for the easy buildout of cities, infrastructure, and industry.

Even worse, roughly one-third of the region's land is made up of islands. Not the sort of flattish, temperate climate islands like Great Britain that can birth a major power, but instead clusters of rugged, jungle-cloaked archipelagos. In all of Island Southeast Asia there are only two places where the land is flat enough to generate traditional cities. The first is Jakarta on the Indonesian island of Java, where a series of formerly separate urban centers have co-mingled into a single sweaty conglomerate. The second is the Manila-Pangasinan corridor on the Philippine island of Luzon, where the rainforest is so thick and the local uplands so close that it has become a melting pot of more ethnicities and languages than most fully globalized cities. And even *if* either of these urban sprawls could fully dominate their respective landmasses, just in the Philippines and Indonesia there are another *ten thousand* inhabited islands.

The geography of mainland Southeast Asia is a bit better, which is to say it is only borderline horrid. There is no single chunk of flat, open land that could give rise to a major power that could dominate the region, but instead smallish pockets that host dense urban sprawls that cannot interact with each other over the land: Hanoi, Ho Chi Minh City (formerly Saigon), Bangkok, and Yangong. The tropics here may have some dry-season advantages, but this isn't northern China with its great wide-opens. Instead the place is a crazy-quilt of thin peninsulas that stretch government resources, and sharp coastal uplift mountains that shelter rebellious groups nearly within sight of cosmopolitan coastal cities. Thailand does have a flattish zone of moderate size, but it is on an interior plateau; its interests are often diametrically opposed to the urbanite lowlanders. In many ways Malaysia has the worst of both worlds: the majority of its population lives dangling at the end of the Malay Peninsula while the majority of its territory is the northern third of the island of Borneo.

Unsurprisingly, *none* of the great powers throughout Earth's human history has ever been birthed here. Even the local powers that have existed in the past — from the Taungoo of Burma to the Kings of Khmer — have never managed to stretch much beyond their core territories, and certainly never out of the region.

It should come as little surprise that local integration has always been difficult, since these pockets of territory have little ability to consolidate independently of each other. Road and rail connections among the mainland countries are thin, and hobbled by high-maintenance costs because of the corrosive impact of the jungle and low freight/weight limitations due to the mountains. This has long made the region the playgrounds of outsiders. Anyone who can reach the region by boat faces little problem conquering the area's disparate coastal communities. Only when the outsiders attempt to extend their control into the interior do things get nasty. In recent centuries the Chinese have held Hanoi, the Dutch Jakarta, the British Yangon, the Americans Manila, the French Saigon — but all of them were bled to the point of frantic desperation when they attempted to push into the bush.

The sole exception to these rather damning characteristics is Singapore. Formed in the 1800s by the British Empire to serve as a way station for European-Indian-Asian trade, Singapore has proven exceedingly capable at leveraging its position on the Strait of Malacca to become a logistical, man-ufacturing, and financial power all out of proportion to its size, boasting a per capita income right up there with the world's most advanced economies. It is most definitely the exception that proves the rule.

To put it in a (tropical) nutshell, Southeast Asia's geography argues for the opposite of success, and there is more than a small body of evidence that the region has missed out on the global development surge of the 1945-2015 period. Indonesia, the Philippines, Vietnam, and Myanmar are poor countries by almost any measure. While Malaysia and Thailand have both eked out industrial bases of moderate sophistication and size, they seem to have plateaued in terms of both economic and human development due to domestic political instability that has wracked them this past decade.[1]

Yet in many ways the area's topographic weaknesses are about to become significant strengths.

Consider this: Nearly unique among the world's major regions, the major Southeast Asian states don't have a history of going to war *with* one another because they cannot easily get *at* each other. Jungles and mountains im-pede not just road and rail, but armies as well. Since the fall of the Khmer Kingdom six centuries ago, Thai and Vietnamese and Burmese powers have done little more than skirmish with one another (when compared to global standards), while Malays and Javanese might as well have lived on different planets. Compare that to the in-your-face horrors of inter-European and inter-Northeast Asian conflict between 1200 and 1945.

As we enter a more mercantile world where old rivalries re-ignite, Southeast Asia simply doesn't have the active history of mutual hostility in the industrial age — or the capacity to engage in hostility — that will so plague nearly everyone else.

The "disadvantage" of local geography has a couple other quirks that will boost the region. Thirty years ago the vast bulk of the Southeast Asian population was engaged in tropical agriculture — a thankless job if there ever was one. In temperate agriculture one has opportunities for investing capital and technology and moving up the value-added scale, shifting up

---

1   Cambodia and Laos are so underdeveloped, poor, and corrupt they are barely worth mentioning. In a footnote.

from ox and sickle to tiller and combine. With efficiency and higher yields comes bigger operations, more profits, and upward social mobility. Such opportunities aren't nearly as omnipresent in the tropics. Each pineapple has to be planted and tended and harvested and boxed by hand. In many crops, from coffee to papaya to bananas to rubber to tea, there simply is no way for the average farmer — much less the average laborer — to improve his lot.

People who work in tropical agriculture are of course not stupid, and so most do what any of us would do: try and get out. Consequently, in recent decades Southeast Asia has had the biggest shifts from rural to urban living of any region. This has flooded the local cities with workers willing to take jobs that pay less than their skill sets would otherwise suggest, making them magnets for companies seeking to limit their labor costs.

The result is a region nearly tailor-made for dollar diplomacy.

Clear local security need. Several of the regional states have weak governments that cannot project power much beyond their core metro regions. The hinterlands and interiors of many of the Southeast Asian states are weak-to-rebellious. A little security assistance in the urban zones that would free up government personnel to deal with the thornier issue of interior pacification might be welcomed so long as it is made clear to both sides that the goal is security *assistance* and not security *takeover*. Signals intelligence, drones, and materiel, yes. Troops on the ground, probably not. Indonesia and the Philippines would in particular need a hand, especially when it comes to Islamist-themed militancy. There could even be some double-taking neck twists as the Vietnamese and Americans find themselves working against the same militant groups.

Opportunities for every type of investor. Southeast Asia runs the gamut from finance and high-tech in Singapore to automotive in Malaysia to computers in Thailand to heavy industry in Indonesia to raw agriculture in the Philippines. Particularly bold (and perhaps unscrupulous) investors will find themselves drawn to Myanmar, where one can literally get in on the ground floor. A domestic military junta deliberately kept Myanmar out of the international mix from 1962 to 2015. Now it is opening, but it needs everything from roads to rail to schools to electricity to ports. In the plus column, Myanmar's Irrawaddy is the region's only navigable river, raising the tantalizing possibility of keeping transport costs low even as the assessable reaches of the country are larger than its tropical, mountainous terrain would suggest. In the minus column, one-third of Myanmar's population are not of the ethnic Burmese majority; they live in that tropical, mountainous terrain, and most have been in a not-so-low-grade state of rebellion for decades. The sort of "security help" that Myanmar is likely to ask for is not of the sort the State Department would normally approve.

Clear local workforce skill/cost advantage. Because of the scads of people in the interior who are attempting to flee tropical agriculture, local labor forces are very attractive because they are higher skilled than their price point would suggest — particularly in Vietnam, which boasts that magic mix of modern urban centers like Ho Chi Minh City and rural zones combined with a far-above-global-average educational standards. Malaysia has proven the best at transforming rural peasants into semi-skilled industrial laborers. Indonesia can by itself provide more assembly work than Mexico. Myanmar's population is coming up from scratch and so works for little more than slave wages.

Clear local workforce concentration advantage. Labor's concentration in coastal urban areas affects the entire development pattern. The national governments need not worry about servicing all their lands, but instead can focus the lion's share of the state's infrastructure and education efforts on dense metro regions. The same is true for any foreign investment. Why build 10 small facilities in 10 small towns that are hemorrhaging people when you can just plop down a single plant in a major city where the labor comes to you? The semiconductor industry in Bangkok epitomizes how well this strategy can work. The Vietnamese are attempting to replicate Thai success in Ho Chi Minh City.

Willing local corporate partners. Regional companies have proven able to metabolize some of this labor concentration locally, generating firms with knowledge and skill sets far beyond most of the developing world with both higher quality and lower costs. But — nearly unique in the developing world — they haven't let their success go to their heads and are not afraid or ashamed to ask for help or additional finances when they need it. The energy sectors of Thailand and Malaysia both integrate well with foreign supermajors — especially American supermajors. Vietnam's energy sector is currently dependent upon Russia, a relationship likely to break down completely once the Tanker and Twilight Wars hit. Throughout the region extra-regional companies regularly use Southeast Asian suppliers for manufacturing of all types. Thailand, in particular, has phenomenal working relationships with a wide range of American manufacturing firms, while Malaysia has some of the world's best intellectual property protection laws.

Clear local financial need. With (again) the notable exception of Singapore, all the Southeast Asian states have soft currencies, and all are capital importers. As global trade and finances go topsy-turvy due to wars and demographic inversions, the region's biggest weakness will be insufficient capital. While many U.S. banking interests have concerns about setting up shop in Beijing or Tokyo or Paris or Berlin or Brasilia or Istanbul or Moscow, Singapore already is a regional hub for global finance and already serves as a regional hub for most major American banks.

Clear manufacturing potential. As the Tanker War unravels Northeast Asian supply chains, much of the world's manufacturing capacity will be forced to relocate. After North America, Southeast Asia is likely to be the region with the biggest gains. It already participates in much of the Asian supply chain system — Korean and Japanese firms are particularly active in the area — and so the Southeast Asians can simply pick up some of the pieces dropped by the Northeast Asians, most notably the Chinese. This rewiring of supply chains is actually better — for both the Southeast Asians and the American companies involved — than it sounds. Southeast Asian cities cannot trade by land efficiently, even within the same country — but they *can* easily trade with each other, even across national boundaries, by *water* via shuttle ships. This enables local supply chains to form that tap lower-than-low-cost, low-skilled labor in the Philippines, Indonesia, Vietnam, and Myanmar; lower than mid-cost, mid-skilled labor in Thailand and Malaysia; and some of the world's most sophisticated labor in Singapore. During Bretton Woods much of this would have been overlooked with European integration or China Inc. able to provide better economies of scale. Remove global trade, however, and Southeast Asia is quite capable of assembling local supply systems without the need of a global rubric. "All" it needs to integrate into the new, shorter supply chain systems is some logistical and financial assistance from ultimate end-users in North America.

Need for moderate regional security that plays to American strengths and preferences. These local maritime supply chains do not need to worry about local maritime threats. The concern is these local maritime supply chains will be caught in the crossfire of the Tanker War. The Southeast Asians will need help with regional naval security (an American specialty). The regional player most interested in American involvement by far would be Singapore, which is simultaneously the regional player that is most dependent upon regional trade as well as the regional player that the United States finds most attractive as a partner: Singapore is possibly the most strategically located country on the planet, its financial status is of huge interest to American business, and its utter lack of a hinterland means that American security commitments can be based on naval assets rather than land entanglements.

Limited energy exposure. The region as a whole is fairly close to energy self-sufficiency. Total regional gross imports are about 3mbpd (Korea alone imports 2.5mbpd), and once local production of refined products are netted out, regional net imports drop by half. In any high oil price scenario, foreign investment would surge into all the region's energy production projects. Brunei is already a minor exporter and Malaysia could become one quickly if its security situation doesn't spin out of control. The investment wave would also significantly boost output in Indonesia, Myanmar, and Vietnam, in that order. Much of that newfound production would undoubtedly flow into the refining centers of Singapore, Thailand, and Malaysia who — for reasons political, economic, and security — would earmark the first portions of every month's refined production runs for Southeast Asian distribution. Somewhat similar to North America, this region will not need to obsess about sourcing crude from a continent away. The Southeast Asians "just" need to take some precautions to ensure that desperate Northeast Asian powers don't try to take their production assets. That concern will greatly encourage the Southeast Asians to offer sweeteners to encourage American involvement in their systems.

Clear local consumption opportunities. Southeast Asia doesn't require an external power to provide consumption. Unlike rapidly aging countries the world over, Southeast Asia is demographically young — in particular the 180 million Vietnamese and 230 million Indonesians. Southeast Asia has a coastal population larger than that of China, and fully half of the region's overall population is under 30 years old. This makes it the one of a handful in the contemporary world that is wealthy enough to purchase American goods yet also poor enough to serve as a manufacturing base for goods for the American market. After the Disorder begins, it will be one of only two.[2]

The worst-case-scenario is pretty bright. Assuming for the moment that the Americans get drawn in to the Tanker War, they could end the conflict in a month with only a minimal expenditure of effort at minimal risk. There's no need for the Americans to engage any Northeast Asian rival in Northeast Asia. Instead it would be far easier for the Americans to engage their foe in the Bay of Bengal and Arabian Sea — well out of range of any possible land-

---

2   Spoiler alert: the second is in the next chapter.

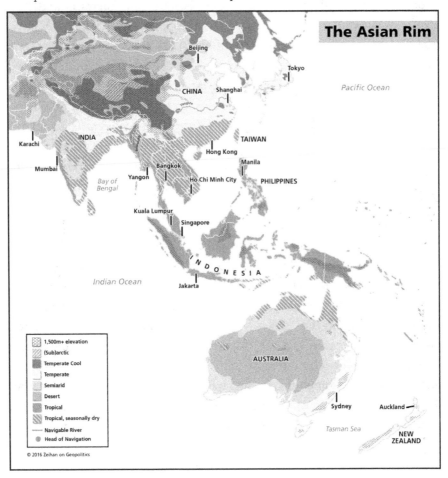

based support. No long-range navy, no tanker convoys. No tanker convoys, no oil. No oil, and that player is out of the war.

There are a couple near-local mitigating factors that make the region even more attractive to dollar-diplomacy-minded American businessmen and bureaucrats.

Minimal input complications. Just to the southeast of Southeast Asia lies Australia and New Zealand, a pair of highly developed Anglo powers. Australia is quite possibly the United States' staunchest ally while New Zealand is a close cultural cousin to both Australians and Americans. As the Southeast Asia countries' collective industrial footprint deepens and expands, they will require more iron ore, more aluminum, more cement, more lumber — all of which and more is found in Australia and New Zealand. Australia can also help square the Southeast Asians' energy circle: it is the world's largest exporter of hard coal, a leading exporter of soft coal, and is on the verge of becoming the largest LNG exporter as well. Unlike Europeans, who will need to re-establish empires to maintain their economies, the Southeast Asians just need to trade with neighbors they've never fought a war with. Even foodstuffs are not a problem. Thailand and Vietnam are consistently among the world's top three rice exporters.[3] With a bit of an economic overhaul Myanmar could undoubtedly return to the ranks of the world's major agricultural exporters. And most of what else is needed — most notably wheat, corn, beef, lamb, fruits, and dairy — can come from the Aussies and Kiwis.

Firm local ally. The leading defense concern of Australia is that some power will prove capable of dominating Southeast Asia and use it to launch a military or economic assault on Australia. In World War II the boogeyman was Japan, and more recently it has become China. With those two powers on opposite sides in the Tanker War the Australians have a vested interest in neither winning. While the Aussies cannot affect the outcome of that conflict, they *can* work to strengthen the capacity of the Southeast Asians — most notably the Indonesians, Singaporeans, and Thais with whom they have the closest relations — to help resist Northeast Asian influence. They will also bring up Southeast Asian topics with the Americans at every meet-

---

3   India typically being the other of the big three.

ing. Every. Single. Time. They. Meet. For the Americans, this isn't annoying in the least. It means that a creative, capable ally is already invested and is willing to run point. Australia isn't so much a target of dollar diplomacy. Instead it will be more of an enabling participant.

Pressing need to compromise. Perhaps most importantly, the Southeast Asians will be eager to make some deals if it means getting the Americans in. Much of the Tanker War will occur in the middle of Southeast Asia, with naval violence likely to erupt regularly in the South China Sea and the Strait of Malacca. Singapore, positioned where those two bodies of water meet, cannot have a modern economy without international financial and supply chain links. The Philippines and Vietnam are likely to be direct targets of Chinese aggression. The Chinese (and maybe the Japanese) are likely to attempt to capture Malaysia's most lucrative sector — offshore oil and natgas production. Nearly all of Thailand's external trade and petroleum imports come in via water, and the Gulf of Thailand's only access to the wider global ocean passes through the South China Sea. The Chinese pipeline corridor through the middle of Myanmar makes the Burmese vulnerable to all sides in the conflict. Indonesia may have a bit of strategic distance from the war, but the Indonesians lack the security, technical, financial, and military capacity to profit from the war without a helping hand. Simply put, all these countries are likely to *ask* the Americans for help. Which means they'll be willing to make concessions to *get* that help. Dollar diplomacy will always be more effective when coercion is at a minimum.

While the rest of the world will soon be struggling — and failing — to secure the basics of food, energy, and stability, while Europeans and the NEA4 will be engaging in industrial re-wirings to keep the lights on, the Southeast Asians will instead boast the perfect mix of factors to fuel the biggest industrialization and mass manufacturing revolution in their history. And the Americans will be a part of it.

Beyond Southeast Asia

Elsewhere on the continent American efforts to commercially penetrate will not be met with nearly the same level of enthusiasm, but that's not the same as saying there won't be notable results.

First, there is a reasonable chance that dollar diplomacy will prove moderately successful in India.

The truth about India is somewhat less spectacular than the common belief, whether in India or the United States. India's overpopulation has landed it with one of the most overregulated, over-bureaucratized systems in the world. Property law — whether physical or intellectual — is weak. Local infrastructure is weak. Local educational standards are weak. Local government is weak. Electricity reliability is weak. Logistics are weak. Construction standards are weak. Cooperation and coordination among India's national, regional, and local governments is weak. Government consistency is weak. It's a long list.

And that doesn't even begin to get into the issue of ego.

It is no surprise that Americans are renowned for being sure of themselves. And considering that as the world breaks down the Americans will keep puttering along, that mindset is unlikely to change. But India has a self-assuredness problem as well. Indians see themselves as one of the world's great powers. I'll leave the discussion of whether that is indeed true to people who wish to get into arguments with Indians, but the simple fact is the Indians are not known for compromising on much of anything that happens within India itself. No matter how nasty the Tanker or Gulf Wars get, India will still be able to secure oil supplies. No matter how much global breakdown the end of Bretton Woods causes, India's economy isn't heavily dependent upon trade and so Indians will not feel all that much pain. There may be economic discomfort, but there will be no burning belief in New Delhi that a new path is required and that such path must include Indians prostrating themselves to the Americans. Dollar diplomacy works best when it isn't being implemented in opposition to the target country's desires. India just isn't likely to be desperate enough apply the strategy en masse.

But there are two reasons that dollar diplomacy is still likely to make at least some headway in India. First, with a population of 1.3 billion, the top slice by any standards — in education, in foresight, in technical aptitude, in wealth, etc. — is still huge. There is absolutely an Indian market to be had that bucks all the trends, and that same top slice of people is the portion most likely to want access to American money, American technology, American supply chains, and the American market. In general they view American participation as a good thing.

Second, India has been so over-bureaucratized for so long that when policy manages to get it right, when the three tiers of India's government manage to align, there is so much pent-up demand that magic can happen. Such an alignment is how Bangalore became a global tech center, and American tech firms would have been fools to pass it up. There will be opportunities for both sides, but they will be much more targeted and shorter term than the other nations where dollar diplomacy will be applied.

One additional region that might prove fertile ground for dollar diplomacy is China, or more specifically the coastal cities of southern China: places like Shanghai, Ningbo, Wenzhou, Fuzhou, Xiamen, Shantou, Shenzhen, Hong Kong, Guangzhou, Macau, and Zhanjiang. All have strong economic and educational cultures. All have a history of cooperation with foreigners. All have their backs to the mountains and no hinterlands, and so cannot possibly make it on their own. And regardless of how the Tanker War resolves, all will be in desperate need of money, food, energy, raw materials, end consumers, and security cover — that last especially, but not exclusively, versus their own former government.

If the Tanker War ends with either a Chinese defeat or a Chinese breakup, all of them will face precisely the same horrid choice: seek out strong foreign sponsors at whatever terms they can manage, or eject over half of their populations to the countryside to avoid mass starvation.

American-style dollar diplomacy checks all the boxes. The United States could serve as a one-stop-shop for everything the southern Chinese need without nearly the historical baggage that Japanese or Taiwanese sponsorship would bring with it.

The third and final location of note is not one where dollar diplomacy will prove successful (at all), but instead a rising complication to American efforts to exploit other Asian locations: Japan.

Win or lose the Tanker War, Japan will remain a powerful, culturally cohesive, physically secure country. Americans bearing cargos of crude or diesel or uranium ore or coal might find some eager business partners in Tokyo, but that isn't the same as high-level economic penetration where all the decisions are made back at American headquarters. From an economic point of view, wartime and post-Tanker War Japan will be even more closed to outsiders than it is now.

In fact, a much bigger problem in Japanese-American relations is about to unfold.

In many ways what is about to happen with dollar diplomacy in Asia is starkly reminiscent of American foreign and economic policy between 1900 and 1941. During that period, American commercial power penetrated deeply throughout many portions of the region, most notably in China's coastal cities, with Washington making no bones about its intent to crowd out any other imperial players who already had interests in the region. This effort reached the point that the Americans were actively — and publicly — moving against long-held Japanese efforts to dominate not just regional markets, but regional energy production sites. Considering that in 1940 Japan was just as dependent upon imported fuels as it is in 2016, and it shouldn't come as a shock that the result was the Japanese attack on American naval assets at Pearl Harbor.

Don't overly read into this comparison, as there are plenty of differences between then and now:

- In contemporary times Japanese energy doesn't come from Southeast Asia (or India) but instead the Persian Gulf, and the Americans aren't likely to do anything to interrupt Japan's convoy efforts unless sorely provoked.

- Since 1990 overall Japanese non-energy economic involvement with the world has steadily eroded. Regional, much less global, involvement is not as critical to Tokyo as it once was; the most dynamic bits of what remains of Japan's international manufacturing connections are fab plants located within the United States itself. Blowing up U.S. military assets would not help with the relevant labor and regulatory talks.

• Japan will have its hands full with China, first during the war and then managing whatever happens to China in the years after. Crushing victory or crushing defeat, that is a project that would require decades of focus. Dogfighting with the Yankees over the Coral Sea would be a supreme distraction from the real work on mainland Asia.

• And, of course, the Japanese fully remember how WWII went and especially how it ended. Tokyo has no desire whatsoever to tangle with a strategically unfettered United States.

But the fact remains that the Americans are about to move into Southeast Asia in force, and will do so while the Japanese are fighting a war of desperation that wouldn't have been necessary if the Americans had stuck to their Bretton Woods commitments. There will be no small sense of betrayal, doubly so should places like Shanghai end up under the American wing.

There will be many within the Japanese political establishment who feel it only right that if the Americans are going to abdicate responsibility, it should be Japan who inherits the region after the war's conclusion, rather than sit back and watch Washington and corporate America initiate a Greater American Co-Prosperity Sphere. That Japan will have likely forged close economic and military ties with Taiwan, the Philippines, Vietnam, and Malaysia as part of the conflict will not only strengthen the sentiment, but give Tokyo some very powerful tools to do something about it.

A war with Japan — either within the confines of the Tanker War or in the years that follow — certainly isn't inevitable, or even likely. But East Asia has always been home to too many peoples with too many interests to be under the thumb of any singular power. Whoever wins the Tanker War, the United States' primary competitor in Asia isn't going to be based in Beijing for much longer.

CHAPTER 13

Dollar Diplomacy in Latin America

As much as it may seem that the world is going topsy-turvy (and it is), and that once firmly-held American fundamentals such as a military presence in the Middle East and upholding Bretton Woods and NATO are going out the window (and they are), there is one element of vintage U.S. foreign policy that the Americans will hang on to with an iron grip: the Monroe Doctrine, a policy that prohibits Eastern Hemispheric activity anywhere in Latin America.

To a degree this certainly feels counterintuitive. If the Americans are finding it hard to get excited about a Russian-instigated German rearmament or a rumble in the Persian Gulf or missile flinging in Asia, why would they feel overly concerned about a region that hasn't seen large-scale imperial European or Asian activity in over a century?

It all comes back to transport. In a world in which everyone is a bit more mercantilist and a degree of autarky is the flavor of the month, protecting internal waterways is a critical national economic and security concern. The water connection between America's two greatest economic zones — the Greater Mississippi and the U.S. East Coast — is the Florida Strait. The strait's proximity to the Gulf of Mexico and the Caribbean Sea forces the Americans to keep both bodies of water on lockdown. Doing so immediately brings into play all tools of American power not just in Mexico, Cuba, Central America, and the Leeward Islands, but also in the South American countries with Caribbean coasts: Colombia and Venezuela. And since the only way any extra-hemispheric power could threaten that lengthy list of concerns is one that had a launching point from somewhere else in South America, it is simpler to draw a line around the entire continent of South America.

The policy of Monroe — dating back to 1823 — is straightforward: Not only is no Eastern Hemispheric power allowed to have a military presence in the Western Hemisphere, but the Americans will take pre-emptive action to prevent any such attempt from occurring.

Pair historical American preference for Latin American exclusivity with increasing economic and energy links among the NAFTA partners with an American military with time on its hands with an American political desire to not go beyond its backyard and you get a perfect storm for heavy — and likely heavy-handed — American penetration throughout the region.

Geography's a Bitch

In most ways that matter, the bulk of Latin America faces even starker geographic challenges than Southeast Asia.

The portions of the South American continent that are jungle — primarily the Amazon Basin — are so hot and so humid and receive so much rainfall and are such dense disease incubators that they have never been able to support civilization above an extremely primitive level. Technically the Amazon is indeed navigable, but its shores are so muddy that population centers and farms and mines are rarities. For the most part, the entire zone is worse than useless as it cannot simply be ignored; the Amazon's fringes are home to a multitude of militant and criminal groups, forcing South American governments to expend scarce resources on patrolling areas that will never prove economically beneficial. And it isn't like these limiting factors end at the edge of the deep jungle of the Amazon Basin. Territories from southern Mexico through Southern Brazil are fully tropical.

The shape of South America in particularly magnifies this problem. Unlike Southeast Asia, where land masses are on the sinuous side, South America is instead a single giant chunk. The geometric difference drastically reduces the ratio of land-to-water access. Southeast Asia's omnipresent islands might (hugely) complicate economies of scale, but at least nearly all of the region's population can attempt to leverage the magnifying effects of maritime transport. Over four-fifths of Southeast Asia's population lives within 60 miles of the coast. For Latin America as a whole, it is only half.

Another piece of topography makes Latin America's situation even worse than this double-punch of climate and geometry suggests: Latin America as a whole is also extremely rugged. Starting at the U.S.-Mexican border, the Sierra Madres fold into the Cordilleras of Central America, and with only a brief hiccup at the Panama Canal Zone become the Andes, which run down the entire spine of South America, comprising the longest contiguous terrestrial mountain system on the planet.

In order to avoid the disease belts of the tropics, most of the region's populations have moved upland into cooler, drier territory. That mitigates the disease problem — and by moving into less humid zones, also to a degree the agriculture problem — but it isolates the region's populations even more. Most Latin American cities are landlocked.

Moving uphill also introduces a new challenge: very few highland regions are flat, and what flat pieces there are tend to be small. Inputs and outputs need to be lugged up and down mountainsides, which means roads have loads of switchbacks (and so are expensive to build and maintain) and rail lines cannot haul all that much if they can be built at all. Any infrastructure operating in one mountain valley cannot naturally flow into another, so there are few economies of scale. Between the lack of space and cost of development, Latin American cities tend to be dense, filthy affairs.

The twin obstacles of tropics and mountains are the bane of Latin America. Mexico, Chile, Peru, and Argentina are mostly mountainous. Venezuela, Belize, and Panama are mostly jungle. Ecuador, Colombia, Brazil, Honduras, Nicaragua, El Salvador, Guatemala, and Costa Rica are both.

Nearly everywhere in Latin America the only way forward is the mass creation of artificial infrastructure to ease the transport problem. Such infrastructure is expensive in flatlands, but regularly costs five or more times as much in highlands because of issues of remoteness and slope. Not only is every investment dollar required to stitch the country together with artificial infrastructure is a dollar not available for industrial or consumer

Global Cities by Elevation

	City	Country	Pop. Density (persons/ sq mile)	Lowest Elevation (feet)	Highest Elevation (feet)
Anglo America	New York City	United States	2826	Sea Level	410
	San Francisco	United States	1755	Sea Level	934
	Los Angeles	United States	2646	Sea Level	5074
	Miami	United States	1096	Sea Level	30
	Minneapolis	United States	544	687	980
	Chicago	United States	1315	579	673
	Denver	United States	305	5130	5470
Europe	Rome	Italy	5804	43	456
	Paris	France	55533	114	486
	London	United Kingdom	11576	Sea Level	69
	Berlin	Germany	9847	92	400
	Stockholm	Sweden	803	Sea Level	174
	Moscow	Russia	10240	495	837
	Geneva	Switzerland	5048	1224	1300
Asia	Seoul	Republic of Korea	42115	69	282
	Tokyo	Japan	16020	16	131
	Beijing	China	3411	100	130
	Singapore	Singapore	20284	Sea Level	540
	Naypyidaw	Myanmar	427	115	377
Latin America	Mexico City	Mexico	15609	7,380	12,890
	Bogota	Colombia	11212	8661	10341
	Buenos Aires	Argentina	37593	Sea Level	82
	Asuncion	Paraguay	11415	300	520
	Rio de Janeiro	Brazil	7037	Sea Level	3,349
	Sao Paulo	Brazil	6424	2392	3,724
	La Paz	Peru	4842	11,942	13,000
	Santiago	Chile	20900	1,312	2,969
	Managua	Nicaragua	6038	180	2,297
	Caracas	Venezuela	6969	2,850	4,600

development, but even successfully roading and railing up one urban area does nothing to help the urban area one mountain line over.

Much of Latin America may be rich in ores and timber, and much more can be transformed via slash-and-burn techniques to raise vast amounts of crops and livestock, but the cost of infrastructure required to make it even theoretically possible doesn't just make regional development among the most expensive in the world, but it oftentimes means the end benefits don't exceed the costs. Such cost/benefit imbalances are particularly hostile in Mexico's desert north, Mexico's jungle south, Colombia's Pacific Coast, Colombia's eastern jungle, the Venezuelan interior, the Bolivian highlands, the Brazilian interior, and almost everywhere in Central America.

This transport problem prevents the locals from generating the economies of scale that make for successful economies elsewhere in the world. And if the Latin Americans cannot integrate internally, they certainly cannot do so across international borders. The result is a "region" that is anything but:

- Central America is made up of a series of isolated city-states. Usable stretches are so few and far between that no two of the region's metro areas can integrate. All are blocked from each other by jungle mountains.

- Most Mexicans have been forced to move upland onto their country's central plateau. The two Sierra Madre mountain chains don't simply retard Mexico City's connections to other Mexican metro regions, but also to both of the country's coasts, and of course the coasts with each other. The result is a fractured network of cosmopolitan urban centers in a sea of rugged landscapes where criminal elements hold sway.

- The Venezuelan capital of Caracas may be only 10 miles inland, but a steep mountain range lies between it and Venezuela's ports. Based on weather (and mudslides and bridge outages), that "short" trip can take upward of 4 hours. Venezuela itself might as well be on a different continent from Brazil. The Amazon jungle is so muddy and thick that not one road connects the two countries' population centers despite 1,300 miles of border.

- Colombia sports a navigable river in the Magdalena, but the country's major cities — Bogota, Medellin, and Cali — are all at least a half-mile above it and so cannot fully benefit from the river's wealth-generating potential or the flat corridor of lands below them. Despite that river and all that coastline, Colombia's population is in effect landlocked.

- Most Chileans live in a single mountain valley just inland from the Pacific with their backs to the Andes. Unlike the jungle-cloaked Andes further north, the Argentine-Chilean Andes are both the tallest mountains in the hemisphere and far enough south to have permanent snow caps. Winter storms regularly sever all road and rail traffic between Chile and Argentina.

- A 2,100-mile stretch of South America's Pacific coast is hard desert, keeping Santiago and Lima (the capital of Peru) as separated as any jungle or mountain. The desert also separates Lima from the bulk of the Peruvians who live high in the Peruvian Andes.

- Bolivia is split between the Medialuna, a crescent of relatively low, relatively fertile land in the country's east; and the Altiplano, a massive highland plateau whose lowest reaches are over 10,000 feet up. At such elevations, infants of European descent have crushingly high mortality rates because of insufficient blood oxygenation. Consequently, the country bears the scars of cultural, ethnic, and wealth splits between the farmers and ranchers of European descent of the lowlands and the poor indigenous of the highlands.

- All of the southern half of Brazil sits on a giant plateau that extends all the way to the coast. The country's commercial capital, Sao Paulo, sits on the one spot where there is a break in the cliffs, so all the interior traffic must funnel to a single road. One result are 24-hour traffic jams that hugely retard economic growth. Another is that all of Brazil's coastal cities are crammed onto tiny plots of land backed by cliffs. This generates breathtaking scenery but means the country lacks a major coastal transport artery even today.

- Reaching out to the neighbors — whether those neighbors are beyond the region, within the region, or even co-nationals — is next to impossible. Most of the population cores in Chile, Ecuador, Bolivia, Venezuela, Colombia, Costa Rica, Nicaragua, Honduras, and Guatemala and Mexico all lack maritime access.

The extreme geographic fracturing produces a multitude of negative outcomes, and considering the changes underway in the international order, *all* of them are about to get worse.

The Politics of a Bad Geography

The economic and political systems of the South American countries are not like the American system. In the United States the early settlers pushed across gaps in the Appalachians and settled in the Ohio, Mississippi, Tennessee, and Missouri River Valleys. They found rich agricultural lands that barely had to be cleared before being brought into grain production. With a few months of work the pioneers could be producing far more grain than they could themselves use. Using the cheap transport capacity of the Greater Mississippi system, the pioneers could ship that excess grain downriver to St. Louis, New Orleans, and then out to the wider world. Shipping depots popped up along the length of the river to help the farmers haul and package the grain.

These depots eventually added services that the farmers found useful — blacksmiths, banks, schools — becoming small towns. Local economic needs led to regional economic development, which became a global economic phenomenon — all without much central planning or taxpayer commitments. As these small towns grew, labor naturally specialized and became more highly skilled, while economies of scale proliferated up and down the rivers, becoming particularly strong and concentrated at both the head and foot of a river's navigation, or where two or more rivers merged. Cities like Pittsburgh, Minneapolis, St. Louis, and New Orleans became easily-replicated examples of the power of the American development experience.

This organic growth and development became the backbone of not just the American economic system, but its political system as well. Smallholders set up around small towns along a unified network granted by nature created a sense of can-do individualism and community that penetrates deeply into the American psyche even today. The concept of local vs. states vs. national government prerogatives, the idea that the individual is the core of the system and the government works in parallel rather than existing to command that individual, the separation of powers made possible by a political constellation that valued a bit of distance between the government and the governed — all this and more may have been envisioned by the Founding Fathers, but their ideas probably wouldn't have worked had the American geography not enabled them.

Such concepts certainly didn't work in Latin America. The geography that rules the United States is flat and open and easy to traverse. The geography of Latin America is anything but: rivers are not navigable and what arable land there is doesn't exist in big chunks like the Greater Midwest, complicating development and largely prohibiting economies of scale.[1] Kept apart by the tyrannies of mountains and jungle, the initial Spanish colonies developed largely in isolation from one another, they tended to be (very) poor, and their economic focus was almost entirely upon extracting mined products for shipment back to the homeland to financially fuel Spain's wars in Europe. The settlers who tended to dominate were those who showed up on Day One with their own cash. It takes time and capital and a lot of effort to hack a farm out of the jungle, not to mention to build the support facilities and mountain roads to make that farm anything other than a subsistence effort. Instead of the poor becoming rich as was the case in the United States, in the bulk of the rest of the hemisphere only the rich — who commanded the poor — could carve something useful out of the wilderness.

Consequently, Latin America is home to some of the world's most unequal societies. Despite the concerns of many Americans as to the relative wealth of the top 1 percent, economic inequality is far starker throughout Latin America than it is in the United States. The typical division is between

---

1   There is one exception to this rule: one area of the Southern Cone is pretty fabulous. We'll get to that in a bit.

a rich class of landowners who feel (with some credibility) that they personally made the country possible, and the poor class who feel (with some credibility) that they've been exploited the whole time. The local Spanish nomenclature for this rich class of people is *jefe*. It roughly translates to someone who is the economic, personal, political, and social boss of you.[2]

Even economic growth in Latin America is sharply self-limiting. Since the preferred regional business — whether foreign or *jefe*-run — tends to be low-valued industries such as tropical agriculture, mining and basic processing, and since population centers are so Balkanized, there is no built-in economic need for higher education or labor specialization (you don't need a doctorate degree to pick coffee beans, and your *jefe* certainly isn't going to help you get one).

This chronic skills shortage does more than limit upward social mobility and individual wealth: Whenever a Latin American country does manage to generate a bit of economic growth, the tiny supply of skilled labor is quickly brought into play and rapidly depleted. Skilled labor costs skyrocket, inflation explodes, and the economy dies back. Similarly, during commodity booms all the ore and grain exports bring in hard currency, sending the local currency sky-high. That appreciation destroys the competitiveness of anything that's more value-added, like manufacturing. The only Latin Americans who can cope with such cycles are those who begin the cycle with the ability to tap overseas labor or markets: the *jefes*. Good times or bad, expansion or recession, everything that happens just deepens the divides.

Lack of capital combined with such social stratification generates extreme *political* divides as well.

The *jefes* believe that since their fiefdoms provide everything from jobs to services to physical infrastructure — and since those fiefdoms would have never existed without *jefe* money, efforts, and foresight — that there is no good reason why each individual *jefe* should not be the one calling the shots in the fiefdoms. Latin American labor, in contrast, sees everything that has been achieved in modern Latin American societies as being achieved by their exploitation. Americans argue about what the United States should and/or could be, Latin Americans argue over who their countries *belong* to.

---

2   The equivalent in Brazilian Portuguese is *caudilho*.

As such Latin American politics take a far more visceral, bare-knuckled, and winner-take-all mentality.[3]

The sorts of personalities who pass as political "moderates" in the United States — people like George W. Bush or Barack Obama — are largely unheard of in South America. Latin American politics teem with character assassination (and sometimes actual assassination). Shifts in administration lead to massive changes in national policy that impact everything from how the constitution reads to whether having a deed to your house or farm means you actually own it. Coups (and counter-coups) are common. And often the military feels obliged to throw coups of its own to prevent the pendulum from swinging too far one way or another (typically introducing a whole new level of instability).

Perhaps of greatest concern is that these challenges are about to get worse.

Countries with navigable rivers have a leg-up on the competition because their baseline transport system is free. Countries with difficult terrain — like most of those in Latin America — tend to always be catching up because they need to shell out scarce capital for the sort of infrastructure that comes easy to others. The volume of capital globally is in the process of contracting because of the global demographic crunch. By 2022 the majority of the developed world's Baby Boomer generation will be in retirement. Any infrastructure that isn't completed by then will face great challenges attracting funding.

The region's economic structure compounds this mounting capital shortage.

Because of the challenges Latin America faces when it comes to integration and economies of scale and wealth and development, most investors — whether domestic or foreign — are fairly picky, favoring very specific sorts of projects. They don't want to deal with any sort of finished goods since the local problems with skilled labor and labor costs and supply chains give almost any part of the world a competitive advantage over Latin America.

---

3   Social historians will note that the Latin American development model has more than a few echoes of the U.S. Deep South model, complete with economic inequality, *jefe* economics, and commodity-driven systems.

Even in Chile and Argentina, which boast the region's deepest wells of skilled labor, labor productivity is one-third less than the OECD average.

Most investors don't even want intermediate products. Not only do Latin American products tend to be below global norms in terms of quality and

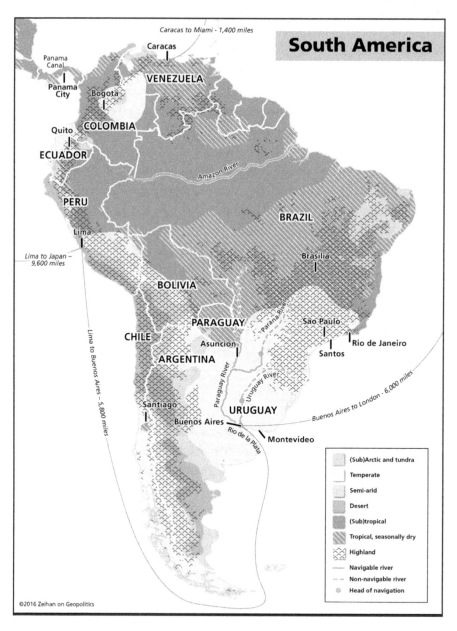

©2016 Zeihan on Geopolitics

above global norms in terms of cost because of infrastructure and skilled labor constraints, but should anything happen to any of that expensive, weak, fragmented, internal regional infrastructure, the investor's *global* supply chain would have a bottleneck in some mountain pass that no one outside of south central Ecuador had ever heard of. Consequently, nearly all investments in Latin America are either into services — a sector in which pent-up demand is massive — or into primary commodities like timber or soy or iron ore, which can be exported for hard currency.

When the Disorder hits, the number of locations around the world that will continue to seek massive supplies of the sorts of inputs that have traditionally attracted capital to Latin America will shrivel, just as the ability of shippers to shuttle such inputs across the globe collapses, just as the amount of capital available globally shrinks. This will be disastrous for a great many players for a great many reasons, but will perhaps be the worst for those countries who once earned their druthers by producing the base materials in the first place. The result will be a triple hit to almost every Latin American country's efforts to claw its way out of the hole that geography has buried them in.

Finally, unlike Southeast Asia, South America it is not on the way to anywhere. South America, especially the southern half, is shockingly remote. The distance from Buenos Aires to London is nearly 7,000 miles. Santiago to Tokyo or Shanghai is about 11,000. And because of the spike-shaped nature of South America, getting around the Andes is quite the chore. The flight from Lima to Sao Paulo might "only" be 2,160 miles — about the distance from New York to Phoenix — but if you want to move cargo and avoid the Andes and Amazon, it's more than a six-*thousand*-mile sail. Any economic development that happens in South America will have to happen because South Americans *make* it happen, rather than the region piggy-backing on someone else's development boom. And since the continent has minimal geographic impetus for development, don't expect any vast regional supply chain network like what is in the process of forming up in Southeast Asia.

The Three Exceptions

Yet Latin America still looks better than the vast bulk of the rest of the planet. Just as most of the region's geographic features argue for its technical backwardness, poverty, runaway inflation, inequality of all types, and all-around poor prospects, a different sort of economic development is about to boom.

It all comes down to three exceptions.

First, the region does not need to worry about war.

The very factors that constrain interaction among Latin America's peoples and urban centers and countries also retard interaction among Latin America's *militaries*. The Latin American geography is so rugged that each and every Latin American country need not fear invasion from any of its neighbors. There is no insecure Russia or Saudi Arabia, nor is there a Japan with the means and need to assault its neighbors, or a Germany that could flip its industrial production from civilian to military goods. The South American geography is so hostile that the last two wars involving meaningful troop movements or territorial exchanges were the War of the Pacific of 1879-1883 among Chile, Bolivia, and Peru, and the War of the Triple Alliance of 1864-1870 among Paraguay, Brazil, Argentina, and Uruguay.

The Latin American states certainly compete, but the vicissitudes of geography limit that competition to the political and cultural — and to a lesser degree, economic — realms. There isn't going to be a war here in the next 30 years. Not even a small one.

For similar reasons Latin America doesn't need to worry about *external* war either. Most of what it has — industrial commodities — can be garnered from other locations at better prices with less sailing time. The Europeans will source what they need from Africa, while the Americans have Canada and the Australians can help out anyone who can sail safely to their shores. Historically, this last-provider feature has condemned most Latin American economies to boom-and-bust cycles, but one definite upside is that the region is fairly uninteresting from an imperial point of view. No one makes a pit stop in Latin America in contemporary times unless they are deliberately going somewhere else in Latin America.

The second major exception is that there is one portion of Latin America that is starkly different from the rest of the region from a geographic point of view.

About midway down the continent's southeastern coast is a deep indentation called the Rio de la Plata — it's an estuary for a combined river system that is the second-largest network of naturally navigable rivers on the planet. More than "merely" providing this region with cheap and safe transport options, it also coincidentally overlays the world's fourth-largest chunk of temperate arable land.

Just about everything else that is true for the rest of Latin America is *not* true for the Plata region. Climate is mild. Tropical diseases are nearly unheard of. Integration is cheap and feasible. The various barriers to human development are low. The countries that formed in this region have traditionally been Latin America's most successful states. Argentina, to finger the most obvious example, was actually the world's seventh-wealthiest society in 1920.

And the fact that one must go back to 1920 to generate that statistic should tell you all you need to know about how nothing about geography is purely deterministic. In the decades immediately after the Spanish Empire's collapse, four states came to share the Plata region: Argentina, Paraguay, Uruguay, and the extreme southern extremities of Brazil. At the time Paraguay was clearly the superior military power, but a gambit to dominate the other three failed, and upward of 90 percent of the country's male population died in The War of the Triple Alliance (1864-1870) and subsequent disease-riddled famine. Demographically, Paraguay only recovered from the sex imbalance in the 1950s. Economically, it never has.

Argentina too is a cautionary tale. Once the cream of the crop, a series of populist-nationalist governments (combine the most extreme negative characteristics of Donald Trump and Bernie Sanders) continually squandered the country's geographic wealth until Argentina literally became the textbook example of how to *not* run a country. The last of those governments only lost power in 2015. I'm not saying that the Plata region will (or won't) do phenomenally well (or badly) in the Disorder. I'm saying that alone in Latin America this region has the geographic building blocks of very successful societies, countries, and economies.

The third and final exception that should keep eyes on the region is that while Latin America is located at the intersection of No and Where, it *is* proximate to the United States — the one major power likely to see its position improve in both relative and absolute terms.

Not only does the United States have a 2,000-mile-long border with Mexico, the Caribbean is directly adjacent to the Gulf of Mexico, giving the Americans easy access to all Central America as well as Colombia and Venezuela. New Orleans is only 850 miles from Veracruz, Mexico's dominant Atlantic port. Houston is half that. And while the trip from San Diego or Miami to places like Santiago or Rio might not be a short hop, those locations not only share time zones with the Americans, they are massively closer to American shores than anywhere else.

These three exceptions combined with Latin America's overall geographic complications not only firmly place Latin America within the Americans' orbit, but also make it custom-made for dollar diplomacy.

The Americans face no security resistance from within Latin America. The inland/highland nature of Latin America means that with the brief exception of Bolivia, Peru, and Chile during the War of the Pacific of 1879-1883 no Latin American power has ever been able to float a navy that proved capable of securing their own coastlines, much less project power beyond the horizon. When the Americans emerged as a significant naval power in the 1890s they were immediately — almost lazily — able to turn all Latin America into an American exclusion zone, quickly excising the Europeans from South America even before the Europeans destroyed themselves in the world wars.

The Americans face no competition from extra-hemispheric powers. If the Americans were able to keep the Western Hemisphere as a zone of exclusive influence when the European empires were still heavily militarized and the American navy was a third-rate fleet, in the coming Disorder the Western Hemisphere might as well be hermetically sealed. No power on the planet can gain access to Latin America without the Americans' express approval.

American penetration into Latin America is largely free of local intra-state security complications. With the notable exception of the Plata region, no two countries with Latin America can threaten each other, so should the Americans partner with any country in the region they do not need to worry about getting sucked into any sort of territorial dispute with a military dimension.

The inability of Latin American countries to decisively settle their internal security concerns increases their need for partnering with the United States. Just as mountain and jungle complicate economic development and the extension of centralized government power, those same features entrench poverty and contribute to huge swathes of lawless territory. This has led Latin American countries to seek out American security assistance in times of Latin American strength. Such assistance has taken the form of American weapons sales to Colombia to battle the FARC, special forces training for Mexican troops in resisting the Mexican drug cartels, and intel transfers to Peru to assist in the fight against the Shining Path. As the Disorder builds, global economic trends will deepen the internal security concerns of many Latin American states — and one of the few approaches on order will be to speak with Washington. Even the crime levels that come about as a result of Latin America's extreme inequality issues encourage Latin American elites to involve the United States.

Latin American countries are poorly positioned to jointly resist American intrusion. With the notable exception of the Plata region, no two countries within Latin America have the infrastructure or economic linkages required to create a meaningful bulwark against any outside power, much less one with the strength and depth of power and options of the United States. With each country needing to carry out any negotiations with the Americans bilaterally, none have much leverage to cut a deal that is anything but what interested American parties desire.

The United States is the only market in town. With the demise of the European common currency, the Chinese yuan, European growth, and Chinese growth the only large-scale market for Latin American outputs is the United States. Even rising demand out of Southeast Asia is more likely to be met by an Australia whose production and shipping costs are lower, and who has a national security interest in making Southeast Asia successful.

The United States is the only option for reaching non-*U.S. markets.* What non-U.S. markets the Latin Americans may wish to access will require a naval power capable of guaranteeing commercial shipments. Only the U.S. Navy has the potential to do so on a global basis. With American buy-in, some Latin American countries may even be able to find new (or maintain old) markets for their industrial commodity exports.

Latin America will desperately need American financial assistance. The need for infrastructure throughout the region is monumental and nearly every single country in the region has been condemned by geography to be capital poor. Whether it is for civic control, connecting population centers, creating ports, breaking land, keeping land fertile, providing utilities, or any other of a host of items that are common in civilized lands, Latin American countries need help with *all* of it — and will always lack the capital to address their needs. The United States is already the world's financial power, and the distance between it and nearly everyone else is about to expand by mammoth proportions. If Latin Americans want capital, there is about to be only one place to go.

Latin America will need the U.S. dollar. In the contemporary period all Latin American currencies are *already* soft currencies, so access to the sole remaining store of value is a perk in and of itself. But even were all Latin American countries ideologically hostile to the dollar (and some are), in the Disorder they will have no choice but to seek it out anyway. First, the U.S. dollar will be the only hard currency with global circulation. Second, all industrial and agricultural commodities of all types — corn (maize), soybeans, bauxite, iron ore, copper, oil, natural gas, literally *every*thing — are almost exclusively bought and sold in U.S. dollars. Anything that increases the exposure of the Latin American export industries to the U.S. dollar will reduce currency risk and somewhat wed Latin American fortunes to the U.S. financial system — the system almost certain to be to be the world's most stable.

The Americans are not simply about to return, but do so in force.

The Good and Bad of Latin American Energy

Because Latin America's topography is so difficult, and because the region's primary source of capital — outsiders — is drying up, no huge development boom looms just off the horizon. Latin America's best hope is to leverage its commodities sector, specifically the commodities that are about to be in sharp shortage. Which brings us directly to the Latin American oil sector. Many Latin American countries are significant oil producers, with the region generating combined net exports of 4.3mbpd. That might not sound like much — and at but 12 percent of global exports it really isn't — but Latin American oil producers have two massive points going for them.

First, neither their production, mid-stream transport, nor their export capacity are threatened by the violence of the Twilight, Gulf, or Tanker Wars. Not only can they sail their cargos to Western Europe without threat, they will even have the option of sailing their cargos up the Pacific Coast of the Americas and then west to Japan to stay out of range of Chinese interdiction.

Second, unlike the Anglo-America that is largely a self-contained energy market, Latin American states are fully exposed to global oil norms — "norms" defined by supply shocks and insufficient productive capacity. American shale producers will not be able to sell directly into that market and so will get no big windfall from hugely higher global oil prices, but Latin American exporters can.

As such, *all* will experience an explosion of foreign (read: American) interest in their energy complexes. As of late-2016, most outside players (read: supermajors) have largely pulled out of this region. Resource nationalism, erratic and hostile contracting terms, and substandard reserves — in some cases all three at once — have soured most investors; the 2015 price slide only cemented feelings that Latin America needed to have a wrenching recession to force belt-tightening of such magnitude that regional political leaders would have no choice but to crawl back to the negotiating table. Ample oil availability in the world's largest oil market due to the shale revolution only deepened the disinterest.

But contract terms that the supermajors would deign to even read when crude is at $50 a barrel will be signed eagerly — even blindly — at $150. Every oil producer in the region will see a massive and sustained surge in first interest, and shortly thereafter, investment. At that $150 price point all will be able to pocket an extra $100 a barrel in pure profit by selling to countries outside of the hemisphere. That windfall will last at least until the three major wars of the Eastern Hemisphere resolve *and* global production capacity and global demand once again reach some sort of balance. In the fastest-case scenario such balance won't occur until at least five years after the shooting starts. Working from current Latin American export levels and assuming absolutely no new investment to spike production, the windfall adds a half a billion dollars a day to the Latin American oil exporters' bottom line. For a region that is consistently capital-starved and riven by internal social malaise, this is nothing less than mana from heaven.

But even this brilliant silver lining has an ominous cloud attached. It all comes back to the region's built-in economic inequality. Guess which class of Latin Americans owns the energy complexes and so benefits from global price rises? Guess which class has to purchase energy and so suffers from global price rises? Far from providing Latin America with a chance to address and heal its economic inequalities, the oil windfall is likely to exacerbate them.

Traditionally, Latin American states have chosen to use energy subsidies to square the circle: Mexico subsidizes gasoline, Argentine subsidizes electricity and natural gas, Venezuela subsidizes … pretty much everything. The costs are about to skyrocket. Shielding the Venezuelan population from the impact of the global carnage to come will run about $100 million a day, or nearly 9 percent of GDP. For comparison, the United States spends one-third that proportion on its military.

Every exporter is about to face a tough choice: Maximize exports in order to maximize income, and to hell with the class divide and social stability? Or maximize subsidies in order to maximize social placidity, and pass up the opportunity for an unprecedentedly epic investment windfall that might provide the boost required to finally overcome some of the region's harsher geographic limitations?

There is no singular "South American" path forward. Each country will make its own decisions based on the unique mix of geographic, political, and economic factors that shape its systems — and never forget that one of those factors is a United States that's about to have a renewed interest in the region.

Venezuela: It Was the Best of Times...

Any discussion of Latin America that has anything to do with energy must begin with the country with the largest production and reserves, the country whose oil output once undermined the Arab oil embargo, the country that has the most upward production potential in the region: Venezuela.

Venezuela possesses oil reserves of some 300 billion barrels. Putting this into scale, not only are Venezuelan oil reserves greater than the total known reserves of the continent of Africa, Venezuela has more oil than Russia or Saudi Arabia. Yet while Venezuela's known reserves have more than *tripled* since 2006, Caracas has seen its oil output *decline* by over 700kbpd. That dichotomy sums up that glory and terror that is the Venezuelan oil patch. The oil is there, but getting it out is a nightmare.

The technical challenges facing the sector are legion. Much of Venezuela's crude is particularly viscous and high in sulfur, often the consistency of toothpaste, in addition to coming from fairly deep deposits requiring a high degree of technical acumen to exploit.

And that's the good stuff. Most of the new reserves of the past decade — which make up the vast majority of those 300 billion barrels — are the ultra-heavy, ultra-high sulfur Orinoco tar deposits. Orinoco output is a gooey solid at room temperature and must be "upgraded" before it can possibly be piped. The upgrading facilities are technically complex and fantastically expensive, and they must be built atop the production sites deep in Venezuela's interior. Rather than upgrade this tar, it is often cheaper and easier to mix Orinoco "oil" with light/sweet crude to form a less mucky medium blend that can — just barely — be piped. But Venezuela produces no light/sweet crude. It must import the stuff, ship it into the interior where it is mixed with the local vintage, and then load the resultant cocktail into pipes for the final journey to the coast. Barrel per barrel the up-front investment costs into the Venezuelan oil sector are typically quadruple or more what they are at more traditional energy sites. As such the Venezuelan state oil monopoly, Petróleos de Venezuela, S.A. (PDVSA) has long bucked Latin American norms, boasting a reputation of considerable technical aptitude.

Or at least it used to.

The year 2002 witnessed an attempted coup, with many of the country's business interests objecting to the populist/socialist policies of then-President Hugo Chavez. Most critically, most of the highly skilled staffers at PDVSA sided with the coup plotters.

The coup's dissolution marked the commencement of a wide-ranging, decade-long purge of anyone with even remotely anti-Chavez leanings, whether they be in management, exploration, production, refining, upgrading, accounting, human resources, or the motor pool. In a few short years PDVSA was an empty shell compared to its 1900s heyday. Its refineries are now in such disrepair that few countries will consider importing their output on quality, quantity, and reliability grounds. The Orinoco projects have degenerated into staff-bloated and engineer-light jokes. Venezuela's plans to export natural gas in liquefied form have been abandoned along with most of its Atlantic offshore blocks. In the aftermath of a politically-driven decision to nationalize some foreign holdings in 2007 — among them ExxonMobil's — most foreign firms have left, taking away not just their investment dollars, but also their much needed technical expertise. Venezuela has fallen so far it even resorted briefly to importing natural gas from regional competitor Colombia simply to keep the electricity on at the country's western oil fields. At the time of this writing, most international airlines have stopped flying to or from Venezuela because they cannot get paid in hard currency. Maracaibo Bay — once host to one of the world's top oil provinces — is plagued by pirates.[4]

Yet the global environment is changing, and that may be all that matters. In a world of oversupplied, cheap crude, Venezuela is a pathetic has-been barely worthy of a map label. But in a world of Eastern Hemisphere supply shocks and expensive oil, Venezuela is a place where every large energy firm on the planet will want to be.

The turnaround will not happen overnight. Eighteen years of Chavismo will be difficult to repair. Any new investment by Western oil majors will first be aimed at stabilizing oil production and rehabilitating transportation and refinery infrastructure. Only then can there be meaningful thoughts about greenfield investments in the Orinoco or offshore. And all of this

---

4   Live on boats, raid the coast to extort, kidnap and rape. Pirates.

will take time. While a half decade should be enough to bring Venezuela back to its pre-Chavez output levels, any new output beyond that point will require scores of billions of investment into new pipes and upgraders and export capacity.

There are two poison pills.

First, Venezuela is *not* a nice place, and I'm not talking about the business-unfriendly attitude of the Chavista government. Venezuela's political culture is the most violent in the Western Hemisphere. Urban poor. Urban gangs. Natives in the jungle. Rangers who take the law into their own hands. Cocaine smugglers. Local politicos who maintain their own militias. Dynasties who maintain their own private armies. Say what you will of the Chavista regime, it has poured oil — a *lot* of oil — on troubled waters and kept the countries' many economic, social, and political cleavages from turning too violent. Even with the recent sixtyfold increase in gasoline prices (a response to the budgetary pressures of low oil prices), the high-end stuff still sells for only 60 cents a gallon.

The most intractable problem is that the Chavista government has handed out tens of thousands — if not hundreds of thousands – of automatic weapons to its supporters. Should the loyalists of the current government find themselves ever cut-off from patronage, they can do something about it. In Venezuela the future of energy subsidies isn't just a political and economic issue, it's a security one as well.

Second, there's a crisis of customers. Very few refineries in the world can take the stuff that Venezuela calls oil: almost all of them are on the U.S. Gulf Coast and all of *those* are retooling to run more of shale's light/sweet blends and less of Venezuela's heavy/sour. Making matters worse, as investment brings more Orinoco crude on-line the quality of Venezuela's overall crude grade will drop even further.

One of three things must happen. First, importers must undergo massive refinery upgrades to be able to turn Venezuelan sludge into useful product. This would result in a very short list of potential customers who would be able to demand substantial price discounts out of the Venezuelans, who have so few potential customers in the first place. The leading would-be customers are those few places with partial infrastructure in place, or the technical capacity to modify what they have: India is the leading candidate in the former category, but the supertanker sail from Venezuela to India is *more* than halfway around the world. It's hard to see such a supply route working in the world-to-come unless there is a naval power far more competent than India or Venezuela ensuring the shipments. Germany is certainly in the top slot for the second category, and Germany and PDVSA did have an oil supply relationship pre-Chavez. But sailing crude into the Northern European war zone is far from a risk-free business proposition.

The second path Venezuelan crude could flow into would be an international multi-step supply chain that blends Venezuela's sludge with higher-quality oil — for example, Algerian Condensate or Bonny Light from Nigeria — to form a medium blend that less-advanced refineries can stomach. With either of the first two options, Venezuela will be part of a complicated, expensive multinational energy supply chain in an era in which simplicity, economy, and bilateral relations will be the norm. Should one piece fall out of place or one country get its knickers in a bunch (or lose its knickers altogether), the entire system crashes and the Venezuelan energy sector simply shuts down because there is nowhere in the world you can store large oil flows for more than a few days. Of potential partners, by far the best option would be Italy, which will be eager to diversify away from Russia, Persian Gulf, and Libyan crudes no matter what happens in the Twilight or Gulf Wars.

There is a third option: partner with the United States.

All three of the American supermajors have extensive experience in the Venezuelan oil patch. All three hold now-underutilized refining capacity on the U.S. Gulf Coast that could take Venezuelan crude. All three have been burned, yet all three would be itching to go back in a high-price environment. And of course the U.S. Navy would be available to help deliver the resultant refined product on to a fuel-hungry world.

There are just two problems. The Venezuelan government loathes the United States and would not consider an American-Venezuelan partnership their first, or second (or third)[5] choice. Second, the primary reason the Americans would be interested is they'd make boatloads of money that Caracas would rather make for itself. Venezuela would in essence be selling

---

5   Or 84th

crude into the American market below $70 a barrel while the Americans would then re-sell the refined product into a global market where crude is at $150 or more.

Unfortunately for Venezuela this is likely the only option they'll have.

Venezuela's energy sector has degraded so much that it cannot thrive unless its exports are managed by a powerful *foreign* force. Global transport logistics and global capital shortages make every non-American option nearly impossible, and the Americans have more than enough leverage to make things go their way. In addition to the tech and capital and experience required to overhaul the Venezuelan oil complex, Venezuela has long been an importer of everything from washing machines to beer to wheat to toilet paper. Two decades of Chavista economic management has devastated not simply the oil sector, but *every* economic sector. Venezuela requires a top-to-bottom overhaul of damn near everything. And the country's internal security situation demands that whoever is doing that overhaul is pretty good at protecting themselves. Venezuela is about to become the poster child for just how effective dollar diplomacy can be.

The U.S. supermajors may not actually own Venezuela, but they will command every part of the production, export, transport, mixing, refining, distribution, and retail process that will actually provide Caracas with its energy income. The only question is whether the Venezuelan government will accede to the inevitable and try to scratch out the best deal possible in a cooperative manner, or resist to the end and risk getting cut out of windfall completely.

Brazil: It Was the Worst of Times...

Brazil's geography is, in a word, unfortunate. Cities like Rio de Janeiro have become famous for the stunning shots of communities clinging to cliff sides and the dramatic views of highlands jutting beyond the coast, but for all pretty postcards they have inspired, these cliffs have long stymied the Brazilian economy. Not one of the Brazilian rivers that flows through populated areas is navigable. Southern Brazil lies atop a plateau, but the plateau slants *in*land, rather than toward the sea. The rivers flow away from the coast (and then south into Argentina), so any coast-based export infrastructure has to scale cliffs. Coastal settlements cling tightly to the country's exceedingly narrow coastal pockets, most of which boast population densities higher than Tokyo, but without a first-world economy to back them up.

Even farming is difficult — clearing tropical biomes is costly and laborious, and farmers lack inexpensive transportation routes to deliver their goods to market. Only the rich Portuguese settlers had anywhere near the resources required to turn these small coastal enclaves into something useful, much less the resources required to jump up on top of the Brazilian Plateau to develop the interior and brute-force some infrastructure to get any product back down the escarpment and out to the wider world. Capital has stayed concentrated within the hands of the elite, wages remained low, and modern Brazil remains shaped by these stark differences in economic opportunities. Consequently, Brazil has emerged as the paragon of South American economic disparity, and indeed has been the most unequal major economy in the *world* since modern data tracking began after World War II. Stay within smell of the Copacabana and you are in Postcard Land, get within smell of anything else and put your camera away.

Brazil's oil sector has not fared much better. In the 2000s Brazil discovered a new set of oil deposits locked in deep offshore reservoirs formed before South America and Africa split into distinct continents. These so-called pre-salt deposits represent one of the biggest new oil plays in the world since the post-Soviet opening. It is the target of an investment effort once expected to top $200 billion. Brazil cannot hope to fund that itself, so it invited foreigners to help out.

That help is not coming. As is common among countries who suddenly discover vast swathes of resources, politicians often spend the money before it is generated. The left-right political split in Brazil is alive and well as it is elsewhere in Latin America. Combine that with soon-to-be-but-not-quite-yet riches and the result was a massive corruption scandal — called Car Wash — that wormed its way deep into the heart of the Brazilian oil sector. As such, foreign firms have sought deposits elsewhere, while the Brazilian political system has drug everything from oil production to foreign contracting into maelstrom of claims, counterclaims, lawsuits, and impeachment hearings that are certain to condemn the country to an economic depression — and that before the Disorder robs the country of cheap foreign capital.

Brazil has three points going for it. First, unlike Venezuela, where the bulk of oil production is onshore and so every aspect of production and transport has become politicized, in Brazil the petroleum is offshore and highly resistant to local disruptions.[6]

Second, Brazilian politics are getting better. At the time of this writing, Car Wash has claimed the sitting president, but her replacement has indicated he has no intention of seeking his own term and is instead attempting to lay the groundwork for a national political reset and reconciliation. As to the specifics of oil, Brazil's left- and right-wingers agree on a couple of critical points. Oil self-sufficiency is a good thing. (The right sees it as an issue of national security and economic pride. The left as a pre-condition of providing the population with energy subsidies.) Both sides of the aisle publicly admit Brazil needs foreign investment to tap the pre-salt, and that supermajors are the only reasonable source for that investment. Already Brazil's Congress has sanded down some of the rougher edges in the country's petroleum laws — foreigners can now directly operate offshore blocks — to lure foreigners back to the pre-salt. There is a reasonable possibility of achieving broad-based reforms just as global prices surge.

Third and most important, Brazil's national oil firm — Petroleo Brasileiro (Petrobras) — is no broken-down has-been like PDVSA. Petrobras is not only the most technically competent state oil major in the world, it is one of the most skilled oil firms of all — it probably ranks second only to ExxonMobil in deepwater operations. Car Wash has only been going on since March 2014 — not long enough to critically damage Petrobras' technical capacity. And it helps hugely that rather than trying to defend its turf, it is Petrobras' voice arguing most loudly for supermajor involvement in the pre-salt.

All of the things that make dollar diplomacy work — logistics, security, technical, and financial assistance — can be applied in Brazil. The supermajors' technical and financial reach is the obvious piece: the Americans

---

6   Or at least technical and security disruptions. Political disruptions the Brazilians have in spades.

writ large are the best at developing systems for harvesting, moving and refining complex oils — something that needs to be taken account when planning in the high-pressure and high-temperature pre-salt deposits. The Americans — more likely via development assistance — can sweeten the pot with some infrastructure and higher education assistance for a country that will always need help with both. Americans can even help with Car Wash; courtesy of post-9/11 anti-terror efforts, the United States has the world's best system for tracking foreign money transfers.

But Brazil is *not* Venezuela. Not only is Brazil a far more technically competent and politically mature system than Venezuela and from that far more resistant to brute force diplomacy and/or arm-twisting, it is also remarkably resistant to some of dollar-diplomacy's less photogenic qualities. Much of the population lives inland, and what doesn't lives in very dense urban centers — neither are places where a quick military raid would make a lick of difference. Moreover, what the Americans are most interested in — the pre-salt oil — is offshore and needs to be connected to onshore processing, refining, and export facilities. There are too many moving parts in too many environments to do any of it without the Brazilians' complete buy-in — and that's even before you consider that the American supers will be forced to (grudgingly) admit that Petrobras may be better at this sort of thing than they are.

And Petrobras will be bringing more to the table than merely the third-largest oil deposits in the Hemisphere. Of all the region's state-owned energy firms, only Petrobras has the technical, logistical, legal, and financial capacity to operate *outside of its home country*. Petrobras already has fingers in the Venezuelan offshore, and the Angolan and Nigerian deepwater.

Petrobras even holds a trump card that could play to Americans' sometimes power-hungry mindset: Petrobras is the only non-American company in the Western Hemisphere with the ability to build out refining capacity on anything other than a decade time frame. Considering the abject shortage of fuel globally, Petrobras could provide the Americans with the capacity to be even *more* strategically powerful.

It will still all come from a slow start — between the constitutional reform and legal gymnastics required to resolve Car Wash and the high technical barriers of pre-salt, don't expect any meaningful Brazilian exports before 2020. And it certainly remains true that the supermajors will own and operate the bulk of the international energy supply system. But the fact remains that it would be more accurate to think of Petrobras as *one of the supermajors* rather than someone that they exploit.

Argentina: Vision of the Future

For decades Argentina has ... been its own special case. The northern territories that are home to the vast bulk of its population are among the world's most fertile. In the same area flow the navigable waterways of the Parana, Uruguay, Paraguay, and Silver (Plata) Rivers — collectively known as the Rio de la Plata region. This is South America's answer to the American Midwest: a large, contiguous piece of high-quality land overlain almost perfectly by an interconnected, navigable waterway network.

Argentina should be a major global power, and for a time it was: as recently as 1920 Argentina was among world's richest countries. It has since been waylaid by politics, particularly those that involve the iconization of Juan Domingo Peron. Peron, and in particular the fawning political ideology that followed his rule, institutionalized a particularly damaging type of politics that mingled aspects of populism, socialism, and fascism.

The most recent incarnation of Peronism ruled Argentina from 2003 to 2015 and, to be blunt, drove the economy into the ground. Peronist policies led to a complete cutoff from global capital markets, a gutting of the country's various pension plans to pay for pet projects, and an end to country's position as a major exporter of a wide variety of agricultural and industrial commodities. In essence Argentina devolved from its previous position as the region's paragon to a state that was gnawing on its bones. In 2012 Buenos Aires nationalized the local branch of Repsol, a Spanish-owned company that ran the Argentine oil sector.

Yet despite all this, Argentina's statist approach has actually landed it with an opportunity that is nearly unique. The Peronist government heavily subsided electricity rates in order to garner public support. Such subsides send demand sky-high, but because of price ceilings no one wants to invest in production, forcing the government to pay full global market prices for imports. To partially address this problem Buenos Aires also set a *minimum price* — $67/boed — that energy firms could earn for selling domestically produced oil and natgas to the government. At the end of the day the government still provides energy to the people at a loss, but it is now a known loss and so private companies have the contract clarity they need to invest.

The result has been not simply a boom in oil and natural gas output, but a boom in *shale* activity. Argentina's shales are among the most geologically favorable in the world: thick, broad, oozing with petrocarbons, and intermixed with most of Argentina's existing conventional oil and natgas deposits and infrastructure — almost all in areas that have more than sufficient freshwater to supply a local shale revolution. At the time of this writing, only Canada and the United States are producing more petroleum from shale than Argentina. And all that under a *Peronist* government.

And now that government is gone. In November 2015 the Peronist government was voted out of office and its successor is if anything staunchly anti-Peronist. Regulations are being revamped, foreigners are being courted, debts are being settled, and in general everything about how Argentina functions is being overhauled.

There is much reason to have hope for Argentina. The country's geographic blessings are such that it wouldn't take a particularly creative or orthodox policy for Argentina to significantly expand its role in global wheat, soy, corn, pork, beef, natural gas, and oil markets in a few short years — and that assumes energy prices stay weak. In a world of oil at $150 or more, precious little of Argentina's long-standing tradition of shooting itself in the foot will matter, even if the Peronists return to power.

Even Argentina's physical remove from the rest of the planet is turning into a positive. Located as it is at the southern end of South America, Argentina is fairly well-positioned to sell into either the Atlantic or Pacific Basin. Any Argentine exports can take their pick of whichever client, price regime, or security regime makes the most sense at the time. And since any Argentine crude exports will be shale-sourced, they will earn the premium that all light/sweet blends do.

Thinking more locally, Argentina is about to reprise its role as a major regional energy supplier. Before 2002 Argentina was the Southern Cone's primary natgas exporter. The flows only stopped because the Peronists so thoroughly destroyed the country's natgas production. All the transmission infrastructure is still in place, but it is either standing idle or instead shipping (much smaller volumes of) Bolivian natural gas. All Argentina needs to be the region's indispensable country is a shale revolution that is already well underway. That's great for everyone. Well, everyone except Bolivia, who can only stand by and watch as lower-cost Argentine natgas destroys Bolivia's largest source of export income.

The opportunities for expansion in agriculture, manufacturing and finance broadly mirror the opportunities in energy. Much of the country needs an overhaul — its industrial base, utility, road, rail, and port infrastructure haven't seen any meaningful maintenance since 2000 — but that is something that can be achieved with local labor at a fairly low cost. The country's low elevations and temperate climate make it the exception to everything that is wrong about the rest of Latin America.

There is but one complication: While Argentina probably has the money and expertise to reformulate any of its economic sectors, it lacks the money and expertise to reformulate all of them *at the same time*. Between all this potential and such an obvious shortfall, American interest in all things Argentine will be deep, broad, and intense — to the point that all the American money, personnel, and tech that will pour in will feel to some like an invasion. And since even in a bad year with a bad government Argentina still looks pretty good, expect sparks to fly at the intersection of companies, governments, Americans, and Argentines.

Trinidad and Tobago: A Bridge to Somewhere

Traditionally Trinidad and Tobago's (T&T) gold isn't so much black, but instead fizzy. T&T is a hemispheric leader not just in natgas, but all the things you can do with it. It sports a large LNG export infrastructure as well as the world's largest ammonia and methanol fabrication and export facilities. Natgas and associated byproducts will continue to form the cornerstone of the domestic energy sector, and therein lies the problem. T&T is too close to the United States, a country that is swimming in *waste* natgas; and since T&T's natgas come from aging offshore deposits, there is simply no way for

T&T to compete in either the American market or any regional market the Americans touch. The competition will be crushing for almost all aspects of T&T's natgas business. The one (massive) exception will be LNG, which will be in such demand in Europe and Northeast Asia that there will be more than enough market for everyone.

There are other bright spots too, one of which involves something T&T had largely written off: collaborative work with Venezuela. T&T boasts one of the very few refineries custom-built to run Venezuelan heavy crude. In addition, many of Venezuela's offshore natgas fields are geologic extensions of T&T's own and so are closer to T&T's *existing* natgas processing centers than they are to Venezuela's *proposed* facilities.

It's an opportunity for both to square some circles. The current Venezuelan government loathes the Americans in general and dollar diplomacy in particular. T&T loves the Americans in general and fully embraces dollar diplomacy since the islanders lack the money and skill sets to manage their own energy sector. Venezuela has huge production potential, but needs vast assistance with processing. T&T's petroleum fields are past maturity, but it has processing infrastructure to spare. Venezuela knows the best way to get its energy products to market is to let the Americans do the heavy lifting, and T&T's facilities provide an opportunity to at least partially cut the Americans out of the effort and claw back at least some of the resultant profits.

Colombia: Getting It Right

Colombia faces a separate set of challenges in attracting investment than many of its neighbors. The bulk of the Colombian economy and population lies in a double corridor, atop the bluffs above the (navigable) Magdalena River. But this corridor accounts for less than one-tenth of the country's land area, with the bulk of the remainder made up of rugged terrain and/or jungle. Colombia's vibrant, cosmopolitan mid-lands have long commanded the country's economic and political systems, while the largely disenfranchised highlanders have existed in a state of open rebellion for decades. The result is a mix of (narco)guerrilla and terror groups, the biggest constellation of which is the Fuerzas Armadas Revolucionarias de Colombia, more commonly known as the FARC.

Colombia's energy reserves lie almost exclusively in the FARC's backyard.

This has forced Colombia to be *very* good. Good at fighting insurgents, even should those insurgents enjoy popular support. Good at protecting oil workers who work in the back of beyond. Good at repairing pipelines that have been subject to daily attacks for decades. Good at producing oil from fields that are past maturity. Good at providing contractual terms to foreign firms so they are willing to overlook both the security concerns and the middling quality and smallish nature of Colombia's energy reserves. All told, Colombia doesn't simply have the best package — in terms of security support, physical infrastructure, local talent, and cooperation with outsiders — of any Latin American country, they have one of the best in the world.

During the past two decades the Colombian electorate had goaded the political establishment into resolving the civil war. One of the results has been a secession of centrist and rightest governments that have ramped up military spending to win the war in conventional terms, proactively seek out American assistance to the same end, and to force the FARC into meaningful negotiations. As a side effect of these governments' alignments, Colombia's business environment has evolved in the opposite direction of most of the continent, becoming more business friendly rather than less even as the country's security concerns have become less intense.

The stage is set for a vast improvement in Colombia's position. In 2016 the FARC rebellion is segueing into a truth-and-reconciliation process that may involve — among other things — mass pardons for some FARC members, prison sentences for others, and an integration of FARC's political wing into the rank-and-file of Colombian society. There is still a long way to go socially, regionally and politically, but much of the heavy lifting has already been done. Colombia's decades-long civil war is nearly over. Rather than being the stand-out in South American politics for its violent political culture, Colombia now stands out in a different way. Most of the rest of the continent is currently struggling with financial crisis caused by low energy prices, while Colombia is flirting — cautiously — with an energy renaissance. And it is doing so on the eve of the greatest increase of energy prices in the modern era.

The biggest challenge to Colombia's energy future is that its petroleum reserves, in a word, suck. Those reserves are less than 1 percent that of neighboring Venezuela's and Colombia's fields are already past maturity. But this isn't new. Despite violence levels and low quality and old fields, between 2003 and 2013 Colombia's oil output nearly doubled due to good state policy, sound sector management, and the presence of a solid national oil company (Ecopetrol). Add in a global price rise and Bogota's goal of reaching a sustainable production plateau of 1mbpd seems reasonable.

That should prove particularly true once you factor in that while Brazilians and Venezuelans and Ecuadorians and Argentines will be drawing up the parameters of what will be fundamentally new relationships with outsiders, that those same outsiders will already be hip-deep in already-operational Colombian projects. It is as if the Colombians went ahead and implemented dollar diplomacy without waiting for the Americans. Relations at the state and corporate levels are cordial, with a bilateral free trade deal already in place. The war's end is already sparking a vast expansion of American corporate interest in all things Colombian. Energy is merely one piece of the overall picture.

And even *that* forecast assumes no meaningful progress on either Colombia's potential shale sector or its nascent Caribbean offshore zones. Colombia may not be destined to be a Latin American Saudi Arabia, but it will be a sort of Latin American North Sea: professional, reliable, friendly to outsiders, and a much-valued part of the solution to the Eastern Hemisphere's energy crisis.

Peru: Inviting Trouble

Neighboring Peru is certainly not an oil power, but its natural gas industry is one of the steadily-growing success stories on the continent. First meaningful production was but 15 years ago. Now Peru not only meets about half of its electricity needs from natgas — bringing power to vast swathes of the interior that until recently had none — but it has enough leftover to fill South America's only LNG export facility. The income from Peru's new Camisea natgas project has been enough to massively accelerate Lima's development priorities, particularly the industrial growth around the capital.

Peru's largest problem in expanding its energy sector is geographic. Camisea and most of Peru's energy deposits are on the wrong side of the Andes chain, presenting the Peruvians with ongoing infrastructure bottlenecks. Luckily the Peruvians can read a map and so are aware of their weakness, and have adopted a mix of regulatory policies designed to attract rather than repel foreign firms. Peru will continue to seek to expand its natural gas sector with an eye toward top-dollar sales to Northeast Asia, but the non-existence of its oil exports will limit the degree to which it can benefit from a higher oil price environment. If anything, Peru will be a net loser. Its 31 million people all need diesel fuel, and Peru produces less than half its needs.

Peru is a country where dollar diplomacy could well toe the line between what is viewed as beneficial and meddling. Peru's ultimate developmental and energy challenge is that the country is evenly split between the Spanish descendants on the rich coast who benefit from cooperation with the Americans, and the natives of the highlands — who just happen to control the natural gas fields — who do not. High global oil prices will only exacerbate social tensions as the costs of subsidies skyrocket, but that is nothing compared to what happens when Lima *invites* American money, security capacity, and diplomatic heft to meddle with Peru's upland communities.

Ecuador: ... and Stay Out!

The challenge for dollar diplomacy in Ecuador will be more visceral.

Ecuador has the third-largest oil reserves in South America — more than triple that of Colombia — but its energy sector has struggled to produce half of Colombia's total output. The discrepancy is largely due to the government's anti-American attitude. In recent years Quito has forced out American operators in favor of Chinese firms as a way of de-Yankifying. The Chinese have used financing terms to depress the price they pay the Ecuadorians, and in a bit of rich irony the Chinese don't even take delivery — they ship Ecuador's crude to the U.S. West Coast and pocket the difference. Based on the conditions of the day, Quito's ideological purity not only costs it $2-$10 a barrel in real-time income, but it has transferred operational control of its production and transport infrastructure to less capable firms that cannot even maintain current output. Add in the increasingly dilapidated status of Ecuador's oil transport infrastructure and Ecuador is in essence locked into a relationship with a loan shark.

The Ecuadorian population is majority of mixed European/indigenous descent — a demographic largely harnessed by the standing government. Higher oil prices would simply mean that Quito would find itself forced to spend its newfound oil income on ever-more-expensive energy subsidies.

Or that's what it looks like without dollar diplomacy. Americans find the wasted potential of Ecuador — in everything from oil to bananas — borderline offensive. And as American companies find themselves with more and more powerful tools, expect them to inject their interests directly into the heart of the Ecuadorian political system. Ecuador will be an example of how intervention can trigger growth and chaos at the same time. In years past mild American intervention has meant a series of coups and counter-coups with Ecuadorian presidents often remaining in office for less than a year. Expect such instability to accelerate as a bitter Ecuador finds itself on the receiving end of American power, while its more pliable neighbors experience the more positive impacts of American intervention.

The Caribbean and Central America: Forced Transition, Forced Integration

The Central American states and Cuba are utterly reliant upon energy imports. For the past decade many have obtained those imports from Venezuela's PetroCaribe program, a program Chavez implemented with an eye toward undermining American influence throughout the region. To a certain degree PetroCaribe has delivered as advertised — several countries in Central America signed on — but at a mammoth cost. Some 240kbpd a day of Venezuelan oil and refined products exports are sold at below-market values, with much of the sticker price deferred with low- to no-interest loans.

Under the Chavista government Venezuela's finances have melted and its ability to simply maintain current output levels is steadily crumbling.

Any change in government in Caracas would almost certainly mean the end of PetroCaribe, leaving all of Central America and the Caribbean in a lurch as the silly financing ends, and regional import prices more than double. On the upside, there will be no shortages for those who can afford to pay. All the former PetroCaribe beneficiaries are located at the beginning of the U.S. Gulf Coast's export systems and be first in line — well, second, after Mexico — to grab U.S. refined products. And while it might be cold comfort, regional product sale prices would still be lower than other buyers who are a hemisphere — and perhaps a war — away.

A deeper discomfort will come from the piercing eyes about to pick apart this entire region; all will find themselves squarely in the sites of U.S. interests. Nowhere will that attention be more focused and sustained than in Cuba. In a more mercantile world there is no way that a country so close to American waterways could remain as hostile to America as Havana has been since 1959. But the Cubans know full well that while an American retrenchment means less American activity in Africa, Asia, and Europe, it also means far more American activity in the Caribbean. Bereft of any foreign sponsor, Havana has chosen to start the normalization process early so as to limit the inevitable economic and political shocks. After all, Havana knows *exactly* what a heavily engaged United States feels like. Cuba was a leading target of dollar diplomacy and related foreign policies back in the day, to the point that it was a de facto American colony from 1898 to 1934.

This hardly means disaster for the Cubans. American funds are already flooding into Cuba to restore Cuban infrastructure and tourist beaches to their 1950s Vegas-style heyday. Next will come a flood of agricultural investment, both to maximize Cuban sugar production as well as displace all non-American food imports. Finally will come the formal integration of Cuba into North American manufacturing supply chains. And should the Cubans sniff at the degree that Cuba is being transformed into a semi-colony, there will always be the balm of a bit of a discount on energy products and the knowledge that an American-leveraged Cuba will be able to eat pretty much all of the Bahamas current tourism market share.

Another big target of dollar diplomacy will be the Caribbean's offshore financial havens. One of the advantages of being the destination for the bulk of the world's capital flight is that there isn't a lot of reason to worry about bank transparency. After all, it isn't like the money fleeing European or Asian or South American domiciles was something that the American tax man could take a piece of — but the environment is changing. In a world where global financial breakdowns are the norm, there is a massive volume of cash in play, and the Americans want all that money to come to *them*. U.S. government pressure, backed by Wall Street, will work to close each and every offshore financial center, with the most fervent efforts reserved for those closest to home. Whether Panama, the British Virgin Islands, or the Caymans, the days of offshore financial centers on America's doorstep are nearly over.

Such intense American attention isn't all bad for the locals. Far from simply seeking to maximize the American advantage, in the belt of countries from Guatemala to Costa Rica, dollar diplomacy will seek to stabilize and strengthen the states themselves because the Americans *want* them to be strong. As Northeast Asian manufacturing supply chains break down due to war and high energy costs, North American supply chains will snake into Central America and Cuba to take their place. Relatively cheaper energy will help maintain social stability while improved manufacturing possibilities will bolster incomes and government revenues — all of which will help the Central American states better stand up to drug smugglers. And none of it is coming from a standing start. Courtesy of CAFTA, almost all the region already has a trade deal with the United States. Cuba is sure to join in in fairly short order.

The Not-So-Absent Superpower

The question isn't "are the Americans coming?" Tourists, aid workers, small businesses, and corporate warriors all are coming to Latin America.

The real question for Latin America is "can we handle what is about to happen?"

Much of the anti-gringo sentiment throughout Latin America exists as a consequence of previous periods of the Americans treating the region like their personal playground.

In those periods various Eastern Hemispheric players may have been in clearly secondary positions to the United States, but they were still able to nibble around the edges. The French and British played where they could throughout the Western Hemisphere right up to World War II. The Soviets' largest KGB station was in Mexico City. The Spanish never truly divorced themselves from the events of their former colonies, enabling a 20th century pseudo-neo-imperial renaissance called the *Reconquista*. More recently the Chinese have come in with boatloads of cash and simply tried to buy everything. The Americans were clearly head and shoulders above all others, but the Latin Americans could at least partially play the various foreign powers against one another.

That's not how it will look this time around. This time the Americans' technological, economic, and financial advantage vis-à-vis Latin America is far larger than it has ever been. This time the various Eastern Hemispheric powers for the most part even lack the capacity to attempt to play at the Latin American table. Not only can no Eastern Hemispheric power reliably reach Latin America without the United States' express consent, all will have far more pressing matters far closer to home. And this time the Latin Americans' best bet for leveraging the Eastern Hemisphere's problems to their own benefit follows an uncomfortably clear path: partnership with the United States.

Here, and nearly alone here, the global superpower will most certainly *not* be absent.

CONCLUSION

Shale New World

The global transition is already well past the point of no return.

American politics have fully flipped in the direction of populism. It isn't simply that Donald Trump was elected president in November 2016, but also that the dominant faction of the Democratic Party has also turned protectionist. The Americans have lost interest in maintaining the global order. The only question is whether the American absence will be deliberate or incidental.

Aging cannot be reversed, or even stalled. The Baby Boomers have been marching into retirement for a decade now, and in another decade nearly all of them will be drawing benefits from the system rather than paying in. Everything from Europe and Japan's financial crises to Brazil's depression are but symptoms of a much wider and deeper capital crunch settling in for the long haul.

Shale has long since turned the corner. Break-even prices are not just globally competitive, but continue to trend sharply down. By the time we reach 2019 shale will even be cost-competitive with most Persian Gulf oil projects.

Shale didn't start the American withdrawal — that began the day the Berlin Wall fell. Shale won't end it either — the Americans won't return until the day the U.S. government decides the chaos and dysfunction of the Disorder unduly impinges upon its interests. But by removing energy dependency — the firmest and most self-interest-driven aspect of U.S. involvement with the wider world — from the mix, shale most certainly accelerates and entrenches the global breakdown.

In the meantime, it is the Western Hemisphere's time to shine. It is a net exporter of both food and energy, so it will not need to grapple with any of the decivilizing trends that are about to so wrack the Eastern Hemisphere. It will barely even bear witness to any of the world's major — or even minor — conflicts to come. And nearly alone among the world's regions, it might not even be starved of capital as the global Boomer generation moves into retirement.

That is all good — and true — but it might be beside the point. For what truly sets apart the Western Hemisphere from the rest of the world is the issue of balance.

The Eastern Hemisphere is spammed with power centers: the Northern European Plain (which is itself home to five major powers), Sweden's Skane, the Eurasian Steppe, the North China Plain, the Ganges Basin, England, the Po Basin, the Pannonian Plain, the Sea of Marmara, Mesopotamia, the Persian Highlands, the Ferghana Valley, the Sichuan Basin, the Indus Valley, Siam, the Seto Inland Sea, the Lower Nile. It's a big list. Just as important, almost *all* of them can easily interact (read: fight) with one another. The result is millennia of history of the rises and falls of this or that power. No one can possibly establish influence over — much less control of — the entire hemisphere.

In contrast, the Western Hemisphere only has a few good locations to grow major powers: the Greater Mississippi Basin, the Columbia Basin of Washington and Oregon, California's Central Valley, the Piedmont of the American Southeast, Canada's Hamilton Peninsula, and the Rio de la Plata zone. Of these the first is more potent than all the others combined, the first four are in the same political authority, and that authority is tightly allied with the fifth. American strategic dominance of the Western Hemisphere isn't simply possible, it is almost automatic. So automatic that American primacy within the hemisphere can occur *without* a formal government policy on the matter.

As the Disorder destroys much of the international stability the world currently takes for granted, the Eastern Hemisphere will become a dangerous place. Without American *government* efforts to stabilize the wider world, American *private* efforts will prefer to operate in safer locales, concentrating the American footprint in a much shorter list of locations where the chaos is far less intense. Southeast Asia looks good. Latin America looks better. Everywhere else, the term free-for-all comes to mind.

Everywhere else, the global superpower's impact will be felt primarily by its absence.

APPENDIX I

Shale and the Changing Face of Climate Change

As I'm sure you've noticed in my demographic and energy analysis, much of what I do is data-driven. But much of the international system — ranging from predicting manufacturing trends to following refugee patterns to inducing state secrets — just doesn't have rich, confirmable data sheets to work from. The world can be messy. That leaves me searching for and studying anecdotes to see if I can stitch together a pattern, and then — preferably — meshing those stories with what data I *can* scrape together to sketch out a fuller picture.

What frustrates me to no end is that on the topic of climate change there is a lot of light not just between the anecdotes and data, but within the data itself. In my experience the light isn't where most people expect it.

First, the basics of climate change. Certain gases are better at trapping atmospheric heat than others. The most prevalent of such heat-trappers is carbon dioxide, the byproduct of pretty much everything that separates modern society from our pre-industrial past. The heat-trapping process is referred to as the greenhouse effect, and it is a very good thing. Without carbon dioxide and other greenhouse gases (GHGs), Earth would be a giant iceball. The environmental concern is too many GHGs could prove as problematic as not enough. Jack up global GHG levels and the Earth warms too much, turning arable zones into barrens, shifting wind patterns, generating superstorms, melting the ice caps, and raising sea levels.

Now let's get my personal politics out of the way. Something is most certainly happening with the climate. I'm an avid backpacker and everyone in that world that I've ever met has a personal story about how the hiking season is getting longer and how snowfields and glaciers are shrinking. My personal stories are from New Zealand and New Mexico, two regions that have nothing in common topographically or climatologically aside from the word "new."

I also chat with folks from a wide variety of industries and geographies on a regular basis, so I understand from people who are in a position to know that things are shifting at the lower altitudes as well. Flooding-related insurance payouts in Florida were up substantially in 2006-2015 despite no significant hurricane activity. Wildfires and beetle activity throughout the American West is up as the region slowly becomes hotter and more arid. Farmers in the Canadian Prairie Provinces have started growing corn, a crop that loves not just long growing seasons, but also heat and humidity. Those are things available aplenty in my home state of Iowa where some days the whole place feels like a gigantic corn incubator, but not so much in the high-latitude, short-summer lands of Saskatchewan.

Every meteorologist I've communed with comments extensively on how weather events are getting kicked up a notch by shifting jet streams. For example, Hurricane Matthew in 2016 didn't just drop more rain on Fayetteville, North Carolina, than any other storm, ever, but dropped more rain in a *day* than the city had received in all but four entire *months* since record keeping began in the 1800s. Something is clearly changing.

Paired with my geopolitical forecasts, my green leanings lead me down a bleak road. As wars spread, as supply chains are disrupted, and as countries find themselves scrambling for the basic inputs of civilized life, nearly all the world's regions will face absolute energy scarcity. The Disorder will leave the governments of more than two-thirds of the world's population with a stark choice: burn coal (which unlike oil or natgas is a local fuel source almost everywhere in the world) for electricity and swallow the emissions, or go without electricity altogether and risk decivilizing.

That's problem No. 1.

Problem No. 2 is that we still don't have a good grip on precisely how this climate change thing works. The issue is that the best available data don't always line up with the anecdotals.

Take a peek at the chart below. The vertical axis denotes the best-estimate global temperature increase from a doubling of the carbon dioxide concentration in the atmosphere (the scientific consensus is that we'll reach that point around 2060). The horizontal axis belts out the scientific studies over time that have studied climate change. Each dot on the graphic, therefore,

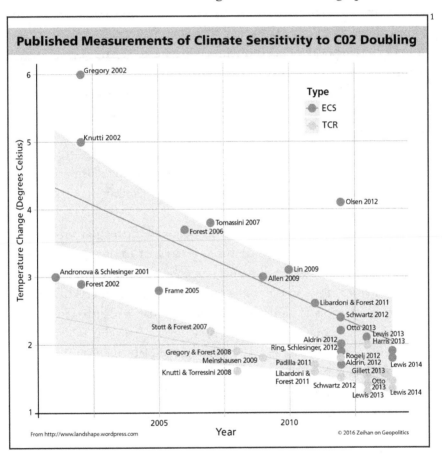

[1]

1   ECS and TCR are two different statistical methods for forecasting global temperature shifts based on carbon dioxide levels. If you like getting into the guts of statistical analysis feel free to dive in here:
https://www.gfdl.noaa.gov/transient-and-equilibrium-climate-sensitivity/

is the best-guesstimate charted out by the year the study was published. As the science of climate change has sharpened, forecasters have *reduced* their estimates for overall temperature increases. The point isn't that this shaded bar is going to reach statistical irrelevance, but instead that our understanding of what makes the climate tick isn't progressing in a straight line.

Even the Intergovernmental Panel on Climate Change — the institution that coordinates global action on global policy and managed the negotiation of the 2015 Paris Climate Accords — puts the global average sea level increase at but 3.2mm per year. If that proves correct, global sea levels in 2100 will be but one foot higher than they are today. Statistically significant, yes, but not exactly apocalyptic. And damnably hard to square with increased Miami flooding that has *already* happened.

I tend to visually squirm when queried on any topic where politics invokes passions, and climate change is no exception. I like to explain. Not argue. For both climate change believers and deniers, climate change has taken on an almost zealous fervor, and me taking the stance of analysis-still-pending earns me few friends. Climate believers think I'm a climate denier. Climate deniers think I'm at best a climate skeptic. I don't think I am either.

I'm climate confused.

I think it is obvious that things are shifting, and the biggest variable that has changed in the past couple centuries is the human presence, so we are probably what's responsible. But that's not the same thing as saying that the data we have access to right now gives us the full picture as to what the pace or consequences of climate change are *or* what is required to head off the supposed consequences. Even the most enthusiastic climate warrior scientists freely admit that we have at best an incomplete understanding about how the biosphere moves, stores, and releases carbon. And on the other side it is devilishly hard to convince someone who is responsible for the pillars of civilization such as electricity producers that they should abandon tried-and-true fossil fuel burning power systems for alternative energy systems that they know from experience are neither as reliable nor affordable.

The details matter hugely, and our understanding just isn't to the point where we have those details.

So where does that leave us?

As my friends in manufacturing, utilities, agriculture, finance, and economic planning tell me, the key to dealing with incomplete understanding is risk mitigation. If carbon emissions are indeed going to shift things around in ways either mysterious or known, if there's more than a negligible chance that the end result could be negative, then taking some preventative steps makes good economic and moral sense.

But there's no need to limit the analysis to the purely environmental. Even if shale helps North America divorce itself from the world's mounting troubles, shale isn't going to provide us with petroleum until the end of time. It's still a finite resource. There's a national security element to green energy. And even if shale is indeed forever and this whole climate change thing is nonsense, diversifying energy inputs is a risk mitigation technique all on its own.

So let's look at the techs available, and see what brings down carbon emissions in the fastest manner. Once we've figured *that* out, we can think about whether that's the path we actually want to take.

The Black and White of Green Energy

Which brings us to problem No. 3.

Available greentechs just don't cut it. There's a profound mismatch between demand patterns for energy and what, when, and how much green systems can produce. It all comes down to the balance among the concepts of supply, demand, energy density, and reliability.

The vast majority of mankind's carbon emissions come from two sources: oil-derived liquid transport fuels and the burning of fossil fuels for electricity production. This is how humanity has done things for good reason. These fuels are not simply relatively easy to source and reliable, but also anyone using them can choose *when* to use them because they are eminently easy to manipulate. Production efforts can be ramped up and down as necessary. Above all, *storage* is simple. Gasoline, diesel, and propane can be kept almost indefinitely in a tank. Coal can literally be left in a pile on the ground.

That's not the case for greentech. A heavy list of factors limit its application.

- *Latitude.* Any zones north of about 42 degrees north latitude — just above Chicago — (or south of 42 degrees south latitude) have too much seasonal variation to enable solar to generate appreciable power half the year. Solar can be brilliant in Phoenix or Santiago, but it is idiotic in Stockholm or Toronto.

- *Climate.* Africa's Gulf of Guinea region or southern China seem to have good solar potential — they are nowhere near 42 degrees north — until you realize that the regions' often-rampant humidity creates a persistent solar-impinging haze and clouds, landing them with some of the world's *lowest* solar radiation ratings.

- *Intermittency.* Even in places with good solar potential, clouds, mist, dust and such often impair power generation on a minute-by-minute basis. Each time local generation proves insufficient, power surges and brown-outs ripple across the electricity-distribution system as some areas get too much power and others not enough. Modifying the U.S. grid so it can handle the ebb and flow of a high-greentech-powered system would run a cool $750 billion. And that assumes there's enough power coming in from somewhere. In the case of larger-scale disruption — say an entire city being under cloud cover — another, more traditional source of power generation needs to be tapped to keep electricity flowing. And of course all throughout the history of humanity, the sun has never once shone at night — so you'll be needing that backup for half the day on average even if everything else is perfect.

- *Supply/demand mismatch.* Peak daily *demand* for electricity is between 4 p.m. and 9 p.m., but peak solar *supply* lies between 10 a.m. and 2 p.m. The lack of match-up means that even if nameplate solar generating capacity could handle all demand, the inability to generate power when it is need-ed forces utilities to operate carbon-burning power generation anyway. Since a coal plant takes 24 (or more) hours to ramp up or down, even large-scale greentech buildouts translate into only negligible reductions in net GHG emissions.

- *Strategic competition.* The best places for solar on the planet are in the Saharan and Arabian Deserts and the Persian highlands. The best place for wind is Siberia. All areas where petroleum is king.

- *Density.* Solar panels take up a great deal of space, particularly if they are not near the equator and must be slanted and separated to capture angled sunlight. Generating 150MW of power from a natural gas-burning facility in the Phoenix area only takes 17 acres of land. Once you take into effect things like panel spacing and angle, getting the same draw from solar would require almost five *thousand* — and that in the U.S. city with the highest solar potential.

- *Transmission.* There certainly are places where the wind is more reliable (Western Iowa, the North Sea, Western Texas come to mind) or where solar radiation is reliably high (the American High Plains, Tibet and the Australian Outback). But this is not the norm. Only 10 to 20 percent of the Earth's surface is ideal for either wind or solar power. Deepening the problem is that most of such areas have shockingly low population densities. Transmitting such green power to cities typically requires so much more infrastructure and related maintenance that transmission costs are triple more traditional carbon-based fuels.

Germany is the poster child for the limitations of a fast-paced buildout with today's less-than-stellar greentechs. The country's Energiewende program is designed to move the country fully away from carbon-based fuels by 2050, and as part of the program the country has installed some 40 gigawatts of solar-generating capacity, technically enough to generate nearly all its normal electricity requirements. However, between Germany's high latitude and persistent cloud cover, the sun rarely shines. All those panels generate but 6 percent of the country's electricity. For public concern reasons the country is shutting down its nuclear power program, and for geopolitical reasons the country is sidelining its natgas-burning power plants. That only leaves wind (which limited by siting concerns is pretty much maxed out already) ... and coal.

Since solar broadly doesn't function in Germany, coal and lignite (a sort of wet, low-quality, locally-produced coal that has the highest carbon foot-

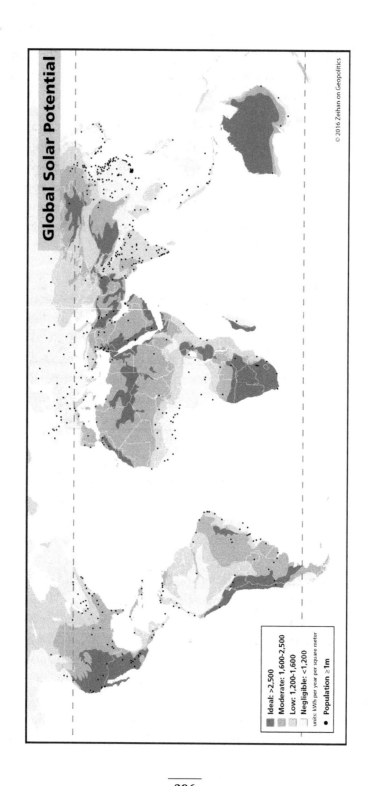

Global Solar Potential

Ideal: >2,500
Moderate: 1,600-2,500
Low: 1,200-1,600
Negligible: <1,200
units: kWh per year per square meter

• Population ≥1m

© 2016 Zeihan on Geopolitics

print of any fuel source) now generate 42 percent of the country's electricity needs. And since it takes so long to ramp up/down a coal/lignite-burning power plant, those plants *keep* burning even on the rare days the sun lights up Germany's omnipresent solar panels. The result? Germany's commitment to solar power has barely nudged the country's carbon emissions. In fact, if not for the 2007-2009 recession, the Energiewende would have made those emissions *rise*.

No wonder that fossil fuels are so strongly represented in global energy patterns. Of all the energy of all forms that humans use, fully 86 percent of it is *not* green. Solar makes up but 0.4 percent of the global primary energy total.

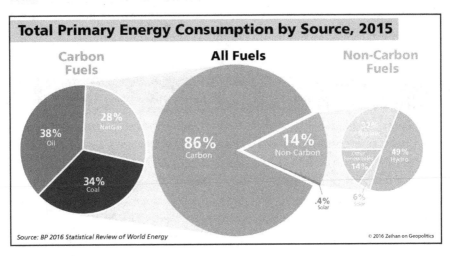

Total Primary Energy Consumption by Source, 2015

Carbon Fuels — **All Fuels** — Non-Carbon Fuels

38% Oil — 28% NatGas — 34% Coal

86% Carbon — 14% Non-Carbon — .4% Solar — 6% Solar — 49% Hydro

Source: BP 2016 Statistical Review of World Energy © 2016 Zeihan on Geopolitics

At least some of these problems could be mitigated with the large-scale application of battery technology. If you can store greentech-generated electricity — especially if you can store it close to demand points — then the timing of when the sun shines is somewhat less important. Reliable, energy-dense battery systems also raise the tantalizing possibility of use in cars and trucks — digging into carbon-heavy transport fuels demand.

Unfortunately, today's batteries suffer their own problems.

The dominant battery system of the day is based upon lithium — a product whose ore is very metal-poor and so its extraction requires massive open pits and/or strip mines along with massively land-, power- and water-intensive processing facilities. Buildouts of such facilities are in progress, but few people understand the required scale. The batteries required to "just" get three hours of grid storage in the United States — an achievement that would be one part of the process of reducing total U.S. emissions by about 10 percent — would take *all* the world's current lithium production for nearly 10 years. If you like batteries, you have to *love* mining.

The energy density issue keeps raising its head. Charging up an electric car to full with a standard 240V power outlet is a 10-hour exercise. Even a Tesla supercharger takes over an hour. Worse yet, the energy density issue stacks with itself. A 5kW residential solar system — about the maximum that can be fitted onto a current suburban home — would require 16 *hours* of full noon-brightness sunlight to charge up a standard electric vehicle (EV). And in the several days it takes to charge your car, you're not getting any power for anything else. Like your house.

Let it Blow

At a glance, wind faces many of the same challenges as solar. Transmission can be a beast of a cost and the wind doesn't always blow, so wind power must be paired with fossil-fuel power. Unless a greentech can generate power 24 hours a day, it is of limited use. And since there are only a handful of good wind channels around the world, wind's upper limit in most places is but a few percent of total electricity generation.

Unless you go higher. Most of the first generation of wind towers were only a few dozens of feet tall. Current towers are around 260 feet, which puts them in stronger and more stable wind currents. The next generation of towers will be higher yet – 330 to 370 feet. At that height, not only are wind currents so stable that they can provide limited baseload capacity (and so enable utilities to actually take carbon-powered systems fully offline), but those wind currents are so omnipresent that all 50 U.S. states could generate significant power from wind, up from only a half-dozen states today.

There are two obstacles. First, engineering. Any structure that is taller than a football field is long isn't exactly child's play to build — or service. Second, the largest obstacle to wind power development to date are community activists who don't want giant towers ruining the view. The newer towers can be seen from over 10 miles away.

There's also the damnably inconvenient truth that batteries are in essence deliberately-stalled chemical reactions, and chemical reactions proceed more slowly in the cold. The effective storage capacity of a battery at temperatures below freezing is less than half that of a battery at room temperature. That fancy Tesla only goes half as far in a northern winter.

These are known problems to the greentech industry, and the smart money is on trying to solve them. But that doesn't mean it is easy or that we have a clear path from here to there.

An example: In late 2016 Korean megafirm Samsung released a new smartphone product, the Note7, boasting a significantly better lithium battery that promised greater energy density. Within a few weeks so many Note7s had caught fire (or exploded) that the American FAA flatly prohibited even having the Note7 on passenger jets. At present we don't know *what* the battery medium that lets us take full advantage of greentech will be. We just know that it won't be lithium.

Abandon All Hope?

Still committed to reducing GHGs? I am. While we are waiting for wind and solar to become more applicable, and for batteries to move into whatever will exist beyond lithium, the trick is to clean up the fuel input mix to something that is less carbon-intensive. Greening the grid in a sustainable, technically-feasible way is the best way to both reduce direct carbon emissions from the power sector *and* to pave the way for wide-scale electric vehicle use.

On this, luckily, we are making a great deal of progress.

Remember back to Chapter 3 where we discussed that in the United States natural gas is a prolific waste product out of the shale fields? And that natural gas is displacing coal out of the American fuel mix? Well, that same natural gas is far less carbon intensive than coal, generating 44 percent fewer carbon emissions. Natural gas's partial displacement of coal has already sliced about 6 percent of emissions out of the power sector on a straight fuel-for-fuel swap.

And that's not the whole story because it is not a straight fuel-for-fuel swap. There's a newish type of power plant called combined cycle (CC). A

CC plant doesn't just burn an input to generate electricity directly, but then also recycles the exhaust to capture the residual heat and generate a secondary electricity feed. Combine natgas with CC and the GHG reduction for the coal-to-natgas changeover isn't 44 percent, but instead 60 percent! Considering that nearly all the natural gas burning power plants the United States has constructed during the past decade are CC, this switchover has had the impact of reducing the power sector's total emissions by 9 percent *with no net increase in electricity costs*. In comparison, the $400 billion build-out for greentech-generating assets since 2005 (inclusive of subsidies) has only reduced power sector emissions by 6 percent for wind and 1 percent for solar.

For climate warriors the thought of using a carbon-based fuel like natural gas — even if it is to displace a far more carbon-intensive fuel like coal — certainly isn't going to sit well. But even here there is a silver lining. Combined-cycle plants have an operational life of only about 30 years. Hopefully as these new CC facilities reach the end of their operational lives in the 2040s, greentech will finally be ready.

Is this ideal? Nope. But it isn't all that bad once you look at it in context.

First is the issue of **net carbon**. Until we can square the energy storage, energy density, and intermittency circles, the absolute maximum the United States can shift from carbon fuels to green-generation is about 20 percent of gross electricity demand. That would be a multi-trillion-dollar build-out using technology that we know is not ready for prime time. You can achieve the same carbon reduction by displacing coal with natgas for a net zero cost. Low-hanging fruit indeed.

Second is **the transport question**. Let's assume the 30-odd electrical vehicle models on the market succeed in eliminating completely *all* competition for like-sized cars, light trucks, and SUVs in their market niches. That only takes away 20 percent of oil demand. Another fifth of oil demand comes from larger SUVs and trucks. Another 20 percent is credited to heavier transport modes — semis, construction and farming equipment, boats, planes, trains.

In everything except that first light-truck/small-SUV/small passenger vehicle category, there are no electric vehicle models available. It is not simply an issue of electricity storage, but of *power* needs. Current electric vehicles simply lack the power to push, pull, or otherwise motivate larger vehicles for long periods of time. A container ship that must go into port to recharge every day is a container ship that no one will ever buy. Batteries simply cannot provide the continual torque required at a weight/duration ratio that still enables the mode of transport to be, well, transportable. In contrast, scaling up a basic internal combustion engine — along with a basic fuel tank — is fairly straightforward. Even with 100-percent conversion, EVs only take us one-*fifth* of the way to life-after-oil.

And that might not even be a net gain from a carbon point of view. Electric cars sound great, but there is a third issue: **what powers your car?** If you have solar panels at home, but you drive to work every day, then your EV's diet is standard grid power — not your clean solar (your car obviously isn't getting any solar-generated electricity when it is parked in your garage at night). All the switchover does is shift the pollution point from your tailpipe to your electricity provider. If you are like most citizens of the planet and coal is your primary source of electricity, you have *increased* your carbon footprint — burning coal kicks out more carbon dioxide than gasoline.

If you're fully committed to getting an EV on environmental grounds, be sure to check out what powers your local grid first because what's on your roof is largely irrelevant. Swapping coal out for shale gas to power the grid in league with EVs not only reduces demand for oil, it would also reduce carbon emissions by another 20 percent.

Those of you who like math probably noticed that in this discussion of the oil markets I've only mentioned three slices of 20 percent each. What's the last 40 percent of oil demand? It's the fourth way that shale helps: **chemicals**. All that waste shale natgas is displacing oil from chemicals manufacture. It has no net impact upon emissions since the end products are chemically identical, but it certainly winnows out the need for oil in the first place — perhaps to the point of reducing oil demand by as much as a complete EV switchover. And we can do that *now*, with current technology.

Finally, there is simple geography. Take a look at a world map. Notice the physical location of the United States relative to the other major advanced countries that have a trillion dollars or so to spend on green tech. The United States is the first world power closest to the equator, which grants it the **most solar potential** by far. Whenever humanity does figure out a way to make solar and batteries work, whenever we do have the possibility of moving beyond shale, that transformation will happen in the United States first.

If the goal is meaningful carbon reductions over a decade-long time scale, then the answer in most places is not solar or wind or electric vehicles, but instead the combination of natural gas displacing coal and efficiency gains from things like LED lights and front-loading washers and smart thermostats and hybrid automobiles. It doesn't have to be sexy to be effective.

APPENDIX II

Other Shale Concerns

What about other shale-based concerns? Community groups and environmental groups have long sought to limit the reach of the shale sector, citing a laundry list of concerns — some completely legitimate, some less so, some not at all. These concerns, and the current status of industry and/or government action, are listed here in order from most to least significant.

Methane leakage: Natural gas is a more intensive greenhouse gas than carbon dioxide, so if methane leaks out of pipe networks it can obviate any progress on the GHG front that might be gained from its replacement of coal in the electricity sector. The magic number for a breakeven is 3% leakage. In 2012 the U.S. government's figure for total leakage was 1.5%. Driving this number down further is an ongoing effort by both government and private interests. The government, rightly, sees it as a greenhouse issue, and recent diplomatic agreements between Canada and the United States seek to specifically minimize methane leakage across the broad swathe of the two country's massive pipe systems. For private interests the concern is more direct: any natgas that leaks out is natgas that isn't being sold for income. A mere 1% leakage rate comes out to 0.7 Bcf/d which wholesales for a half billion dollars per year. There are two primary means of meaningfully reducing leakage: better well completions to stop leakage at its source and improved pipeline monitoring to detect leaks in the distribution system.

Earthquakes: Every frack job forces liquid into a solid object to break it up. This, by definition, is seismic activity — the informal translation is fracking causes earthquakes. However, the force emanating from fracks is miniscule, rarely being less than the amount of energy released from the swinging of a sledgehammer, and even that occurs on the other side of a mile of solid rock. There have been a grand total of one seismic events globally caused by fracking, which occurred in the United Kingdom when some moron fracked a fault line.

This does not, however, mean that there is no link between seismicity and the shale sector — just that it the link is not to fracking. Instead, the link is to water *disposal*. At some point the water used in fracking cannot be recycled any longer, and it must be disposed of. Considering how many thousands of wells that are fracked annually, this all adds up to billions of gallons of water (almost one-third as much as U.S. golf courses use). You're certainly not going to simply dump it in a river, so most of this water is put into specially designed deep-injection disposal wells two or more miles underground where there is no chance of it ever mingling with anything that anyone would ever care about.

Problem: unlike fracking where most of the small amount of water used is pulled right back out (and so aside from the microfractures there is no change to the overall geology), in a disposal well thousands of times as much water is injected and *left behind*. This causes distortions in the local geology which do indeed trigger small earthquakes[1]. This is by far the most significant direct environmental impact the industry has, and why the smart money is figuring out how to use less water, how to avoid frack stages that are not necessary, how to recycle as much water as possible to reduce the volumes that ultimately need to be disposed of, and how to identify geologies for safe disposal where the buckling of that geology will not trigger quakes that can be felt on the surface.

Water usage: Many shale plays are in arid environments, leading to conflicts among farmers, city planners and county regulatory bodies over who

---

1 Technically the jury is still out on this point, but at the time of this writing the scientific consensus in Texas and Oklahoma is rapidly moving from correlation to causation.

has access to the surface water required for the fracs. Somewhat ironically, operators prefer *not* to use surface water as it is contaminated by a host of bacteria and algae and purifying said water requires extensive treatment — not to mention heavy transport costs for shipping water to well sites. The industry's preferred solution is a mix of recycling used fluids and especially tapping in-ground water levels well below the potable water table. Most regions have a subsurface brackish water layer in excess of 2000 feet down. This water a) has no bacteria or algae, reducing treatment costs, b) it is on-site, eliminating trucking costs, c) it is already saline, reducing input costs and d) operators need to drill through it anyway, so they already have access to it by dint of their existing operations. Add in the technical and operational changes brought on by microseismic, the use of water tanks, and the broadscale shift from conventional production to shale production, and the overall volume of what is used - per barrel of American oil produced - has shrunk by over 85% during the past decade. Additionally, if you consider the total volume of water used across the entire process of production to transport to consumption in the energy sector, shale natgas is by far the least water-intensive fuel source, using less than one-tenth the water needed for coal or nuclear, and one-hundredth that of ethanol.

Fracking denudes the landscape and is loud: In 2012 a densely exploited shale field used less than 5% of the land area for drilling operations. Once work was completed, all that remained of the work site was a plug and pipe outlet not much bigger than a king sized bed. However, as pad drilling has replaced single-well drilling, the surface footprint per barrel produced has steadily shrunk. There are now fewer than a quarter the number of drilling sites compared to 2008 to tap the same land area. In addition, changes in water usage (above) have reduced the need for trucks by over three-quarters, vastly easing the burden on local roads, with the commensurate reduction of traffic, traffic-related noise and the need for truck parking lots at each drilling site. In addition, with fewer pads producing more petroleum per pad, collection systems have become concentrated with fewer, larger pipes requiring fewer right-of-ways to gather the petroleum for transport via truck lines. All told the operational footprint is more than an order of magnitude smaller in 2016 compared to 2007.

Toxicity: There are concerns that the fluids used to frac a well are toxic. While specific ratios vary from well to well, much less field to field, on average frac fluid is 90% water and 9.5% inert sand. Of the remaining 0.5% over 90% are typically items that exist in the average kitchen (i.e. not classified by governments as toxic) with the most common additive being sodium chloride (table salt). The push within the industry is to do an end run around this entire topic by shifting the fluid composition so that it is entirely non-toxic. Since 2013 the (more than a little creepy) fad among chemical execs is to be filmed drinking the chemical mix.[2]

Drinking water contamination: Many shale wells drill down through the potable water layer on their way to the petroleum-rich layers that the operators seek so there are concerns that the frack fluids or extracted natgas could leak into the water table. Such occurrences are improbable to say the least as the water table is typically within 400 feet of the surface and most frack zones are over vertical mile down under layers of impermeable rock (remember, shale rock doesn't give up anything unless it is pulverized). The *only* route for possible contamination is up the well shaft itself. Wells are designed to funnel all the oil/gas (and frac fluids) through the pipe (after all, that's the entire point of oil and natgas extraction). What leakage which might occur is trace natgas which comes up the well-shaft but not within the pipe. Operators address this potential leakage by encasing the pipe in concrete wherever it is within 100' or so of the potable water layer. According to the Obama administration's EPA report on water contamination, while there have been cases where leakage has occurred, such events are statistically insignificant when compared to the millions of frac jobs completed in the United States. In essence the report was a somewhat limp-wristed rubber stamp of the industry's long-held assertions that shale wasn't a meaningful threat to water supplies, and aside from some fairly

---

2   Have fun on YouTube.

mild directives — almost all of which had been part of the industry's best practices for over two years — did not call for further actions.[3]

If there was going to be a concerted effort from the left to shut down the shale sector, it was going to happen under the Obama administration. Instead, the White House has (quietly) encouraged natural gas wherever it has been feasible, a boon to shale in all its geographies. While the White House has opposed international *import* petroleum pipelines like Keystone, it has enthusiastically — if, again, quietly — supported a multitude of international *export* pipelines of natural gas to both Mexico and Canada.

---

3   You can find the entire report here:
https://www.epa.gov/hfstudy/hydraulic-fracturing-water-cycle.
Incidentally, those YouTube videos which show people lighting their tap water on fire are all in areas that first produced oil and natural gas over a century ago. The EPA, backed up by a century of newspaper archives, believes that this methane contamination predates the shale revolution and fracking by decades.

APPENDIX III

Oil and Natural Gas Data

A few notes on energy data from the research desk: Unfortunately, there is no single, standardized source for all aspects of global energy data. We built these tables using data we believe best represent a country's energy sector, but circumstances forced us to do this using multiple sources that don't always agree. We sought to keep the data as consistent as possible, relying particularly heavily on the BP Statistical Review of World Energy 2016 for production, consumption, and reserves while focusing on the Joint Oil Data Initiative (JODI), a country-level self-report system, for much of the trade data. As such, these data points must be considered approximate and demonstrative rather than technically authoritative — part of why we rounded most data points to the nearest 100,000 barrels. Most of our crude oil figures include natural gas liquids (NGLs).

Approximate Global Crude Oil and Product Data

Region	Country	Crude and NGL			Products			Total Consumption	Reserves (billion bbls)
		Production	Exports	Imports	Production	Exports	Imports		
Greater Russia	Azerbaijan	800	700	-	100	-	-	100	7.0
Greater Russia	Belarus	-	-	-	-	-	-	100	0.2
Greater Russia	Russia	11,000	5,100	100	6,400	3,100	-	3,100	102.4
Greater Russia	Ukraine	-	-	-	-	-	200	200	0.4
Central Asia	Kazakhstan	1,700	1,300	-	400	100	-	300	30.0
Central Asia	Turkmenistan	300	-	-	200	-	-	100	0.6
Central Asia	Uzbekistan	100	-	-	-	-	-	100	0.6
Central Europe	Czech Republic	-	-	100	200	100	100	200	-
Central Europe	Poland	-	-	500	600	200	100	500	0.1
Central Europe	Slovak Republic	-	-	100	100	100	-	100	-
Northern Europe	Norway	1,900	1,200	-	400	400	100	200	8.0
Northern Europe	Sweden	-	-	400	500	300	200	300	n/a
Northern Europe	United Kingdom	1,000	700	1,000	1,300	500	700	1,600	2.8
Western Europe	Austria	-	-	200	200	100	100	300	-
Western Europe	Belgium	-	100	700	700	500	500	700	n/a
Western Europe	France	-	-	1,200	1,300	400	900	1,600	0.1
Western Europe	Germany	-	-	1,800	2,200	500	800	2,300	0.1
Western Europe	Italy	100	-	1,400	1,600	600	300	1,300	0.6
Western Europe	Netherlands	-	-	1,300	1,300	2,300	1,900	800	0.1
Western Europe	Portugal	-	-	300	300	100	100	200	n/a
Western Europe	Spain	-	100	1,400	1,300	400	300	1,200	0.2
Western Europe	Switzerland	-	-	100	100	-	200	200	-
North Africa	Algeria	1,600	600	-	600	600	100	400	12.2
North Africa	Libya	400	200	-	100	-	100	200	48.4
SubSaharan Africa	Angola	1,800	1,700	-	100	-	100	100	12.7
SubSaharan Africa	Equitorial Guinea	300	200	-	-	-	-	-	1.1
SubSaharan Africa	Nigeria	2,400	2,200	-	-	-	400	400	37.1
SubSaharan Africa	South Africa	-	-	400	500	100	200	600	<0.1
Eastern Mediterranean	Egypt	700	200	100	500	-	400	800	0.3
Eastern Mediterranean	Greece	-	-	500	600	300	100	300	<0.1
Eastern Mediterranean	Israel	-	-	300	300	100	100	200	<0.1
Eastern Mediterranean	Jordan	-	-	100	100	-	100	100	-
Eastern Mediterranean	Turkey	-	-	500	600	200	500	800	0.3
Persian Gulf	Iran	3,900	1,100	-	1,800	500	100	1,900	157.8
Persian Gulf	Iraq	4,000	3,000	-	400	-	100	700	143.1
Persian Gulf	Kuwait	3,100	2,000	-	1,000	700	-	500	101.5

Data in thousand barrels per day, except reserves which are in billion barrels.
Countries in **bold** are those where conflict and crises will most directly impact energy supply.

Approximate Global Natural Gas Data

Region	Country	Natural Gas				Of Which: LNG		Reserves (TCF)
		Production	Exports	Imports	Consumption	Exports	Imports	
Greater Russa	Azerbaijan	1.9	0.8	-	1.1	-	-	41
	Belarus	-	-	1.8	1.8	-	-	-
	Russia	61.6	19.2	0.9	43.2	1.4	-	1,140
	Ukraine	1.8	-	1.6	3.0	-	-	21
Central Asia	Kazakhstan	1.2	1.1	0.7	0.8	-	-	33
	Turkmenistan	7.0	3.7	-	3.3	-	-	617
	Uzbekistan	5.6	0.7	-	4.9	-	-	38
Central Europe	Czech Republic	-	2.7	3.5	0.8	-	-	-
	Poland	0.6	2.8	3.9	1.8	-	-	3
	Slovak Republic	-	4.2	4.6	0.4	-	-	1
Northern Europe	Norway	11.7	11.0	-	0.6	0.5	-	66
	Sweden	-	-	0.1	0.1	-	-	-
	United Kingdom	4.0	1.4	4.4	7.0	-	1.4	7
Western Europe	Austria	0.1	3.7	4.3	0.8	-	-	-
	Belgium	-	2.4	4.0	1.6	0.1	0.4	-
	France	-	0.5	4.3	3.8	-	0.5	-
	Germany	0.8	6.7	13.7	7.9	-	-	1
	Italy	0.7	-	5.9	6.5	-	0.6	2
	Netherlands	5.3	4.9	3.6	3.9	-	0.2	24
	Portugal	-	-	0.5	0.5	-	0.2	-
	Spain	-	0.5	3.1	2.7	0.1	1.3	-
	Switzerland	-	1.0	1.3	0.3	-	-	-
North Africa	Algeria	8.3	4.0	-	3.6	1.5	-	159
	Libya	1.5	0.6	-	0.4	-	-	53
SubSaharan Africa	Angola	-	-	-	-	-	-	11
	Equitorial Guinea	0.6	0.5	-	0.2	0.5	-	1
	Nigeria	4.8	2.7	-	1.8	2.7	-	180
	South Africa	0.1	0.4	4.0	0.5	-	-	-
Eastern Mediterranean	Egypt	4.3	-	-	4.6	-	0.3	65
	Greece	-	-	2.5	0.3	-	0.1	-
	Israel	0.8	-	-	0.8	-	-	6
	Jordan	-	-	0.2	0.2	-	0.2	-
	Turkey	-	0.1	4.7	4.6	-	0.7	-
Persian Gulf	Iran	22.1	0.8	0.9	18.5	-	-	1,201
	Iraq	2.3	-	-	0.7	-	-	130
	Kuwait	1.6	-	-	1.9	-	0.4	63

Data in billion cubic feet per day, except reserves which are in trillion cubic feet
Countries in bold are those where conflict and crises will most directly impact energy supply

Approximate Global Crude Oil and Product Data

Region	Country	Crude and NGL			Products			Total Consumption	Reserves (billion bbls)
		Production	Exports	Imports	Production	Exports	Imports		
Persian Gulf	Oman	1,000	800	-	200	-	-	200	5.3
	Qatar	700	500	-	600	500	-	300	25.7
	Saudi Arabia	12,000	7,200	-	2,500	1,200	600	3,900	266.6
	United Arab Emirates	3,900	2,400	-	800	1,000	100	900	97.8
	Yemen	-	-	-	-	-	-	100	3.0
Southeast Asia	Australia	400	200	300	500	-	500	1,000	4.0
	Brunei	100	100	-	-	-	-	-	1.1
	Indonesia	800	300	400	1,000	100	500	1,600	3.6
	Malaysia	700	400	200	700	500	600	800	3.6
	Myanmar	-	-	-	-	-	100	100	-
	Papua New Guinea	-	-	-	-	-	-	-	0.2
	Singapore	-	-	900	1,000	1,900	2,600	1,300	-
	Thailand	500	-	900	1,300	300	100	1,300	0.4
	Vietnam	400	100	-	100	-	100	400	4.4
South Asia	India	900	-	3,900	4,900	1,200	500	4,200	5.7
	Pakistan	100	-	100	300	-	200	500	0.4
Northeast Asia	China	4,300	100	6,700	11,100	800	1,500	12,000	18.5
	Japan	-	-	3,400	3,500	400	1,100	4,200	<0.1
	Korea	-	-	2,800	3,000	1,300	800	2,600	n/a
	Taiwan	-	-	800	900	300	400	1,000	<0.1
North America	Canada	4,400	3,200	700	1,900	600	600	2,300	172.2
	Mexico	2,600	1,200	-	1,300	200	800	1,900	10.8
	Trinidad and Tobago	100	-	100	100	100	-	-	0.7
	US	12,700	500	7,400	18,200	4,100	2,100	19,400	55.0
South America	Argentina	600	-	-	700	-	100	700	2.4
	Bolivia	100	-	-	-	100	-	100	0.2
	Brazil	2,500	700	300	2,100	100	600	3,200	13.0
	Chile	-	-	200	200	-	100	400	0.2
	Colombia	1,000	700	-	300	100	100	300	2.3
	Ecuador	500	400	-	100	-	100	300	8.0
	Peru	100	-	100	300	100	100	200	1.4
	Venezuela	2,600	2,000	-	1,200	600	200	700	300.9

n/a - not available

Sources: JODI, BP Statistical Review 2016, OPEC, EIA, UNCOMTRADE, IEA Headline Global Energy Data, various national statistical agencies, calculations and estimates

© 2017 Zeihan on Geopolitics

Approximate Global Natural Gas Data

Region	Country	Natural Gas				Of Which: LNG		Reserves (TCF)
		Production	Exports	Imports	Consumption	Exports	Imports	
Persian Gulf	Oman	3.4	1.0	-	2.5	1.0	-	24
	Qatar	17.6	12.2	-	4.4	10.3	-	866
	Saudi Arabia	10.3	-	-	10.3	-	-	294
	United Arab Emirates	5.4	0.7	2.6	6.7	0.8	-	215
	Yemen	0.3	0.2	-	0.1	0.2	-	9
Southeast Asia	Australia	5.1	3.3	0.7	2.5	3.3		123
	Brunei	1.2	0.8	-	0.4	0.8		10
	Indonesia	7.3	2.8	-	4.5	2.1	0.1	100
	Malaysia	6.1	3.3	0.9	3.8	3.3	0.2	41
	Myanmar	1.9	1.3	-	0.3	-	-	19
	Papua New Guinea	-	-	-	-	.9	-	5
	Singapore	-	-	1.2	1.2	-	0.3	-
	Thailand	3.8	-	1.3	4.9	-	0.3	8
	Vietnam	1.0	-	-	1.0	-	-	22
South Asia	India	3.2	-	1.7	4.8	-	1.7	53
	Pakistan	4.1	-	0.1	4.2	-	0.1	19
Northeast Asia	China	12.9	-	2.9	15.8	-	2.5	136
	Japan	0.4	-	11.9	12.3	-	11.9	1
	Korea	-	-	4.2	4.2	-	4.2	-
	Taiwan	-	-	1.8	1.8	-	1.8	-
North America	Canada	15.9	7.6	1.9	9.9	-	0.1	70
	Mexico	4.4	-	1.9	6.4	-	0.6	11
	Trinidad and Tobago	4.0	1.9	-	2.1	1.6	-	12
	US	74.2	4.9	7.4	75.3	0.1	0.3	369
South America	Argentina	3.5	-	0.6	4.6	-	0.6	12
	Bolivia	2.0	1.6	-	0.4	-	-	10
	Brazil	2.2	-	1.6	4.0	-	0.7	15
	Chile	0.1	-	0.3	0.4	-	0.3	1
	Colombia	1.1	-	-	1.0	-	-	5
	Ecuador	-	-	-	0.1	-	-	-
	Peru	1.3	0.5	-	0.8	0.5	-	15
	Venezuela	2.5	-	-	3.3	-	-	198

n/a - not available

Sources: JODI, BP Statistical Review 2016, OPEC, EIA, UNCOMTRADE, IEA Headline Global Energy Data, various national statistical agencies, calculations and estimates

Acknowledgments

And now for some massive shout-outs.

In prosecuting *The Absent Superpower* I've tapped the knowledge and skills of more people than I can count or credit, and any effort to enumerate them undoubtedly will leave out many. That said, there are a spectacular few about whom I would be remiss if I failed to gush. In no particular order ...

- Let's start with the Bureau of Economic Geology at the University of Texas. It is one of the painfully few groups within American academia that studies shale not simply as geological phenomena but also from a developmental point of view.

- Chapter Three would have proven impossible without the Southern Company crew for (patiently) walking me through the ins and outs of the American electrical system.

- Huge kudos to anyone who has ever passed through the doors of the U.S. Department of Energy's Energy Information Agency (EIA). EIA has long been the best source of energy-related information on the United States and the wider world, and I have been dependent upon its skills, knowledge, insights, and data for as long as I've been doing this analyst thing. It is made up of far and away the most competent and underloved people in the federal government.

- Carrie Hladilek was kind enough to help get me started on this project with the down-low on the mechanics of shale and the innovations that keep cropping up throughout the industry. Carrie works at Dura-Bar, a specialty metals firm whose products are used throughout a wide swathe of American industry — not to mention shale completions. So thank you to Carrie for sharing your knowledge, and thank you to Dura-Bar for sharing your shale expert with me for a few days.

- Very little of the energy-related work I do would have been possible without the expertise of David Nicklin and Marlin Downey. Not only did both selflessly share insights from decades of involvement in the American energy complex, but both also shared decades of contacts without the least bit of arm-twisting. Wow!

- The intern crew: Travis Cady, Taylor Land, and Kathryn Wallace. All three helped me explore the reach, depth, and breadth of every aspect of the energy markets and so delineate this book's wide-ranging scope. Best of luck tackling your new careers!

- Everything that is not text in this book is the handiwork of Adam Smith of SevenThirteen Creative, who regularly takes untold gajillions of bits of information and cheerily and breezily turns them into the graphics you see throughout my work. The cover? That's Adam too.

- Big thanks to Brienne Diebolt Brown for agreeing to reunite with me as my editor after a decade-plus hiatus.

- We all owe a debt of gratitude to Lori Slaughenhoupt McDaniel for assaulting every misplaced word, erroneous part of speech, and sloppy bit of punctuation that foolishly crept into the final draft.

- The man who handled *Absent*'s formatting and layout is one Scott J. Doughty, and he did so with a speed that can only be described as breathtaking.

Last and most certainly not least, to my crew:

Melissa Taylor has been directing the research side of my operation for two years now. Not only is her work impeccable, she isn't shy in the slightest in telling me when I'm wrong. Good for the ego? No. Good for everything else? Absolutely.

My analytical and logistics chief, Michael Nayebi-Oskoui, not only proved instrumental in gaming out the Gulf and Twilight Wars, but also in keeping this entire beast of a project on track. Without Michael, *Absent* probably would have gotten published around 2256.

My partner of 13 years is one Wayne Watters. He does double duty as our organization's financier as well as providing me with my daily sanity check.

And finally, Susan Copeland, who is not only our indispensable admin, but undoubtedly the most bad-ass den mother to ever grace this earth.

Geopolitical Strategist Peter Zeihan is a global energy, demographic and security expert who marries the realities of geography and populations to a deep understanding of how global politics impact markets and economic trends, helping industry leaders navigate today's complex mix of geopolitical risks and opportunities. With a keen eye toward what will drive tomorrow's headlines, his irreverent approach transforms topics that are normally dense and heavy into accessible, relevant takeaways for audiences of all types.

Zeihan founded his own firm — Zeihan on Geopolitics — in 2012 in order to provide a select group of clients with direct, custom analytical products. Today those clients represent a vast array of sectors including energy majors, financial institutions, business associations, agricultural interests, universities and the U.S. military. Prior to his independent life, Zeihan put in stints at the U.S. State Department, the DC think tank community, and Stratfor, one of the world's premier private intelligence companies, where he served as vice president of analysis.

He regularly contributes to a wide array of media including the *New York Times*, the *Washington Post*, Forbes, the Associated Press, Bloomberg News, CNN, CNBC, Fox News, National Public Radio, Market-Watch, and others.

His freshman book, *The Accidental Superpower*, debuted in 2014.